CW01510630

The Makers of British Foreign Policy

Also by T.G. Otte

MILTARY INTERVENTION: From Gun Diplomacy to Humanitarian Intervention (*co-editor*)

PERSONALITIES, WAR AND DIPLOMACY (*co-editor*)

DIPLOMATIC THEORY FROM MACHIAVELLI TO KISSINGER
(*with G.R. Berridge and Maurice Keens-Soper*)

The Makers of British Foreign Policy

From Pitt to Thatcher

Edited by

T.G. Otte
Lecturer in International History
University of the West of England
Bristol

First published 2002 by
PALGRAVE
Houndmills, Basingstoke, Hampshire RG21 6XS and
175 Fifth Avenue, New York, N.Y. 10010
Companies and representatives throughout the world

PALGRAVE is the new global academic imprint of
St Martin's Press LLC Scholarly and Reference Division and
Palgrave Publishers Ltd (formerly Macmillan Press Ltd).

ISBN 0–333–91579–8 hardback

This book is printed on paper suitable for recycling and
made from fully managed and sustained forest sources.

A catalogue record for this book is available
from the British Library.

Library of Congress Cataloging-in-Publication Data
The makers of British foreign policy : from Pitt to Thatcher /
  edited by T.G. Otte.
    p. cm.
  Includes bibliographical references and index.
  ISBN 0–333–91579–8
    1. Great Britain—Foreign relations—18th century. 2. Great
Britain—Foreign relations—19th century. 3. Great Britain—
Foreign relations—20th century. I. Otte, Thomas G.., 1967–

DA470 .M35 2001
327.73'0092'2—dc21

                                                    2001036877

10   9   8   7   6   5   4   3   2   1
11   10   09   08   07   06   05   04   03   02

Printed and bound in Great Britain by
Antony Rowe Ltd, Chippenham, Wiltshire

Contents

Preface and Acknowledgements

The essays brought together in this volume seek to offer fresh assessments of the course of modern British foreign policy, and its underlying motivations. They do so by studying this subject through the prism of the personalities of those Prime Ministers and Foreign Secretaries who exercised a profound influence on the formulation and direction of British foreign policy. This personality-centred approach allows for a more thorough understanding of the continuities in Britain's foreign relations as well as the changes wrought by the upheavals of the twentieth century. The essays assess Britain's place in international politics as well as the geostrategic and domestic, economic and financial constraints placed upon policy-makers in London; and in so doing they also analyse the foreign policy decision-making process.

Inevitably, a collection such as this has to be selective. Not every Foreign Secretary could be included; many indeed, such as Lord Malmesbury or the Earl of Iddesleigh, or more recently Selwyn Lloyd, receive no or only little mention. To such charges the editor must plead guilty. It is a matter of great personal regret to me that, for example, Lord Lansdowne, an unjustly underrated Foreign Secretary, could not be included. Similarly, readers might wonder why the great war-time leaders, such as the younger Pitt or Winston Churchill, were omitted from this collection. There is no easy answer to this. The abundance of literature on the subject apart, ultimately I decided that the exigencies of war, though not to be ignored, none the less demand separate treatment; and that the historical analysis of Britain's diplomatic tradition ought firmly to be in the foreground of this volume. To redeem these omissions, and to offer an overarching framework, the chapters on individual makers of foreign policy are preceded by a chronological and thematic intro-ductory survey of British foreign policy from the Protestant Succession to the Maastricht treaty of 1991. For this introduction the editor alone is responsible.

Extracts from unpublished Crown copyright material and private office papers held at the Public Record Office at Kew are quoted by permission of the Controller of Her Majesty's Stationery Office. Other copyright materials are quoted by permission of: Birmingham University Library; the Bodleian Library; the British Library; the Syndics of Cambridge University Library; the Master, Fellows and Scholars of Churchill College, Cambridge; the National Trust; and the Most Hon. The Marquess of Salisbury. My sincerest apologies are due to anyone whose copyright I may have infringed unwittingly.

T.G.O.
Bristol, December 2000

Notes on the Contributors

Nigel J. Ashton is a Lecturer in International History at the London School of Economics. He has published widely on aspects of mainly post-1945 British foreign policy, and is the author of *Eisenhower, Macmillan and the Problem of Nasser* (1996).

C.J. Bartlett is Emeritus Professor of International History at the University of Dundee. Among his publications are *Castlereagh* (1966), *The Global Conflict, 1870–1970: The International Rivalry of the Great Powers* (several editions), (ed.) *Britain Pre-eminent: Studies of British World Influence in the Nineteenth Century* (1969), *Defence and Diplomacy: Britain and the Great Powers, 1815–1914* (1993), and *A Special Relationship: Anglo-American Relations after 1945* (1996).

Jeremy Black is Professor of History at the University of Exeter. Among his many publications are *A System of Ambition?: British Foreign Policy, 1660–1793* (1991), *Pitt the Elder* (1992), *British Foreign Policy in an Age of Revolutions, 1783–1793* (1994), and *Convergence or Divergence: Britain and Europe* (1995).

John Charmley is Professor of Diplomatic History at the University of East Anglia, Norwich. He is the author of, among others, *Chamberlain and the Lost Peace* (1989), *Splendid Isolation?: Britain and the Balance of Power, 1874–1914* (1999).

David Dutton is a Senior Lecturer at the University of Liverpool. He is the author of *Austen Chamberlain: Gentleman in Politics* (1985), *Sir John Simon* (1993), (ed.) *Statecraft and Diplomacy in the Twentieth Century* (1995), *Anthony Eden: A Life and Reputation* (1997), and The *Politics of Diplomacy: Britain and France in the Balkans in the First World War* (1998).

Richard S. Grayson is the author of *Austen Chamberlain and the Commitment to Europe: British Foreign Policy, 1924–29* (1997). He is now the Director of the Centre for Reform, the Liberal Democrat think-tank, and a special adviser to the leader of the Liberal Democrats.

Sean Greenwood is Professor of History at Christchurch College Canterbury. He has published widely in the field of post-1940 international history. Among his publications are *Britain and European Integration since the Second World War* (1996), *The Alternative Alliance: Anglo-French Relations before the Coming of NATO, 1944–1948* (1996), and *Britain and the Cold War, 1945–1991* (2000).

Greg Kennedy is a Lecturer in Defence Studies at the Joint Services College/King's College London. He is the author of (ed. with Keith Neilson) *Far-Flung Lines* (1997), (ed. with Keith Neilson) *Incidents and International Relations: Personalities, Perceptions, and Power, 1750–1950* (2001), and *Imperial Crossroads: The Influence of the Far East on Anglo-American Relations, 1932–1939* (2001). He is also reviews editor of the *Northern Mariner*.

Keith Neilson is Professor of International and Military History at the Royal Military College of Canada, Kingston, Ontario. His numerous publications include *Strategy and Supply: The Anglo-Russian Alliance, 1914–1917* (1984), *Britain and the Last Tsar: British Policy and Russia, 1894–1917* (1995), (ed. with Greg Kennedy) *Far-Flung Lines* (1997), and (ed. with Greg Kennedy) *Incidents and International Relations* (2001).

Thomas G. Otte is a Lecturer in International History at the University of the West of England. He has published widely on aspects of mainly pre-1914 international history, and is the co-editor of *Military Intervention: From Gunboat Diplomacy to Humanitarian Intervention* (1995), *Personalities, War and Diplomacy* (1997) and *Diplomatic Theory from Machiavelli to Kissinger* (2001). He is also the reviews editor of *Diplomacy and Statecraft*.

Paul Sharp is Professor of International Relations at the University of Minnesota, Duluth. His *Thatcher's Diplomacy: The Revival of British Foreign Policy* was published by Macmillan in 1997. He is the convenor of the International Diplomatic Studies Group (DSG).

1
'It's What Made Britain Great': Reflections on British Foreign Policy, from Malplaquet to Maastricht

T.G. Otte

Britain has had the same foreign policy objective for at least five hundred years – to create a disunited Europe. In that cause we fought with the Dutch against the Spanish, with the Germans against the French, with the French and Italians against the Germans, with the French against the Italians and Germans. [...] Humphrey thinks that it is, in fact, current policy. It was necessary for us to break up the EEC, ... Now that we're in, we were able to make a pig's breakfast out of it. [...] ... and the Foreign Office is terribly happy. It's just like the old times. [...] This all strikes me as the most appalling cynicism, and I said so. Sir Humphrey agreed complacently. 'Yes Minister. We call it diplomacy. It's what made Britain great, you know.'

The Complete Yes Minister

The theme of this book – the making of British foreign policy and the country's place in the world – has generated much historical research and debate. Indeed, it seems a powerful stimulant to the historian's imagination as well. Assumptions about carefully laid plans and fixed principles or, alternatively, expositions of the country's epic decline and of the flaws of British statecraft abound. These are by no means the exclusive preserve of more recent literature. Already at the end of the nineteenth century, such a shrewd observer as Albert Sorel felt justified to pronounce that British foreign policy-makers had always been guided by one *pensée constante*: 'to extend their maritime empire, and to contain, to eliminate even if they had the means, that of France.' At the end of the twentieth century, the distinguished German scholar Michael Stürmer praised Britain for having 'exercised so masterfully' the role of balancer in Europe during the nineteenth century.[1] Similarly Aaron L. Friedberg's incisive study of British power around 1900 is based on the premise of Britain's 'unique role as the independent, detached arbiter of world affairs'.[2] British writers, too, have been tempted to overstate either the extent of Britain's power and influence or its decay. Thus, Arnold Toynbee, in one of his masterly Chatham House *Surveys*, stated that 'Britain had, indeed, been the arbiter of Europe from before the close of the War of the Spanish Succession till after the close of the Napoleonic Wars. But, in the course of the hundred years, 1815–1914, the balance of power in Europe and in the world had been turned against Britain by the industrialization of Germany and the United States.'[3] This not only exaggerates Britain's position in eighteenth-century European diplomacy, but also the constraints placed upon her in the aftermath of the reconstitution of Europe in 1815. More recently, Corelli Barnett's study *The Collapse of British Power* takes the empire as 'the greatest power in the world' as its starting point.[4]

These examples are but a small, almost random, selection from the extant literature. They do, however, serve to instil a degree of caution when assessing Britain's place in the world and the underlying principles of the country's foreign policy. In his memoirs Sir Edward Grey, Britain's longest-serving twentieth-century Foreign Secretary, indeed refuted all talk of 'far-sighted views or large conceptions or great schemes' as guiding Britain's foreign relations.[5] This, however, ought not to be construed into an assumption of an altogether haphazard foreign policy-making process, subject only to the expediencies of the moment without the guiding hand of 'grand strategic' objectives. Not infrequently, especially post-Cold War writers, echoing Dean Acheson's famous West Point speech in 1961 about Britain's search for a post-imperial role, have commented upon the absence of a strategic vision in recent foreign policy.[6] True, as one former senior British diplomat noted on reviewing his professional experiences with policy-makers, talk of grand designs is 'the sort of idea that is apt to make the British wince'.[7]

Certain principles and patterns of behaviour can nevertheless be distilled from the past record of Britain's external relations. Four components of foreign policy, which helped to underpin Britain's international position, can readily be identified. The most prominent of these is the use of *armed force* to project British power. Until the inter-war period Britain's naval power was the main means of protecting the country's imperial possessions, and of containing, through the threat or the actual imposition of a naval blockade, any potentially hegemonial power on the continent of Europe.[8] In the post-Second World War era successive British governments came to regard Britain's international influence as resting prominently on her nuclear capability and the, albeit now limited, global reach of her armed forces.[9] Most writers on international affairs hold it as axiomatic that 'wealth is usually needed to underpin military power'.[10] Britain's *financial capacity*, then, forms the second element of foreign policy. During the eighteenth and nineteenth centuries, the commercial empire and the head-start proffered by Britain's advanced stage of industrial development were convertible into political coinage. As these advantages evaporated in the course of the twentieth century, Britain's financial capacity was transformed from a facilitator of to a constraint upon foreign affairs.[11] Closely linked to this is the third component of British global strategy, the *mobilization of imperial resources*. Especially during the two world wars, but already in earlier conflicts, the raw materials and manpower reserves of the empire enabled Britain to sustain major war efforts for prolonged periods of time. Interwoven with these components of 'hard power' is a fourth, less tangible, hardly quantifiable, but no less crucial component: *(alliance) diplomacy* in both peace and war-time.[12] Diplomacy was employed as a means to forge combinations with other powers, or groups of powers, with the aim of containing any power striving for Continental predominance and threatening Britain's vital sea-lines of communication or the independence of the strategically important Low Countries opposite the south-eastern coast of the British Isles. Implicit in this schematic exposition is the understanding that underlying the history of British foreign policy there is a complex relationship between European commitments and extra-European interests.

Britain, or rather pre-Union England, emerged as a European great power at the close of the seventeenth century. Since the loss of the last remaining parts of France in 1558 English involvement in European affairs had been inter-mittent; indeed during the restoration period the Stuart kings tended to follow France's lead, though it would be misleading to describe them as clients of the French.[13] However, the succession to the throne of the *stadhouder* of the United Provinces of the Netherlands, Prince William of Orange, transformed the country into a European power. The new king's European connections and commitments, and the diplomatically better-versed Dutch entourage with which William surrounded himself, forced English politicians to acquaint themselves with European matters. The king's efforts to assume full control over foreign policy were no doubt aided by the fact that English and Dutch interests were largely identical. William's concern with defending the 'liberty of Europe' against the hegemonial ambitions of Louis XIV not only demonstrated a comprehensive strategic vision; it also combined English with Dutch interests, and identified these with the interests of Europe. Thus, the Anglo-Dutch involvement in the Nine Years' War (1689–97) was aimed at forcing the French king to recognize the Protestant succession in England (hence its old title of War of the English Succession), and to protect English trade, whilst simultaneously securing the Low Countries against France. The dispatch of a naval squadron to the Mediterranean in order to increase pressure on France's southern flank by supporting Savoy, moreover, was an indication of William's keen geostrategic understanding of the realities of European affairs. Indeed, during the quarter of a century following 1688 England took a leading part in a series of Continental land-wars. England's involvement in the War of the Spanish Succession (1701–14) was largely to safeguard the gains made in the Nine Years' War against the renewed threat posed by Louis XIV, who seemed to have installed French power from Gibraltar to Antwerp.[14]

Already in the course of the Nine Years' War the size of England's army had increased threefold, and her navy was by now the strongest in Europe. The growth of the armed forces continued for much of the eighteenth century. At the end of Queen Anne's reign the standing army had become an accepted fact of political life. Indeed, army interests gained a clearly recognizable parliamentary presence at Westminster.[15] England, or rather now post-1707 Britain, was the main beneficiary of the Peace Treaty of Utrecht of 1714 which brought the Spanish war to a conclusion. French ambitions were contained with the Dutch 'Barrier' re-erected and Savoy enlarged in the south. In terms of European politics, the Pacification of Utrecht prevented the disruption of the emerging balance of power and restored the principle of flexibility based on 'alliances and alignments'.[16] More importantly still, the 1714 settlement recognized Britain's naval superiority. The newly acquired naval bases at Gibraltar and Minorca created a new balance of power in the Mediterranean which rested on Britain's naval presence there. Britain emerged from the war with a numerically and technologically superior navy, whose organization also was superior to those of other European navies, and a large number of merchantmen and privateers.[17] The Admiralty Board's 'intelligence' system provided the information required to organize and coordinate Britain's global ship movements. The need to gather accurate information, not least about the Stuart Pretender and his supporters on the Continent, also provided a further impetus for the proper institutionalization of a diplomatic service.[18] Britain's rise to great power status on the back of the military successes in the wars around 1700 was financed through import duties and indirect taxation. National debt, however, rose substantially between 1688 and 1714; the annual debt charges in 1714, indeed, were 15 times those of 1688.[19] The wars, in fact, transformed Britain from a largely free-trade country to a *de facto* protectionist one.[20] Foreign reactions to imposed import duties and petitions from concerned traders at home, in turn, created further demand for collecting and collating accurate information.

Britain's Continental connections and commitments were reinforced by the Hanoverian accession in 1714. The combination of the new king's primarily German interests and the now clearly discernible decline of Britain's long-standing ally, the Netherlands, produced a shift in Britain's European diplomacy. The Anglo-French alliance of 1716 instrumentalized France's diplomatic influence in northern Europe to check Russian and Swedish threats to George's Hanoverian possessions – during the Nordic War the latter, indeed, were expanded to the North Sea. The combination with

France also maintained the Dutch 'Barrier' against possible French expansion in north-western Europe, whilst simultaneously helping to stabilize the domestic positions of both Hanoverian king and the Orleans regency in France. The French alliance remained 'the sheet anchor of British foreign policy' until the 1730s.[21]

Britain's diplomatic and commercial ties with Europe grew steadily in the quarter of a century after 1714. None the less, Britain's main concern lay with the transatlantic trade with the North American colonies and the expansion of British influence and commerce in the East and West Indies. Cooperation with France in European affairs notwithstanding, Britain's overseas expansion hampered that of France and began to undermine the latter's maritime commerce. The growth of British commerce was not only one of the distinct features of this period, it also began to have a greater impact on the country's foreign policy than before. The war with Spain in 1739 was caused largely by orchestrated political pressure by commercial interest groups seeking redress for the exclusion of British merchants from trade in Spanish America, with Captain Jenkins famously presenting 'his [bottled] ear and his grievances at the bar of the Commons'.[22] The war, moreover, set in motion developments in the Western hemisphere which would only come to a conclusion some eighty years later with Canning's recognition of the Latin American republics and the simultaneous promulgation of the Monroe Doctrine as the principal guideline of United States (US) hemispheric policy in 1823.

In terms of Britain's relations with Europe, the years 1740 to 1763 witnessed the high-water mark of her Continental commitments. The outbreak of the War of the Austrian Succession (1740–48) marked the beginning of a period of instability in European affairs which transformed Britain's international position. The ensuing Austro-Prussian struggle for mastery in central Europe complicated her position on the Continent. For whichever side were to emerge as the dominant force in German politics, either of the two military monarchies at the heart of the German empire would have become the *de facto* guarantor of Hanover. Britain entered the war on Austria's side primarily against France, and only to a lesser extent against the young robber-king from Prussia, though Hanoverian interests were strongly anti-Prussian.[23] In return she obtained a promise of territorial advantages for Hanover, and guarantees that the Dutch East India Company would cease trading from Oostend in the Austrian Netherlands. Britain's ongoing colonial and commercial rivalry with France thus became interlinked with Hanover's precarious strategic position in the Hapsburg–Hohenzollern conflict. Any hopes that Austria might act as an effective Continental counterweight to France remained unfulfilled. Not only did Austria not recover sufficiently, the Diplomatic Revolution of 1756, burying the old Hapsburg–Bourbon animosity, turned upside down Britain's containment policy towards France, since Austria, the guardian of the Dutch

'Barrier', was now allied with France. On the other hand, Prussia's startling rise under Frederick II to the rank of a European great power handed British foreign policy a more viable strategic tool than Austria could ever have been – Prussia 'as Britain's "continental sword"'.[24] With the Treaty of Westminster of January 1756 Prussia was tied to the policy of defensive European alliances which Britain continued to pursue.

In the course of the Seven Years' War (1756–63) Britain mobilized her superior financial resources to subsidize Prussia and the various north German armies fighting under Prussian military leadership. Indeed, without the annual subsidy of £670 000, agreed in April 1758, Frederick's bid for central European dominance would very likely have come to an abrupt end.[25] It was not the first time that Britain's financial power had proved to be an asset in international politics. Already during the 1740–48 war, the British government had undertaken to finance Austria's war effort through a secret annual subsidy of £300 000, whilst also providing British-paid Danish and Hessian troops to aid the Austrian Empress Maria Theresia. These complex arrangements 'proved a house of cards'.[26] During the Seven Years' War, by contrast, the strategy pursued by the Elder Pitt, who was largely responsible for the war effort, was altogether more successful. It created a military stalemate on the Continent, so preserving the Hanoverian possessions, whilst at the same time allowing Britain to concentrate on overseas naval and military operations against France.[27]

Together with the settlement of 1714, the 1763 Paris Peace Treaty was one of the cornerstones that defined Britain's international position in the eighteenth century. She was now established as the greatest colonial power; French competition in India was all but eliminated; Canada had been retained; and British dominance in North America and the West Indies was confirmed, though French fishing rights off Newfoundland still entailed the possibility of a future French naval challenge in the Atlantic.[28] The net balance of the war for Britain was, however, not uniformly positive. The drying up of Britain's subsidies for Prussia, and her eventual abandonment of Frederick after Pitt's resignation in 1761, left behind a legacy of suspicion of a 'perfidious Albion' which lasted well into the twentieth century.[29]

The conclusion of the Seven Years' War created a new balance of power in Europe, with a strengthened Prussia now clearly established as a European great power and French and Austrian power and prestige in decline. British diplomacy after 1763 was largely shaped by the continued maritime and commercial rivalry with France. Indeed, in light of Britain's relative aloofness from European affairs, the French recovery in the late 1760s was of significance. France's acquisition of Corsica in 1768 counterbalanced Britain's naval strength in the Mediterranean.[30] Moreover, the diversion of Britain's military and financial resources in order to deal with civil unrest in the North American colonies furnished France with the long-sought opportunity to redress the overseas imbalance in Britain's favour. In fact, the War of

American Independence (1777–83) was also a major Anglo-French-Spanish (-Dutch) colonial war. Nevertheless, Britain's war effort in America had a European dimension to it. As in the Seven Years' War the country's superior, albeit by now strained, financial resources were mobilized to hire predominantly German troops to augment the British forces operating in North America.[31] Even Russia was approached at the end of 1775 with a view to hiring 20 000 troops. Such efforts came to nothing, as did the proposal to let Emperor Joseph II of Austria mediate a settlement to the conflict. More importantly, the Fourth Anglo-Dutch War in December 1780, the first between the two erstwhile allies for over one hundred years, diverted vital resources from the main theatre of war, and so contributed to the loss of North America.[32]

Still, within a decade after the Treaty of Versailles of January 1783, which concluded the American War, Britain re-emerged as the key power in a complex system of alliances and coalitions ranged against France. Failures of French strategy, indeed France's international paralysis owing to her mounting internal problems after 1787, no doubt contributed to the reassertion of British influence in Continental affairs.[33] Of greater importance, however, were the naval reforms which rendered the Royal Navy a more efficient war-fighting force. The abolition of the cumbersome division of Britain's diplomatic machinery into a Northern and Southern Department, and their merger into a new Foreign Office in 1782, also enhanced the effectiveness of diplomatic communication and foreign policy-making.[34] Not least, Britain achieved her post-war international recovery through commercial and financial recovery. The explosion in demographic and industrial growth gave Britain the edge over other European powers. The free trade treaties with France and other Continental countries after 1786 reinforced Britain's advantageous commercial position.[35] Efforts to safeguard British access to open Continental markets were part of the younger Pitt's foreign policy strategy. With the Anglo-Prussian alliance of April 1788 Britain also re-entered formally European politics. Pitt recognized the alliance with post-Frederician Prussia as an instrument for maintaining peace and stability in Europe – a key aspect of 'our continental system'.[36] It was also a conscious effort to revert to earlier attempts to contain France, with Prussia now assuming the role then played by Austria.

The escalation of the French Revolution into a European conflict in 1792/93 fundamentally changed the power structure of Europe. The outbreak of the Revolutionary Wars propelled Britain to the head of a series of anti-French coalitions. Unlike in the mid-century wars against France, however, attempts simply to subsidize the military efforts of Britain's allies fell stillborn in view of their fundamental weakness. Instead, Britain found herself in a near-total war on land and at sea that lasted intermittently until 1815. The experience of the Napoleonic Wars was crucial for the further development of Britain's foreign relations. Organizing and conducting the war effort placed great pressures on the country's economic resources, but it did not overstrain its capacity to bear them. Increased productivity in agriculture and industry as well as the global financial networks of British merchants and bankers helped Britain prevail over Napoleon's bid for Continental supremacy. London-based banks largely financed the war efforts of the Continental allies.[37] Nevertheless, the strain on Britain's national finances was considerable, nearly quadrupling national debt (from £240m in 1793 to £900m in 1815), and unbalancing the budget. Direct taxation (income tax was introduced for the first time in 1799) accounted for 35 per cent of all additional, war-induced expenditure, significantly more than the 17 per cent during the First World War. Above all the war was financed through a series of government loans, amounting to a total borrowing of some £475m.[38] Annual debt charges for the decade after 1815 stood at £32m. Indeed, the financial impact of the Napoleonic War resembled that of the First World War.[39] The Napoleonic Wars also left an imprint on British diplomatic strategy towards Continental Europe after 1815. Castlereagh, one of the central figures in British politics after Pitt and 'the least British of British Foreign Secretaries', set a tradition of cooperating with European governments. His personal experience of conducting a war against Napoleon's Continental empire with a coalition, beset with deep-seated rivalries and suspicions was crucial. It sharpened his understanding of the importance of constant and close diplomatic contact. Castlereagh's efforts to continue the alliance into the post-war period were guided by the idea that allied unity was the best means of preserving the peace of Europe, which he deemed to be Britain's greatest interest.[40] Thus Castlereagh's policy made a major contribution to the emergence of the nineteenth-century 'congress system'.

Britain had, however, by no means become a predominantly European power. She still had major interests overseas; and most of Britain's trade was with extra-European areas, most notably with Latin America.[41] The peace settlement of 1814–15 had not so much enlarged Britain's colonial empire, but it led in the longer term to further colonial expansion. With the Cape Colony and the formerly French islands of Mauritius, the Seychelles and Maldives, as well as the former Dutch possessions along the Straits of Molucca with Singapore, now in British hands, Britain had significantly improved her control over the strategic lines of communication with India. This in turn provided a further incentive, by the assertion of naval power, to place her strategic control on an even firmer footing. The gains of Heligoland, Malta and the Ionian Islands, moreover, reinforced Britain's naval position in the North Sea and the Mediterranean, though assumptions of naval supremacy must be regarded as misleading. Until the middle of the nineteenth century Britain was able to defend her maritime and commercial empire, and to maintain her naval advantage at minimal expense to the Exchequer.[42]

Despite the growing importance of Britain's overseas interests and possessions, British foreign policy was never truly isolationist. On the contrary, Britain's imperial position was always dependent upon her relations with the other European great powers, and was thus linked to the Continental balance of power. For reasons of national and imperial security, as well as maritime interests, a policy of strict isolation was never a practical option. To secure the British Isles against the threat of invasion and to safeguard British trade in north-western Europe it was still imperative to keep the Low Countries out of the hands of any foreign power. Moreover, in light of the successful development of steam navigation in the Red Sea and the Persian Gulf, Britain's position in the Mediterranean gained a new significance. The future of the Turkish Straits thus became a major concern for British defence planners and policy-makers throughout the nineteenth century. Active involvement in European affairs, then, not only helped to preserve the stability and the peace of Europe, but also to safeguard vital British interest on the Continent and its periphery. An active European diplomacy is closely associated with Castlereagh's name. None the less, his concept of European politics focused on general balance of power considerations. He was reluctant to intervene in the internal affairs of smaller countries in order to uphold or restore their conservative social and political order, as was advocated by the Continent's leading statesman, the Austrian chancellor Prince Metternich. Britain 'decline[d] being a party to any League or Concert in the nature of a general guarantee.'[43] The clash between the 'extreme doctrine of intervention', favoured by the Eastern conservative monarchies of Austria, Russia and Prussia, and Britain's minimalist conception led to the *de facto* collapse of the 'congress system'.[44] Especially under Castlereagh's successor, George Canning, Britain's European policy was more aloof. This, however, did not preclude intermittent cooperation with Continental governments in defence of specific interests. Anglo-Russian cooperation in the Greek Question in 1826–27, for example, led to the creation of an independent Greece, whilst simultaneously preserving Turkish control over the Straits. Canning's diplomacy, then, was not one of strict non-intervention in Europe. Like Castlereagh he wished to preserve the territorial arrangements of 1815, and with it the containment of France. But it was rather a policy of limiting the occasions for intervention.[45]

Palmerston's attitude towards Europe was more akin to Castlereagh's than to that of Canning. The last Whig Foreign Secretary has repeatedly been accused of having acted on a mistaken preference for blustering demagoguery over sound diplomacy. Yet, there was more to Palmerston than the bravado of 'Don Pacifico' fame. Both in its conception and in its legacy, Palmerston's robust foreign policy was more complex. Its boldness and its hectoring tone were aimed at maintaining British prestige on the Continent, and to preserve as much as possible the European *status quo*. His frequently provocative stance took Britain to the brink of war with France over the Belgian crisis in

1831 and again in 1840 over French meddling in Egypt. *Au fond*, however, Palmerston was anxious 'at all costs to avoid a European war'.[46] His risks were calculated risks; and his brinkmanship ultimately bore fruit. Furthermore, Palmerston's legacy was long-lasting, setting the course of British foreign policy until the beginning of the twentieth century. It was Palmerston who initiated the two instruments of international law that were to define Britain's position in Europe for nearly the next seventy years: the 1839 treaty guaranteeing Belgian neutrality and independence, and the closure of the Turkish Straits in the London Convention of 1841.[47]

British foreign policy since 1815 was motivated by fears of French ambitions to overturn the Vienna Settlement of 1815, and by fears of Russian expansionism in the Near East and central Asia. These strategic concerns did not preclude cooperation with either of the two potential enemies. The rapprochement with Russia in 1826 and 1839–41 helped to maintain some degree of stability in the Near East. But cooperation with St Petersburg was intermittent, and limited to situations which seemed to threaten the stability of Europe. Thus, Anglo-Russian diplomatic cooperation during the 1848 revolution was an exercise in crisis management to preserve the *status quo*.[48] Fears of France were less pronounced, and there was more fluctuation in Anglo-French relations than in those with Russia. Still, Palmerston's liberal Quadruple Alliance with France, Spain and Portugal of 1834, envisaged 'as a powerful counterpoise to the Holy Alliance of the East',[49] could never conceal the latent antagonism with France, and slowly faded away. It did not prevent, nor did it survive, the Anglo-French clash over Egypt in 1840. The Egyptian landlink between the Mediterranean and the Red Sea was too important a factor in British imperial strategy. Palmerston's Conservative successor, Lord Aberdeen, agreed that France was the most likely threat. His response, however, was to push hard for 'a cordial, good understanding', '*une entente cordiale*'. But this latest rapprochement, too, failed to allay even Aberdeen's underlying suspicions of France. The 'scares' of a French invasion in the mid-1840s were real enough. At any rate, the *entente* did not survive the fall of French premier Guizot, who was personally associated with this policy.[50]

British fears of French revisionist ambitions grew more acute, especially after Napoleon III's seizure of power. General mistrust of Bonapartist, expansionist designs was only briefly outweighed by more immediate and pressing concerns about the possibility of Russia gaining control over the Turkish Straits. The ninth Russo-Turkish war drew Britain into an uneasy alliance with France in 1853. The descent into the Crimean War (1853–56), the first major war in Europe since the defeat of Napoleon Bonaparte in 1815, owed more to diplomatic blunders than to firm political resolve.[51] Russia's defeat in the war removed the Russian threat to Constantinople and Turkey's Balkan provinces, albeit only temporarily. The war's legacy for British foreign policy, however, was ambiguous. In terms of imperial strategy, the diversion of Russian expansionism from the Balkans to central Asia in the 1860s served to increase pressure on India. But the war also affected the underpinning of Britain's international position. The exigencies of war finance stretched Britain's financial resources. The sudden end of the 'quick victory' illusion not only necessitated heavy borrowing in order to salvage the country's wrecked military reputation, but also substantial lending to the Piedmontese and Turkish allies, though a revival of the eighteenth-century practice of hiring foreign troops was rejected as unrealistic. Ultimately, the finance of the Crimean War was predominantly pragmatic, achieved through a mixture of taxation and borrowing. Total war expenditure came to £69.3m, and the net creation of national debt during the war years to £39.7m.[52] The British army's dismal performance in the Crimea led to renewed calls for a radical reform of the armed forces. But these demands soon lost resonance with the public and the political elite alike. In the end, Britain lacked the political will to create and maintain a European-style standing army. Ambitions to be a continental European power thus ran counter to an unwillingness to meet the necessary financial costs.

Until the Crimean War, Britain had been able to maintain her international position 'on the cheap'. With the war this period came to an end. In fact, during the 1860s Britain's economic position became less favourable, and declined in relative terms as compared to the now rapidly industrializing France and Germany.[53] Successive British governments lost confidence in Britain's ability to influence Continental affairs. Thus, during the post-Crimean international crises British policy-makers were reluctant to overstep Britain's apparently limited strength. Napoleon III's involvement in Italy, his acquisition of Nice and Savoy in 1859, and his rearmament programme in the 1860s helped to foster traditional concerns about French expansionism. The uneasy Crimean alliance thus came apart, whilst relations with Russia and Austria were strained. Britain's own perceived weakness, then, was compounded by external, diplomatic constraints. Together these two factors restricted Britain's ability and willingness to act. British aloofness allowed Russia and Prussia to quash the Polish uprising against Russian rule in 1863. Cooperation between the two Eastern powers affected the alignment of the European powers, as it gave Bismarck a free hand in central Europe, and so achieve German unity under Prussian leadership. When in 1864 Bismarck engineered a German–Danish War over the future of the duchies of Schleswig and Holstein the aged Palmerston's government was divided internally, and internationally isolated; and so forced to let matters run their course.[54]

It has been argued that the years 1863–64 marked the end of the Palmerstonian, interventionist era in British foreign policy, and the beginning of consistent isolation.[55] Not only had Palmerston 'finally met someone who was his superior in the art of bluff',[56] his successors also misread the Bismarck phenomenon and the developments in Germany. In 1815 Castlereagh had allied Britain with Russia and Austria to contain France. In the aftermath of the Danish and Austro-Prussian wars (1864 and 1866)

Palmerston and his successor, the Conservative Lord Stanley, regarded a strong Prussia as necessary 'in order to control those two ambitious and aggressive powers, France and Russia'.[57] In light of the recently established Anglo-Prussian dynastic ties, through the marriage of Queen Victoria's eldest daughter to the Prussian crown prince, such a rationale certainly gained plausibility. Even Stanley's Liberal successor, the Earl of Clarendon, though mistrustful of Bismarckian methods, regarded German unity as inevitable. None the less, British foreign policy in this period was not at all consistently non-interventionist. French claims to the Grand Duchy of Luxembourg as compensation for Prussian gains in the 1866 war against Austria led to British diplomatic intervention. The Anglo-Prussian combination put a stop to any French expansion; and in guaranteeing Luxembourgeois neutrality and integrity in the treaty of London of 1867 Britain entered into fresh Continental commitments. Moreover, whilst punctiliously neutral in the Franco-Prussian War in 1870, Foreign Secretary Lord Granville intervened to safeguard the neutrality of Belgium against both belligerents. The treaty of August 1870 strengthened Britain's 1839 commitment to Belgium.[58] Earlier in the century Canning and Palmerston had rejected 'fixed resolutions for eventual probabilities' or 'engagements with reference to cases which have not wholly arisen'.[59] Now Britain was committed to a definite course of action in the event of a future invasion of Belgium. Whilst post-Palmerstonian British foreign policy, then, can not justly be called strictly isolationist, it was nevertheless only cautiously interventionist. British interests on the Continent were preserved, but at the price of limiting their scope.

The changing political structure of Britain after the extension of the franchise in 1867, moreover, affected the framing and executing of foreign policy. The rising middle class's greater concern for budgetary stringency began to outweigh the aristocracy's traditional appreciation of Europe's significance for British interests, though between Canning and Grey only three Foreign Secretaries sat in the House of Commons. Victorian finance pursued strictly economic ends.[60] Between the Crimean War and the Boer War, Britain's national debt fell steadily. With the reduction in government expenditure, the size and preparedness of Britain's army declined. The relative insignificance of Britain's armed forces compared with the mass armies of France and Prussia-Germany, and the inapplicability of naval pressure against the dominant Continental powers further restricted Britain's ability to interfere in Europe. The prevailing economizing consensus, indeed, created a mindset that would ultimately contribute to Neville Chamberlain's problems in the late 1930s. The desire of mid-Victorian public opinion for abstention sapped the ability of governments to lead with confidence.

The 1860s, however, were not only the decade of Sadowa and Sedan, but also of Gettysburg. The sense of Britain's precarious diplomatic position in Europe was compounded by her perceived military vulnerability in North America. Strained relations with the US, Lord Clarendon argued, 'to a great extent paralyses our action in Europe. There is not the slightest doubt that if we were engaged in a Continental quarrel we should immediately find ourselves at war with the United States.'[61] The strengthening of British North America through confederation was one step towards improving Britain's strategic position in the Western hemisphere; the improvement of Anglo-American diplomatic relations by removing US grievances, such as the still outstanding *Alabama* claims, was another. Compensating America, Chancellor of the Exchequer Robert Lowe remarked, was cheaper than financing a future war.[62] As Paul Kennedy has argued, the British decision to accept the *Alabama* arbitration, and Clarendon's earlier efforts to bring about mutually beneficial troops reductions on the continent marked the beginning of the 'tradition of appeasement' as a policy of rational and peaceful compromise.[63] Britain's prestige and her international position had rested on her willingness to intervene in European affairs diplomatically or by force. Her international self-effacement after 1863–64 marked the nadir of British influence in Europe. Bismarck, the new strongman on the Continent after 1870, indeed, declared 'that England had ceased to be a political power'.[64]

Britain's influence in Europe only revived with Disraeli's return to power in 1874. The Tory Disraeli consciously followed the policy of the Whig Palmerston. The latter's 'concerted movement to preserve the peace of Europe' against France during the Near Eastern crisis of 1840 provided the model.[65] His decision to purchase the majority of the Suez Canal shares in 1875 was more than a *coup de théâtre*. Britain's control of the canal fused into one British India and the country's position in the eastern Mediterranean: 'It is now the *Canal & India*; there is no such thing to us now as India alone', Disraeli's Lord Chancellor pointed out.[66] Acquiring the controlling share over the canal transformed Britain's strategic landscape. Thus, when Russian armies appeared outside Constantinople at the close of the Russo-Turkish War of 1877–78, it was Russia's anticipated ability to project her power into the eastern Mediterranean that spurred Disraeli into action. The Disraeli–Salisbury policy during the war was a fortuitous combination of bravado and shrewd diplomacy. The dispatch of a naval squadron to Besika Bay at the entrance to the Dardanelles and the movement of troops in the Mediterranean appeared to take Britain to the verge of war with Russia. Simultaneous diplomatic cooperation with all the powers ensured that Russia remained isolated, thus reducing the risk of war.[67] The Anglo-Turkish convention of June 1878, moreover, handed Cyprus to Britain, and so enhanced her strategic position in the Mediterranean. Britain's diplomatic triumph at the Berlin Congress in 1878 remained short-lived. None of Disraeli's successors could resolve the underlying tension between active European involvement and a policy of eschewing Continental entanglements. Gladstone epitomized this dichotomy in late-Victorian British foreign policy. In A.J.P. Taylor's pungent phrase, Gladstone's 'zest for financial economy inclined him towards Cobden [that is, non-intervention]; his moral fervour tempted him to universal interference'.[68] A strong moral element also underpinned his earnest efforts 'to strive to cultivate and maintain, ay, to the very uttermost, what is called the concert of Europe; to keep the Powers of Europe in union together'.[69] Granville, who had a keener understanding of the realities of power politics, somewhat tempered Gladstone's moralistic posturing. Ultimately even Gladstone had to acknowledge 'that Disraeli's world ... was now the real world of international relations'.[70] His efforts to revive the Concert failed. Indeed, it is difficult properly to speak of a Concert of Europe thereafter, until the Balkan Wars of 1912–13. Ironically, Britain became more dependent upon other European powers. After Britain 'drifted' into the occupation of Egypt in 1882 without any formal compensation for France, relations with Paris were irreparably strained for a generation. Moreover, the advance of Russian power in central Asia steadily gained momentum; so much so that by 1884 Russia was encroaching upon Afghan territory. During the Penjdeh crisis in March 1885 war with Russia seemed imminent. With relations with France and Russia strained, Britain now became more reliant upon Germany.[71]

Lord Salisbury, who virtually dominated British diplomacy until 1900, tacitly acknowledged this dependence on Bismarck by leaning towards the German-led Triple Alliance without, however, formally joining it. On the contrary, like Castlereagh, Canning and Palmerston, he consistently maintained that British involvement in Europe had to be determined on a case-by-case basis. He eschewed firm alliances, but nevertheless skilfully manipulated relations between the other European powers. His nuanced diplomacy and his calculated risks bore fruit in that they split the *Dreikaiserbund* of the three eastern monarchies of Germany, Austria and Russia – the combination that could hurt British imperial interests most. Salisbury has, therefore, aptly been described as 'un diplomate de la classe de Bismarck'.[72] Yet, at the turn of the century, Salisbury's *beau ideal*, the 'free hand', had become something of an illusion. Salisbury could manipulate, but not abate, the existing tensions between the great powers of Europe. The underlying problem for British diplomacy at the close of the nineteenth century was that British governments saw European affairs in light of Britain's imperial interests. Continental governments, by contrast, viewed colonial problems in terms of the general great power constellation in Europe. As a result, British diplomacy tended to regard agreements on issues arising from the geostrategic periphery as a means to reduce European frictions, which in turn could impinge on Britain's overseas interests. The European powers judged the value of any agreement with Britain by its utility in forcing Britain to take part in Continental affairs. Thus, Anglo-German alliance talks in 1898 and 1900–01 came to nothing, and the Anglo-French *entente* after 1904 was plagued by different interpretations as to the nature and extent of the understanding.

The term 'end of isolation', then, is partially inappropriate. The realignments with the US, Japan and France between 1901 and 1904 were the result of a settlement of outstanding overseas problems within a strictly defined regional framework. The search for such settlements was given fresh impetus by Britain's inability to deal with the double crisis of 1900, the Boer War and the Boxer crisis in China. The 'Black Week' in December 1899 dealt a severe blow to Britain's military prestige, such as it was. Moreover, Britain's military debacle coincided with the end of a long upswing of the economic cycle. By the time of the 1901 budget, war expenditure amounted to £153m, double that of the Crimean War; national debt, which had gradually been reduced during the previous decade, rose to £688m.[73] War finance was a pragmatic mixture of public loans or Treasury bills, as well as increased direct and indirect taxation. Still, the fact that the loans were nine times oversubscribed underlined the nation's underlying financial strength.[74] In terms of British foreign policy and imperial strategy, however, the financial constraints reinforced the belief amongst policy-makers in Whitehall that, in light of the growth of foreign navies, Britain's naval supremacy was seriously imperilled. The 'Two-Power-Standard', established in the Naval Defence Act of 1889 as the benchmark against which the margin of Britain's national and imperial security was to be measured, could no longer be maintained. The diplomatic corollary to these naval developments was that 'our hitherto followed policy of "splendid isolation" may no longer be possible'.[75]

In the second Hay–Pauncefote treaty of 1901 Britain effectively relinquished the Western hemisphere to the custodianship of the US. The treaty 'is one of the great treaties of the twentieth century', laying the foundations for the rapid improvement in Anglo-American relations.[76] But it came at the price of conforming British policy in the Western hemisphere to that of the US. The alliance with Japan of 1902 was even more dictated by naval considerations. It created a new naval balance of power in the Far East, one of the storm centres of international politics around 1900. The alliance was conceived of by Lansdowne as a defensive act of policy safeguarding Britain's interests in the Far Eastern region, without involving any commitments in Europe. Ironically, then, the Anglo-Japanese alliance re-emphasized Britain's aloofness from Europe. It did not mark the 'end of isolation'.[77] It did, however, establish a new pattern of regional agreements. The *entente* agreements with France of April 1904 similarly settled a series of strictly colonial disputes, mostly in Africa and Asia. At its core was France's recognition of Britain's occupation of Egypt, in return for British support for French aspirations in Morocco. For as long as the future of Morocco remained unsettled, Britain was pledged to support France; and as France's strongest rival for influence in Morocco was Germany, any future clash between the two countries over north-west Africa brought with it the risk of a Continental war. Britain's pledge of diplomatic support for French ambitions in Morocco, therefore, contained within it the seeds of a *de facto* Continental commitment.[78] The 1907 agreement with France's ally Russia on spheres of influence in central Asia reinforced the existing ties with France.[79] The *entente* agreements reduced traditional rivalries in the geostrategic periphery. This, in turn, allowed for a redeployment of the Royal Navy in the North Sea and the Channel to ward off Germany's mounting naval challenge to Britain's naval dominance.[80] The reduction of overseas rivalries was also accompanied by a tightening of imperial bonds. It was reflected in the growing influence of Alfred Milner's ideas which stressed the importance of Britain's imperial interests and the unrealized potential of the empire. The tightening of imperial bonds, however, was not merely confined to heady rhetoric. In more practical terms, the newly created Dominions made a contribution to imperial defence.[81]

In the pre-1914 *'l'inquiétude de l'Europe'*,[82] caused by the growing division of the Continent, between the Franco-Russian alliance and the German-led Triple Alliance, Britain was the decisive factor in the European equilibrium. Remaining outside the two alliances, Grey's diplomacy performed a delicate balancing act to contain a nervously restless Germany by supporting France, without, however, encouraging the latter to provoke Germany into an act of aggression. The staff talks with Paris which laid the groundwork for joint military and naval operations in the event of a Continental war were thus aimed largely at reassuring France of British support. Yet, such support was by no means a foregone conclusion, not least because of deep divisions within the Liberal administration of the day. Indeed, the Haldane mission to Berlin in February 1912, albeit ultimately unsuccessful, and the colonial talks between London and Berlin in 1912–13 demonstrated Britain's readiness to come to terms with Germany.[83] Compromise on political issues, such as the naval race with Germany, was preferable to an Anglo-German naval war in the North Sea, the outcome of which could conceivably expose a weakened Britain to a superior Franco-Russian naval combination. None the less, when Germany decided to take the 'calculated risk' of a Continental war in July 1914, Britain's *entente* partners were still too weak in Europe.[84] Germany's catastrophic decision-making, thus, transformed the *entente* and its implicit Continental commitments into a firm military alliance.

The First World War accelerated the process of social and economic change in Britain; indeed, it fundamentally transformed the country. Britain's war aims and war-time alliance diplomacy to some extent reflected this. Prime Minister Herbert Asquith publicly rejected any expansionist aims: 'We do not covet any people's territory, we have no desire to impose our rule upon alien populations. The British Empire is enough for us. All ... that we wish for ... is to be allowed peaceably to consolidate our own resources.'[85] Still, like her pre-1914 foreign policy, Britain's alliance diplomacy during the war was a balancing act. To keep the war-time coalition together the conflicting interests of Britain's allies had to be reconciled with each other. The result was a series of often conflicting agreements, such as the Treaty of London of 1915, which encouraged Italian aggrandizement in the Adriatic and the eastern Mediterranean, and the Anglo-French Sykes–Picot agreement of 1916 on the future of Turkey's Asiatic dominions from which Italy had originally been deliberately excluded.[86] British plans for post-war Europe also required a balancing act. Germany's power base had to be reduced, primarily by eliminating German militarism as a power-political factor. Yet, on the other hand, Germany herself was not to be eliminated as a factor in the future European equilibrium. Active planning for a post-war European order only began in August 1916.[87] Safeguarding economic security against Germany on the basis of close Anglo-French economic ties was an important aspect of Britain's war plans. These aimed at restoring the pre-war international trading system, and with it, the key position of the City of London as the world's financial centre. Such ambitions, however, could not hide the fact that the war-effort carried the country to the brink of ruin. 1917 was the crisis year, with France exhausted and Russia eventually leaving the war. Britain now effectively led the war against the Central Powers, before the US finally assumed the role of financier of the Allied war effort.[88] While Britain's naval blockade slowly strangulated the German economy, Britain's own economy was beginning to show signs of strain. By 1917, British overseas investments were nearly depleted, or had been offered as securities against US loans. Previously, these investments had helped to balance the chronic trade deficit to produce a surplus in the balance of payments. Thus, the economic underpinning of Britain's international position was gradually weakened by the war effort.

Ironically, when the war ended, Britain's position in world politics seemed to be much enhanced. The British empire was at its largest after substantial territorial additions, especially in the Middle East. Its most recent rival, Germany, and Russia, the traditional rival, were both weakened as a result of military defeat; and France was weakened by war-induced internal problems. Yet, this state of affairs was highly deceptive. The defeat of Germany only briefly obscured the problem of the balance of power in Central and Eastern Europe. Japan's further rise during the war already indicated potential future problems in the Far East; and, more importantly, in the long term Britain could not match the vast power potential of the US and the Soviet Union. Moreover, the war had placed a massive strain on the country's financial resources. In the last year of peace Britain's national finances showed a surplus of £4.8m. By 1918, the Treasury had to make up for a shortfall of £1988.8m. The war had been financed through short-term borrowing and increases in mostly direct taxation. As a result, national debt rose nearly ten times between 1913 (£19.9m) and 1918 (£189.9m); indeed the increase by 1919 (£270m) was nearly fourteen-fold. Throughout the 1920s debt charges remained well in excess of £300m *per annum*. Debt servicing as a percentage of total government expenditure peaked in 1925 at 41.6 per cent. It continued to hover around the 40 per cent mark until 1931, slowly to decline further until 1939, by which time it still accounted for just over a quarter of total gross expenditure.

The 1914–18 war, then, had exacerbated the mismatch between Britain's reduced financial base and an enlarged British empire, what Basil Liddell-Hart later termed 'imperial overstretch'. The strategic imperative of debt reduction affected foreign policy-making. In contrast to the pre-war period, Treasury assessments of the availability of funding now set the parameters for defence planning, most notoriously in the Ten-Year Rule which effectively blocked major armament projects until 1932 (though even then full-scale rearmament did not start until 1938). The Treasury's dominance no doubt hampered the formulation of a sound strategic policy, but it did so 'simply because it suited the Cabinet's ends'.[89] Nevertheless, the financial impact of the First World War expedited the breakthrough of the Treasury's dominance of late twentieth-century British politics. Clearly, as Paul Kennedy concluded, the 'economic consequences of the war ... were extremely deleterious for Great Britain's world power status'.[90] In 1921–22, at the Washington naval conference, Britain gave up all claims to naval supremacy, and accepted in principle parity with another power, the US. The Two-Power Standard had been consigned to the past. Moreover, the simultaneous decision to bow to American pressure not to renew the 1912 Anglo-Japanese alliance was the first instance of British foreign policy conforming with US policy outside the Western hemisphere. The decision to drop the alliance with Japan was an acknowledgment of America's increased leverage over Britain since the war.[91] But it was also fully in the logic of developments set in motion by the Hay–Pauncefote Treaty of 1901.

Britain's international position was further weakened by the prevailing Treasury tendency to view the post-war world largely in terms of the Edwardian period. The rigid orthodoxy of Winston Churchill, as Chancellor of the Exchequer from 1924 to 1929, epitomized this. His decision to return the country to the gold standard in 1925 ended in failure six years later. Aspirations for Sterling to be the leading international trading currency thus proved to be illusory, as did hopes for a liberal international finance and trade regime. Neither survived the shock waves of the world depression of 1929–31. Still, it would be overly simplistic to reduce inter-war British foreign policy to economic determinants.[92] The granting of universal adult suffrage after the war substantially changed the domestic environment in which policy-makers operated. Public revulsion at the carnage of the world war, no doubt, provided a strong incentive for successive governments to cut defence expenditure. Moreover, the nature of 'mass' politics made it necessary to court votes in the centre ground of politics, resulting in higher civilian expenditure throughout the inter-war period in an effort to appease the newly enfranchised sections of society.[93]

The desire to pare down overseas commitments did not translate into a general withdrawal into isolation. As already during the 1880s and with the pre-war *ententes*, diplomacy had to provide the security that Britain's armed forces could no longer safeguard unilaterally. The formulation of a conscious European diplomatic strategy is associated especially with the name of Austen Chamberlain. Chamberlain, aided forcefully by his Permanent Under-Secretary Sir Eyre Crowe, succeeded 'in reestablishing the ascendancy of the Foreign Office' over Britain's external relations, after its influence had declined during the Lloyd George years.[94] It was a last flowering of the Office's relative independence. Thereafter prime ministerial influence over foreign policy-making grew steadily. To some extent Chamberlain's European diplomacy naturally evolved from the policy of mediation between France and Germany, initiated by the first Labour government in 1924. British intervention was crucial in securing French acceptance of the Dawes Plan on the reorganization of Germany's finances and reparations payments to the Allied powers. The resultant agreement of August 1924 brought to an end the immediate post-war European hangover. But in removing French leverage over Germany it also marked the end of French predominance on the Continent in the immediate aftermath of the war.[95] Anglo-French friction was abated during the francophile Chamberlain's tenure of the Foreign Office. Yet, all governments during the inter-war years eschewed any binding military commitments – a fact which was somewhat concealed by the Locarno Pact of 1925. The prominent part played by Chamberlain in negotiating the mutual and collective guarantees of the *status quo* in Western Europe seemed to suggest a renewed Continental commitment on the part of Britain. In reality, the Baldwin government showed little interest in any military underpinning of Britain's diplomatic undertakings. Indeed, in light of the restricted nature of the military enforcement envisaged under the pact, Locarno ultimately weakened the 1919 peace settlement – not least because it also left the back door open for German expansion in Eastern Europe. Furthermore, as Locarno was a pledge against 'aggression', it forced France to abandon all offensive plans against Germany, while Britain was able to avoid a repetition of the pre-1914 Anglo-French staff talks. The uncertainty about Britain's support, in turn, increased British leverage over France. Locarno, then, created a new balance between France and Germany with Britain acting as umpire. On Chamberlain's part, to no small degree encouraged by the Foreign Office's historical adviser, Sir James Headlam-Morley, it was a conscious attempt to return to Castlereagh's equilibrist European Concert diplomacy.[96] Locarno undoubtedly contributed to the stabilization of European affairs, just as the Washington Treaty had done as regarded Far Eastern matters. In so doing, both treaties allowed Britain to concentrate on more pressing domestic and imperial issues, while maintaining a relative aloofness from international affairs. Both treaties disguised Britain's underlying strategic weakness. The efforts of British governments until the early 1930s to achieve multilateral disarmament agreements were a more reliable indication of Britain's real position; and the attempted consolidation of the empire through protectionism was a clear pointer as to the country's real interests.

At any rate, an equilibrist policy was only possible for as long as the Continental powers accepted the need to maintain the European balance, and for as long as no major extra-European threat to Britain's imperial interests emerged. The acceleration of the revisionist dynamics of German and Italian policies, and Japan's embarkation upon an expansionist policy on the Asian mainland, undermined the strategy of aloof equilibrism. The energetic rearmament by the revisionist powers further exacerbated the existing mismatch between Britain's global interests and her limited military and naval capabilities. Worse still, especially Germany's decision to build up a large bomber fleet now rendered the British Isles acutely vulnerable in the event of a Continental war. These constraints help to explain Britain's reluctance to lead League of Nations action against Japanese aggression in Manchuria in 1931; her acquiescence, indeed her secret condoning, of Italian expansion in East Africa; and her generally passive response to German rearmament and renewed revisionist drive. Thus, by 1937–38, a Continental commitment could no longer realistically be avoided. Two factors prevented this for the time being: Britain's lack of military, financial and industrial readiness for conflict; and the personality of Prime Minister Neville Chamberlain. During his premiership the Foreign Office's influence on policy making was eclipsed, circumvented indeed, to a hitherto unprecedented degree.[97] Traditional assumptions of Chamberlain's appeasement as a policy of weak-kneed retreat in the face of dictators must clearly be regarded as no longer tenable. Chamberlain's policy was neither feeble, nor did it surrender unilaterally to the pressure generated by Hitler and Mussolini. It amounted to an attempt to adapt his half-brother's diplomatic strategy of the mid-1920s to the changed circumstances of the late 1930s, and to salvage its equilibrist Concert rationale. Certainly, appeasement meant satisfying most of Germany's self-proclaimed grievances. But it did so by intervening diplomatically in Continental affairs, if possible in anticipation of Hitler's actions. Though fearful of another war, Chamberlain did not pursue 'peace at any price'. Concessions to Germany had to be limited and commensurate with the interests of Britain's national and imperial security. Moreover, Chamberlain clearly seems to have had the ambition of binding Germany into a general European settlement, a new form of European concert, with Britain again acting as umpire, albeit now in closer cooperation with Germany. Thus, during the Czech crisis of 1938, much to his intense chagrin, Hitler not only had to accept British and European diplomatic intervention, but was also forced at the Munich conference to co-guarantee rump-Czechoslovakia's new frontiers. Munich also demonstrated that, if Hitler proved recalcitrant, Italian influence at Berlin could be exploited with advantage in an effort to restrain Hitler. However reasonable such a rationale, ultimately it rested on an 'incorrect interpretation' of the nature of the Hitlerite regime in Germany.[98] In addition, firm opposition to Hitler, even at the risk of war, would have been impossible without domestic cooperation with the Labour Party, which was anathema to Chamberlain.[99] Chamberlainite appeasement was narrow-minded and ruthless in pursuit of its goals. The Prime Minister was impervious to advice from other sources, unwilling, perhaps even unable, to reflect on the developing diplomatic dynamics. In early 1939, the option of a firm military alliance with France was rejected, nor was the possibility of collaboration with the Soviet Union seriously explored. In this way, neither was Mussolini deterred from acting as Germany's jackal, nor was Hitler contained: there was nothing now to stop renewed conflict in Europe. For Britain, moreover, 'Munich' had become 'a traumatic experience in world politics'.[100] Never again would a British Prime Minister want to be seen clutching Chamberlain's rolled umbrella – with disastrous consequences in the mid-1950s, when Anthony Eden drew the wrong historical parallels when faced by a Middle Eastern tinpot dictator over the future of the Suez Canal.

Britain emerged from the Second World War with 'an unassailable nominal membership of the triumvirate of world powers'.[101] In the harsh light of the post-war dawn, it soon became clear that the country's status as the third world-power was impossible to sustain. The war had weakened the financial underpinning of Britain's international position to a greater extent than had been anticipated before 1939. The war-time debts to the United States of nearly £4bn ($16bn) could realistically only be reduced in the long term. Nearly two-thirds of Britain's overseas debts were to members of the Sterling bloc, especially India and Egypt. To finance the war, and to offer securities for loans, around £1.1bn of British pre-war overseas investments had to be liquidated. This, in turn, reduced regular income from interests and dividends by over 70 per cent (from £168m in 1938 to around £50m in 1946).[102] The year 1940 was, in many respects, 'the fulcrum of the twentieth century', as David Reynolds has argued. Britain's pre-eminence in the Western world passed to the as yet still neutral US.[103] By November 1940, Britain was effectively bankrupt, and there was little alternative to 'putting all our cards on the table' before the Americans.[104] For Britain to survive the lonely struggle against the Axis powers; to retain the empire; and ultimately to defeat the Axis, the US had to be brought into the war. US policy towards Britain during the crucial year 1940–41, however, was not remarkable for its altruistic qualities. It exacted a heavy political and economic price for American assistance. Churchill, the war-time Prime Minister, accepted it. Considerations of morality apart, in light of the alternatives of either outright submission to Nazi Germany, or an uneasy coexistence as Hitler's offshore junior partner, he had little realistic choice.[105] Whereas in earlier wars Britain had usually acted as the main financier of allied war-efforts, she fought the Second World War with the aid of America's economic power. As in earlier wars, foreign manpower was still crucial to Britain's success. Without mobilizing imperial manpower reserves, and, equally crucial, without the Soviet Union's numerical superiority, the outcome of the war might have been different. Both, however, came at a price: recognition of Russia's pre-dominance in Eastern Europe, and the acceleration of centrifugal processes within the empire. Already in 1941–42 the British government was forced to promise Indian independence after the war; and after 1945 the 'white' dominions began to lean towards the US rather than the 'mother country'.

At the end of the war the chronic mismatch between Britain's international interests and capabilities had grown considerably. By 1947, now without American 'Lend-Lease' aid, Britain faced a 'financial Dunkirk'. Hopes of maintaining Sterling as the world's second reserve currency had to be buried. A mild recession in America in 1949 led to renewed pressure on Sterling, and forced the Attlee government to devalue the Pound by nearly 30.5 per cent. The 1949 devaluation set the precedent for the fateful post-war British reliance on a depreciating currency to pass on increased costs.[106] Greater still was the disparity between British interests and the outcome of the war in Europe. Yet, assumptions of an abrupt fall from great power status are misleading. The main theme of post-war British foreign policy is rather one of constant attempts to adapt to the changed international setting.[107] Ernest Bevin, perhaps Britain's most unlikely Foreign Secretary, developed a new great power strategy for the post-war world, which established the basic pattern of much of late twentieth-century British foreign policy. Bevin was the main architect of post-1945 Western security arrangements. The impetus for some form of West European economic and military organization was provided by Britain.[108] Still, the experience of 1940 had demonstrated that the Continental nations were no longer able to defend their territorial integrity against the massive onslaught of a determined adversary. A Western European alliance, then, could be no substitute for the active military involvement of the US in Europe's defence, with an Anglo-American 'special relationship' at its core. Bevin's role in encouraging American financial assistance to Europe and military commitment to its defence in the shape of the North Atlantic Treaty Organization in 1949 was crucial. NATO and the American Marshall aid programme provided the necessary diplomatic and economic underpinning of British and West European security and recovery. Bevin's strategic foreign policy revolved around two further considerations: the consolidation of the remainder of Britain's overseas imperial possessions on a narrower and more realistic basis, and the creation of an independent British nuclear deterrent. Britain, then, was to play a leading role in inter-national politics, acting in alliance with the US against the Soviet Union, whilst maintaining a large degree of independence from the US.

By the mid-1950s, under the dual impact of the Korean War and the Suez crisis, Britain's great power strategy had unravelled. Increased defence expenditure halted her economic recovery, at a time when France, and even more so West Germany, grew rapidly. The full extent of Britain's fragile economic position was revealed by Prime Minister Anthony Eden's Suez adventure. The rapid plummeting of the value of the Pound in the wake of US opposition to the Anglo-French military intervention forced the British government to seek the assistance of the International Monetary Fund (IMF) in order to prop up the ailing currency, and ultimately to abort the military operation. Britain was no longer able to act unilaterally. Never again would a British government openly defy the US on a major international policy issue. It is instructive, for example, to note that even Margaret Thatcher's rapid military response to the Falklands crisis in 1982 was accompanied by strong diplomatic lobbying in Washington to get the US 'on side'.[109] Suez dealt a major blow to Britain's international prestige. One outward sign of Britain's decline was the fact that after 1956 there were to be no more international great power conferences involving Britain. These would eventually be replaced by superpower summits. It was the US and the Soviet Union who now dominated the international agenda.

With the loss of regional influence in the Middle East, the process of winding up the remainder of Britain's imperial concerns was accelerated, deftly summarized by Prime Minister Harold Macmillan's 'wind of change' speech at Cape Town in February 1960. In 1964 all military commitments 'East of Aden' were relinquished. By that time, the Anglo-American 'special relationship' had significantly improved since the dark days of Suez, not least because of the resumption of nuclear cooperation between the two countries, which had ceased in 1946.[110] But it was a lop-sided relationship. Macmillan's Polaris deal with President Kennedy at Nassau in November 1962 in effect locked Britain into a relationship of complete nuclear dependence on the US – a dependence that has lasted to the present day.[111] Ironically, economic considerations apart, the need to restore and maintain British influence with the US provided a further impetus for Macmillan's two bids to join the newly developing European Economic Community (EEC).[112] While Britain was preoccupied with Korea and Suez, France and Germany had jointly initiated the process of European integration which steadily gathered pace. Britain's half-hearted attempt to counter the supranational EEC by creating the European Free Trade Area (EFTA) as an inter-governmental rival, ultimately failed. When she eventually joined under Edward Heath in 1973, British foreign policy had to be coordinated more closely with her new Continental partners, and within a new institutional framework. Yet these institutions themselves, and the main planks of EEC activities, were the product of a carefully balanced compromise between the original founder members of the EEC. The Community's main emphasis on agricultural protectionism was somewhat at odds with Britain's mainly commercial and free-trading interests. Britain's entry into Europe, therefore, occurred under unfavourable conditions, especially as regarded British budgetary contributions.[113] The timing of Britain's joining of the EEC was doubly unfortunate. Not only did Britain appear a somewhat reluctant latecomer, her entry also coincided with the oil crisis of 1973 in the wake of the Middle Eastern war of that year. The ensuing global recession reduced the chances of structural reforms of the European institutions, and minimized the economic benefits the larger EEC market would have offered. Thus, from the very outset, Britain's relationship with the rest of 'Europe' was strained, burdened moreover by deep divisions over 'Europe' within the political class and the wider public at large.

Heath's European policy was more complex than his rhetoric seemed to suggest. It was a 'calculated strategy of national self-advancement';[114] a policy of selective engagement, advocating political and economic cooperation, whilst abjuring Europe-wide social legislation. Ironically, then, despite Heath's later vilification, especially in his own party, there has been a significant element of continuity in British European policy since Heath. Expectations amongst the smaller Continental nations that Britain would act as a much needed counterweight to the dominant Franco-German axis remained unfulfilled; and President Pompidou's notion of a London–Paris–Bonn triangle at the heart of EEC decision-making did not survive Heath's premiership.[115] The Wilson–Callaghan government was noticeably cooler on European cooperation in its rhetoric, but in practice continued Heath's selective Europeanism. Callaghan's 'Atlanticist' efforts to bridge the gap between the US and the EEC, particularly on trade matters, were fully in line with the logic of post-war British foreign policy. His Atlanticism and his efforts to renegotiate Britain's contributions to the community's budget (the 'British Budgetary Question' (BBQ)), however, were countered by a revived Franco-German axis.[116] The Schmidt–Giscard partnership created a new dynamic in European affairs to which the British government seemed conceptionally unable to respond. Moreover, Britain's reluctant Europeanism was undermined by the country's economic weakness. On balance, the Labour government's economic record was creditable enough. The budget deficit that Chancellor of the Exchequer Denis Healey inherited in 1974 was transformed into a surplus of £1.2bn in 1978. Inflation, though still high, had been brought under control. Nevertheless, this could not off-set the humiliation of having to accept the stringent conditions on which a $3.9bn credit was granted by the International Monetary Fund to bale Britain out during the Sterling crisis of 1976.[117] At least in the short term it appeared as if Britain could no longer 'pay her way'. The country's economic decline, the ambassador at Paris argued in his valedictory dispatch in March 1979, 'has been such as to sap the foundations of our diplomacy'.[118]

This trend was undoubtedly reversed during the ten years of Margaret Thatcher's premiership, so much so that she could make an open bid for a leadership role in the Western alliance in 1986/7.[119] None the less, British aspirations for international influence and the reality of British power remained uneasily matched; and Margaret Thatcher's foreign policy record is mixed. On Europe, there was a broad continuity between Callaghan's cool approach and the abrasive stance adopted by *la fille d'épicier*. Like her predecessor, indeed like every British leader since Callaghan, she had to face the inescapable necessity of reconciling the demands of domestic and European constituencies. Her public stance often appeared to border on the nationalistic, such as in her Bruges speech in September 1988. The tone might have been more strident, in substance it differed little from Heath's and Callaghan's utterances.[120] In practice, she was 'in one sense, a stronger integrationist, but, in another, the opposite'.[121] She ascribed to institutionalized Europe 'a wider strategic purpose' as a safeguard, alongside NATO, of the freedom of Europe.[122] For this reason, and because it chimed in with the prevailing deregulatory economic doctrine of the day, she accepted the creation of a single European market, even though this meant giving up Britain's veto power over trade-related matters. Her signature of the Single European Act at the Luxembourg summit in December 1985, then, marked no departure from Britain's policy of selective European engagement. Still, she probably failed to grasp, or perhaps ignored, the wider, federalist ambitions of the Franco-German axis during the Kohl–Mitterrand years, and its Brussels outrider, the EC commission under Jacques Delors. Their idea of a single European currency to complement the single market was initially resisted by Thatcher. Ultimately she bowed to Cabinet pressure, and agreed to Britain joining the European Exchange Rate Mechanism (ERM) at Madrid in 1990.[123] In Anglo-European relations, the year 1991/2 may well turn out to be a watershed. Britain's 'opt-out' from certain provisions of the Maastricht Treaty of December 1991 signalled a continuation of selective Europeanism. The withdrawal from the ERM in September 1992 – under somewhat embarrassing circumstances for the new Prime Minister John Major, who had vowed to move Britain closer to 'the heart of Europe' – further reduced British involvement in Europe.[124] Whether Maastricht, and everything it symbolizes, will prove to be a Cartesian blueprint for the future Europe, or merely a 'marginal comment on the flow of Europe's history', remains to be seen.[125]

The contrast between a tough line on some issues, such as the Falklands, and a compromising stance on others, such as Rhodesia, Hong Kong and Ireland, also characterized Thatcher's handling of post-imperial problems. The military success in the Falklands campaign unquestionably lifted the morale of a nation plagued by economic woes. Margaret Thatcher's close personal rapport with the leaders of the two superpowers further increased Britain's international standing. Close relations with both President Reagan and Soviet leader Mikhail Gorbachev allowed her briefly to act as a conduit in East–West relations, a role which had eluded Winston Churchill in the early 1950s.[126] Thatcher's personal reception in Eastern Europe and her relations with Gorbachev ensured that British foreign policy played an effective part in the final stages of the Cold War era. Still, Britain's real influence in East–West relations became apparent when President Reagan agreed to the ultimately abortive Reykjavik deal in 1986 abolishing all nuclear weapons, without consulting his nuclear-armed ally in Downing Street. Thatcher's 'very special relationship' with Reagan notwithstanding, the Anglo-American 'special relationship' remained lopsided, as the US invasion of Grenada, a Commonwealth member, showed. A mutually beneficial relationship with the US continues to exist, especially in the fields of intelligence and (nuclear) military cooperation. British and American diplomatic and military strategies could smoothly be coordinated during the Gulf War in 1990–91, and again in 1999 during the Kosovo campaign. Indeed, Britain's contribution to the Gulf War was of no small significance, in sharp contrast to that of the other Europeans. Her leading role in the Kosovo conflict may well have been decisive in ensuring its outcome. Nevertheless, British talk about a 'special relationship' underlines Britain's relative dependence on the US: 'Strong countries do not need to make such claims; they get what they want without them.'[127]

Britain at the beginning of the twenty-first century is operating from a smaller power base than in 1945. The empire has vanished; and British foreign policy has to safeguard a more limited range of interests. Is Britain, then, doomed to become 'an off-shore irrelevance' unless she embraces a federal European future?[128] This seems unduly pessimistic. It is also a misreading, both of the nature and traditions of British foreign policy, and of the realities of institutionalized Europe. Since the seventeenth century British foreign policy has been characterized by a continuous and careful balancing of overseas interests and European commitments. Atlanticist and offshore sentiments will continue to exert a strong attraction by virtue of Britain's geographical position and cultural heritage. But Britain's global influence is inextricably linked to her ability to influence European affairs. The gradual dislocation of the Franco-German axis since Germany's reunification in 1990 offers a strategic opportunity to widen British influence, and to achieve the reforms Heath and his immediate successors strove in vain to achieve. Europe itself seems to have passed the high-water mark of federalism. For Britain, and for the other Europeans, '"Europe" is more than a geographic notion but less than an answer'.[129] British foreign policy will have to continue to balance, sometimes no doubt uneasily, European engagement with Atlanticist reflexes and interests in the pursuit of furthering Britain's global influence. It is what made Britain great; and it may yet keep her moderately so.

Notes

1. A. Sorel, *L'Europe et la Révolution Française* (8 vols, Paris: Plon, 1906), vol. i, p. 340; *Guardian Weekly* (9 August 1992), as quoted in C.J. Bartlett, *Defence and Diplomacy: Britain and the Great Powers, 1815–1914* (Manchester: MUP, 1993), p. 3.
2. A.L. Friedberg, *The Weary Titan: Britain and the Experience of Relative Decline, 1895–1905* (Princeton, NJ: Princeton UP, 1988), p. 152.
3. A.J. Toynbee, *The Eve of War, 1939* (Oxford: Royal Institute for International Affairs, 1958), p. 47.
4. C. Barnett, *The Collapse of British Power* (Gloucester: Allan Sutton, reprinted 1987), pp. 67–8. For the parallel debate on cultural values and economic decline cf. M.J. Wiener, *English Culture and the Decline of the Industrial Spirit, 1850–1880* (Harmondsworth: Penguin, 1985).
5. Viscount Grey of Fallodon, *Twenty-Five Years, 1892–1916* (2 vols, US edn, New York: Frederick A. Stokes, 1925), vol. i, p. 6.
6. For example, W. Wallace, 'Foreign Policy and National Identity in the United Kingdom', in *International Affairs*, vol. lxvii, no. 1 (1991), esp. pp. 78–80. For an insider's view on the subject cf. J. Coles, *Making Foreign Policy: A Certain Idea of Britain* (London: John Murray, 2000), ch. 3.
7. N. Henderson, *Channels and Tunnels: Reflections on Britain and Abroad* (London: Weidenfeld & Nicolson, 1987), p. 78.
8. P.M. Kennedy, 'The Influence and Limits of Sea Power', *International History Review*, vol. x, no. 1 (1988), pp. 2–17.
9. J. Baylis, *British Defence Policy: Striking the Right Balance* (London: Macmillan, 1989), pp. 30–6; for a general survey cf. M.L. Dockrill, *British Defence Policy since 1945* (Oxford: Blackwell, 1988).
10. P.M. Kennedy, *The Rise and Fall of the Great Powers: Economic Change and Military Conflict from 1500 to 2000* (London: pb.ed. Fontana, 1989), p. xvi.
11. D.C.M. Platt, *Finance, Trade, and Politics in British Foreign Policy, 1815–1914* (Oxford: Clarendon Press, 1968), p. xvii; S. Pollard, *The Development of the British Economy, 1914–1980* (London: Edward Arnold, 3rd edn 1983), p. 7.
12. On the distinction between 'hard' and 'soft power' cf. J.S. Nye, Jr., *Bound to Lead: The Changing Nature of American Power* (New York: Harper Collins, 1991), pp. 188–201, though Nye's analysis does not include diplomacy.
13. K. Feiling, *British Foreign Policy, 1660–1672* (London: Macmillan, 1930), pp. 218 and 358; J.M. Black, *A System of Ambition?: British Foreign Policy, 1660–1793* (London: Longmans, 1991), pp. 24–7.
14. S.T. Bindoff, *The Scheldt Question to 1839* (London: Allen & Unwin, 1945), pp. 130–1.
15. J.H. Plumb, *The Growth of Political Stability in England, 1675–1725* (Harmondsworth: Penguin, 1969), pp. 125–7.
16. H.G. Pitt, 'The Pacification of Utrecht', in J.S. Bromley (ed.), *The New Cambridge Modern History* (Cambridge: CUP, 1970), vol. vi, p. 479.
17. J. Black, 'The British Navy and British Foreign Policy in the First Half of the Eighteenth Century', *Studies in History and Politics*, vol. iv, no. 4 (1985), pp. 137–55.
18. D.B. Horn, *The British Diplomatic Service, 1689–1789* (Oxford: Clarendon Press, 1961), pp. 1–11.

19. Unless otherwise noted, all statistical data in this chapter were taken from B.R. Mitchell and P. Dean, *Abstract of British Historical Statistics* (Cambridge: CUP, 1962), pp. 386–99.

20. R. Davis, 'The Rise of Protection in England, 1689–1786', *Economic History Review*, 2nd ser., vol. xix, no. 3 (1966), pp. 306–7.

21. J.F. Chance, *The Alliance of Hanover: A Study of British Foreign Policy in the Last Years of George I* (London: John Murray, 1923), p. vi; R. Hatton, *Diplomatic Relations between Great Britain and the Dutch Republics, 1714–1721* (London: Anglo-Dutch Society, 1950), pp. 53–61.

22. H.W.V. Temperley, 'The Age of Walpole and the Pelhams', in A.W. Ward et al. (eds.), *The Cambridge Modern History* (Cambridge: CUP, 1909), vol. vi, p. 66.

23. Black, *System of Ambition?*, p. 36.

24. D.B. Horn, *Great Britain and Europe in the Eighteenth Century* (Oxford: Clarendon Press, 1967), p. 129.

25. For a detailed assessment of this complex relationship cf. K.W. Schweitzer, *Frederick the Great, William Pitt, and Lord Bute: The Anglo-Prussian Alliance, 1756–1763* (New York: St Martin's Press, 1991), pp. 78–80; P.H. Wilson, *German Armies: War and German Politics, 1648–1806* (London: UCL Press, 1998), pp. 266–8.

26. M.S. Anderson, *The War of the Austrian Succession, 1740–1748* (London: Longmans, 1995), pp. 78–9.

27. J. Black, *Pitt the Elder* (Cambridge: CUP, 1992), pp. 165–225; B. Williams, *The Life of William Pitt, Earl of Chatham* (2 vols, London: Longmans, Green & Co., 1913), vol. i, pp. 356–7, and vol. ii, pp. 1–34.

28. For details, cf. Z.E. Rashed, *The Peace of Paris, 1763* (Liverpool: Liverpool UP, 1951), pp. 192–212.

29. D.E. Showalter, *The Wars of Frederick the Great* (London: Longmans, 1996), pp. 309–11.

30. British influence in the Mediterranean was, however, by no means checked by these developments, cf. M.S. Anderson, 'Great Britain and the Russo-Turkish War of 1768–1774', in *English Historical Review*, vol. lxix, no. 1 (1954), pp. 39–58.

31. C. Ingrao, 'The Hessian Mercenary State and the American Revolution', *Studies in History and Politics*, vol. iv, no. 4 (1985), pp. 113–22.

32. A.C. Carter, *Neutrality or Commitment: The Evolution of Dutch Foreign Policy, 1667–1795* (London: Edward Arnold, 1975), pp. 97–105; P.W. Schroeder, *The Transformation of European Politics, 1763–1848* (Oxford: Clarendon Press, 1994), p. 40.

33. Cf. Black, *System of Ambition?*, p. 222, who argues convincingly that the French collapse in 1787 'was the last act in the American War and a testimony to the greater potency of British resources'.

34. C.R. Middleton, *The Administration of British Foreign Policy, 1782–1846* (Durham, NC: Duke UP, 1977), pp. 19–21. A useful insight into the 'old system' can be gleaned from Williams, *Pitt*, vol. i, pp. 325–30.

35. J. Black, *British Foreign Policy in an Age of Revolutions, 1783–1793* (Cambridge: CUP, 1994), pp. 101–12; J. Ehrman, *The British Government and Commercial Negotiations with Europe, 1783–1793* (Cambridge: CUP, 1962).

36. Lord Malmesbury's phrase, as quoted in Sir R. Lodge, *Great Britain and Prussia in the Eighteenth Century* (Oxford: Clarendon, 1923), p. 212; cf. Wilson, *German Armies*, pp. 291–3.

37. For example, Baring's remitted £57m to the Continental allies during the war, and the London Rothschilds were solely responsible for the subsidies during the 1815 campaign; cf. W.H.B. Court, *A Concise Economic History of Britain* (2 vols, Cambridge: CUP, 1954), vol. ii, p. 143; D. Wilson, *Rothschild: A Story of Wealth and Power* (London: André Deutsch, rev. edn 1994), pp. 56–8.
38. These loans also created a new market in government securities, cf. D. Kynaston, *The City of London* (2 vols, London: Pimlico, 1995), vol. i, pp. 24–5.
39. Court, *Economic History*, vol. ii, pp. 146–9.
40. C.J. Bartlett, *Castlereagh* (London: Macmillan, 1966), pp. 5 and 157–61.
41. D.C.M. Platt, *Latin America and British Trade, 1806–1914* (London: Charles Black, 1972), pp. 23–4; *idem, Finance, Trade, and Politics*, pp. 308–16.
42. C.J. Bartlett, 'Statecraft, Power and Influence', in *idem* (ed.), *Britain Pre-eminent: Studies of British World Influence in the Nineteenth Century* (London: Macmillan, 1969), pp. 173–4.
43. Castlereagh to Stewart (no. 27), 4 December 1820, Public Record Office, FO 7/148.
44. D.L. Hafner, 'Castlereagh, the Balance of Power, and "Non-Intervention"', *Australian Journal of Politics and History*, vol. xxvi, no. 1 (1980), p. 77.
45. H.W.V. Temperley, *The Foreign Policy of Canning, 1822–1827: England, the Neo-Holy Alliance, and the New World* (London: Bell & Sons, 1925), pp. 452–4.
46. R. Bullen, *Palmerston, Guizot and the Collapse of the Entente Cordiale* (London: Athlone Press, 1974), p. 338.
47. C.K. Webster, *The Foreign Policy of Palmerston, 1830–1841: Britain, the Liberal Movement and the Eastern Question* (2 vols, London: Bell & Sons, 1951), vol. ii, pp. 780–1.
48. W.E. Mosse, *The European Powers and the German Question, 1848–1871, with Special Reference to England and Russia* (Cambridge: CUP, 1958), pp. 19–20; K.A.P. Sandiford, *Great Britain and the Schleswig-Holstein Question, 1848–1864: A Study in Diplomacy, Politics, and Public Opinion* (Toronto: Toronto UP, 1975), pp. 25–8.
49. As quoted in H.C.F. Bell, *Lord Palmerston* (2 vols, Hamden, CT: Archon Books, reprinted 1966), vol. i, p. 148.
50. M. Chamberlain, *Lord Aberdeen: A Political Biography* (London: Longmans, 1983), pp. 387–8; S. Mastellone, *La politica estera del Guizot (1840–1847)* (Florence: La Nuova Italia, 1957), pp. 103–6.
51. J.B. Conacher, *The Aberdeen Coalition, 1852–1855: A Study in Nineteenth Century Party Politics* (Cambridge: CUP, 1968), pp. 233–69.
52. For further details cf. O. Anderson, *A Liberal State at War: English Politics and Economics during the Crimean War* (London: Macmillan, 1967), pp. 201 and 220–8.
53. Cf. P.T. Marsh, *Bargaining on Europe: Britain and the First Common Market, 1860–1892* (New Haven, CT: Yale UP, 1999), pp. 8–16.
54. K.A.P. Sandiford, 'The British Cabinet and the Schleswig-Holstein Crisis, 1863–4', *History*, vol. lviii, no. 194 (1973), pp. 360–83; W.E. Mosse, 'Queen Victoria and Her Ministers in the Schleswig-Holstein Crisis, 1863–4', *English Historical Review*, vol. lxxviii, no. 3 (1963), pp. 263–83.
55. Mosse, *European Powers*, p. 164.
56. John Charmley's chapter in this volume, (Chapter 4, p. 93).
57. Palmerston to Russell, 13 September 1865, as quoted in D. Southgate, *'The Most English Minister': The Policies and Politics of Palmerston* (London: Macmillan, 1966), p. 519; R. Millman, *British Foreign Policy and the Coming of the Franco-*

Prussian War (Oxford: Clarendon Press, 1965), pp. 35–6; K. Hildebrand, 'Grossbritannien und die deutsche Reichsgründung', in E. Kolb (ed.), *Europa und die Reichsgründung, 1860–1880* (Munich: Oldenbourg, 1980), pp. 18–21.

58. M.R.D. Foot, 'Great Britain and Luxembourg 1867', *English Historical Review*, vol. lxvii, no.3 (1952), pp. 352–79; Lord E. Fitzmaurice, *The Life of Granville George Leveson Gower, Second Earl Granville, K.G., 1815–1891* (2 vols, London: Longmans, 1905), vol. ii, pp. 34–44.

59. Canning to Ward (no. 6), 8 July 1826, FO 50/19, as quoted in Temperley, *Foreign Policy of Canning*, p. 471; Palmerston to Clanricarde (no. 6), 11 January 1841, in H.W.V. Temperley and L.M. Penson (eds), *Foundations of British Foreign Policy from Pitt to Salisbury* (Cambridge: CUP, 1938), doc. no. 33, p. 137.

60. H.C.G. Matthew, 'Disraeli, Gladstone, and the Politics of Mid-Victorian Budgets', in *Historical Journal*, vol. xxii, no. 3 (1979), pp. 615–43; V. Cromwell and Z.S. Steiner, 'The Foreign Office before 1914: A Study in Resistance', in G. Sutherland (ed.), *Studies in the Growth of Nineteenth Century Government* (London: Routledge, 1972), p. 169.

61. Clarendon to Queen Victoria, 1 May 1869, in G. E. Buckle (ed.), *The Letters of Queen Victoria*, 2nd ser, (3 vols, London: John Murray, 1926), vol. i, pp. 594–5.

62. For details cf. T.W. Balch, *The Alabama Arbitration* (Freeport, NY: Books for Libraries Press, reprinted 1969); K. Bourne, *Britain and the Balance of Power in North America, 1815–1908* (London: Longmans, 1967), pp. 294–307.

63. P.M. Kennedy, *Strategy and Diplomacy, 1870–1945* (London: Fontana, 1989), p. 21.

64. Disraeli to Lady Bradford, 26 November 1875, in Marquess of Zetland (ed.), *The Letters of Disraeli to Lady Bradford and Lady Chesterfield* (2 vols, London: E. Benn, 1929), vol. i, p. 307.

65. Derby diary, 8 May 1877, in J.R. Vincent (ed.), *The Diaries of Edward Henry Stanley, 15th Earl of Derby (1826–1893), between September 1869 and March 1878* (London: Royal Historical Society, 1994), p. 216.

66. Cairns to Disraeli (confidential), 29 January 1876, Hughenden Mss, Bodleian Library, Dep. Hughenden 91/3.

67. Cf. W.N. Medlicott, *The Congress of Berlin and After: A Diplomatic History of the Near Eastern Settlement, 1878–1880* (London: Frank Cass, 2nd edn 1963), pp. 137–47; M. Svartz, *The Politics of British Foreign Policy in the Era of Disraeli and Gladstone* (London: Macmillan, 1985), pp. 82–103.

68. A.J.P. Taylor, *The Trouble-Makers: Dissent over Foreign Policy, 1792–1939* (London: Hamish Hamilton, reprinted 1964), p. 57.

69. W.E. Gladstone, *Midlothian Speeches 1879*, reprinted edn by R.D. Foot (New York: Humanities Press, 1971), p. 115.

70. C.C. Eldridge, *England's Mission: The Imperial Idea in the Age of Gladstone and Disraeli* (London: Macmillan, 1973), pp. 246–7; but cf. also P.W. Schroeder, 'Gladstone as Bismarck', *Canadian Journal of History*, vol. xv, no. 2 (1980), pp. 163–95. Gladstone's view of Granville's role was naturally somewhat different, R. Shannon, *Gladstone: Heroic Minister, 1865–1898* (London: Penguin, 1999), pp. 252–3.

71. R. Robinson and J. Gallagher, *Africa and the Victorians: The Official Mind of Imperialism* (London: Macmillan, 2nd edn 1981), pp. 286–7.

72. W.N. Medlicott, 'La Grande-Bretagne et l'Europe', in M. Beloff et al. (eds), *L'Europe du XIXe et Du XXe Siècle (1870–1914): Problèmes et Interprétations Historiques* (2 vols, Milan: Marzorati, 1962), vol. ii, p. 557.

73. Sir B. Mallet, *British Budgets: 1887–88 to 1912–13* (London: Macmillan, 1913), p. 168; Lady V. Hicks Beach, *Life of Sir Michael Hicks Beach (Earl of St. Aldwyn)* (2 vols, London: Macmillan, 1932), vol. ii, pp. 118–20, 137–40 and 166–8.

74. Memo, Hamilton, 'Forecast of financial position', 14 June 1900, PRO, T 168/48; D. Lieven, 'Dilemmas of Empire, 1850–1918', *Journal of Contemporary History*, vol. xxxiv, no. 2 (1999), pp. 172–3.

75. Kerr to Selborne (secret), 20 October 1900, in D.G. Boyce (ed.), *The Crisis of British Power: The Imperial and Naval Papers of the Second Earl of Selborne, 1895–1910* (London: The Historian's Press, 1990), pp. 123–6; K. Neilson, '"Greatly Exaggerated": The Myth of the Decline of Great Britain before 1914', *International History Review*, vol. xiii, no. 4 (1991), pp. 699–701.

76. J.A.S. Grenville, 'Great Britain and the Isthmian Canal, 1898–1901', *American Historical Review*, vol. lxi, no. 1 (1955), p. 69.

77. G.W. Monger, *The End of Isolation: British Foreign Policy, 1900–1907* (London: Thomas Nelson, 1963), p. 62; I.H. Nish, *The Anglo-Japanese Alliance: The Diplomacy of Two Island Empires, 1894–1911* (Westport, CT: Greenwood, reprinted 1976), pp. 229–32.

78. T.G. Otte, 'The Elusive Balance: British Foreign Policy and the French Entente before the First World War', in A. Sharp and G. Stone (eds), *Anglo-French Relations in the Twentieth Century: Rivalry and Cooperation* (London: Routledge, 2000), pp. 16–17.

79. B.J. Williams, 'The Strategic Background to the Anglo-Russian Entente of August 1907', *Historical Journal*, vol. ix, no. 3 (1966), pp. 360–73.

80. E.L. Woodward, *Great Britain and the German Navy, 1898–1914* (London: Frank Cass, new edn 1964), pp. 100–21; S.R. Williamson, *The Politics of Grand Strategy: Britain and France Prepare for War, 1904–1914* (London: Ashfield Press, 1990), ch.9. For a revisionist view, cf. C.H. Fairbank, 'The Origins of the Dreadnought Revolution', *International History Review*, vol. xiii, no. 2 (1991), pp. 246–72.

81. W. Nimocks, *Milner's Young Men: The 'Kindergarten' in Edwardian Imperial Affairs* (London: Hodder and Stoughton, 1970); A.S. Thompson, 'The Language of Imperialism and the Meanings of Empire: Imperial Discourse in British Politics, 1895–1914', *Journal of British Studies*, vol. xxxvi, no. 2 (1997), pp. 147–77.

82. P. Renouvin, *La Crise Européenne et la Première Guerre Mondiale* (Paris: Presses Universitaires de France, 1962), p. 183.

83. R. Langhorne, 'The Naval Question in Anglo-German Relations, 1912–1914', *Historical Journal*, vol. xiv, no. 2 (1971), pp. 359–70; but cf. G. Schmidt, 'Great Britain and Germany in the Age of Imperialism', *War & Society*, vol. iv, no. 1 (1986), pp. 31–51.

84. D. Stevenson, 'Militarization and Diplomacy in Europe before 1914', *International Security*, vol. xxii, no. 1 (1997), pp. 125–61; K. Hildebrand, 'Julikrise 1914: Das europäische Sicherheitsdilemma', *Geschichte in Wissenschaft und Unterricht*, vol. xxxvi, no. 7 (1985), pp. 469–502.

85. Asquith speech at Cardiff, 2 October 1914, in *idem*, *The Justice of Our Case and the Duty of Every Man* (London: Liberal Publication Department, 1914), p. 28.

86. Cf. I. Friedman, *The Question of Palestine, 1914–1918: British–Jewish–Arab Relations* (London: Routledge & Kegan Paul, 1973), pp. 97–118; V. Rothwell, 'Mesopotamia in British War Aims, 1914–1918', *Historical Journal*, vol. xiii, no. 2 (1970), pp. 279–80.

87. E. Goldstein, *Winning the Peace: British Diplomatic Strategy, Peace Planning, and the Paris Peace Conference, 1916–1920* (Oxford: Clarendon Press, 1993), pp. 9–13.

88. For details cf. K. Burk, *Britain, America, and the Sinews of War* (London: Allen & Unwin, 1985).

89. J. Ferris, *Men, Money, and Diplomacy: The Evolution of British Strategic Policy, 1919–1926* (Ithaca, NY: Cornell UP, 1989), p. 29; cf. M. Wright, 'Treasury Control, 1854–1914', in Sutherland (ed.), *Nineteenth Century Government*, pp. 218–20.

90. Kennedy, *Strategy and Diplomacy*, p. 97.

91. E. Goldstein, 'The Evolution of British Diplomatic Strategy for the Washington Conference', in *idem* and J.H. Maurer (eds.), *The Washington Conference, 1921–1922: Naval Rivalry, East Asian Stability and the Road to Pearl Harbor* (London: Frank Cass, 1994), pp. 4–34.

92. G. Martel, 'The Meaning of Power: Re-thinking the Decline of Great Britain', *International History Review*, vol. xiii, no. 4 (1991), pp. 691–2.

93. M. Cowling, *The Impact of Hitler: British Politics and British Policies, 1933–1940* (London: CUP, 1975).

94. E. Goldstein, 'The Evolution of British Diplomatic Strategy for the Locarno Pact, 1924–5', in B.J.C. McKercher and M.L. Dockrill (eds), *Diplomacy and World Power: Studies in British Foreign Policy, 1890–1950* (Cambridge: CUP, 1996), p. 135; cf. E. Maisel, *The Foreign Office and Foreign Policy, 1919–1926* (Brighton: Sussex UP, 1994), pp. 83–4.

95. Cf. S.A. Schuker, *The End of French Predominance in Europe: The Financial Crisis of 1924 and the Adoption of the Dawes Plan* (Chapel Hill, NC: University of North Carolina Press, 1976).

96. Chamberlain to d'Abernon, 15 May 1925, *Documents on British Foreign Policy*, 1st ser., vol. xxvii, no. 325; cf. Headlam-Morley, 'The Problem of Security' [February 1925], in *idem*, *Studies in Diplomatic History* (London: Methuen, 1930), pp. 146–71. For the background cf. Goldstein, 'Evolution', pp. 122–7.

97. D.C. Watt, 'Chamberlain's Ambassadors', in McKercher and Dockrill (eds), *Diplomacy and World Power*, (Cambridge: CUP, 1996), p. 169.

98. R.A.C. Parker, *Chamberlain and Appeasement: British Policy and the Coming of the Second World War* (New York: St.Martin's Press, 1993), p. 346; cf. R. Overy, 'Germany and the Munich Crisis: A Mutilated Victory', *Diplomacy & Statecraft*, vol. x, nos 2–3 (1999), pp. 191–215.

99. Cowling, *Impact of Hitler*, pp. 387–90.

100. B.W. Schaper, *Het trauma van München* (Amsterdam and Brussels: Elsevier, 1976), p. 269.

101. R. Jenkins, *British Foreign Policy since 1945: The Seventh Annual Lecture under the Thank-Offering to Britain Fund* (London: OUP, 1972), p. 12.

102. Details in A. Cairncross and B. Eichengreen, *Sterling in Decline: The Devaluations of 1931, 1949 and 1967* (Oxford: Clarendon, 1985); also A.E. Hinds, 'Imperial Policy and Colonial Sterling Balances, 1949–1956', *Journal of Imperial and Commonwealth History*, vol. xix, no. 1 (1991), pp. 24–44.

103. D. Reynolds, '1940: Fulcrum of the Twentieth Century', *International Affairs*, vol. lxvi, no. 4 (1990), pp. 325–50; *idem*, 'Rethinking Anglo-American Relations' in ibid., vol. lxv, no. 1 (1988), pp. 106–7.

104. Cadogan diary, 11 November 1940, in D. Dilks (ed.), *The Diaries of Sir Alexander Cadogan, O.M., 1938–1945* (London: Cassell, 1971), p. 335.

105. D. Reynolds, 'Churchill the Appeaser? Between Hitler, Roosevelt and Stalin in World War Two', in McKercher and Dockrill (eds), *Diplomacy and World Power*, (Cambridge: CUP, 1996), pp. 197–220; B.J.C. McKercher, *Transition of Power:*

Britain's Loss of Global Pre-eminence to the United States, 1930–1945 (Cambridge: CUP, 1998), pp. 299–301. For a critical view of Churchill's policy cf. J. Charmley, *Churchill: End of Glory* (London: Hodder & Stoughton, 1993), esp. pp. 431–41.

106. B. Pimlott, *Hugh Dalton* (London: Macmillan, 1986), pp. 481–5; K. Middlemass, *Power, Competition, and the State: Britain in Search of Balance, 1940–1961* (London: Macmillan, 1986), pp. 153–7; S. Newton, 'The 1949 Sterling Crisis and British Policy Towards European Integration', *Review of International Studies*, vol. xi, no. 3 (1985), pp. 169–88.

107. For a slightly different view cf. D. Reynolds, *Britannia Overruled? British Policy and World Power in the 20th Century* (London: Longmans, 1991), p. 298, who identifies as the principal feature the 'motif ... of "decline, revival and fall"'.

108. M.L. Dockrill, 'British Attitudes towards France as a Military Ally', *Diplomacy & Statecraft*, vol. i, no. 1 (1992), pp. 67–9; G. Warner, 'The Labour Government and the Unity of Western Europe, 1945–51', in R. Ovendale (ed.), *The Foreign Policy of the Labour Government* (Leicester: Leicester UP, 1984), pp. 61–82; J. Baylis, 'Britain, the Brussels Pact and the Continental Commitment', *International Affairs*, vol. lx, no. 4 (1984), pp. 615–29.

109. L. Freedman and V. Gamba-Stonehouse, *Signals of War: The Falklands Conflict of 1982* (London: Faber & Faber, 1990), pp. 134–9 and 154–62; N. Henderson, *Mandarin: The Diaries of an Ambassador, 1969–1982* (London: Weidenfeld & Nicolson, 1994), pp. 442–68.

110. S.J. Ball, 'Military Nuclear Relations between the United States and Great Britain under the Terms of the McMahon Act, 1946–58', *Historical Journal*, vol. xxxviii, no. 2 (1995), pp. 439–54; M. Gowing, 'Nuclear Weapons and the "Special Relationship"', in W.R. Louis and H. Bull (eds), *The 'Special Relationship': Anglo-American Relations since 1945* (Oxford: Clarendon Press, 1989), pp. 124–6.

111. For an excellent discussion of the Nassau deal, cf. C.A. Pagedas, *Anglo-American Strategic Relations and the French Problem, 1960–1963: A Troubled Partnership* (London: Frank Cass, 2000), pp. 244–56; also A. Horne, *Macmillan* (2 vols, London: Macmillan, 1989), vol. ii, pp. 427–53; G. Warner, 'The Anglo-American Special Relationship', *Diplomatic History*, vol. xiii, no. 4 (1989), pp. 490–2.

112. Pagedas, *Troubled Partnership*, pp. 177–8; M. Camps, *Britain and the European Community, 1955–1963* (Princeton, NJ: Princeton UP, 1964), pp. 274–312.

113. J. Campbell, *Edward Heath: A Biography* (London: Pimlico, 1994), pp. 361–3; A. Volle, *Grossbritannien und der europäische Einigungsprozess* (Bonn: Europa Union Verlag, 1989), pp. 13–19.

114. Reynolds, *Britannia Overruled*, pp. 245–6.

115. Volle, *Grossbritannien*, pp. 19–20; P. Limagne, *La Ve république de Charles de Gaulle et Georges Pompidou* (Paris: Editions France-Empire, 1978), pp. 346–7.

116. At Brussels the 'BBQ' was also known as the 'Bl**dy British Question'. Cf. R. Jenkins, *A Life at the Centre* (London: Pan Books, 1992), p. 491; also H. Simonian, *The Privileged Partnership: Franco-German Relations in the European Community, 1969–1984* (Oxford: Clarendon, 1985), pp. 265–9.

117. For details cf. K. Burk and A. Cairncross, *'Goodbye, Great Britain': The 1976 IMF Crisis* (New Haven, CT: Yale UP, 1992); D. Healey, *The Time of My Life* (Harmondsworth: Penguin, 1989), pp. 427–33.

118. Henderson to Owen (confidential), 31 March 1979, *The Economist* (2 June 1979), reprinted in N. Henderson, *Channels and Tunnels: Reflections on Britain and Abroad* (London: Weidenfeld & Nicolson, 1987), pp. 143–58; cf. D. Owen, *Time to Declare* (Harmondsworth: Penguin, 1992), pp. 277–8.

119. P. Sharp, *Thatcher's Diplomacy: The Revival of British Foreign Policy* (London: Macmillan, 1997), pp. 196–7.
120. For a different view, cf. J.W. Young, 'Conservative Governments and the Challenge of Europe, 1984–97', in A.M. Birke et al. (eds), *An Anglo-German Dialogue: The Munich Lectures on the History of International Relations* (Munich: K.G. Saur, 2000), pp. 261–2.
121. H. Young, *This Blessed Plot: Britain and Europe from Churchill to Blair* (London: Macmillan, 1998), p. 357.
122. M. Thatcher, *The Path to Power* (London: Harper Collins, 1995), p. 347.
123. M. Thatcher, *The Downing Street Years* (London: Harper Collins, 1993), pp. 719–24; N. Lawson, *The View From No.11: Memoirs of a Tory Radical* (London: Corgi Books, 1993), pp. 928–35.
124. S. Hogg and J. Hill, *Too Close to Call: Power and Politics – John Major in No.10* (London: Little, Brown and Co. 1995), pp. 77–9 and 187–8. Again, in his insistence on the importance of nation states, their institutions and traditions, Major did not differ in substance from his predecessors.
125. A.S. Milward, *The European Recovery of the Nation State* (Berkeley, CA: UCP, 1992), p. 444.
126. Sir P. Cradock, *In Pursuit of British Interests: Reflections on Foreign Policy under Margaret Thatcher and John Major* (London: John Murray, 1997), pp. 86–90; M. Gorbachev, *Memoirs* (London: Doubleday, 1996), pp. 160–1 and 498–501. For a more critical assessment, cf. G.R. Urban, *Diplomacy and Disillusion at the Court of Margaret Thatcher: An Insider's View* (London: I. B. Tauris, 1996), p. 95.
127. K. Burk, inaugural lecture, University College London, October 1996, published as 'A yoke that's wearing thin', *Times Higher Education Supplement* (6 December 1996), p. 18.
128. Sir R. Denman, *Missed Opportunities: Britain and Europe in the Twentieth Century* (London: Cassell, 1997), p. 278.
129. T. Judt, *A Grand Illusion?: An Essay on Europe* (London: Penguin, 1996), p. 141.

2
Pitt the Elder and the Foundation of an Imperial Foreign Policy

Jeremy Black

William Pitt the Elder (1711–78), First Earl of Chatham, is an important figure in the development of British foreign policy. He is also interesting for the study of the subject both because his career serves as a useful reminder of the powerful domestic political configurations that can guide policy, and because the issue of 'America or Europe?' as the priority in British policy that he posed and also sought to resolve is one that has returned to haunt us today.

There are several problems in judging Pitt's attitudes and influence. First, and most importantly, the material available for judging both policy formulation and Pitt himself is far less than was the case with policy-makers a century later. Secondly, Pitt was in office as one of the two Secretaries of State responsible for the conduct of foreign policy from December 1756 until April 1757 and from July 1757 until September 1761. He also played a major role as head of the ministry from July 1766, although the post he held, as Lord Privy Seal, did not give him any direct role, and serious ill health from February 1767 ensured that his formal leadership of the ministry until the following year was nominal. For much of the rest of his career, Pitt was a critic, often a bitter one, of the government, and this involved denunciations of foreign policy. As opponents pointed out, there were major problems of consistency in Pitt's stance, and that is a reminder of the centrality of political considerations in his career and attitudes.

These considerations varied in nature and intensity, but, at the risk of considerable simplification, Pitt can be located as an opponent both of the role of dynasticism in foreign policy formulation and of European issues in policy prioritization. The two were linked in his hostility to ministers whom he felt paid too much attention both to the concerns of George II (ruled 1727–60) as Elector of Hanover as well as king, and to the possibility of constructing a

European alliance system that would protect Hanover and, more generally, restrain the ambitions of other powers, particularly France.

In place of this, Pitt appealed to a sense of national interest that was not expressed through or in the monarch, and to a national identity conceived of in terms of Britain as a maritime power with an active trans-oceanic destiny. Such interests and identities had been offered before, but mostly in terms of literary rhetoric, for example in the press campaign against Sir Robert Walpole in 1738–39 for an alleged failure to stand up in defence of British interests in the Caribbean against Spanish depredations. With Pitt, they were to come centre stage in the discussion of foreign policy.

Pitt's first parliamentary sallies on foreign policy occurred over Spanish depredations both in 1738 and in 1739. The government had negotiated a settlement of the disputes with Spain, the Convention of the Pardo of January 1739, but this was strongly attacked by opposition politicians in the Commons' debate on the Convention on 8 March 1739. Aside from condemning it as ignominious and a betrayal of national interests, Pitt also objected to referring Britain's right to freedom of navigation to negotiators, because, he claimed, this was treating as equal two very different situations:

> On the part of Spain, an usurpation, an inhuman tyranny claimed and exercised over the American Seas; on the part of England, an undoubted right by treaties and from God and Nature, declared and asserted in the resolutions of Parliament.[1]

This firm conviction and strong assertion of national rights commanded popular support. Pitt also clearly linked this with Parliament, a position he was to maintain throughout his political career. In February 1743, Pitt was to speak on behalf of motions pressing the government to disclose correspondence with Vienna, Berlin and The Hague, as a way to expose the actions that would help government policies answerable to Parliament.

The war with Spain (1739–48) proved less successful than Walpole's critics (such as Pitt) had suggested, but he, not they, took the blame and fell in 1742. The Carteret ministry that followed in 1742–44 took a more active stance in foreign policy and moved towards support of Maria Theresa of Austria and opposition to France in the War of the Austrian Succession that had broken out when Frederick II ('the Great') of Prussia attacked Austria in 1740. An active member of the opposition, Pitt was convinced that such interventionism was designed to serve Hanoverian, not British, interests. In the Commons, on 10 December 1742, Pitt attacked what he claimed were unnecessary alliances and for engaging in Continental quarrels, and criticized George II for being most interested in aggrandizing Hanover and for being paid by Britain to do his duty as Elector and support Maria Theresa. His remarks constituted a powerful attack both on the conduct of the king and on the readiness of the ministry to defend national interests.

At a time of rising national feelings, Pitt therefore advanced a definition of loyalty based on the furtherance of national interests, rather than on the defence of the Protestant Succession, and the interests were presented as not arising from royal initiatives. The Protestant Succession had been the keynote of Whig claims for identity and support since the expulsion of James II in 1688, but it had compromised Whig ministries by obliging them to consider the particular interests of foreign monarchs, first William III and then the Hanoverians. The issue was brought to the fore as Britain came to take an active role in European power politics. Thus, on 1 December 1743, Pitt unsuccessfully proposed the rejection of the Address of Thanks when he claimed that the original reasons for British intervention in the war had been distorted, and that Parliament was being ignored.

Pitt's bitter critiques of Hanoverian influence had to be abandoned after February 1746 when Pitt joined the government, first as joint Vice-Treasurer of Ireland and from May as Paymaster General. As such he found himself obliged to defend government policy in the Commons without the power to direct it. Britain was at war with France until 1748, but the focus of British efforts had changed and was easier to defend. In place of Carteret's desire to redraw boundaries and George II's wish to act against Prussia, the ministry was now concentrating on a traditional theme – the defence of the Low Countries. Subsidized foreign troops – a bugbear of Pitt in opposition – were clearly designed to protect the Low Countries, and thereby British security, rather than to further secret goals. The traditional non-interventionist agenda seemed less relevant, and Pitt's move into government can be related to this shift.

Pitt remained Paymaster until 1755, and played an active role in refuting opposition criticisms that national interests were being ignored. The charges that had been brought against Walpole were repeated. In February 1750, twenty years after Walpole had been criticized on the same head, the opposition complained that France, with whom peace had been negotiated by the Treaty of Aix-la-Chapelle of 1748, had failed to fulfil her undertaking to destroy the defences of Dunkirk. Pitt replied that the sole alternative to negotiation was war, that Britain was in no state for conflict, that the motion was dangerous, as it would incite popular pressure, and, in response to the claim that he had formerly adopted the same position, added:

> upon some former occasions I have been hurried by the heat of youth, and the warmth of debate, into expressions which, upon cool recollection, I have deeply regretted ... Nations, as well as individuals, must sometimes forbear from the rigorous exaction of what is due to them. Prudence may require them to tolerate a delay, or even a refusal of justice, especially when their right can no way suffer by such acquiescence.[2]

The following January, the opposition attacked the Anglo-Spanish commercial treaty of October 1750, in which the Spanish claim to a right to search British merchantmen had not been explicitly denied. Pitt defended the treaty, arguing that he had been wrong to criticize Walpole in 1739 for failing to secure the same repudiation:

> I have considered public affairs more coolly and am convinced that the claim of *no search* respecting British vessels near the coast of Spanish America can never be obtained, unless Spain were reduced as to consent to any terms her conqueror might think proper to impose.[3]

Pitt also defended the treaty on the grounds that it would serve as a basis for better Anglo-Spanish relations. It had been a commonplace of opposition arguments that good relations with either France or Spain were impossible and that they were to be regarded as enemies. In contrast, for many decades, ministers had argued not only that good relations were possible, but also that they were essential to prevent the development of a hostile Bourbon pact. The resulting alliances and policies had been presented by opposition politicians as a craven failure to defend national interests, but in 1751 Pitt rejected this legacy of polemical analysis.

Although it is easy to appreciate why charges of hypocrisy were advanced, there was also a measure of flexibility that reflected Pitt's response to domestic and foreign circumstances, and that contrasted with his increasing inflexibility in the 1760s and 1770s. In Walpole's last years as minister, Pitt foolishly underestimated the difficulties of defeating Spain, but he was not alone in that and in 1751, as over Dunkirk the previous year, he did not shirk the unpleasant task of explaining the limits of national power, even if he knew he could rely on a solid parliamentary majority. Passed over in the ministerial reshuffle of 1754, Pitt moved into opposition at the same time as Anglo-French relations deteriorated. Fearing attack by France and/or her then ally, Prussia, on Hanover, George II sought the support of subsidy alliances with Hesse-Cassel and Russia. In September 1755, however, Pitt made it clear in response to ministerial approaches for him to rejoin the government that he would only return to office if he could also play a major role in policy formation. On 2 September, Newcastle met Pitt. The Duke reported the next day, 'There was such a firm resolution, so solemnly declared, both as to persons, and things; that, if complied with, must produce a total change of the present system, both as to measures and men.' Pitt said

> that, if it was expected, that he should take an *active part*, in support of measures, he must be enabled to do it; which he could not think, the calling him to the Cabinet Council, would, in any degree, do. That the House of Commons was now an assembly of atoms; that the great wheels of the machine were stop'd – that *this* could not be thought sufficient to

put them in motion ... that I did not know the state of the House of Commons; which he might say without vanity, he did, better than any body ... that the business of the House of Commons could not go on, without there was a minister (a subordinate one, perhaps) which should go directly between the King and them ... that he could not, and would not, take an *active part* in the House of Commons, without he had an *office of advice*, as well as of *execution*; – and that was the distinction he made thro'out the whole conversation – that he would support the measures which he *himself* had *advised*; but would not, like a lawyer, talk from a *brief*. ... if I could be induced to part with some part of my sole power; to that I replied, that I know of no such sole power; that my present situation was not my choice, but the King's command.

Pitt told Newcastle of the proposed treaty with Russia: 'this measure, might, in time of peace, be approved, as a measure for preserving the peace; but that, at present, it was the establishing a subsidiary system; which was destructive to this country, it might alienate the peoples from the present royal family'. The Duke said it was necessary to defend Hanover

if attacked (as in this instance) for English causes; but that that defence should be separated from the object of the Continent. Mr Pitt said, that was impossible; and would understand, both Russian and Hessian treaties, as singly entered into, on account of Hanover. And what disservice must it do the King, and His Royal Family, when the people of England saw, that they could not enter into a war, for the support of their own rights, without exposing themselves to such consequences? and he repeated what he said to your lordship, that Hanover could only suffer by being, perhaps for a time, in the possession of some other Prince; and that even an indemnification would be better given, afterwards, than such expenses entered into beforehand.

He would not back a subsidy treaty with Russia as it would limit the country's ability to fight France.[4]

As George II did not want Pitt as Secretary, while the treaty with Russia was seen as essential to prevent Prussia from attacking Hanover, there was no possibility of an agreement on these terms. The protection of Hanover was not a priority for Pitt, and as a result he was passed over for a Secretaryship of State. On 13 November 1755, Pitt launched a major attack in the Commons, condemning the Hanoverian focus of foreign policy and subsidy treaties, and the past failure to take sufficient note of the defence of North America, stressing the importance of the navy, and offering a very Whiggish account of the royal position – 'the King owes a supreme service to his people'.[5] Pitt was dismissed as Paymaster and made little impact with his parliamentary attacks. He returned to the ideas and language of his earlier hostility to Walpole and Carteret: the ministry could be trusted neither with the constitution nor the country.

Instead, it was the failure of Admiral Byng to prevent the French from capturing Minorca, then a British colony, in June 1756, that led Pitt to office, as the discredited ministry feared parliamentary attack. Pitt became Secretary of State in a ministry headed by the Duke of Devonshire. As his fellow Secretary, Robert, Fourth Earl of Holdernesse, was in the House of Lords, Pitt became the leading government spokesman in the Commons.

Political weakness prevented Pitt from implementing the 'Patriot' programme which would have blocked subsidy treaties designed to obtain the support of Continental rulers, although the King's speech to Parliament on 2 December 1756, written by Pitt, promised that 'the succour and preservation of America cannot but constitute a main object of my attention and solicitude'.

However, on 17 February 1757, Pitt had to support a request for funds for the defence of Hanover and its ally, Frederick the Great: Prussia's western flank was threatened by the French advance into Germany. Support for an 'Army of Observation', composed mostly of Hanoverians and Hessians, was presented as a means to enable George to fulfil his engagements with Frederick. Pitt's success was due to his skill in presenting support for unpopular Hanover as a means to back the Protestant Hero. However, in 1757, French forces overran Hanover and forced the Duke of Cumberland, the commander of the 'Army of Observation' to sign the Convention of Klosterseven which left the French in control. This revealed the limited value of Hanover in great power diplomacy, and the vulnerability that came from lacking a large army and not being an island.

The political crisis of the spring and summer of 1757 led to Pitt losing office and then returning in a ministry headed by the Duke of Newcastle. This success, despite his lack of strong party backing, can be seen as a consequence of Pitt's public reputation,[6] as well as of the inability of Newcastle's Old Corps Whigs to cope with a serious crisis without support. As a result, Newcastle accepted Pitt's rise to office, and thus a measure of responsibility. Pitt was more influential than hitherto in large part because he dominated the Cabinet, although he did not interfere in the detailed work of other departments.

The Seven Years' War (1756–63) was the most successful war Britain fought during the century; it saw the decisive defeat of French power in Atlantic waters, North America and India. Supporters of Pitt argued that his policies were in large part responsible. They claimed that the government's commitment of resources to the struggle against France in Germany, including, from 1758, troops was in the national interest because it contributed to success elsewhere, and was thus different from the policies and achievements of earlier ministers. The *Monitor*, an influential Pittite London newspaper, in its issue of 12 May 1759 stated that Pitt was always in a condition to improve the arms of his country's allies to the national interest, by feeding them with such succours and supplies only, as the connection of their war influenceth the measures to be pursued, in favour of his own country; and to keep clear of those ruinous continental measures, which were taken in favour of the Dutch and the House of Austria [;]

the last a criticism of the more interventionist policies during the Nine Years' War (1689–97 for Britain), and the wars of the Spanish (1702–13 for Britain) and Austrian Successions (1743–48 for Britain).

Support for Hanover was a sensitive matter for Pitt, because of his contradictory obligations to the government and towards Patriot and Tory opinion. In the winter of 1757–58, however, Pitt played a major role in securing a political settlement that tied the defence of Hanover to British direction and identified it with the Prussian alliance, a policy he had anticipated in Parliament when supporting the grant for the Army of Observation. The British took over much of the cost of the Army of Observation and agreed to provide a subsidy to Frederick. His ability to win parliamentary support reflected Pitt's skilful presentation of policy. This greater commitment was George II's price for repudiating the Convention of Klosterseven.

In 1758, Pitt first came to be associated widely with victory, an association that made it easier for him to appear to represent the national destiny. His role in pressing for and organizing a substantial military effort in North America designed to conquer Canada was well known and he was given much of the credit for British success. Contemporaries contrasted British success with the less brilliant trans-oceanic operations of the War of the Austrian Succession, when the colonial campaign was clearly a sideshow compared to the war in the Low Countries. The contrast was to be even clearer by 1759, when the French navy was defeated near Lagos in Portugal (18–19 August) and in Quiberon Bay (20 November), and their army at Minden in Germany (1 August) and outside Québec (13 September). Despite the threat of invasion, which was ended by victory at Quiberon Bay, Pitt was determined to maintain substantial forces in North America to retain the initiative and in Germany to prevent defeat. Pitt had freed Britain from the mesmerised state of 1756, when the prospect of French invasion had led to an essentially reactive strategy.

War-time foreign policy focused on strategy and the dynamics of alliance politics. It also entailed preparing for peace, which was often closely linked to strategy and alliance politics. As eighteenth-century conflicts between major powers commonly ended in compromise settlements, there was generally a political cost to taking the responsibility for negotiations. This was especially so in Britain where mistaken notions of national capability, engendered in part by opposition polemic, such as the parliamentary attacks on Walpole in which Pitt had participated, made any peace contentious.

When Parliament met on 13 November 1759, Pitt warned that it would be impossible to negotiate a peace that pleased everyone in Britain. In late 1759, he actively pressed for negotiation, and it was not until the following February that he decided both that it was worth fighting on for another campaign and that Britain should seek to retain the whole of Canada. His readiness in late 1759 to return Louisbourg and other gains was not common knowledge, but it helped to ensure that when he subsequently adopted the pose of firm opponent of national sell-out his attitude commanded little respect among other ministers.

In 1760, the French in New France (Canada) capitulated as a result of the British advance on Montréal, and Pitt took an active role in supporting the dispatch of more troops to Germany. It was not so much a matter of conquering America in Germany, a claim often made, but one that overlooks the limited extent to which the French could intervene in North America; but rather holding on to America in Germany, in other words preventing French gains in Germany that would have to be exchanged for Canada in the subsequent peace treaty.

George III, who came to the throne on 25 October 1760, had already become disillusioned with Pitt's attitudes, but Pitt continued in office. Far from George's determination to rely on his favourite, John, Third Earl of Bute, and to end the war, making rivalry and Pitt's speedy fall inevitable, Pitt remained in office, and was the minister responsible for unsuccessful Anglo-French peace negotiations in the summer of 1761. And yet Bute's position and British relations with the Bourbons were to be the crucial issues that drove Pitt from the ministry, although the fundamental cause was his unwillingness to compromise, and his refusal to accept the views of others.

In the negotiations of 1761, Pitt showed that he lacked a mastery of the conciliatory diplomatic arts. The papers he sent to Paris were thought offensive both by colleagues and by the French ministry. At a Cabinet meeting on 14 August 1761, a draft reply by Pitt was criticized as 'too long and too irritating'. Pitt refused to alter it, leading Hardwicke to comment that nations might 'be writ ... into perpetuating a war'.[7]

The aggressive and long-winded style that made Pitt's parliamentary speeches so distinctive was not suitable for diplomacy. Pitt had no experience as a diplomat and his instinctual distrust of the Bourbons may have exacerbated the consequences of a naturally autocratic temperament. Accepting that Pitt's style could be excessively harsh, it is still worth pointing out first that he moderated his attitude during the negotiations and, more importantly, that it would have mattered less had the Bourbons been prepared to settle. Instead, France was able to win Spanish support and therefore decided to fight on. Pitt was to break with his ministerial colleagues in October 1761 over relations with Spain, not the previous summer over negotiations with France. That reflected his willingness to settle with France if satisfactory terms could be obtained. Arguably Pitt delayed the offer of reasonable terms until too late, but the lengthy negotiations that had marked the end of the wars of the Spanish and Austrian Successions suggest that a quick peace was difficult to obtain and, the following year, without Pitt, the pacific ministry was still to find peace negotiations with the Bourbons difficult and very divisive. To a certain extent, Pitt was castigated in the summer of 1761 as a result of his reputation, rather than as a consequence of his actions. Nevertheless, his tendency to believe that he alone could be relied on to defend national interests had been accentuated.

The failure of negotiations with France forced the ministry to confront the possibility of war with Spain. In the Cabinet in September 1761, Pitt pressed for an immediate declaration of war, arguing that delay would be dangerous. The other ministers disagreed. They did not want to widen the war, were especially concerned about the possible financial burdens, and hoped that Spain would not take action against Britain. They doubted that Britain had sufficient grounds to attack, and proposed pressing Spain to deliver a categorical assurance of her friendly intentions. There was the danger that to attack Spain would only drive the Bourbon courts closer together. Pitt was unwilling to agree or to abide by the majority Cabinet decision. On 2 October 1761, Pitt attended the Cabinet for the last time as Secretary. He argued that Britain must attack Spain while she was unprepared for war and, when the other ministers reiterated their views, claiming that it was not the moment to attack, and that to do so would consolidate the Bourbon Family Compact, Pitt delivered his valedictory assessment of his years as Secretary. A Cabinet minute recorded:

Mr. Pitt, in his speech, recapitulated his own situation, called (as he was without having ever asked any one single employment in his life) by his Sovereign; and he might say in some degree by the voice of the People, to assist the state, when others had *abdicated* the service of it, that he accordingly came, had gone through more difficulties than ever man did; that (though he supposed it might be good fortune) he had succeeded in his measures taken for the honour, and interest of the nation; that, in the execution of these measures, he had met with great obstructions from some (hinting at principal persons) who did not wish the success of them. That there was hardly one expedition which he had proposed, though the most probable and at last attended with the best success, that had not been before treated as chimerical and ridiculous. That he was loaded with the imputation of this war being *solely* his; that it was called his *war*; that it had been a successful one; and, more than hinted, that the success was singly owing to him; that the case was otherwise now; he saw what little credit he had in the Council, from an union of opinion of some of the greatest persons in this kingdom; he knew the little interest he had either in Council or Parliament ... that the papers he had in his bag (meaning my Lord Bristol's letter and Mr. Wall's paper) fixed an eternal stain on the

Crown of England, if proper measures were not taken upon it; that it would be criminal in him, as Secretary of State, to let this affair sleep in his office. Spain is now carrying on the worst specie of war she can for France covers her trade; lends her money and abetts her negotiation. This puts you actually in war with the whole House of Bourbon. That he could not acquiesce in sending no answer to Spain; that he could agree to no answer, but what was contained in his paper. That in his station and situation he was responsible; and would not continue without having the direction; that this being the case, nobody could be surprised that he could go on no longer; and he would repeat it again, that he would be responsible for nothing but what he directed.[8]

Pitt's resignation on 5 October 1761 stemmed from his unwillingness to follow a policy that he believed to be wrong. As was predicted at the time, Pitt was to be vindicated in part by the outbreak of war with Spain that winter. However, his attitude to the conduct of government was unacceptable to his Cabinet colleagues. The cooperative nature of British ministries was the product of the absence both of party government based on a party organization and of unchallenged royal direction that could be delegated to a favourite. This cooperative element produced stress for ministers who found the process of winning support difficult, and Pitt did not appreciate that he might have to yield to the views of colleagues whose assumptions were not dishonourable. In light of a growing national desire for peace and the individual grievances of particular ministers against him, Pitt's determination to force the pace for war was inappropriate. That determination, at once egoistic obstinacy and honourable single-mindedness, made Pitt a difficult man to work with, both in office and out.

Pitt's resignation and the continuation of the war helped cause a bitter controversy over national goals and policies. In 1762, Bute's growing determination to break with Frederick II and to reopen negotiations with France helped to ensure that the vindications of Pitt's past policies produced by the former minister and by his supporters were unwelcome. In addition, what had been initially a rift ostensibly only over the question of how best to confront the Bourbon alliance became a more wide-ranging difference of opinion over the entire direction of government policy. George III was closely identified with a specific 'patriotic' agenda, the rejection of his grandfather's tradition of intervention in German affairs. Pitt's trumpeting of the value of such intervention during the Seven Years' War compromised his reputation in 1762 at a time of growing isolationism and helped to anger the government. In the Commons on 12 May 1762, Pitt pressed for the maintenance of good relations with Prussia and claimed that Continental interventionism had been practised by great British rulers, such as Elizabeth I. He declared:

When I give my advice to the House I consider myself as giving my advice to the crown ... The Continental Plan is the only plan otherwise all Europe will be interdicted by these haughty oppressions of the House of Bourbon from receiving you whom they affect to treat as an overgrown pirate from their ports. Increase of power must be continued with increase of commerce or both will dwindle. The best the speediest issue, is to continue your full forces on the Continent this year: ... this will bring you a speedy, a sober and a well understood and permanent peace.

... I am convinced this country can raise 12, 13, 14 or even 15 million the next year: I know it without seeking information from bundles of papers and accounts ... The only question is whether grievous and permanent as that tax must be, it is not to be preferred to the perpetual dishonour of the nation, the aggrandisement of the enemy, the desertion of your allies, all which tend to an inglorious and precarious peace ... Think of your greatness in every part of the world ...

The moment you withdraw your troops there are 140,000 French to be employed in the Low Countries. I rejoice at the extinction of parties ... [9]

Pitt had reverted to his attitude of 1738–39: criticizing a ministry trying to follow a prudential foreign policy, and to maintain or obtain peace, on the grounds that it was betraying national interests, while at the same time failing to discuss the implications of his policy, especially in financial terms. This was an obvious contrast to his prudential defence of foreign policy after the War of the Austrian Succession; but peacetime exigencies were different to those of the more volatile war-time political atmosphere.

In 1762, the Bute ministry managed to negotiate the best terms that Britain was ever to obtain in a peace treaty prior to the Vienna peace settlement of 1814–15. To Pitt, they were unsatisfactory because, he claimed, the ministry could have obtained better terms and because they did not end the danger of a Bourbon *revanche*, although it is not clear how fears on that head could have been assuaged. Pitt's opposition to the terms of what was to be the Peace of Paris of 1763 was to play a major role in fostering his image as a defender of national interest, but accounts of the reception of his Commons speech on 9 December 1762 reveal that he made little impact. Pitt was especially scathing about France being allowed a continued share of the Newfoundland fishery, and argued that it, and the return of Guadeloupe and Martinique, gave France the means to recover from her losses and to threaten Britain's maritime and commercial position anew.

The problems of domestic office led to Bute's resignation in 1763, and to that of his successors, George Grenville in 1765 and Charles, Second Marquess of Rockingham in 1766. Succeeding Rockingham as head of a reconstituted ministry, Pitt, who went to the Lords as Earl of Chatham, found peacetime leadership of a poorly united ministry very difficult. The sense of national unity that he had been able to benefit from, and to foster, during the Seven Years' War was absent.

Chatham devoted most of his attention to attempting to reverse the breach with Prussia that he blamed on Bute. In holding an evil adviser responsible, Chatham reflected a strong tradition of political thinking that had been seen in attacks on Walpole, a tradition that attributed much to sinister intentions and that combined naturally with Chatham's paranoia. This, however, led both to a failure to probe causes sufficiently and to a misguided belief that a change in leadership would right the situation, a characteristic of eighteenth-century thought about international relations. Although it was attractive to blame the breach with Frederick in 1762 on Bute, it was substantially due to an absence of shared interests that had been disguised by the consequences of the fortuitous diplomatic changes of 1756. The leading states of eastern and central Europe – Austria, Russia and Prussia – had risen in relative power since the 1680s. They had also, especially Austria and Prussia, from the 1710s, become less interested in western Europe and its rivalries. Frederick was essentially interested in a Russian alliance. Once he had achieved that in 1764, Frederick was not interested in diluting his influence by including Britain, a move that would also raise the danger of involvement in British confrontations with the Bourbons.

Chatham had hoped that Britain would benefit from the Prusso-Russian realignment of 1762, and the failure to do so had led him to feel that Bute's abandonment of the Prussian alliance was as much evidence of his failure to defend national interests as the peace terms with the Bourbons. Back in office, Chatham's enthusiasm for a triple alliance with Prussia and Russia took no note of the actual state of relations. There was a naive sense that in office he could invigorate the government and thus obtain success, as if only will-power was required, the last a delusion that can be seen at several stages in his career. The veteran envoy in Berlin, Sir Andrew Mitchell, was much better informed and his accurate prediction that Frederick would reject the approach was proved correct. Rebuffed in September 1766, Mitchell found Chatham unwilling to accept Frederick's refusal, and he was ordered in November to make another approach, which had a predictable fate on 1 December. The Duke of Grafton observed, 'Mr. Pitt's plan was Utopian ... he lived too much out of the world to have a right knowledge of mankind'.[10]

As Chatham had intended to approach Russia via her Prussian ally, the failure of this approach spelled the end of his system. The chances of a Russian alliance were slight anyway because George III was opposed to granting Russian demands for a peacetime subsidy and for a commitment to assist Catherine the Great in any war with Turkey. George's attitude was more realistic than that of Chatham. Relations over the previous half century had revealed that Russian rulers and ministers would only accept British diplomatic initiatives on their own terms.

Britain sought stability in Europe. Alliance with an aggressive power was not the way to achieve it. Furthermore, the financial cost of a Russian alliance scarcely accorded with the exigencies of post-war retrenchment.

In 1767, Chatham's health collapsed, probably as a combination of stress and depression, and he did not return to politics until late 1769. Over the following years, he focused on alleged governmental supineness in the face of Bourbon aggression. In 1770, he called in Parliament for an inquiry into the failure of the Grafton ministry to prevent the French acquisition of Corsica: it had been bought from Genoa in 1768 and popular opposition had been crushed. The Spanish expulsion of an English settlement from the Falkland Islands during the recess provoked eight speeches from Chatham between November 1770 and February 1771. He pressed for a strong navy and the vigorous pursuit of national interests. Refused French support and influenced by a major British naval armament, Spain backed down, denying Chatham the opportunity to attempt a campaign similar to that directed against Walpole in 1738–39. In his speech on 22 November 1770, Chatham cited the Convention of the Pardo of 1739 and his advice for war with Spain in 1761, rather than his defence of the Anglo-Spanish treaty of 1750. Chatham felt at ease, asserting national interests and criticizing the ministry.

From late 1773, Chatham became very concerned about the increasingly volatile situation in Britain's American colonies. On 20 January 1775, he warned the Lords that France might exploit the situation. Chatham pressed for conciliation and was prepared to envisage the abolition of parliamentary taxation of America, but he was fixedly against American independence. The integrity of the British empire, the political, strategic and economic interdependency of different parts that he saw so clearly, would be destroyed by independence. Like most politicians and commentators, Chatham felt that economic and political strength were related, that the monopoly of American trade supported British power, and that, without political links, it would be impossible to maintain economic relationships. Chatham was depressed by the outbreak of war, and his reputation improved as the attempt to crush the revolution foundered. In 1777, he wrote to his nephew Thomas:

> I tremble for news from America. Till the event (which in every alternative must be ruin) is known, the date of England's greatness seems protracted for a few days. Sad tenure, of more public happiness and prosperity than Providence has ever given to a nation, and infatuated counsels have ever thrown away.[11]

On 20 November 1777, Chatham pressed for peace with America, which he declared could not be conquered, and for preparations against the Bourbons. He claimed that his policy would lead the Americans to reconciliation with Britain and he was still opposed to independence. Chatham made his last parliamentary appearance on 7 April 1778 in response to a motion by the

Duke of Richmond for an address to George III calling for the withdrawal of troops from America and the resignation of the ministry. The Duke argued that Britain had to recognize American independence in order to free herself for the imminent war with France.

Chatham replied that Britain could wage both struggles simultaneously, and claimed that the abandonment of the colonies would be a national humiliation and would lead to national ruin. Richmond replied that the country could not fight France and the Americans successfully. Chatham then rose to speak but collapsed and was carried from the Chamber. He died on 11 May.

There was a definitely heroic note to his collapse in the Lords and it struck many contemporaries in that light. The heroic image was to be propagated visually, most obviously in Jonathan Singleton Copley's picture *The Death of Chatham*, which was reproduced in engravings, particularly that by Francesco Bartolozzi, published in 1791. This contributed directly to Chatham's subsequent reputation as the advocate for empire. As the chronological survey already provided indicates, there was in fact sufficient variety in his positions to lead to widespread charges of inconsistency, but these were submerged in hindsight, which always seeks for an overall impression. The highpoints of his career that attracted subsequent attention were his direction of British policy during the Seven Years' War and his attempts, in opposition, to prevent the break up of Britain's Atlantic empire. Pitt's criticism of the Peace of Paris appeared prescient in light of the French entry into the War of American Independence in 1778. His clear sense that national identity entailed maritime strength and trans-oceanic expansion and that these required conflict with the Bourbons seemed further vindicated by the French Revolutionary and Napoleonic wars in which Britain fought France in 1793–1802, 1804–14 and 1815. Furthermore, Pitt the Elder was linked in posterity to his second son, Pitt the Younger, war-leader against the Revolutionary French and Napoleon, and both were seen as stalwarts of national strength.

This image burned bright during the nineteenth century and for most of the twentieth, a situation that reflected the continued vitality of empire. Pitt emerged as hero in a number of biographies, and his position was even more strongly asserted in popular works such as national histories. The Seven Years' War was seen as a period of heroic achievement, as in G.A. Henty's adventure story *With Wolfe in Canada: The Winning of a Continent* (1887).

When that vitality ebbed a lack of interest in military or diplomatic history and, instead, a preference for social history ensured that little attention was devoted to Pitt's role in both foreign policy and war. Nevertheless, his reputation was affected by revisionism, with Richard Middleton suggesting that Pitt was less dominant in the ministry and less successful than was generally argued. By focusing on the execution of policy and drawing heavily on administrative papers, Middleton, however, underrated the politics of leadership in which he was so important.[12]

These politics related to the internal dynamics of the ministry, to the politics of parliamentary support and popular opinion, and to the role of Pitt in creating a foreign policy tradition. This was the tradition of empire. Clearly there were many reasons for the shift in foreign policy attitudes towards a greater engagement with the non-European world, but, if they have to be associated with a single politician, then Pitt is the man.

Pitt's resignation in 1761 was important as it helped to anchor a presentation of him as a man willing to sacrifice himself for the cause. It was crucial that he resigned over war with Spain, rather than the continuance of subsidies to Prussia and other aspects of Continental interventionism. As a consequence, success in the war with France, with which Pitt was closely associated, was not compromised, as far as most contemporaries were concerned, by Continental interventionism. Instead, Pitt was associated, in 1762 and subsequently, not only with a war with Spain that appeared inevitable in hindsight, but also with a war that brought great success in 1762. This success, and continued victories over France in 1762, especially the capture of Martinique, lessened public concern over the failure to secure peace in 1761.

This was important in the anchoring of a public perception of Britain as a necessarily imperial maritime power. The situation in 1761 was in fact very dangerous. It was difficult to be optimistic about the position on the Continent. There was little reason for confidence that Frederick II would be able to hold off his assailants for ever or to negotiate a satisfactory peace. Spain was a major power whose energies had not been dissipated by recent conflict, and Portugal appeared as a vulnerable British ally. Although France had been gravely weakened as an imperial power by the collapse of her position in Canada and India, she had felt able to reject British terms in 1761.

Yet, by then, the success with which Pitt was associated had helped to redefine Britain. There had initially been no plan to conquer the French empire, still less that of Spain, understandably so as in 1755 the conquest of French India, Canada, West Africa and of much of the French West Indies seemed unrealistic. Yet, once won, gains appeared both necessary and natural. By the close of 1759 Britain really did rule the waves, and optimism about her naval capability and potential grew. This helped to make a maritime foreign policy appear normative. The reconceptualization of Britain, and her role in the world, was one of the major changes that took place in the mid-eighteenth century. The choice in policy was no longer largely defined in terms of Continental interventionism versus a Tory, agrarian withdrawal from abroad, albeit one that was tempered by a degree of 'blue water' raiding and cheap colonialism, as had been the case in the first half of the century. Instead, 'blue water' was transformed into Britain's destiny. It was to be a feature in which the state invested heavily and took a major role. This was seen most clearly in the dramatic shift in the dispatch of regulars abroad. Prior to the Seven Years' War, very few regulars were sent to Canada and India, and in military terms the direct trans-oceanic British impact was essentially naval. This altered with the dispatch of the regulars that conquered Canada, Bengal and the Carnatic.

Britain's engagement with the trans-oceanic world changed greatly as there was a far greater endorsement of far-flung colonies as opposed to bases. Trade was to be complemented by settlement and, in Bengal, by the revenues of territorial control.

Political leadership by Pitt in the mid and late 1750s and by George III in the early 1760s played a major role in the shift in the conception of the national destiny as more of the world was brought within Britain's real and imaginative grasp. Their determination to break with the systems they confronted was important. However, any single explanation of what was a complex and multifaceted shift must be suspect. The imaginative re-creation of Britain as a global state with a maritime destiny reflected an interaction of shifts in attitude and changes in political contexts and policies. The failure of the Duke of Newcastle's European collective security system project in 1755–56 was crucial. That was also a failure not only of policy and of an understanding of European international relations, but also of Europe as a definition of British identity and interest.

After the Seven Years' War successive ministries were to adopt an attitude to interventionism that was very different from those prior to the war. Yet the aura of an imperial state did not provide an answer to the problems that might face Britain. The trans-oceanic amphibious operations helped to set the political tone for discussion of potential British military action for the next three decades. As the War of American Independence involved no hostilities in Europe, apart from the unsuccessful Bourbon siege of Gibraltar and their capture of Minorca, and Britain did not intervene in the Austro-Prussian War of the Bavarian Succession (1778–79), the generation of ministers and generals who faced in 1793 the problems of coordinating significant Continental operations against revolutionary France had no recent experience on which to look back. In addition, the fortuitous success of 1762 was important in leading to an absence of any serious widespread critique of the commitments assumed to arise from Britain's apparent maritime destiny. There was little public sense that the war had been a risk. The glow of success had shadowed the problems and failures of the early stages of the conflict with France. This attitude led to a post-war confidence, indeed complacency, that was to have serious consequences for Britain's international position.

Notes

1. R. Chandler, *The History and Proceedings of the House of Commons from the Restoration to the Present Time* (London, 1743), vol. xi, pp. 32–3.

2. William Cobbett, *Parliamentary History of England from ... 1066 to ... 1803* (36 vols, London, 1806–20), vol. xiv, p. 694.
3. Cobbett, *Parliamentary History*, vol. xiv, p. 801.
4. Newcastle to Lord Chancellor Hardwicke, 3 Sept. 1755, British Library, Additional Manuscripts (hereafter BL. Add.) 32857 fols 408–20.
5. Horace Walpole, *Memoirs of King George II*, edited by John Brooke (3 vols, New Haven: Yale University Press, 1985), vol. ii, pp. 69–72.
6. P. Langford, 'William Pitt and Public Opinion, 1757', *English Historical Review*, 88 (1973), pp. 54–80.
7. Philip Yorke, *Life and Correspondence of Philip Yorke, Earl of Hardwicke* (3 vols, Cambridge: Cambridge University Press, 1913), vol. iii, pp. 318–21; P.D. Brown and K.W. Schweizer (eds), *The Devonshire Diary. William Cavendish Fourth Duke of Devonshire: Memoranda on State of Affairs 1759–1762* (London: Royal Historical Society, 1982), p. 111.
8. Cabinet minute, 2 October 1761, BL. Add. 32929 fols 21–2.
9. James West MP, report on parliamentary proceedings in Newcastle papers, 12 May 1762, BL. Add. 32938 fols 186–8; papers of James Harris MP, diary 12 May 1762, London, History of Parliament transcripts.
10. W.R. Anson (ed.), *Autobiography and Political Correspondence of Augustus Henry, Third Duke of Grafton* (London: John Murray, 1898).
11. Chatham to Thomas Pitt, 25 September 1777, BL. Add. 69288 no. 35, no fol.
12. *The Bells of Victory: The Pitt–Newcastle Ministry and the Conduct of the Seven Years War* (Cambridge: CUP, 1985).

3
Castlereagh, 1812–22

C.J. Bartlett

Henry Kissinger and Lord Strang (an influential British diplomat of the mid-twentieth century) offer very different assessments of Castlereagh as a foreign minister. Kissinger thought him 'out of tune not only with his contemporaries but also with the entire thrust of modern British foreign policy. He left no legacy; no British statesman has used Castlereagh as a model.'[1] In contrast Strang credits Castlereagh with enduring influence over British diplomacy right down to the 1940s and 1950s:

> Castlereagh was the founder of a tradition of firm but conciliatory diplomacy of which the true heirs were Salisbury, Grey, Eden, and Bevin, in comparison with the challenging ... or merely nagging diplomacy of a Canning, Palmerston, or Lord John Russell.[2]

The late Professor W.N. Medlicott concedes that 'there are many interesting parallels between [Britain's] post-war problems after 1815 and 1945', but contends that in Bevin Britain had 'a tough and forthright negotiator more reminiscent of Palmerston or Churchill than of Castlereagh'.[3]

To explain the place and the long-term influence of an individual in the making and conduct of British foreign policy is by no means a straightforward task. Each inherits much from the past, and finds him/herself the focus of intense contemporary internal and external pressures, especially in periods of crisis. Moreover his/her successors may well be more interested in establishing their own image and not standing in the shadow of their predecessors. Even personalities such as Wellington or Aberdeen, whose thinking on foreign affairs suggests no little continuity from Castlereagh, have left frustratingly little explicit evidence of their debts to him. Castlereagh's association in the minds of so many with reaction at home and abroad also discouraged overt invocation of his name – even by conservatives. An exception was Robert Cecil, the future Third Marquess of Salisbury, who, as a journalist in the 1850s, felt free to take his own line. He provided a penetrating, sympathetic – but not uncritical – study in the *Quarterly Review* of January 1862. Yet even Cecil concluded that Castlereagh's influence died with him 'through his failure to attract devoted followers'. On the other hand he credited him with laying down 'landmarks of policy which have lasted through many revolutions of opinion and are respected still'.[4] Perhaps he should also be credited with identifying and highlighting others.

When Castlereagh took over the Foreign Office in 1812, he was no stranger to revolution, war, and Britain's interests in Europe and the wider world. For much of the 1790s he had been involved in the defence of Ireland from rebellion and French invasion. His political skills had been honed in carrying through the Union of the Irish and British parliaments. As President of the Board of Control from 1802 he had become familiar with the costs as well as with the advantages of the British presence in India, not to mention the negative (as well as the positive) ripple effects from the Indian Ocean to Egypt. He served twice as Secretary of State for War between 1805 and 1809; had grappled with problems of military finance, manpower, supply, and strategy, and been much involved in the first phase of the Peninsular War. His political apprenticeship in London in the 1800s had given him insights into the handling of Parliament and the mysteries of government and ministerial infighting in Whitehall. There had been setbacks, but breaks from office had given him leisure to reflect on the interaction between home and foreign affairs, and the importance of clear priorities in the management of British interests abroad. At the same time he gained a reputation for aloofness. Croker likened him to 'Mont Blanc', a splendid but unapproachable summit. Yet there was also a more accessible and amiable side to his character. As Leader of the House of Commons he steadily earned a reputation for 'good humour' and 'agreeable manners'. Indeed Brougham thought him the only gentleman in the Cabinet. Above all he was at his best in one-to-one or small group discussions in which he displayed a remarkable mixture of patience and perseverance, conciliation and firmness.[5]

Over and above his own qualities, Castlereagh's position was enhanced by the state of parties in the Commons at the time. His bitter critics, however eloquent and incisive, could not carry real weight as long as the majority of MPs preferred the current ministry under Liverpool to the only alternative – a Whig–Radical coalition. This, it was widely believed, could not be trusted to offer sufficient protection to the interests of the landed classes and other bastions of the existing order. Domestic concerns weighed more heavily with the majority of MPs than 'who ruled whom and how' in Europe as long as Britain herself was secure. Thus, Castlereagh, although he was sometimes reminded by Liverpool and others of hostile feeling at home on the subject of treaty commitments, or involvement which might delay the reduction of taxes at home, could still negotiate in Paris and Vienna with a degree of freedom which no future Foreign Secretary was to enjoy. Articulate critics at home might influence future interpretations of his foreign policy, but they mattered little at the time.

Castlereagh, in fact, received more guidance from previous generations than from his contemporaries. The First Lord Melville had contributed to the long-running debate over the relative importance of the balance of power in Europe as opposed to empire building and the acquisition of new markets overseas. Britain, he argued, needed a world strategy to fight France – given the latter's command of so much of Europe. As early as 1796 he insisted that 'the way to defeat France is to take all her colonies and destroy her trade'. Britain, meanwhile, would draw ever more resources from overseas, and with these she could compensate for her inability to create a great Continental army by subsidising allies to play the main part in the land war.[6] Castlereagh, while agreeing in principle, anticipated many difficulties in practice. As he was to display so often in his career, he preferred to examine each problem from many angles and to make allowance for the unexpected. Memoranda composed during the brief peace with France in 1802–03 stressed the huge costs of recent conflicts. He was wary of further war with France unless it was inescapable. Britain needed time to rebuild her financial strength. The government had to be assured of solid public support and high national morale. The efficacy of colonial and economic warfare could not always be guaranteed. He argued that dealings with Continental allies required deeper British understanding of the interests and priorities of indispensable partners and so maximize their support. Already there were strong indications of how Castlereagh would act as Foreign Secretary from 1812.[7]

Grenville and Pitt had earlier given some thought to the problems of closer cooperation with allies and the long-term security of Europe – areas in which Castlereagh was to earn the greatest distinction. Both men were much preoccupied with the balance of power in Europe and (on a more positive note) with the development of some sort of ongoing collaboration between the victors. Grenville, as Pitt's Foreign Minister in 1797, and Pitt himself in 1805 both believed that the great (and so far unattained) alliance, which alone could defeat France, should continue after the war. Some sort of Concert of Europe was needed to uphold the peace settlement, and promote a more stable and orderly state system.[8]

Pitt's more ambitious ideas are to be found in his response to a heterogeneous set of proposals from Tsar Alexander I. In his memorandum of 19 January 1805, Pitt replied that a durable peace would depend on the dissolution of the French empire created in Europe since 1792, with France itself reduced to 'its former limits'. The states restored or created by this action should be assured of 'security and happiness' in their own right, and 'at the same time should constitute a more effectual barrier in future against encroachments on the part of France'. He specifically identified central Europe as a region whose weaknesses and divisions had encouraged and facilitated French aggression. Finally he wished to see 'a general agreement and guarantee for the mutual protection and security of different powers, and for re-establishing a general system of public law in Europe'. Means had to be found to 'frustrate future attempts to disturb the general Tranquillity'.[9] Grenville, it is interesting to note, was to argue forcibly in the House of Lords on 4 November 1813 that there was 'neither safety nor peace for England ... [to be found] but with the safety and peace of Europe'. Castlereagh could not have put it better himself – indeed, given his ponderous speeches in Parliament, he would probably not have said it half so well.

Nevertheless, whatever Castlereagh's debts to Pitt and Grenville, he was confronted with enormous difficulties when trying to implement their vision, and in updating their ideas (with the addition of some of his own) in the light of development of events since 1805. In the process he could expect to find few effective allies at home. Even those who continued to count themselves followers of the late William Pitt did not necessarily share the international aims of the master, or did so only in so far as they were deemed relevant to the narrow national interests of Britain. Difficulties continued with Britain's Continental allies – even at the height of the struggle against Napoleon. Austria had serious conflicts of interest with both Russia and Prussia. In addition to their own divisions the three Continental powers could also agree at times on policies which ignored the interests and needs of Britain. Such behaviour confirmed traditional British suspicions: alliances should be concluded only for immediate and specific objectives. Such feelings were very evident during the long-drawn-out negotiations to produce a peace settlement in 1813–15. Security for the homeland and the empire, peace in Europe, lower taxes and minimal foreign commitments represented the sum of the thinking of most politicians.

Castlereagh could count on a handful of loyal aides and – most valuable of all from 1814 – the backing of the Duke of Wellington, now a leading military figure in Europe, especially after Waterloo. Both men agreed that conflict on the scale of the Napoleonic Wars was not in the interest of Britain, or of any state which had cause to fear the revival of destructive revolutionary forces. Wellington was also well aware of Britain's dependence on the mass armies of her three allies. In several (though not all) of post-1815 crises he was to be a strong advocate of close cooperation with war-time partners.

The Foreign Secretary's shortage of allies at home could, however, be partially offset by other advantages. Castlereagh was at the conference table in person, a position that a lesser Foreign Secretary, Lord Clarendon, was subsequently able to exploit at the Congress of Paris in 1856 against no less a Prime Minister than Lord Palmerston. In Castlereagh's case, the length and complexity of the proceedings (they were spread over more than eighteen months) offered further protection. The relative slowness of communications between London and Paris – and more particularly when the talks were centred in Vienna – necessitated some freedom of choice. In practice he demanded, and was given more discretion, both because of his expertise and because he was second only to the Prime Minister himself in the Cabinet. As a trusted Leader of the House of Commons (as well as Foreign Secretary) he was as indispensable as any minister could be.

Castlereagh's first great challenge, the exploitation of Napoleon's invasion of Russia in 1812, demanded little in the way of original thinking. What was required was a grasp of the realities of the moment, and a readiness to take tough and unpopular decisions. Britain was fearful of Russia's ambitions both in the Baltic and at the expense of Turkey and Persia. Even as Franco-Russian relations deteriorated, some influential Russians still hoped for a new settlement with Napoleon (a second Tilsit). Perhaps Russia could become the fulcrum of a balance of power between France and Britain. What Castlereagh could do was to encourage the Turks and Swedes to make peace with Russia. In 1813 even the Persians came into line. These treaties enabled Russia to concentrate primarily on the war with France. In addition Norway (then under Danish sovereignty) was promised to Sweden, although Castlereagh knew full well that this would be unpopular in the British Parliament. Sweden, however, was needed as an ally against France, as a supplier of naval stores to Britain, and might even be made more resistant to Russian influence.

Metternich, the crucial policy-maker in Vienna, also required delicate handling. Past Austrian defeats at the hands of France, and fears that Russian influence in eastern Europe might surpass even that achieved by the Polish partitions, meant that Metternich was less interested in another war with Napoleon than in negotiating a peace which would establish a true balance of power between France and Russia. If Liverpool thought Austrian behaviour 'abject', and Castlereagh agreed that Metternich was too submissive to the wishes of Napoleon, the Foreign Secretary also showed some understanding of Metternich's fears and hopes. Even so his patience was sorely strained by Metternich's continuing efforts to reach an agreement with Napoleon, one of which would adversely affect certain major British interests, and especially those maritime rights which were the key to the Royal Navy's ability to control neutral trade with the enemy. The year 1813 saw other disappointments, with Austrian and Swedish entry to the war complicating rather than diminishing allied suspicions and dissension. Castlereagh commented:

> The risk of treating with France is great, but the risk of losing our continental Allies and the confidence of our own nation is even greater ... with respect to the Continent we must sustain and animate those powers through whose exertions we can alone hope to improve it [the situation], taking care, in aiming at too much, not to destroy our future means of connexion and resistance.[10]

Castlereagh, however, was sufficiently sanguine to re-read Pitt's Concert proposals of 1805, and to pass on his latest thoughts to the Tsar.[11]

At the same time he could not ignore the relative ease with which Britain could be sidelined and ignored in the deliberations of Russia, Austria and Prussia. Notwithstanding the allies' dependence on British subsidies, they concluded an armistice with Napoleon in June 1813. Castlereagh's representatives at allied headquarters failed to exert as much influence as he had hoped. Castlereagh himself made several attempts in writing to underline the need for unity at a moment when 'We now have the bull close pinioned between us.' Allied cooperation should also continue after the war. On the other hand he disturbed some of his allies by his reference to the current war of peoples (after the example of the French): it was no longer a simple 'game of statesmen' with professional armies. To Castlereagh's dismay, however, the next major act of the allies was to offer Napoleon the 'natural frontiers of France' in their Frankfurt peace proposals of 9 November 1813. He was equally outraged by their continuing neglect of prime British interests such as the expulsion of France from Holland and Antwerp, and by their readiness to include Britain's maritime rights in the proposed peace talks.

Matters came to a head with an allied dispatch on 5 December 1813 requesting the appointment of one person with plenary powers to represent Britain at expected negotiations with France. This was the origin of Castlereagh's lengthy presences in Europe in 1814–15. His first concern was allied unity to effect the defeat of Napoleon; his second and much longer task was the negotiation of an enduring peace settlement. Similarly it was early in 1814 that he began to emphasize the importance of ongoing personal contacts with the leading allied figures, notably Alexander I and Metternich. These, he contended, would best promote mutual understanding, develop a sense of united purpose, and ensure continuing cooperation in the management of peace as well as war. Lord Ripon, who attended Castlereagh on the first mission, recorded the Foreign Secretary's thoughts on the difficulties he expected to face at the allied headquarters in Basle. He laid special emphasis on those which were caused by '… the want of an habitual confidential and free intercourse between the Ministers of the Great Powers, *as a body* … many pretensions might be modified, asperities removed, by bringing the respective parties into unrestricted communications common to them …'[12] This was an advance on the ideas outlined by Grenville and Pitt in their sketches of a future concert.

Castlereagh had also informed his subordinates in Europe in February 1814 that British interests did not require assertion by chicane or dexterity: a steady and temperate application of honest principles would be 'her best source of authority'. Although this might suggest naivety or hypocrisy, it has to be remembered that Britain could not long remain a Continental military power once the war was over (the army occupying France was withdrawn in 1818). Great as were her economic and naval powers, these would need time to make an impact in an emergency. Thus a reputation for disinterestedness – in so far as that quality was ever attainable – might invest British diplomacy with more authority than recourse to backdoor and other underhand methods. Clausewitz, the Prussian expert on war, might seem an unlikely admirer, but such was his dismay over the determination of some of his countrymen to impose a punitive peace on France that he found hope for the future in the open-handedness and cool style of the British. They would play the better role 'because they do not seem to have come here with a passion for revenge ... but rather like a master who wishes to discipline with proved coldness and immaculate purity'.[13] This was praise indeed, though in fairness it must be added that the British could comfortably act in this way since, by a fairly early stage in the peace-making process, they had achieved their main objectives. They wished to preserve the new *status quo*.[14]

Castlereagh's faith in the value of his personal contacts with Alexander and others, plus his own persuasive skills in camera, were naturally linked to Britain's usefulness to the other powers. His early and continuing success with Metternich owed much to the latter's fears of Russia's growing power in the heart of Europe. Both men had a vested interest in a satisfactory balance of power. Admittedly their relationship was threatened by disagreements over the appropriate response of the great powers to the revolutions of 1820–21. Yet it was quickly revived when the Greek revolt against the Turks renewed fears of further Russian advances at the expense of the Ottoman empire, so that by 1822 the understanding between the two men was as strong as it had ever been. Castlereagh found it much more difficult to work with Alexander I. At the time of their first acquaintance in 1814 Castlereagh had encountered the Tsar in buoyant mood, elated by the size and success of his armies. He was determined to secure acceptance of Russia as a civilized and truly European power, and therefore entitled to exercise major influence in the heart of Europe and over the political future of France. Some leading Russians were equally ambitious, though with rather different priorities. They anticipated a renewal of competition with Britain, a view well expressed by General Kutuzov in 1812. Asked by a British diplomat why the French had been allowed to leave Moscow unmolested, the commander-in-chief had replied:

> I am by no means sure that the total destruction of the French emperor and his army would be such a benefit to the world; his succession would not fall to Russia or any other Continental country, but to that power which already commands the seas, and whose domination would then be intolerable.[15]

Anglo-Russian rivalry, in short, had merely been put on hold for the time being.

Alexander's readiness to listen to Castlereagh was greatly increased when Napoleon launched his surprise (and initially successful) counter-offensive in February 1814. A less confident Tsar was persuaded to take more account of the views of his allies. Thus Castlereagh was at last able to conclude the comprehensive alliance which he had been seeking since September 1813. The Treaty of Chaumont was signed on 9 March 1814. Castlereagh's position was further improved by Wellington's advance into south-western France and by a promise from London of £5m in further subsidies, with additional money if Britain was unable to match the 150 000 troops promised by each ally. A delighted Castlereagh wrote that assistance on this scale would, he trusted, 'put an end to any doubts as to the claim we have to an opinion on Continental matters'. Furthermore, the allies agreed to continue the alliance for 20 years after the defeat of Napoleon for security against any future French attempt to upset the peace settlement. True, he was unable to realize Pitt's 1805 hope of a general territorial guarantee by the powers. The allies more modestly promised to strive for 'the equilibrium of Europe', and reserved to themselves the right 'to concert together [on the defeat of France] ... as to the means best adapted to guarantee to Europe and themselves reciprocally, the continuance of the peace'.[16]

Napoleon's determination to fight on from 1813 had thus worked mostly to Castlereagh's advantage. The restoration of the Bourbons (tempered by a modest constitution) also gave Castlereagh reason to hope that in due course France might learn the wisdom of moderation at home and abroad. He thus pressed for allied restraint in the peace settlement. To deprive France of significant territories would damage the new regime in the eyes of its people, and further inflame desires for revenge. Most of the French colonies and commercial posts captured by the British were therefore returned. On the other hand French possession of the Low Countries could not be tolerated. As Lord Harrowby remarked, 'Antwerp and Flushing out of the hands of France are worth twenty Martiniques in our own hands'.[17] It has often been forgotten that Nelson's victory at Trafalgar had not permanently put an end to the fear of a French invasion, the British being particularly alarmed by the French naval build up in Antwerp in the last years of the war.

Castlereagh hoped that a union of the Low Countries (Belgium having formerly belonged to the Habsburg empire) would create a more effective defence in the event of any future French bid to revise their north-eastern frontiers. The union was pushed through against some Belgian objections and reservations on the part of Lord Liverpool (the union in fact lasted only until the early 1830s). Captured colonies were also returned to the Dutch to enrich the Netherlands, while the purchase of the Cape of Good Hope from the Dutch for £2m had a double strategic significance. The Cape was a crucial base on the most used British route to the East, while the compensation was used to strengthen the new Dutch border against France. Strategic needs were similarly reflected in British insistence on the possession of such islands as Malta, Mauritius and St Lucia. In addition, and in response to direct pressure from Wilberforce and anti-slave trade campaigners (who had also won the ear of other ministers), Castlereagh took up the cause for abolition in talks with

France. There was a considerable outcry at home when France was allowed five years' grace before the trade was stopped. Castlereagh, however, complained that this aggressive campaign had simply provoked French national pride and led to a passionate public outcry. This might have been avoided by quiet diplomacy.

The first Peace of Paris signed on 30 May 1814 met most of Britain's direct needs, but the task was only half complete given Castlereagh's belief that there would be no security against war or revolutions without a comprehensive peace settlement. There were those in Britain, however, who could not see why their country should be so deeply involved in the future of distant and obscure parts of the Continent in which they had little direct interest. This was the view of some Cabinet ministers. In any case the patience of Liverpool and some ministers was being sorely tried by the absence of their Leader of the House of Commons for long periods between December 1813 and November 1815, and especially from the start of the Congress of Vienna in September 1814. Furthermore, some of his dealings resulted in extra calls on a hard-pressed Treasury at a time when Britain was still at war with the US. It is therefore not unreasonable to suggest that while others in his place might have agreed to some British involvement in European affairs, they might well have adopted a more selective and warier approach.

Castlereagh (though less visionary than Gladstone or Woodrow Wilson) was a man with a mission, and one can only marvel at his persistence and industry in the face of so many obstacles – at home and abroad. He had few experts to help him, the best being Joseph Planta (his private secretary), Lord Clancarty and Edward Cooke, the last-named suffering a breakdown from overwork in Vienna. Planta in the poorly organized Foreign Office was still complaining of overwork in 1822. Experience soon persuaded Canning, Castlereagh's successor, that the Foreign Office with the 'Lead' in the Commons was 'too much for any man'. Gentz, the Congress Secretary, was best placed to offer an objective verdict. He was astonished by Castlereagh's industry and his patient dealings with the other leading figures in Vienna: his qualities as a diplomat were outstanding.[18] Captain Gronow, an avid collector of news and gossip in Paris during one phase of the peace talks, described Castlereagh as the 'pre-eminent star', but so overloaded with business that he made up for lack of sleep by relaxing and dozing in a bath for an hour or two each day. Gronow was further impressed by the simplicity of his dress, compared with most of the English in Paris, visitors and army officers alike. On a subsequent occasion in Britain he recalled Castlereagh's extraordinary aplomb in the face of a major riot.[19]

Often Castlereagh prevailed against Metternich and Alexander I by sheer persistence, greater stamina, superior mastery of the subjects under discussion, and astonishing self-control. In return he could deploy lengthy and elaborate counter-arguments, verbally or on paper. To indications in 1818 that the European monarchies might be tempted to intervene in some way or other in the crisis between Spain and her rebellious South American colonies, Castlereagh came up with no less than 43 comments and queries on the wisdom and practicability of their proposals. Liverpool at one stage in the lengthy search for peace wrote impatiently to his Foreign Secretary arguing the case for an early, however imperfect, peace. What was needed, he contended, was a sufficiently long interlude during which the genie of revolution could be firmly restoppered in its bottle, thus reducing the danger that the next war would take on the character of those which had ravaged and destabilized Europe since 1792. Castlereagh was at one with him in such fears, but believed that a comprehensive and just peace would prove the better solution. A new balance of power should leave no power – not even France – seriously aggrieved. Given such promise of international stability, and coupled with the creation as far as possible of strong and stable regimes within the most important or potentially troublesome states, the danger of further wars and revolutions would be much reduced. He favoured, for instance, a modest constitution in Bourbon France in the hope that this would lead to moderate policies at home and abroad.

So ambitious a settlement, unfortunately, was not easily attainable. Relations between the powers continued to worsen despite the start of the Congress of Vienna in the autumn of 1814. Deep differences still existed between Austria on the one hand and Russia and Prussia on the other over territory and areas of influence in Eastern Europe. Russia posed the most serious problem, because she was already in occupation of the larger part of Poland and seemed determined to dictate the fate of Saxony to the exclusive advantage of Prussia. There would, in short, be no equilibrium in Central Europe, especially given Russian military power in Poland. For a time even Castlereagh seemed resigned to defeat. By December 1814 his own standing from Vienna to London was at its lowest ebb. He was rescued by several new developments. One was the ending of the war with America; another was the readiness of France to support the Austrian and British position on Saxony, while the reaction of several lesser states helped to persuade Alexander that it was time to be conciliatory if he wished to retain his title as the great Christian liberator and peacemaker of Europe. Although the secret alliance of France, Austria and Britain was not called upon to act, it is interesting to note that in this instance Liverpool was willing to back Castlereagh. Peace with the US was one factor, but he also welcomed the polarization of France and Russia: fears of a deal between Paris and St Petersburg were much diminished. For Castlereagh there had been some improvement to the European balance (Prussia gave up part of Saxony to the great relief of Austria), while France's readiness to work with Britain and Austria surely contributed to his later conviction that even Napoleon's brief bid to regain power (the Hundred Days) should not be allowed to obstruct ultimate French admission to the new Concert.[20]

The widespread sense of insecurity seemed justified when Napoleon's Hundred Days were accompanied by signs of a revival of 'Jacobinism' in vulnerable parts of Europe. Fortunately Britain's larger role in the Anglo-Prussian victory at Waterloo added to her standing on the Continent. Unfortunately it also encouraged many in Britain (including some in government) and Prussia to demand ruthless punishment and an overall weakening of France for the foreseeable future. Liverpool wrote in July 1815, 'The prevailing idea in this country is that we are fairly entitled to avail ourselves of the present moment to take back from France the principal conquests of Louis XIV.'[21] Bathurst added on 25 August that 'The public could never be made to understand why we should be severely taxed, in order to preserve the integrity of France.'[22] Liverpool sent further punitive proposals for the weakening and control of France. Meanwhile the British press, by the violence of its demands against France, was encouraging the Prussians to persist with their own extreme demands.[23] Fortunately Castlereagh's views were shared by the Tsar and Wellington. London was bluntly told that the best securities against war and revolution lay in the survival of the Bourbon dynasty. The latter should be spared the humiliation of large surrenders of territory, which might have damaging effects on the standing of the Bourbons among the French people. The terms envisaged by the Cabinet were not severe enough to cripple France: they would only inflame the grievances of her people. The differences, which had been evident between Castlereagh and Cabinet colleagues for some time, had finally come to a head. Fortunately it resulted in a victory for Castlereagh and Wellington over the treatment of France.[24]

Castlereagh spelt out his long-term intentions towards France to Liverpool in August 1815. It was, he insisted, 'not our business to collect trophies [from France], but to try to bring the world back to peaceful habits'. France might once again become a 'useful rather than a dangerous member of the European system'. In the meantime some French fortresses would be occupied by the allies until the French had given 'protracted proofs of having ceased to be a revolutionary state'. The second Peace of Paris was somewhat harsher than the first, but these were described as not being 'against France as a nation, but against France as the concentration of military Jacobinism'. Kissinger, writing in 1957, observed that 'At no other time in his career did Castlereagh show to greater advantage than in his battle for the equilibrium of Paris.'[25]

The attainment of a complementary objective soon followed, and one that was of even greater importance to Castlereagh. This was the Quadruple Alliance of 20 November 1815. For him this was to form the keystone of future European stability and security, and for that reason he was anxious that it should be a permanent union. The alliance, as finally drafted, was less ambitious. A general guarantee of all Europe against aggression, as suggested by Pitt in 1805, was a step too far for most in Westminster and Whitehall.

The alliance was directed against any future French aggression and French acceptance of rule by a Bonaparte in any shape or form. Mutual aid within the Quadruple Alliance was agreed, but Britain would not pledge herself to maintain the Bourbons on the French throne. Even a revolution in France required the allies to do no more than 'concert among themselves … the measures which they may judge necessary'. Article VI laid down the obligations of the signatories. They would meet at fixed periods to consult common interests, and to consider such measures which, 'at each of these periods shall be considered the most salutary for the repose and prosperity of nations and for the maintenance of the peace of Europe'. Credit should also be given to the contributions of the representatives of other leading powers. F.H. Hinsley reflected in the early 1960s – one of the tenser periods of the Cold War – that 'The impressive thing about the behaviour of the Powers in 1815 is that they were prepared, as they had never previously been prepared, to waive their individual interests in the pursuit of an international system.'[26] Contemporary sceptics of the high-mindedness of the peacemakers included Clausewitz and Gentz.[27]

Even this modest, though novel Treaty of Alliance (and especially Article VI), prompted the Cabinet to remind Castlereagh in November 1815 that only the exceptional international conditions which Britain had experienced since 1789 enabled the government to accept such commitments. Although the Commons approved the treaty by 240 votes to 77 in February 1816, this should not be taken as evidence of great enthusiasm for the settlement. It was the dissidents who were moved by strong feelings, and who seized the opportunity to denounce the alliance as a threat to the liberties of Europe – and perhaps even to those of Britain herself. Indeed foreign issues over the rest of Castlereagh's career, and especially his readiness to cooperate with the autocracies, supplied useful hostages to opponents intent on blackening and discrediting the government.

Nevertheless, Castlereagh's relations with the autocracies and his responses to the revolt of Spain's South American colonies, the Greek rising against the Turks, the Spanish and Italian revolutions in the early 1820s, plus sundry experiments in limited constitutional government, continued to be directed towards the avoidance of war and a major revival of revolutionary activity in Europe. In so far as his responses were influenced by what might loosely be characterized as ideological, only Bonapartism at one pole and 'Jacobinism' at the other were non-negotiable. His pragmatic flexibility with respect to the many intermediate possibilities confused many (British and European) contemporaries whose thinking was much less flexible. Too much attention was paid (and still is by some writers) to tactical moves, and too little to the underlying strategic continuity in Castlereagh's policies as defined above. Tactical failures did not necessarily mean strategic failure. Castlereagh's rich experience of politics had left him with few illusions as to how much influence one minister could hope to exercise. He once warned the Tsar of the dangerous and unpredictable consequences which might follow if a statesman 'were permitted to regulate his conduct by the counsels of his heart instead of the dictates of his understanding'.

'Counsels of the heart' nevertheless sometimes asserted themselves, especially with reference to his hopes of an enduring and effective Quadruple Alliance. Precious too was his faith in regular meetings of key ministers and even heads of state, impelled by the twin aims of identifying critical problems, and acting in concert in their solution. Indeed as late as 1818 he disturbed Cabinet colleagues when, writing in a moment of exhilaration from the Congress of Aix-la-Chapelle, he described the Congress system as 'a new discovery in the European Government, ... giving to the counsels of the Great Powers the efficiency and almost the simplicity of a single State'. This was not in accord with the guidance given to him by the Cabinet before his departure to the Continent. As it was he soon conceded that the 'existing state of European relations may possibly not endure beyond the danger which originally gave them birth, ... but it is our duty, as well as interest, to retard if we cannot avert, the return of a more contentious order of things.' In the same document he claimed that he was indulging in no 'blind confidence' in the trustworthiness of other powers, but he was determined that 'our own missions abroad' should not provoke disputes. Britain's insular position, her naval supremacy, and her network of overseas bases enabled her to pursue in safety 'a more generous and confiding policy'.[28]

It was on the basis of such calculations that he clung to his hope that the powers could be persuaded to deal with each other with greater frankness and honesty. Thus French activity in Buenos Aires in 1820 was characterized as flowing from 'some of the dregs of that old diplomacy which so long poisoned the body politic of Europe', and which he now (too optimistically) thought much reduced – at least in 'the councils of the Quadruple Alliance'. Given the strength of his commitment to the alliance, one should be wary of interpreting his famous and much quoted State Paper of 6 May 1820 as if it signalled a fundamental change of policy. It was above all an exercise in damage limitation at home in response to domestic critics of counter-revolution. After all, circumstances might change and the tenuous links with the European despots might then be reactivated. It is also possible that some of the more insular passages on the subject of the alliance might have been influenced (or even written) by colleagues anxious to distance themselves from powers whose main preoccupation seemed to be the suppression of moderate as well as extreme opponents of the existing political order.

Two months later (11 July 1820) Castlereagh and Canning each spoke in a foreign affairs debate. Where the latter stressed his support for 'the extension of liberty and liberal institutions throughout the world', Castlereagh openly and unashamedly asserted that 'the honour of every individual power who was a party to that holy alliance [a synonym for the most extreme reactionary states when used by his critics at home] ... was untainted'.[29] Meanwhile he was signalling to Metternich and others his disapproval of the use of the alliance as 'an union for the government of the world or for the superintendence of the internal affairs of other States'; especially if supposed revolutionary threats to neighbours were illusory. The alliance was not intended to deal with 'every possible danger'. What mattered was that Britain should be found in her proper place 'when actual danger menaces the system of Europe'. The Austrian ambassador noted several intimations from Wellington in the spring of 1820 that the British Cabinet for the time being wished the alliance to sleep. Yet as unrest grew in several parts of Europe, so Metternich and Castlereagh through secret exchanges (and finally through a secret meeting in Hanover in October 1821) were able to proceed with a better understanding of each other's needs and thinking. Neither wished the turbulence in Spain to lead to great power intervention, and each hoped to prevent further extensions of Russian and French influence. Castlereagh wished to see Italy remain within the Austrian orbit, while doing his best to persuade Vienna to keep its coercive actions to a minimum. He even believed that the Iberian Peninsula as a whole might benefit from moderate constitutions – a compromise between the claims of the two monarchs and their opponents. He was less sympathetic to the Neapolitan revolution of July 1820.

At times it seemed as if the tenuous ties with Vienna must break. Castlereagh accepted that this might prove unavoidable, especially when he found it impossible to provide a cogent – or indeed an entirely honest – defence of his policy at home. Nor was he able to reassure the European courts at this time. Nevertheless he hoped to rescue something from the wreck. The Greek question, while increasingly dangerous, helped to revive his relationship with Metternich. It also opened the Tsar's eyes to certain harsh realities. Though described by the Russian historian, Sergei Soloviev, as 'the Agamemnon of tsars', Alexander I was less interested in great adventures than personal prestige and the cultivation of his image as the great Christian peacemaker in Europe. If a Russian war with Turkey over the Greek revolt was the worst nightmare of Castlereagh and Metternich, carefully worded personal appeals to the Tsar helped them to buy time. These included warnings of the dangers of new revolutions, and the need to uphold the alliance.

In the middle of 1821 it seemed that the crunch would come at the proposed congress in Verona. Professor Derry writes that the 'Congress of Verona would have exposed growing tensions between Castlereagh and his allies', but adds that 'this is not to say that his whole work collapsed in his personal tragedy'.[30] Had he lived he might have been able to adjust to new circumstances. He was always appreciative of the unpredictability of international politics. Before his breakdown and suicide on 12 August 1822, he was busy with ideas to tackle the problems posed by Spain's rebellious American colonies, and by the Spanish as well as the Greek revolutions. Nor had he seemingly despaired of finding some common ground with the other powers. Among the options under review was recognition of the Greeks as belligerents and the creation of a 'qualified Greek government'. He was, however, reluctant to do more than was absolutely necessary. Aberdeen was firmly put in his place in 1821 when he urged a more positive policy on behalf of Greece. Castlereagh opposed 'portentous Experiments, especially in an age when half the World is at Sea in search of the means of self-government'. He feared Russian subversion of the Turkish empire. His own reliance on agreement between himself, Metternich and the Tsar seemed to be vindicated when the latter dismissed Capodistrias in 1822, the most revisionist of his advisers.[31] The value of personal links had not been exhausted. But following his death, there was no question of Britain trying to seize the initiative at Verona as envisaged by Castlereagh.

Canning's proclamation of the philosophy of '… every nation for itself and God for us all', might seem to mark a change as decisive as the death of his predecessor. Robert Cecil concluded in 1862 that Castlereagh, despite his success in mastering 'an appalling storm', had failed to inspire 'that intense personal devotion which has united so many great statesmen with their political supporters. Therefore his influence died with his own death.'[32]

Yet it would be surprising if some of those with first-hand experience of the traumatic years down to 1815 (and the fear that they might all too easily return) had not reacted to new crises in Europe in ways similar to those adopted by Castlereagh. Even Canning had written to his mother in 1819 lamenting the degree to which the times were still 'out of joint', and how Britain might be adversely affected by unrest in Europe.[33] Peel said the same in 1820.[34] Wellington, ever fearful of anything that might cause a new war, was particularly troubled by the Greek revolt against the Turks, especially when it broadened into a Russo-Turkish war during his Premiership of 1828–30. Russia herself might succumb to revolution as a result of the costs of a new conflict. He wavered between thoughts of drastic action and a reluctance to act at all. It was left to Aberdeen as Foreign Secretary to initiate the moves, which finally led to some international dialogue and an independent Greece in 1832.[35]

Admittedly Castlereagh's successors and secret admirers were not tempted to involve Britain so deeply in the affairs of Europe. Whatever their worries, they were not confronted with such immense and seemingly never-ending dangers as had been the case from 1793 to 1815. Nevertheless they shared his conviction that it was imperative to prevent a revival of French, Napoleonic and revolutionary threats. Clear echoes of Castlereagh's strategies can be found in the international thinking of such conservatives as Wellington, Aberdeen and Malmesbury (and also in the analyses provided by J.W. Croker, and the historians, Sir Archibald Alison and James Froude). War and/or revolution in Europe could have the most damaging imperial and domestic consequences for Britain. Muriel Chamberlain notes that Aberdeen as Foreign

Secretary 'favoured the old flexible balance of power system which he had learned from Castlereagh and which he had sometimes defended in the House of Lords'.[36] It is true that the three eastern powers did not always respond in the way that he wished, while his own use of old allies and the Concert of Europe was highly selective.

Chamberlain entitles one chapter of her valuable biography of Aberdeen, 'A Conservative Abroad'. This covers the 1830s. Elsewhere, in her *'Pax Britannica'? British Foreign Policy, 1789–1914*, she asks if there was an 'Alternative Tradition?' with Wellington and Aberdeen as the 'obvious heirs' to Castlereagh in contrast to Palmerston as the follower of Canning's approach, a tradition which in his case became increasingly chauvinistic and even bombastic.[37] Wellington and Croker are good examples of those who feared the potential knock-on effects of war with another power. Thus they feared that war over Oregon with the US would soon be followed by war with France. The cost of such conflicts would impose enormous strains on the British economy and thus stability of the existing political and social order, not least in Ireland.[38]

Aberdeen was highly critical of Whig foreign policy in the 1830s. He complained that they were too inclined to favour Orleanist France under a constitutional monarchy, and to spurn the conservative powers. With other Tories he welcomed the displays of unity shown by the eastern powers at Münchengrätz and Berlin in 1833 'against the disorganising and revolutionary policy of the present Governments of Britain and France'. Conservative unity gave Europe its best promise of peace and stability.[39] The Tory preference for evolutionary change, and then often only as a last resort, did not satisfy Palmerston. Yet his alignment with the despotic powers against France in the Near Eastern crisis of 1839–41, and his belief in 1849 that the continued inclusion of Hungary in the Habsburg empire was essential to the proper working of the balance of power, would surely have earned approval from the ghost of Castlereagh.

Wellington, Aberdeen and some other Tories did not wish to side with the conservative powers in all circumstances, despite their fears of France and revolution. Such entanglements ran counter to their preference for a free hand when possible. Nor did they intend to supply useful ammunition to their critics at home. They showed flexibility in 1830 when faced by revolution in France and renewed talk of another 1789. Wellington himself finally agreed to recognize the new Orleanist regime in France – if only as the least bad option. But once out of office, the Tories made much of the pro-French leanings of the Whig Cabinet. It was even thought possible that the Whigs (with Palmerston in the Foreign Office) might join France in a war against one or more of the eastern powers to advance the revolutionary process in Greece, Italy and Spain. This was at a time when Britain herself was grappling with the explosive subject of parliamentary reform.

In an interesting letter to Croker in September 1833 Wellington outlined the foreign policy he would have followed had he retained office after 1830. He had, he wrote, hoped to buy time until circumstances would permit the reversal of the Belgian revolt from Dutch rule. This was a breach of the Vienna Settlement which had set up a united Netherlands to add to the obstacles to renewed expansion by the French on their eastern frontiers. Aberdeen for a time had shared this interest in reunification.[40] France continued to excite alarm, and in 1845 he assured Peel that Britain could count on the Habsburgs in a 'real emergency'. Unfortunately Russia was a different matter, having too many ambitions of her own to be treated as a reliable partner. Thus Aberdeen avoided a direct reply in 1842 when St Petersburg pressed for what in effect would have been a revival of the old Quadruple Alliance. As for Prussia, he deemed her too weak to be of much consequence.[41] He felt amiable relations with the eastern powers were sufficient for Britain's purposes, especially as they were unlikely to render Britain any assistance outside Europe. It was essential, therefore, for Britain to try to remain on reasonable terms with France and the US.

Aberdeen's efforts to maintain an *entente* with Orleanist France, however, were strained by a naval race in the early 1840s, while the revival of Bonapartism in the person of Louis Napoleon from 1848 suggested that the old war-time alliance might once again have its uses.[42] Thus a new crisis in the Near East in 1853 found Aberdeen and some other Tories deeply reluctant to believe the worst of Russia, given their fears of France. In contrast to liberal and radical demands for a crusade to overthrow the strongest of the despotic powers (such a victory, they claimed, would make the cause of progress unstoppable elsewhere), Aberdeen privately feared catastrophe. He described worsening Anglo-Russian relations over Turkey as 'incredible' and 'unintelligible'. Talk of war seemed insane. The Prince Consort shrewdly commented just after the outbreak of the Crimean War that for Aberdeen this was 'like a civil war; like a war between England and Scotland'. Indeed by June 1854 Aberdeen was wondering if Napoleon might exploit the conflict to revise the Treaty of Vienna. In the autumn he was also alarmed by the deteriorating relations between Austria and Prussia. 'For all this may at last end in a revolutionary war greatly to the desire of many here [in Britain] and elsewhere.'[43]

The Admiralty continued to keep a close watch on French naval policy during the war. If Croker conceded that Russia was not blameless in the Near East, he still accused the radicals of seeking war against Russia as 'the dernière resource of monarchy'. He, too, feared Napoleon III and suspected the existence of a secret European revolutionary party. Two historians, Alison and Froude, agreed that the war might lead to wider and more serious consequences. In October 1854 the Duke of Argyll questioned the purpose of the war, a war which he feared was being guided by an over-excited British public.[44] Later, in 1859, Malmesbury (the Tory Foreign Secretary) and others tried to reverse the Franco-Austrian drift towards war over the future of northern Italy. They clearly wished to avoid any weakening of the Habsburg empire – a reliable and necessary defender of the *status quo*.

The 15 years following the end of the Crimean War, however, belonged to Napoleon III, Cavour and Bismarck. This reached a climax with the German victory over France in 1870–71, an outcome which was seen by many as promising to create a rather better balance than that which had existed since France's revival as a leading power from the mid-1850s. The 1870s were to witness at least one major individual effort to approach international affairs in the spirit of Castlereagh. During the Near Eastern crises of 1875 and 1878 Lord Derby as Foreign Secretary strove to maintain high politics as the preserve of experts. He wished to exclude as far as possible the emotional vagaries of public opinion, and restrain political leaders such as Disraeli who (in his opinion) thought too much in terms of prestige abroad or popularity at home. He favoured 'pacific, free-trading mid-Victorian values'; not 'the alien world of honour and prestige'. This was the thinking which lay behind his secret diplomacy (official and unofficial) to avert a war with Russia. His dealings with the Russian ambassador resemble Castlereagh's secret exchanges with Metternich. Derby, however, did not share his distant predecessor's passion for great power cooperation. He believed foreign policy had usually prospered most when Britain chose the path of isolation.[45] Even so many of the key elements in Castlereagh's thinking and diplomatic methods were still evident in some Tory ranks. Admittedly this may often have been evidence of Castlereagh's success in identifying British needs and interests, and the best means of securing them, rather than in the existence of a 'school' as defined by the future Lord Salisbury. Yet imitation, whether conscious or not, is an impressive form of flattery. His emphasis on patience, conciliation and compromise was also echoed by many of his successors.

Castlereagh encouraged such an approach to relations with the US.[46] As Foreign Secretary in 1812 he had been one of those ministers who had blundered into the war of 1812 with the US. Apart from the issues at stake, there was a widespread tendency in Britain to belittle the US, and to insist that serious negotiation was almost impossible with a government composed of leaders of the mob and lacking men of honesty and principle.[47] The ensuing conflict, however, had been sufficiently inconvenient, especially while Britain was at war with Napoleon, for him to decide that however ungentlemanly, unpredictable, and aggressive the North Americans might seem, an uneasy coexistence was preferable to another war. The growth of Anglo-American trade was likely to offset commercial rivalry and disputes. Furthermore, although Canada had been successfully defended in the war of 1812, and severe damage had been inflicted on the American economy, the British had been happy to settle for a draw at the end of 1814. It was also becoming apparent that it could only be a matter of time before the US – in terms of population, resources and enterprise – would pose a serious challenge to British interests in the New World, particularly with respect to

Canada with its much smaller population. Castlereagh opted for a policy of conciliation, patience and civility, and trusted to the healing effects of time. In due course his successors, with varying degrees of reluctance, reached the same conclusions.

The Rush–Bagot agreement of 1817 was the first step towards the creation of the 'undefended frontier' between the US and Canada, and progress was made on a number of other issues. True, much remained unresolved, while Castlereagh himself wished to limit American expansion and influence as much as possible. When questions were raised on the future of Santo Domingo, he unhesitatingly noted that it would be better for Britain if ruled by 'Negroes' rather than Americans. Nevertheless he had set the tone of British policy for such Tory successors as Wellington, Aberdeen and Malmesbury. Although Canning, and more so Palmerston, were highly critical of the 'Yankees' in private, even Palmerstonian abuse was often the prelude to further concessions. From the 1870s it was accepted that the Americans could take Canada if they were so minded, and in the early 1900s the Admiralty agreed that the Americans could build the world's largest navy if they chose. If the policy of retreat by the 1900s had fallen short of an *entente*, Theodore Roosevelt in particular had come to believe that Britain and the US had many international interests in common. If Britain faltered as a great power, the US might have to step in as her supporter and even successor. Castlereagh himself could hardly have expected such a measure of progress towards coexistence, but he can be credited with making the right assumptions as early as 1815.

On the subject of the British empire and other parts of the world, Castlereagh emerges as a relatively modest imperialist. Indeed he might be described as leaning towards a 'blue water' empire – an empire based on selective rather than total occupation. His qualifications to Dundas's enthusiasm for colonial warfare have been noted above. He proudly asserted to the Commons in 1816 that Britain 'had acquired what in former days would have been thought romance'; the keys of every military position needed for the security of the empire. These included Gibraltar, Malta, the Cape of Mauritius, Ceylon, Bombay and Calcutta (Singapore was added from 1819), Halifax and Bermuda. With respect to Latin America, after a false start with military failure at Buenos Aires and the Rio de la Plata in 1806–07, he was content to rely on the 'silent and imperceptible operation of our [at that time] illicit commercial intercourse'. Further military intervention was likely to be costly and counter-productive. By the time of his death he had seen the Spanish colonies make great progress to independence: recognition had become a matter of time and method rather than of principle.[48] He had gone far enough for recognition by Canning to be only a matter of timing. Latin America was to form part of the empire of free trade.

Edward Ingram is a notable critic of Castlereagh's reluctance to become actively involved in the defence of Persia against further Russian advances.

Instead, and Canning after him, he gave priority to Europe and the Near East, thereby allowing Persia to become dependent on Russia.[49] In due course their successors were to accord a higher priority to this region, with Palmerston arguing that events in Europe and India's north-western areas could not fail to influence each other. Yet it can be argued that Castlereagh was right to give priority (as matters stood in the years 1812–22) to the search for peace and stability in Europe. As Salisbury once reminded an overactive Viceroy of India, Lord Lytton, he should leave some problems to occupy his successors.

It is obvious that Castlereagh had been exceptionally fortunate in being in power at the time he was. He represented the richest of the powers at a critical moment in the history of Europe. He was fortunate, too, that the war-time allies, despite their many differences with each other, had many important interests (and fears) in common. Though often criticized for his neglect of liberalism and nationalism, Castlereagh was not 'out of tune' with the most powerful forces in the Europe of 1814–15. These largely prevailed for another 40 years. To have built on the foundations recommended by some Whigs and many Radicals would have been building on sand. It is also evident that whatever verdict one passes on Castlereagh's policies, he had, by his own criteria, been successful. It is true that another in his place would probably have been more selective and therefore less interested in continuing cooperation with the other powers. It could be argued that Castlereagh had involved Britain more deeply in Europe than was strictly necessary. On the whole Europe proved a less dangerous place until 1848 than he had anticipated. Peace had been kept by the weaknesses, divisions and fears of the other powers as much as by the treaties concluded in 1814–15. Above all the balance of power favoured the defenders of the *status quo* until the late 1850s.[50]

Nevertheless one can credit Castlereagh (and his Continental counterparts) with a major contribution to the relative peace which ensued. If France was restrained mainly by her own weakness and frequent isolation, the peace terms had been judicious and constructive. If the statesmen were often guided by more selfish motives than they professed, Castlereagh himself (once he began to be reappraised by historians from the mid-nineteenth century onwards) has by and large continued to maintain his standing among scholars as a great foreign minister. He appreciated that much might be gained by an attempt to understand the needs and thought patterns of others; that one might secure more in the long run by judicious compromises; that to strive for too much (like Napoleon) could be the most damaging of courses; and that given the intractable nature of some problems it was better to seek refuge in a *modus vivendi*, or simply agree to differ rather than generate still more ill-feeling by persisting in futile controversy.

The degree to which a policy-maker can make a difference is often very limited, but a well-informed choice among even a limited number of options is still important. Similarly personal skills and qualities, the ability to strike the right balance between firmness and conciliation, the mastery of facts and ability to argue a case, and even superior stamina and sense of purpose can influence the final outcome. At the same time one should never lose sight of Castlereagh's debt to the relative advantages enjoyed by Britain over the other powers. It was often possible to be inventive, urbane and conciliatory in the shadow of the world's strongest economy and largest navy.

Notes

1. Henry Kissinger, *Diplomacy* (New York: Simon and Schuster, 1994), p. 91.
2. Lord Strang, *Britain in World Politics* (London: Faber & Faber and Andre Deutsch 1961), pp. 110, 344.
3. W.N. Medlicott, *British Foreign Policy since Versailles, 1919–1963* (London: Methuen, 1968), p. 294.
4. Cited by Robert Taylor, in *Lord Salisbury* (London: Allen Lane, 1975), p. xi.
5. C.J. Bartlett, *Castlereagh* (London: Macmillan, 1966), pp. 162–5.
6. M. Fry, *The Dundas Despotism* (Edinburgh: Edinburgh University Press, 1992), Chapter 6 and pp. 207ff.
7. Lord Londonderry, *Memoirs and Correspondence of Viscount Castlereagh* (London, 1848–53) [hereafter *CC*] v, 29–82.
8. See J.M. Sherwig, 'Lord Grenville's Plan for a Concert of Europe, 1797–9', *Journal of Modern History* vol. 32, no. 2 (1962), pp. 284–93; for Pitt's memo of 19 January 1805, see K. Bourne, *The Foreign Policy of Victorian England, 1830–1902* (Oxford: Clarendon Press, 1970), pp. 197–8.
9. *CC*, xi, 125–9.
10. *CC*, ix, 32.
11. Bartlett, *Castlereagh*, pp. 125–6.
12. *CC*, xi, 125–9.
13. R. Parkinson, *Clausewitz* (London: Wayland,1970), pp. 35, 287–8.
14. Bartlett, *Castlereagh*, pp. 116–17.
15. E. Ingram, *Britain's Persian Connection 1798–1828* (Oxford: Clarendon Press, 1992), p. 203.
16. Sir C.K. Webster, *British Diplomacy, 1813–15: Select Documents Dealing with the Reconstruction of Europe* (London: Bell, 1921), p. 166; *CC*, xviii, 419; A. Thiers, *Histoire du Consulat et de l'Empire* (Geneva: C.L. Gruaz 1845–69), xvii. 53–5.
17. Webster, *British Diplomacy*, pp. 123–8; Report on the *MSS of Earl Bathurst, Historical MSS Commission* (1923), p. 261.
18. C.K. Webster, *The Foreign Policy of Lord Castlereagh, 1812–15*, (London: Bell, 1931), p. 379; *Dictionary of National Biography*, iv, 1004–5; xv, 1284; xix, 1121–3.
19. C. Hibbert (ed.), *Captain Gronow, 1810–60* (London: Kyle Cathie, 1991), pp. 166, 224.
20. For varied reactions at home to the peace settlement, see John Gore (ed.), *The Creevey Papers* (London: Batsford, 1963), p. 112: Lord Holland wrote on 17 October 1814, 'The peace, ... satisfies no one class of people. Those who hate France think enough had not been done to reduce her power of mischief, and those who feel some sympathy (as he did himself) with her from a recollection of the original case in which she engaged, ... lament her humiliation, and resent yet more the triumphs of her enemies.' A king restored caused 'every sprig of Royalty [to become] ... more insolent and insupportable'.

21. C.D. Yonge, *Life and Administration of Robert Banks, Second Earl of Liverpool* (London, 1868), ii, 193–6.
22. *CC*, x, 500–1.
23. Bartlett, *Castlereagh*, pp. 154–8.
24. Col. G. Gurwood, *The Dispatches of the Duke of Wellington, 1799–1818* (London: John Murray, 1835–8), xii, 596–601; *CC*, x, 484–91; G. Pellew (ed.), *The Life and Correspondence of Henry Addington, Lord Sidmouth* (1847), iii, 131–7.
25. H. Kissinger, *A World Restored* (London: Weidenfeld & Nicolson, 1957), p. 180; see also his *Diplomacy* pp. 81–2.
26. F.H. Hinsley, *Power and the Pursuit of Peace* (Cambridge: Cambridge University Press, 1963), p. 197. See also Douglas Dakin's thoughtful assessment of the Congress of Vienna, chapter 1 in Alan Sked (ed.), *Europe's Balance of Power, 1815–48* (London: Macmillan, 1979).
27. C.J. Bartlett, *Peace, War and the European Powers* (London: Macmillan, 1996), pp. 9–10; see also p. 45 for an overview of the avoidance of great power wars between 1815 and 1854.
28. *CC*, xi, 104–7; Webster, *The Foreign Policy of Castlereagh, 1815–22*, (London: Bell, 1925), pp. 509–12; C.J. Bartlett, *Great Britain and Sea Power*, (Oxford: Oxford University Press, 1963), pp. 63–5. See also below, for Castlereagh and his speech on strategic bases to the House of Commons in 1816.
29. *Hansard*, new series, ii, 385, 392; iv, 1355–62, 1365–76; see also *Hansard*, xl, 498.
30. J. Derry, *Castlereagh* (London: Allen Lane, 1976), pp. 211, 219.
31. M. Chamberlain, *Lord Aberdeen* (London: Longman, 1983), p. 201.
32. Sir A. Alison, *The Lives of Lord Castlereagh and Sir Charles Stewart* (1861), ii, 342. Both Disraeli and Lord Stanley congratulated Alison on his work. John Derry, *Castlereagh*, p. 8, notes Aberdeen's praise of and thanks to Castlereagh as his mentor.
33. W. Hinde, *Canning* (London: Collins, 1973), p. 282.
34. L.J. Jennings (ed.), *The Correspondence and Diaries of J.W. Croker* (1884), i, 170.
35. See especially, Chamberlain, *Aberdeen*, Chapter 13.
36. Ibid, pp. 304–5.
37. M. Chamberlain, *'Pax Britannica'? British Foreign Policy, 1789–1914* (London: Longman, 1988), p. 77.
38. Chamberlain, *Aberdeen*, pp. 269, 272. See also C.K. Webster, *The Foreign Policy of Lord Palmerston, 1830–41* (London: Bell, 1951), ii, 785–7 for Lamb from Vienna on Austria as Britain's natural ally of France as the natural foe; in 1830s.
39. Chamberlain, *Aberdeen*, p. 272.
40. For the alarm of Wellington and others, see Chamberlain, *Aberdeen*, chapters 14 and 16; J. Brooke (ed.), *Wellington's Political Correspondence, 1833–4* (London: HMSO, 1975), pp. 301–23.
41. Chamberlain, *Aberdeen*, p. 305; also pp. 302ff.
42. Bartlett, *Great Britain and Sea Power*, pp. 288–9.
43. See J.B. Connacher, *The Aberdeen Coalition, 1852–5* (Cambridge: Cambridge University Press, 1968) pp. 393, 436, 440–4; Sir T. Martin, *The Life of the Prince Consort* (London: Smith Elder, 1875–80), iii/ 13, 21, 47, 56; A.C. Benson and Viscount Esher, (eds) *The Letters of Queen Victoria* (London: John Murray, 1908) first series, iii, 82–3. For Aberdeen's desperate efforts to avoid war, see Chamberlain, *Aberdeen*, pp. 472–500.
44. For other critics of war against Russia and their greater distrust of France see, for example, Jennings (ed.), *J.W. Croker*, iii, 256, 315, 317, 319–21, 329–30, 373–4;

W.H. Dunn, *James Froude* (Oxford: Clarendon, 1961–3), i, 203, 206. Note also Graham on French plots and ambitions; see Chamberlain, *Aberdeen*, p. 472.

45. J. Vincent (ed.), *A Selection from the Diaries of the 15th Earl of Derby, 1869–1878*, (London: Royal Historical Society, 1994), pp. 14–31, 337, 392–6, 427–8.

46. For comprehensive coverage, see Bradford Perkins, *Castlereagh and Adams, Britain and the United States, 1812–23* (Los Angeles, CA: California University Press, 1964), passim.

47. D. Gray, *Spencer Perceval* (Manchester: Manchester University Press, 1963), pp. 172, 451.

48. Bartlett, *Castlereagh*, pp. 71, 250.

49. E. Ingram, *The Beginning of the Great Game* (Oxford: Clarendon Press, 1979), pp. 31–44.

50. See Bartlett, *Peace, War and the European Powers*, pp. 1–52 for an overview of the reasons for the avoidance of great power wars between 1815 and 1853.

4
Palmerston: 'Artful Old Dodger' or 'Babe of Grace'?

John Charmley

The charge most commonly levelled against Palmerston was best expressed by that master of political invective, Disraeli, in an election address in 1857: 'He is the Tory chief of a Radical Cabinet. With no domestic policy, he is obliged to divert the attention of the people, from the consideration of their own affairs, to the distraction of foreign affairs. His external system is turbulent and aggressive, that his rule at home may be tranquil and unassailable.'[1] More recently, it has been argued that 'the truth was more or less the opposite of this familiar charge', and that Palmerston's external liberalism was a genuine manifestation of Britain's own liberalism.[2] The Third Marquis of Salisbury, writing in 1896, came to a not dissimilar conclusion, without regarding it as a matter of commendation: 'Palmerston was a disciple of Canning, and with him believed that foreign policy should follow your political proclivities'; this had led to the 'dangerous errors of 1846–1856', chief of which was the transformation of Russia into an antagonist.[3] The assumption of the primacy of domestic politics in Palmerston's foreign policy takes us along a familiar line: the outsider to Whig politics who used foreign affairs to advance his own career; Salisbury's assertion of the primacy of ideology leads to the conclusion that Palmerston's greatest achievement was to saw off the branch upon which he had been sitting.

Of Palmerston's importance in setting the pattern for British foreign policy in the nineteenth century there can be no doubt. As *The Times* put it in its obituary tribute: 'John Bull' thought that 'he could do anything and he would do anything ... He was supposed to have his pocket full of constitutions, to have a voice in half the Cabinets of Europe, to have monarchs past reckoning under his thumb'.[4] Palmerston became the symbol of Britain's mid-Victorian success. To those, like Richard Cobden, who objected that the Crimean War would ruin the real foundation of that success, Britain's commercial prosperity, Palmerston replied: 'we went to war for the liberties of Europe, and not for the purpose of gaining so much per cent on our exports'. In his usual *de haut en bas* style, he explained that the Crimean War was not about 'increasing the export of our commodities'; it was a war 'for the maintenance of the liberty and independence of nations, and for the maintenance of that balance of power, which however the hon. Gentleman may treat it with contempt and sneer at, because he does not understand it – everyone else considers to be a point deserving of assertion'.[5] To his fellow countrymen, who wanted their prosperity translated into power and prestige, Palmerston was the personification of these things; his personality imprinted itself upon the popular imagination, as it did upon British foreign policy.

Diplomacy was the last part of the British governmental machine to succumb to bureaucratization and in Palmerston's day much depended upon the Foreign Secretary himself. The workload at the Foreign Office was punishing.[6] It contributed to the early deaths of Castlereagh and Canning, and exacted a heavy toll from all its occupants. It took an exceptionally strong constitution to bear its burden for long, and great assiduity to master its detail; Palmerston possessed both qualities, which gave him an unusual degree of control over foreign policy. It was not until the late 1840s that he would meet a real challenge, and that was from the monarchy, which could not compete with his parliamentary mastery. After Grey's retirement, none of the Prime Ministers he served could control Palmerston, and his habit of conducting diplomacy by private letter effectively circumvented his Cabinet colleagues, most of whom paid little attention to foreign affairs except at times of crisis.[7] Palmerston had learned from Canning's example the importance of the Fourth Estate, and he always took great care to stay on good terms with the press, to whom he fed information and which, in return, fêted him. Palmerston could be the most charming of men, when he wanted, but he was fond of getting his own way and not particular about the means he employed to achieve his desired ends. The question that exercised the Chancelleries of Europe in 1830 was similar to the one that has puzzled generations of students: what were those ends?

For most of the previous half century, British foreign policy had been in the hands of the Tories. Wellington was a man personally known to the sovereigns of the Quintuple Alliance, and his devotion to the Vienna Settlement of 1815 could be taken for granted. All that was known of the new premier, Lord Grey, was that he was an incorrigible Whig. With revolutions having broken out in France and in the Netherlands, the autocrats of Europe feared lest Britain should fan the flames by placing itself at the head of some sort of liberal crusade.[8] From this perspective, Palmerston's appointment to the Foreign Office seemed to offer some reassurance. He had been a member of every Tory government between 1808 and 1828, spending most of that period as Secretary at War.

At the age of 46 Palmerston's career was remarkable for its private sexual athleticism rather than for any public achievements. Ambitious young men seldom spend 20 years in minor political office. Palmerston himself had expected Grey to offer him the leadership of the House, but happily accepted the Foreign Office. Despite Sir Charles Webster's moralistic dismissal of the very idea that a woman of such loose morals as Princess Lieven could have been responsible for suggesting the idea to Grey, it seems as though her preference for her old *beau* helped sway her current one.[9] However, the Princess's hopes that Palmerston would pacify the fears of Europe's autocrats were as wide of the mark as it was possible to be; for the next 25 years, Palmerston would be one of their greatest sources of anxiety.

Napoleon used to ask of his generals 'Is he lucky?'; Palmerston would have passed this test; he was always lucky. German reactionaries stigmatized him as the 'Devil's son', and there were times when his opponents at home must have concurred. His high-handed style threatened ruin on at least three occasions before nemesis struck in 1864; and even then, he survived unscathed.

Palmerston was fortunate even in the timing of his arrival at the Foreign Office. The July Revolution in Paris created a natural counterpoise to the Holy Alliance powers. The detestation of Tsar Nicholas I for the revolution meant that the new French monarch, Louis Philippe, would not be able to follow his predecessor by allying with the autocratic powers; it also meant that the French had no choice other than to look to London for support. This was a situation tailor-made for Palmerston's gift for bullying. France's diplomatic isolation gave Palmerston two ways of intervening in Continental politics at little or no cost: he could either ally with France to form a liberal counterpoise to the Holy Alliance; or else he could foster discussions between all the powers at conferences in London, which allowed him to play the role of mediator.[10] In 1830, Palmerston had reacted to the July Revolution in France by declaring to his brother-in-law: 'Let us drink the cause of Liberalism all over the world';[11] but unlike some of his new Whig colleagues, Palmerston was no uncritical francophile. France could be used to support liberal causes, and cooperation with her was a way of restraining her ambitions; but Palmerston never trusted the home of the revolution of 1789.

Palmerston was also lucky that domestic circumstances allowed him a relatively free rein. Soon after taking office, he likened himself to 'a man who has been plumped into a mill-race, scarcely able by all his kicking and plunging to keep his head above water'.[12] With the Belgian crisis added to those in Portugal and Greece, there was plenty of work even for a man of Palmerston's enormous stamina; there was certainly too much for other ministers to follow. Grey, who kept a watchful eye on his new Foreign Secretary, found himself unable to intervene as often as he would have liked because of his preoccupations with parliamentary reform and keeping the Cabinet together; the other two ministers with an interest in foreign policy,

Lords Lansdowne and Holland, having proved too indolent to take on the post of Foreign Secretary, were insufficiently assiduous to keep up with Palmerston. Holland, whose francophilia made him deeply critical of Palmerston, was 'so little Master of the details' and 'so childishly, nervous and uncomfortable at the dread of not being able to speak' even in the sedate atmosphere of the Lords, that Palmerston would always have the beating of him.[13] He was by far the most experienced minister in a government full of men whose party had spent most of the previous three decades out of office. When Princess Lieven told Palmerston's mistress, Lady Cowper, in January 1831 that 'Palmerston is adorable, *controlling* foreign affairs in every sense of the word', few could have dissented from her conclusion; even fewer would have agreed with her first adjective.[14]

Palmerston was also fortunate in other ways. By the time he became Foreign Secretary the great powers had agreed to a conference on the Belgian issue taking place in London, and an armistice had already been agreed between the Belgians and the Dutch; it had already been decided that Belgium would have to be separated from the Netherlands. Not only were the remaining questions mostly second order, over which compromises were more likely to be reached, but France's diplomatic quarantine made it easy for Palmerston to exploit her for his own purposes. When William I looked as though he might make headway against the rebels in 1831, Palmerston was able to use the French army to support the Belgians. When it looked as though the French would not evacuate Belgium unconditionally, he wrote to Granville, the British ambassador in Paris: 'One thing is certain – the French must go out of Belgium or we have war, and war in a given number of days.'[15] Aware that the French were reading his correspondence, Palmerston was trying to frighten the French. Bluff was always his weapon of choice, and like many bullies, he was skilful in using it; he knew Louis Philippe would not risk provoking a war in which the Holy Alliance powers might intervene.

Palmerston's caution about French ambitions in Belgium should not detract from his belief in the liberal alliance and its importance for British foreign policy. As he told the Commons in March 1832: 'The interest of England was the maintenance of general peace throughout Europe, and this object was … most easily, most safely, and most securely to be attained by the maintenance of a firm and strict alliance between France and this country.'[16] However, Palmerston used France for British interests, and those Tories who criticized him for allowing the French army into Belgium in August 1831, were swiftly quieted when the French later withdrew. As Lord Holland concluded, sadly, Palmerston was not 'so averse to Anti-Gallican and anti-revolutionary systems as I had once hoped.'[17]

Because France was diplomatically isolated, Palmerston enjoyed the luxury of being able to cooperate with her on his own terms; the chief of these was that France should not profit by her intervention in any liberal cause. When Austria and France almost came to blows in early 1831 over Metternich's desire to suppress the liberal revolts in the Italian provinces, Palmerston found it impossible to 'side with France in a contest the result of which may be to extend her territories'.[18] The other main limitation on Palmerston's liberalism was Britain's military weakness in areas beyond the reach of sea power; as the Poles and other oppressed European nationalities would discover, for all Palmerston's willingness to lecture, he could bark but not bite.

The limitations imposed on Palmerston's diplomacy by Britain's relative want of military power were exposed clearly in 1832 when the Ottoman Sultan, Mahmoud II, asked the European powers for help against his rebellious vassal, the Egyptian Pasha, Mehmet Ali. Like all good liberals, Palmerston despised the Ottoman empire as corrupt and enfeebled, but he wished to help the Sultan to avoid France's Egyptian protégé gaining the upper hand. Unfortunately for Palmerston's hopes, the British fleet was already at full stretch off the coasts of Belgium and Portugal, and so no action was taken. Palmerston later called the failure to intervene the most 'tremendous blunder' that 'has happened since I have been in this office'.[19] The British Cabinet refused its aid to the Sultan, but Tsar Nicholas I of Russia did not, and this led to the treaty of Unkiar Skelessi (8 July 1833) which Palmerston thought converted Turkey into a Russian protectorate. This was followed up by a renewal of the Holy Alliance in the Convention of Münchengrätz in August.

Palmerston was even less fond than most men of being checked, and although he could do nothing in the East, French assistance did enable him to respond in the West. Britain's involvement in the tangled affairs of the Iberian Peninsula was, for Palmerston, a clear-cut case of support for constitutionalism against autocracy. The Whigs supported the cause of Dõna Maria in Portugal against her uncle, Dom Miguel, who enjoyed support from the Holy Alliance. Palmerston made strenuous efforts to persuade Ferdinand VII of Spain to recognize the new order in Portugal, but the wily old Bourbon hated the very word constitution and refused recognition, despite the fact that Miguel supported the pretender to the Spanish throne, Don Carlos, against Ferdinand's infant daughter and designated successor, Isabella II. After Ferdinand's death in September 1833 his widow, the Regent Maria Cristina sought to shore up her position by aligning with the new order in Portugal, and she looked to France and Britain for support. From this situation emerged the Quadruple Alliance of April 1834, which Palmerston represented as a riposte to the new Holy Alliance.[20] Caveats need to be entered about the extent to which the alliance was much more than a riposte to Russia, and it was certainly an example of another technique of Palmerston's diplomacy – cooperating with another power in order to restrain it. What the alliance actually did was to allow Palmerston to gain a public triumph at little cost; but it did deliver some positive objectives from the liberal point of view.

Palmerston had wanted to intervene in Portugal but had been prevented by lack of support in the Cabinet; Spain's willingness to intervene there enabled Palmerston to act by proxy. He had also been worried about the French fishing in the troubled waters, and by allying with Louis Philippe, who had no other ally on offer, he sought, and gained, a measure of control over French policy in the Peninsula. Symbolically the alliance established unity between the four powers and represented their common commitment to liberal ideas and institutions. But in a Spanish context, liberalism did not necessarily mean what it did in Britain; as Sir George Villiers, the British Minister in Spain commented in 1836: 'Words which it is necessary to apply to things here, because there are no others, do not represent the same ideas as when applied elsewhere.'[21]

The Quadruple Alliance may be described as Palmerston's masterpiece in the original sense of the word, as marking the end of a long apprenticeship. In July 1834 Grey, tired out with the effort of managing business, his colleagues and his own temperament, resigned. His replacement was Palmerston's old friend Lord Melbourne, brother of Lady Cowper, Palmerston's long-time mistress and future wife. With 'Caro William' (as he was known in the close-knit Lamb family circle) there would be no deference and no need to find a footing for a working relationship.[22] Indeed, Palmerston had already shown that he was willing to sacrifice old intimacies in order to get his way. Princess Lieven, who had been so satisfied with her part in getting her former lover to the Foreign Office, found herself leaving England in May as a result of having crossed Palmerston once too often. When his choice for British ambassador to St Petersburg, Stratford Canning, was refused by the Tsar, Palmerston, suspecting the hand of the Princess had been at work, refused to nominate any other successor, with the effect that by mid-1834 it became necessary to recall the Russian ambassador – and her husband. It was a foretaste of what those who sought to cross Palmerston could expect.

Palmerston's masterful and domineering temperament did not endear him to his subordinates. The future Lord Granville, who served as his Under-Secretary in 1840, described how elusive his chief was: 'He comes down very late, having kept quantities of people waiting for him … The clerks detest him, and have an absurd sort of fancy that he takes pleasure in bullying them.'[23] They were not the only ones subjected to Palmerston's bullying. When the Whigs came back to power in early 1835 after Peel's 'Hundred Days' Palmerston refused to take any office save his old. In a characteristically pugnacious letter to Melbourne he proclaimed that 'I consider myself to have conducted our foreign relations with great success during four years of excessive labour', and attributed the move against him to Holy Alliance and Tory intrigues.[24] Melbourne was overborne, as he always would be.

If Melbourne's premiership increased Palmerston's tendency to treat British foreign policy as his sole preserve, so too did the death in early 1837 of

William IV. It was constitutional practice to submit all important despatches in draft to the monarch before sending them. Palmerston had usually done this with William IV, although latterly he tended to send copies where he had thought it important to expedite the despatch of business; he had also sent the King selected incoming despatches; with the young Victoria he deemed neither of these practices necessary.[25]

If an increasingly preremptory manner set the tone for Palmerston's second period at the Foreign Office, then its main theme had been foreshadowed by the removal of Princess Lieven – Russophobia. To Palmerston, as to many British liberals, Russia represented the antithesis to their own country: backward, autocratic and repressive. Russia was not only the gendarme of Europe, she was also an aggressive and expansionist power in central Asia. Since the treaty of Turkmanchi of 1828, British politicians had worried about growing Russian influence over Persia and Afghanistan, with popular fears about the danger to the north-west frontiers of British India being aroused by works such as de Lacy-Evans' *Practicability of an Invasion of British India* (1829).[26] In Palmerston's view, Nicholas I was 'ambitious, bent upon great schemes, determined to make extensive additions to his dominions', all whilst 'labouring to push his political ascendancy far beyond the range of his Ukases' and 'animated by the same hatred to England which was felt by Napoleon'. Britain, Palmerston declared was the friend of 'national independence' and the enemy of 'all conquerors', so it was natural that an Anglo-Russian antagonism should exist.[27]

It was fortunate for Palmerston that the two countries whose ambitions he feared the most, France and Russia, could never make common cause because of their ideological disagreements; this gave him the luxury of dealing with Britain's chief rivals *seriatim*. But Palmerston never forgot that France was a liberal power, and he rejected overtures from Metternich for an alliance on the ground that this would estrange Britain and France, which would mean the abandonment of 'all the objects we have been striving for during the last five years'. Palmerston's attitude towards France was not altered by the rise of the Anglo-Russian antagonism, and he continued to treat her as he did some of his mistresses. Where France could be useful, as in Belgium and Spain, he would use her, without making any concessions to French patriotic feeling or allowing Louis Philippe to gain those diplomatic victories which might have strengthened his regime. Palmerston could never resist scoring diplomatic points, even at the expense of friendly powers, and when France tried to go beyond the role he had allotted her, Palmerston was ready to slap her down, even if it meant cooperating with Russia and forcing his own policy on an unwilling Cabinet. The most graphic example of this came in the form of the second Mehmet Ali crisis in 1839–40.

After Unkiar Skelessi, Palmerston changed his mind on the subject of the future of the Ottoman empire. Rejecting the 'nonsense which people talked about Turkey being in decay' as being the result of 'mistaking a metaphor for an argument',[28] Palmerston sought to give the Turks a breathing space in which to carry out the internal reforms their empire needed; in the meantime he sought a way of reducing Russia's special influence at Constantinople. As early as 1835 Palmerston had come up with the idea of a general European guarantee of Turkey's territorial integrity, but it was not until the circumstances caused by the renewal of war between the Sultan and Mehmet Ali in 1839 that it made any headway.[29]

Palmerston hated Mehmet Ali, regarding him as 'nothing but an ignorant barbarian, who by boldness, cunning and mother-wit, has been successful in rebellion';[30] according to his mood he saw the Pasha as an agent either of Russian or of French influence in the Levant. So, when in 1839 Mahmoud II took steps to deal with Mehmet Ali, Palmerston approved, and when Mehmet's armies vanquished those of the Sultan and marched on Constantinople, he was correspondingly alarmed; fortunately for Palmerston, he was not the only one. Metternich, who naturally regarded anything which threatened Austria's vulnerable southern borders as dangerous, acted swiftly to try to bring about a concert of the powers to achieve a 'European' solution to the problem. Palmerston seized the opportunity this offered to press ahead with his own plan to neutralize Mehmet Ali, proposing that the powers should demand his removal from Syria. To this last condition all the powers, bar France, eventually agreed, but given the francophile views of the Whig Cabinet this should have been enough to spike Palmerston's guns, not least because Lord Holland let the French know just how much opposition to Palmerston's plans there was in the Cabinet.[31]

The French, like Lord Holland and many of Palmerston's colleagues, assumed that the Foreign Secretary would have to climb from his high horse through lack of international support – it seemed inconceivable that, given his view of Russia, he would be willing to act with the Tsar, and it was equally improbable that Nicholas would alter his policy of keeping the Eastern Question in his own hands;[32] yet this was what happened. Nicholas, concerned at the prospect of an Anglo-French-Austrian alignment against him in the Levant, grasped the opportunity to drive a wedge between Britain and France by agreeing to support Palmerston's stand against Mehmet Ali. Palmerston, seeing the opportunity to put Unkiar Skelessi into commission, agreed to Russia's suggestion in September that they should conclude a pact which would guarantee the future security of the Straits and put an end to Mehmet Ali's ambitions.[33]

Palmerston spent the best part of the next nine months trying to get Russia, France and Austria to cooperate, but the French proved obdurate, as did his own colleagues. The main opposition inside the Cabinet came from Holland, whose French connections made him a danger to Palmerston's plans, and from the new Lord Privy Seal, Clarendon, whom Palmerston suspected of intriguing to replace him at the Foreign Office.[34] The crucial moments came in July 1840.

On 4 July Palmerston told his colleagues that the moment for 'immediate decisions' had been reached: either Britain would cooperate with the other powers, bar France, against Mehmet Ali, or she would have to leave the Russians supreme at Constantinople because the Tsar would certainly stand by the terms of Unkiar Skelessi. After the meeting, Melbourne told Palmerston that he doubted whether he would be able to carry his colleagues with him.[35] Palmerston was obdurate, not to say obstinate, and he offered to resign rather than give way, telling Melbourne on 5 July 1840 that 'the object to be attained is of the utmost importance for the interests of England, for the preservation of the balance of power, and for the maintenance of peace in Europe'. He warned Melbourne that if Britain drew back from cooperation with the other powers because of France 'we shall place this country in the degraded position of being held in leading-strings by France', which was 'a principle of policy which is not suitable to the power and station of England'.[36] Conscious that Palmerston's resignation 'must lead at once to the dissolution of the Government', Melbourne persuaded him to postpone his resignation.[37] Melbourne could cope much more easily with threats from Holland and Clarendon to resign, and by allowing them to sign a note of dissent at the Cabinet on 8 July, he was able both to let Palmerston have his way and to keep his government together. On 15 July Britain, Russia and Austria signed a convention providing for Mehmet Ali's forcible removal from Syria and for a joint guarantee of Turkey's integrity; France found herself isolated and humiliated. It was little wonder that the popular verdict was that Palmerston exercised 'an absolute dominion at the Foreign Office, and deals with all our vast and complicated questions of diplomacy according to his own views and opinions'.[38]

For the next month and a half Palmerston resisted all efforts by his colleagues to water down his policy, and steadfastly refused French offers to compromise. When military action was launched against Mehmet Ali, it went smoothly, and Palmerston could justify his policy – if not its tone. Throughout the crisis, both parties in the Cabinet had profusely leaked information to the press, but there was no doubting upon whose side popular opinion settled. Palmerston had begun his transmogrification into the personification of John Bull. That he had humiliated the French, weakened the liberal regime of Louis Philippe and upset the liberal *entente* was of little account to Palmerston beside the satisfaction of winning his point. The fact that Anglo-French relations, so promising in 1830, were at their nadir a decade later, counted for nothing with Palmerston; France, after all, had nowhere else to go. In the final year of the Melbourne administration, he took a similarly high hand with the US, China and Afghanistan, much to the alarm of many of his colleagues. The diarist George Greville spoke for many when he commented that: 'Considering the immensity of the stake for which he is playing ... it is utterly astonishing he should not be more seriously affected than he appears to be with the gravity of the situation.'[39]

Sir Charles Webster's verdict that Palmerston had 'set the course of British foreign policy for a generation' is no exaggeration.[40] The Convention of 1841, to which France adhered, governed control over the Straits for the rest of the century, and Palmerston's policy of supporting the integrity of the Ottoman empire would be pursued by his successors until the 1880s, and arguably the 1890s. Palmerston's 'doctrine' that 'we should reckon *upon ourselves*; and act upon principles of our own', also set the tone of British foreign policy into the 1860s, whilst his view that 'the system of England ought to be to maintain the liberties and independence of all nations', and that she should 'throw her moral weight into the scale of any people who are spontaneously striving for freedom', established the tenor of liberal foreign policy for far longer than that.[41] For all his declaration in 1848 that 'we have no eternal allies and no perpetual enemies',[42] Palmerston's liberalism led him inexorably to prefer constitutional states to autocracies, even if his strong sense of national pride would not let him subordinate Britain's interests to those of any other power; all these attitudes commended him to a British public opinion which shared them.

Palmerston spent his years in opposition between 1841 and 1846 profitably. Freed from the restraints of official duties, he spent much of his time in the Commons, cultivating MPs. As a resolute and vocal critic of Aberdeen's diplomacy, Palmerston established himself as a favourite within his own party. His marriage to Lady Cowper in 1839 had provided him with a partner who provided at Gloucester House a *salon* which did much to replace Holland House after Lord Holland's death in 1840, and to which selected MPs, Peers and journalists were invited. The result was that Palmerston was, by 1845, much better known, and much more popular, within his own party.

This new popularity within the Liberal ranks was not universal. Some of those who had served with him in the 1830s had come to distrust him, and when Sir Robert Peel resigned because his Cabinet was divided over the issue of the repeal of the Corn Laws in December 1845, Lord John Russell, the new Whig leader, found it impossible to form a government because the Third Earl Grey refused to serve if Palmerston went to the Foreign Office. Once the Tories had split irrevocably over the Corn Laws and a Whig government was inevitable, and Palmerston duly became Foreign Secretary once more; but his situation was very different from what it had been under Melbourne. As Guizot wrote to Princess Lieven, most of the political world wanted a 'continuation de la politique de lord Aberdeen', and viewed Palmerston with suspicion. Guizot's fears that under Palmerston the spirit of national rivalry and 'd'amour-propre personnel' would be revived,[43] proved only too correct; where he was wrong was in assuming that Palmerston's colleagues and hostility of the monarchy would be able to restrain the headstrong Foreign Secretary.

The most spectacular result of Guizot's mistrust of Palmerston was the fiasco over the Spanish Marriages, when French suspicions of British intentions led to a major diplomatic row between Paris and London. Anticipating the usual Palmerstonian refusal to let France have what Guizot thought was her proper influence in Spain, he decided to take precipitate action.[44] The marriage of the young Spanish Queen and her sister was a matter of concern to the great powers, and during Aberdeen's time at the Foreign Office he and Guizot had come to an agreement on the matter; this provided for the Infanta to marry Louis Philippe's son, the Duc de Montpensier, but only after the Queen herself was married and had produced an heir. If the British did not want Louis Philippe's grandson to sit on the Spanish throne, the French did not want Prince Albert's cousin, Leopold of Saxe-Coburg. The mention of the latter by Palmerston in a letter to the British ambassador, Bulwer, aroused all Guizot's suspicions, and he pressed ahead with the marriages. Montpensier married the Infanta, but only a few minutes after the Queen married the Duke of Cadiz, an effeminate grandee who was unlikely to father an heir to the Spanish throne.[45]

However, even in defeat Palmerston was fortunate. Despite their distrust of him, both the Queen and Lord John Russell agreed that Guizot had acted dishonourably, and even the pacific Aberdeen had to tell the indignant Princess Lieven that 'the mischief is done' and that it meant the 'rupture, for the present, of all our friendly intercourse and cordial understanding'.[46] Palmerston's handling of the issue had alienated the Spanish and the French, but British public opinion blamed Guizot for the breakdown of the *entente cordiale*.

Palmerston's dogmatism in preaching the virtues of constitutional government to both the Spanish and the Portuguese governments did little for Britain's relations with either country. The sharp and overbearing tone which Palmerston took with the Portuguese Queen particularly offended his own monarch, who whilst she deplored conditions in Portugal, thought that Palmerston's tone was 'likely only to irritate without producing any effect'.[47] This verdict might be applied more generally to Palmerston's diplomacy, and Metternich's view by 1847 was that 'abandoned by France and defeated on every diplomatic field, England now finds herself alone and paralysed in the face of the Continental Powers'.[48] Exaggeration though this was, it was significant that when, in 1846, Russia extinguished the nominally independent Polish Republic of Cracow in defiance of the Vienna Settlement and without consulting its other signatories, Palmerston did not join with France in making a joint protest. Without a complaisant France, Palmerston risked finding himself in much the same position as Canning had occupied before 1826, in which rhetorical invocations of English liberal superiority served to disguise diplomatic isolation. From this prospect he was saved by the revolutions of 1848.

The year of revolutions on the Continent had two effects on Palmerston: in the first place the downfall of the autocratic regimes seems to justify his lectures to them, and his rhetorical support for the liberal regimes in France, and especially Switzerland, refurbished his credentials with the Radical wing of the Liberal Party; in the second place, it began the process of shaking Palmerston's own confidence in the continuation of the Vienna system.

Palmerston was, in fact, no great friend of the Continental revolutionaries: he distrusted the Lamartine government in France and tried to extract from it a statement that it would not pursue an aggressive foreign policy. He believed Austria to be a European necessity and refused to countenance Hungarian separatism; and although in response to the revolt in northern Italy, he sponsored the idea of a northern Italian state, that was only because he thought losing Lombardy would 'strengthen Austria', whose 'importance' he never lost sight of.[49] The fact that European conservatives were ready to identify Palmerston as the cause of all their woes, thus demonstrating they had learned nothing from their fate in 1848, simply served to make him the darling of the English Radicals. Palmerston was not averse to taking the credit for events over which he had had little control; for him 'the connection between publicity and diplomacy was fundamental; an unsung triumph was only half a triumph'.[50]

Thus, 1848 was a seminal year for Palmerston: henceforth his personal popularity would be his main bulwark against his critics, which would make his diplomacy even more reckless than it had been before; and, becoming convinced that the Vienna Settlement could not hold much longer, he would seek ways of profiting from any changes in it.

Palmerston's new popularity came at an opportune moment. By 1848, the Queen was telling Russell that she 'had no confidence' in Palmerston, and that he made her 'seriously anxious and uneasy for the welfare of the country and for the peace of Europe in general'.[51] She complained not only about his policies, but also about his attitude towards her. She accused him of opening her private letters from other monarchs, and of sending off despatches of which she had not approved.[52] The Queen's complaints put Russell between the proverbial rock and a hard place. As far back as July 1846 Guizot, who was an acute observer of the English political scene, had recognized that in the confused state of the British party system after the fall of Peel, Palmerston could end up leading the Protectionists in the Commons if he fell out with the Whigs.[53] Russell made precisely the same point in March 1850 when Prince Albert pressed for Palmerston's removal: 'he was very popular with the Radical part of the House of commons as well as with the Protectionism so that either would be ready to receive him as their leader; he was therefore most anxious to do nothing which would hurt Lord Palmerston's feelings, nor to bring about a disruption of the Whig Party.'[54] However, Palmerston's own high-handedness was to offer his enemies the opportunity they had long sought to dismiss him.

In January 1850, Palmerston suggested that the British fleet should be sent to blockade the Piraeus in an attempt to make the Greek government pay attention to the claims of a Gibralterian Jew, Don Pacifico, who was seeking compensation for damage done to his property. The whole business was a trumpery affair, but it gave Palmerston an opportunity to vent his spleen against King Otto and the Greek government. France and Russia, as the co-guarantors of Greece, protested against Britain's action, and on 19 June the House of Lords supported a censure motion against the government; Palmerston offered to resign. But as usual, Palmerston's luck was in. Russell would have loved to have removed Palmerston, but could not do so in response to an opposition censure motion; he would have loved to have abandoned Palmerston to a richly deserved obloquy, but could not do so without having to offer the resignation of his government; there was no alternative to toughing it out in the Commons.

Palmerston's criticisms of Aberdeen's foreign policy in 1828 and 1829 had first signalled his parliamentary rise, but it was their unexpectedness as much as their excellence which had won them attention. Palmerston had no great reputation as an orator, and when he rose on the evening of 25 June to defend himself against his critics, no one expected that he would sit down four hours later with the plaudits of the House ringing in his ears. Palmerston knew when to make the speech of his career. In place of the point-scoring and the levity, which often marked his speeches, this one was a 'calm and reasoned defence of all his foreign policy' for the past 20 years.[55] He celebrated the success of English liberalism in reconciling liberty with order, contrasting it effectively with the fate of Continental conservatism, which, by insisting on order above liberty had, in effect, lost both. He defended his actions in detail and in general, finishing with a peroration which won him a permanent place in the quotation books, contending that it was his aim that the British subject, 'as the Roman, in days of old', should hold himself 'free from indignity' when he 'could say *Civis Romanus Sum*'.[56] Gladstone's criticism of this as offensively implying that the Englishman was, like the Roman of old, a member of a 'conquering race' and a 'privileged caste', missed the point. However offensive Gladstone found such sentiments, most of his fellow countrymen shared them. The government won the debate with a majority of 49, but that was hardly the most significant thing about it. Palmerston's astonishingly effective performance placed him, as the usually critical Clarendon conceded, 'on a pinnacle of popularity at home' and settled the question of whether he should remain at the Foreign Office: 'Lord John must either go on with him or go *out* with him.'[57] He was, by Grey's pained admission, 'the most popular man in the country'.[58]

Palmerston had now succeeded to a remarkable extent in taking over Canning's position: he was detested by the Court and distrusted by his

Cabinet colleagues, whilst being admired by the Commons and immensely popular in the country at large. This led to a stalemate. For much of the next 18 months the Court would press for Palmerston's removal to some other office, and for the whole of that time Palmerston would coolly refuse all requests from Russell, whilst simultaneously driving the Queen to distraction by his behaviour. As the author of the Russell government's one great parliamentary success, Palmerston considered himself untouchable, and it was not in his character not to ride his success for all it was worth. But, as every successful bully must, he knew when to 'knock under'.

On 28 July the Queen finally lost patience with Russell's prevarication. Acknowledging the difficulty of removing Palmerston, she nevertheless demanded that he should do so, saying she had 'no confidence' in a Foreign Secretary who exposed her 'to insults from other nations' and 'the country to the constant risk of serious and alarming complications'.[59] The Queen submitted a memorandum from her old adviser, Baron Stockmar, setting out her conception of how a Foreign Secretary should behave. But if she hoped this would provoke Palmerston into open revolt, she had underestimated her man. In an interview with Prince Albert on 14 August he protested his anguish at having upset the Queen and promised to amend his ways, particularly with regard to letting the Queen see despatches before they were sent.[60] He then proceeded to behave exactly as he always had, managing to outrage the Queen in October by his obvious approval of the manhandling of the Austrian General Haynau by draymen at Barclays Brewery.[61]

Those who counselled caution to the Queen on the grounds that Palmerston was bound to over-reach himself were vindicated in early December 1851. Palmerston's official response to the coup of Louis-Napoleon Bonaparte was neutral, but in a private conversation with the French ambassador, Count Walewski, he made plain his personal approval of Napoleon's action. Normanby, the British ambassador in Paris, complained about Palmerston's actions to the Court, and the Queen insisted that Russell finally confront the errant Foreign Secretary. Russell attempted to bribe Palmerston with another Cabinet post and a British peerage, but he would have neither, which meant that Russell had to dismiss him. His fall was 'regarded by a public unacquainted with the peculiar circumstances which had led to it, as a victory for the old diplomacy, and as a triumph for all the forces of absolutism'.[62]

Palmerston never again held the Foreign Office, but that did not mean that his influence over British foreign policy ended in December 1851. In February 1852 he had his 'tit for tat with John Russell', bringing down the government over the Militia bill, and paving the way for the first Conservative government since Peel. He was duly offered, and refused, a post by the new Prime Minister, Derby, and when the Aberdeen coalition was formed in December 1852, he became Home Secretary; the Queen would not have him back at the Foreign Office. However, the collapse of the Aberdeen government in 1855 in the middle of the Crimean War made him the 'man whom public opinion indicated unmistakably to be the necessary premier'.[63] With one short exception in 1858–59, Palmerston was Prime Minister for the rest of his life, and although, strictly speaking his actions lie outside the study of the work of British Foreign Secretaries, it would be an incomplete account of his influence on British diplomacy which made no reference to them, especially since his position as Prime Minister 'enabled him to dominate ... Britain's external policy'.[64]

Clarendon summed up the 'total change that has taken place in Palmerston's position': 'He has no colleagues to fear or to upset; he has attained the object of his ambition; he can't act upon his impulses at the Foreign Office; he is more immediately responsible to Parliament than he ever was before ... The Queen, therefore, must not persist in thinking him the Palmerston of old. He has put off the old man and become "a babe of grace".'[65] This was too optimistic by half: the Queen had not ceased to distrust Palmerston, and he had not ceased giving her good reasons to do so. One reason for the Court's unwillingness to see Palmerston as Prime Minister was that 'he was known to entertain ulterior views, upon which he was agreed with the Emperor of the French'; or, as the Queen put it more bluntly: 'He would make a new map of Europe.'[66]

In Palmerston's opinion the Crimean War was not simply about the future of the Ottoman empire, it was linked to the views which he had been formulating since the impact of the Year of Revolutions. Palmerston's *'beau ideal'* had been expressed in a memorandum circulated to his colleagues on 19 March 1854, a few days before the British declaration of war on Russia. In it he drew up a plan of partition for the Russian empire which would have resulted in a Napoleonic 'remaniement de la carte de l'Europe': Finland and the Aaland Islands would be restored to Sweden; the Baltic provinces would be ceded to Prussia; Poland would be transformed into an independent 'substantive kingdom'; Austria would be compensated for her loss of Lombardy by the acquisition of Moldavia and Wallachia, and the Crimea and Georgia would return to Turkey.[67] He told Clarendon in 1855 that 'the main and real object of the war was to curb the aggressive ambition of Russia. We went to war not so much as to keep the Sultan and his Mussulmans in Turkey as to keep the Russians out of Turkey.'[68] As he explained to Derby's son, Lord Stanley, whom he hoped to entice into joining his administration, he looked forward to the Russians being driven out of Poland, Finland and the Caucasus. Stanley declined the offer, coming away with the impression that 'he looked forward to a long, and ultimately a revolutionary war'.[69] Despite Lansdowne's dismissal of these schemes as 'day-dreams', there was a general congruence between them and Napoleon III's objectives, and many Liberals, including Lord John Russell, found themselves in general agreement that Britain's war aims needed to be wider than Aberdeen wanted.[70] Lord Aberdeen said plaintively that 'We have the plan sketched out for a thirty years' war';[71] with Napoleon's help it took much less time than that to alter the map of Europe. As Baron Stockmar had warned Granville in 1852: 'Napoleon's system in foreign affairs was *La France et la violence*. This system the nephew believes himself to be predestined to revive.'[72]

The young Lord Robert Cecil had a better appreciation of Napoleon III's aims and objectives than Palmerston did: 'A Napoleonic throne must drag with it Napoleonic traditions', he wrote in 1860. He saw the necessary primacy of domestic politics in the Emperor's diplomacy: 'He has profited by his uncle's glory: he cannot renounce his uncle's system. He has nothing save the one gewgaw of military distinction to offer as a bribe to the fierce political passions which his bayonets hold in check.'[73] For Palmerston to imagine that he could use Napoleon's France in the way he had used Louis Philippe's was a miscalculation with far-reaching consequences.

As it transpired, Napoleon was unwilling to push the Crimean War to the conclusion which Palmerston wanted, and by the end of the war Britain's relations with her ally, and with Austria, were strained.[74] However, Napoleon and Palmerston did have in common a desire to use the breakdown of the Vienna system to sponsor liberalism in Italy and Germany. In supporting French patronage of Cavour's Italian ambitions, Palmerston was acting entirely in character. He wanted to use French military forces for ends he judged worthy, and cooperation with France was seen as a way of providing the 'diplomatic trammels'[75] necessary to prevent Napoleon profiting from his exertions. There was also a second reason for Palmerston's support for Italian liberalism, which takes us to the circumstances out of which Disraeli's famous accusation arose; there were excellent domestic reasons for backing Cavour and Napoleon.

Palmerston's effortless election victory of 1857 had been followed in 1858 by the rude shock of being ejected from office because he had 'truckled' to Napoleon III by agreeing to take action against liberal refugees in England. It was a lesson to the old politician in two senses: in the first place it did not do to offend his core constituency by deviating from the firm diplomacy for which he was famous; and in the second place, keeping a liberal coalition together was a difficult business. The Italian war of unification gave Palmerston a chance to profit from these lessons.

The proximate cause of the Liberal union of June 1859 was the prospect of war in northern Italy. Liberals of whatever shade could all agree that Derby's government seemed pro-Austrian and needed to be replaced with one which would take a properly liberal line. Liberals could unite around this cause in a way they could not about the other great progressive cause of the day, par-liamentary reform.[76] In this narrow sense, there was something to be said for Disraeli's accusation that Palmerston's diplomacy served a domestic political purpose, even if it was not the one Disraeli imagined; the true function of foreign affairs was to unite the Liberal Party. This was particularly true of Palmerston and his new Foreign Secretary, Russell. As early as September 1859 Granville was writing that 'whereas we all feared danger from the disunion of the two great statesmen, our chief difficulty now is their intimate alliance'.[77] Disunited totally on the question of parliamentary reform, Palmerston and Russell were at one on the Italian question. As Clarendon, who had been kept from the Foreign Office by this unnatural alliance, put it cattily: 'John Russell has neither policy nor principles of his own, and is in the hands of Palmerston, who is an artful old dodger and whose monomania about Austria has reached the point of phrenzy.' Clarendon's fear that England would end up being 'dragged wherever the Emperor chooses to go'[78] was falsified, not by Russell's skilful diplomacy, but by the march of events.

Napoleon III had wanted a northern Italian federation which would have been a French client state, and by July 1859 when it looked as though this would indeed be the result of the Austro-Sardinian war, Palmerston was 'deeply mortified and annoyed', fearing that the 'treaties of 1815' had been destroyed to France's profit.[79] The revolts in central Italy, combined with Garibaldi's successful war against the kingdom of the Two Sicilies, did create something approximating to a kingdom of Italy, which allowed Palmerston and Russell to take a great deal of unwarranted credit.[80] However, Palmerston's desire to be 'very Austrian north of the Alps, but very anti-Austrian south of the Alps',[81] betrayed the sort of insular liberal logic which led him to favour German unification whilst supposing that it need have no great effect upon the balance of power. Palmerston acknowledged that it 'is greatly for the interests of Europe that Austria should continue to be a great Power in the centre of the Continent', but he sponsored actions which were bound to weaken it.

Granville thought that the great lesson of the Italian crisis was that Russell 'has had a lesson that the Cabinet will support the Queen in preventing him and Pam acting on important occasions without the advice of their colleagues';[82] this was over-optimistic. If the diplomacy of the last Palmerston government was 'inept, often irresponsible, and frequently inconsequential',[83] this had much to do with the fault-line between 'Palmerston and John Russell on foreign affairs; generally backed by Gladstone, and opposed by all the rest of the Cabinet.'[84] Most ministers disliked the congenital activism of the two 'dreadful old Men', but this did nothing to dissuade Palmerston and Russell, despite the increasingly obvious fact that Napoleon's aims and those of the British Cabinet were far from identical.

The difficulties attending an Anglo-French alliance were sharply demonstrated in 1863 in the aftermath of the Polish revolt against their Russian overlords. Feeling in Britain was very strong against the Alvensleben Convention, concluded in February 1863 and which allowed the Russians to pursue Polish rebels into Prussian territory, but Napoleon III's suggestion that the two powers should act in concert with Austria to 'break up the Coalition against the liberties of Poland', aroused Palmerston's fears about French ambitions. He suspected that where Britain was taking her stand on the 1815 Vienna Settlement, which Russia was breaking, Napoleon wished to tear it 'into tatters' with a view to redrawing the map of Europe according to Bonapartist principles.[85] The result was that Britain declined to cooperate with France and instead addressed a firm note of remonstrance to Russia, in Palmerston's eyes 'the real culprit' in the affair. However, the Russians refused to be cowed by diplomatic protests, and since Palmerston was unwilling to go as far as Napoleon III, he had no alternative except to content himself with barking and not biting.

It was the same fear of Bonapartist ambition which prompted Russell and Palmerston to turn down Napoleon's suggestion in November 1863 of a general European congress to revise the Vienna Settlement. It was, however, rather late in the day for Palmerston to be realizing that support for the Vienna treaties and Napoleon III were mutually incompatible. Napoleon did not easily forgive Palmerston for balking him of his great ambition, and exacted his revenge in the Schleswig-Holstein crisis.[86]

As Foreign Secretary at the time when the future of Schleswig and Holstein had first threatened to disturb the peace of Europe in 1848, Palmerston was expert enough on the question to be able to say with confidence that 'the connection and Relations of Denmark, Sleswig [sic] and Holstein to each other have been so various, and so complicated that you may pick out historical events to bear any conclusion you may wish to entertain'.[87] The 1850 London Protocol had declared the integrity of the King of Denmark's dominions to be a matter of 'European interest'; Britain was a signatory of that treaty, and with Palmerston and Russell in charge of British diplomacy, there was little chance that Britain would not try to intervene. Palmerston told the Commons on 23 July 1863 that if any 'violent attempt were made' to overthrow Danish rights in the Duchies 'those who made the attempt would find in the result, that it would not be Denmark alone with whom they would have to contend';[88] Palmerston was a master of bluff, but this time he had miscalculated.

Although there was a large section of public opinion which sympathized with gallant little Denmark and vociferously supported Palmerston, he conspicuously lacked support elsewhere. Most Cabinet ministers shied away from their leader's activism, and there was little likelihood that their backbenchers would demand action; many Radicals had 'become passive, adopting enough of a Cobdenite gloss' to give the government a decidedly 'Manchester' tinge.[89] The Queen, who was 'very German' on the issue, added her weight to those who opposed any British intervention on behalf of Denmark.[90]

The external constraints on British action were even greater – and mostly self-inflicted. The fate of the Duchies was a 'European' question in as far as it involved the question of the sanctity of treaties and the balance of power.[91] British fears about the ambitions of Napoleon III had already driven a wedge between the two Crimean allies: Napoleon's disappointment at Britain's response to his suggestions for a European Congress ensured that he would not support Palmerston. Russia, which might in other circumstances have been disposed to intervene to keep the balance of power in the Baltic, was not willing to intervene against Prussia and Austria, especially since anything which upset the Crimean system was bound to work out to Russia's benefit; Tsar Alexander II had no incentive to help Palmerston. Austria, which owed Palmerston no favours, was pledged to act with Prussia. Palmerston believed that Prussia was too weak and too divided internally to secure hegemony in Germany, and that British menaces would secure her diplomatic retreat; but, in Bismarck, he had finally met someone who was his superior in the art of bluff.

Palmerston and Russell failed to persuade their colleagues or the Queen to back the use of force. They were successful in convening a conference on the question of Schleswig-Holstein, but when it broke down in June and hostilities between Austria, Prussia and Denmark resumed, they tried unavailingly to avoid the inevitable; speaking in the Lords on 6 July, Russell admitted that there was nothing Britain could do to help the Danes.[92]

Derby had stigmatized Russell's policy as one of 'meddle and muddle', alleging that as a result of it 'this country is now in such a position that its menaces are disregarded, its magniloquent language is ridiculed and its remonstrances are treated with contemptuous indifference by the small as well as by the great Powers of the Continent';[93] even after allowance has been made for the asperity of party politics, it is difficult to dissent from this as a general verdict on the diplomacy of the last Palmerston government. If Britain moved into a period of isolationism for the next decade, that was largely the result of Palmerston's failures.

However, that was not the real legacy of Palmerston. Isolationism soon proved irksome to a country conscious of its own wealth and position, particularly to one nurtured on the bluff and bluster of Palmerston; time softened the impact of Schleswig-Holstein and lent a tincture of rose to 'Pam's' earlier triumphs. Gladstone's Liberal Party declined to take up its Palmerstonian inheritance, but Disraeli was not so fastidious. A diplomatic style that had allowed an old Tory to unite a Liberal Party could be used by a younger Tory to attach a larger electorate to the Conservative Party after 1867. The contingent nature of Palmerston's successes, like their diplomatic and temporal context were not replicable, but that would not prevent Disraeli, and many of his successors, from making the attempt.

There was a dramatic unity about Palmerston's diplomacy. His last government has been called the 'last Whig' government as far as foreign policy was concerned,[94] but the argument here has been that his diplomacy was of a piece; nineteenth-century 'Whig' foreign policy was Palmerston's. It believed in the extension of liberal principles on the Continent by moral example and by lecturing; it believed in non-intervention, except when the

French could be persuaded to act as a catspaw for liberalism; above all it believed in activism on liberal principles. But, as Salisbury later remarked, 'Politics is a matter of business', and 'similarity of religious faith' was 'no more indicative of a useful ally than similarity of political faith would be'. Looked at from that angle Castlereagh had been correct to align British policy with Russia and Austria because it had enabled France, Britain's real rival, to be kept in check: 'but Palmerston would be guided by common sympathies instead of by common interests', the result of which, 40 years on, was that 'we have not kept France, – she is more our enemy than ever. But the feud with Russia remains.'[95] It would take another Whiggish Foreign Secretary to remedy that situation and set Britain on a course where she would again intervene in Europe.

Notes

1. G.E. Buckle, *The Life of Benjamin Disraeli, Earl of Beaconsfield, vol. IV* (London: John Murray, 1910–1920), p. 74.
2. E.D. Steele, 'Palmerston's foreign policy and Foreign Secretaries 1855–1865', in K.M. Wilson (ed.), *British Foreign Secretaries and Foreign Policy* (London: Croome Helm, 1987), pp. 25–6.
3. G.P. Gooch and H. Temperley, *British Documents on the Origins of the War 1898–1914, vol. VI*, Salisbury to Mr. Iwan-Muller, 31 August 1896, (London: HMSO, 1928) p. 780.
4. H.F.C. Bell, *Lord Palmerston, vol. II* (London: Longmans, Green, 1936), p. 420.
5. K. Bourne, *The Foreign Policy of Victorian England, 1830–1902* (Oxford: Clarendon, 1972), p. 329.
6. C.K. Webster, 'Palmerston at work', in A. Coville and H. Temperley (eds), *Studies in Anglo-French History* (Cambridge: CUP, 1935), pp. 74–8.
7. R. Bullen, *Palmerston, Guizot and the Collapse of the Entente Cordiale* (London: Athlone Press, 1974), pp. 65–6.
8. G. Le Strange (ed.), *Correspondence of Princess Lieven and Earl Grey, vol. II* (1890), Lieven to Grey, 31 August 1830, p. 73.
9. Sir Charles Webster, *The Foreign Policy of Palmerston 1830–1841, vol. I*, (London: G. Bell, 1951), pp. 309–14; H.W.V. Temperley (ed.), *The Diary of Princess Lieven* (London: G. Bell, 1925), p. 167; K. Bourne, *Palmerston: the early years* (London: Allen Lane, 1982) pp. 330–1.
10. G. Henderson, *Crimean War Diplomacy* (Glasgow, 1947), pp. 162–4.
11. Bourne, *Palmerston*, p. 314.
12. K. Bourne (ed.), *The letters of the third Viscount Palmerston to Laurence and Elizabeth Sullivan 1804–1863* (1979), p. 248.
13. A.D. Kriegel (ed.), *The Holland House Diaries 1831–1840* (1977), 5 August 1831, p. 24.
14. Lord Sudely (ed.), *The Palmerston-Lieven Correspondence 1828–1856* (1943), p. 24.
15. Bourne, *Foreign Policy*, Palmerston to Granville, 16 August 1831, p. 219.
16. Bourne, *Foreign Policy*, p. 32.
17. Holland diary, 20 December 1831, p. 100.
18. Bourne, *Foreign Policy*, Palmerston to Granville, 11 March 1831, p. 218.
19. Webster, *Palmerston I*, Palmerston to F. Lamb, 22 May 1838, p. 283.

20. R. Bullen and F. Strong, (eds), *Palmerston: Private Correspondence with Sir George Villiers as Minister to Spain 1833–1837* (1985), pp. 10–13 for the background.
21. Bullen, *Palmerston, Guizot*, p. 22.
22. L.G. Mitchell, *Lord Melbourne 1779–1848* (1997), pp. 204–7.
23. Lord E. Fitzmaurice, *Life of the Second Earl Granville, vol. I*, (London: Longmans, 1905), Lord Leveson to Lord Granville, 10, 20 March 1840, p. 29.
24. Webster, *Palmerston II*, Palmerston to Melbourne, 14 April 1835, pp. 839–40.
25. Bourne, *Palmerston* pp. 436–7.
26. See Edward Ingram, *The Beginning of the Great Game in Asia 1828–1834* (Oxford: Clarendon, 1978), for more detail.
27. Webster, *Palmerston II*, Palmerston to Melbourne, 8 June 1835, pp. 841–3.
28. F.S. Rodkey, 'Lord Palmerston's Policy for the Rejuvenation of Turkey, 1839–1841', *Transactions of the Royal Historical Society, fourth series, vol. XII, 1929*, p. 171.
29. There are excellent accounts in Webster, *Palmerston II*, pp. 583–95, and in Bourne, *Palmerston*, pp. 564–70.
30. Bourne, *Palmerston*, p. 576.
31. There are many accounts of the crisis, the best are at: Webster, *Palmerston II*, pp. 621–776; Bourne, *Palmerston*, pp. 576–620; H.W.V. Temperley, *Britain and the Near East The Crimea* (London: G. Bell, 1936).
32. The best account of Russian policy remains Philip E. Mosely, *Russian Diplomacy and the Opening of the Eastern Question in 1838 and 1839* (Cambridge, MA: Harvard UP, 1934).
33. Mosely, pp. 82–92.
34. Fitzmaurice, *Granville I*, Leveson to Granville, 11 December 1840, p. 30.
35. Webster, *Palmerston II*, Melbourne to Palmerston, 4 July 1840, p. 857.
36. Bourne, *Foreign Policy*, Palmerston to Melbourne, 5 July 1840, pp. 243–6.
37. Webster, *Palmerston II*, Melbourne to Palmerston, 6 July 1840, pp. 857–8.
38. H. Reeves (ed.), *The Greville Memoirs, vol. IV* (London: Longmans, 1888, p. 307.
39. Reeves, *Greville Memoirs IV*, p. 308.
40. Webster, *Palmerston II*, p. 780.
41. Bourne, *Palmerston*, p. 627, citing Palmerston to F. Lamb, 21 March 1838.
42. *Hansard*, 3rd series, vol. xcvii, cols. 122–3, 1 March 1848.
43. J. Naville (ed.), *Lettres de François Guizot et de la Princesse de Lieven* (Paris, plon, 1964), Guizot to Lieven, 8 August 1846, p. 246.
44. Naville, *Guizot-Lieven Corr.*, Guizot to Lieven, 18 July 1846, p. 224; Guizot to Lieven, 24 July 1846, p. 229; Lieven to Guizot, 25 July 1846 pp. 231–2; Guizot to Lieven, 8 August 1846, p. 246.
45. Bullen, *Palmerston, Guizot*, pp. 87–147.
46. E. Jones-Parry (ed.), *The Correspondence of Lord Aberdeen and Princess Lieven, vol. I* (London: Camden Society, 1938), Aberdeen to Lieven, 16 November 1846, p. 264.
47. B. Connell (ed.), *Regina v. Palmerston* (London, 1962), p. 48.
48. Bell, *Palmerston I*, p. 398.
49. A.J.P. Taylor, *The Italian Problem in European Diplomacy 1847–1849* (1934), p. 92.
50. Bullen, *Palmerston, Guizot*, p. 57.
51. A.C. Benson and Viscount Esher (eds), *The Letters of Queen Victoria, vol. II, 1844–1853* (London: John Murray, 1907), Memorandum by the Queen, 19 September 1848, pp. 231–2.
52. Bell, *Palmerston I*, pp. 437–8.
53. Naville, *Guizot-Lieven Corr.*, Guizot to Lieven, 21 July 1846, p. 227.

54. Benson and Esher, *The Letters of Queen Victoria, vol. II, 1844–1853*, Memorandum by Prince Albert, 3 March 1850, p. 279.
55. Bell, *Palmerston, vol. II*, p. 26.
56. House of Commons, Debates, *Hansard*, 3rd series, vol. cxii, columns 443–4, 25 June 1850.
57. Sir H. Maxwell, *The Life and Letters of George William Frederick, fourth earl of Clarendon, vol. I* (London: Edward Arnold, 1913), Clarendon to G.C. Lewis, 28 June 1850, p. 311.
58. Bell, *Palmerston II*, p. 28.
59. Benson and Esher, *Letter of Queen Victoria II*, Victoria to Russell, 28 July 1850, pp. 305–6.
60. Connell, *Regina v. Palmerston*, pp. 123–4.
61. Bell, *Palmerston II*, p. 40.
62. Fitzmaurice, *Granville I*, p. 52.
63. Fitzmaurice, *Granville I*, p. 93.
64. E.D. Steele, 'Palmerston's foreign policy and Foreign Secretaries 1855–1865', in K.M. Wilson (ed.), *British Foreign Secretaries and Foreign Policy* (1987), p. 25.
65. Fitzmaurice, *Granville I*, Clarendon to Granville, 16 September 1855, p. 120.
66. Benson and Esher, *Letters of Queen Victoria, volume III*, memorandum by Prince Albert, 3 February 1855, p. 120; Steele, p. 34 for the Queen's comment.
67. G.P. Gooch, *The Later Correspondence of Lord John Russell, vol. II* (London: Longmans, 1925), pp. 160–1; W. Baumgart, *The Crimean War 1853–1856* (London: Edward Arnold, 1999), p. 28.
68. W.E. Mosse, *The Rise and Fall of the Crimean System, 1855–1871* (London: Macmillan, 1963), p. 1, citing Palmerston's memorandum sent by Clarendon to Cowley, 26 September 1856.
69. J.R. Vincent (ed.), *Disraeli, Derby and the Conservative Party. The Political Journals of Lord Stanley 1849–69* (New York: Barnes & Noble, 1978), memorandum on Public Affairs, November 1855, p. 136.
70. Paul W. Schroeder, *Austria, Great Britain and the Crimean War. The Destruction of the European Concert* (Ithaca: New York State UP, 1972), p. 151.
71. S. Walpole, *The Life of Lord John Russell, volume II* (London: Longmans, 1889), p. 214.
72. Fitzmaurice, *Granville I*, Stockmar to Granville, 19 February 1852, p. 59.
73. P. Smith (ed.), *Lord Salisbury on Politics* (Cambridge: CUP, 1972), pp. 128–9, quoting from Cecil's article in *The Quarterly Review*, April 1860.
74. Mosse, *Crimean System*, pp. 46–52.
75. David F. Krein, *The Last Palmerston Government. Foreign Policy, Domestic Politics and the Genesis of 'Splendid Isolation'* (Iowa, 1978), p. 22, citing Palmerston to Russell, 2 August 1861.
76. Krein, pp. 6–8; Paul Scherer, *Lord John Russell: a biography* (Cranbury, N.J., 1999) pp. 266–9; Angus Hawkins, *Parliament, Party and the Art of Politics in Britain, 1855–59* (London: Longmans, 1987), pp. 260–1; Fitzmaurice, *Granville I*, Granville to Palmerston, 27 May 1859, pp. 329–30.
77. Maxwell, *Clarendon II*, Granville to Clarendon, 13 September 1859, p. 197.
78. Maxwell, *Clarendon II*, Clarendon to the Duchess of Manchester, 7 January 1860, pp. 206–7.
79. Fitzmaurice, *Granville I*, Granville to the Prince Consort, 13 July 1859, p. 351.
80. Derek Beales, *England and Italy 1859–60* (London: Thomas Nelson, 1961) pp. 166–73.

81. Fitzmaurice, *Granville I*, Palmerston to Granville, 30 January 1859, p. 325.
82. Fitzmaurice, *Granville I*, Granville to Argyll, 31 August 1859, pp. 357–8.
83. Krein, *The Last Palmerston Government*, p. 4.
84. Fitzmaurice, *Granville I*, Granville to Lord Canning, 16 December 1859, p. 360.
85. W.E. Mosse, *The European Powers and the German Question 1848–71* (Cambridge: CUP, 1958), pp. 114–21.
86. Mosse, *German Question*, pp. 138–43; K.A.P. Sandiford, *Britain and the Schleswig-Holstein Question 1848–64* (Toronto: Toronto UP, 1975), pp. 86–9.
87. Gooch, *Later Correspondence of Lord John Russell, II*, Palmerston to Russell, 30 October 1851, p. 52; see also Ragnild Hatton, 'Palmerston and "Scandinavian Union"', in K. Bourne and D.C. Watt (eds), *Studies in International History* (London: Longmans, 1967), pp. 119–44.
88. Bourne, *Foreign Policy*, pp. 368–70 for the main text.
89. Krein, *The Last Palmerston Government*, p. 12.
90. W.E. Mosse, 'Queen Victoria and her Ministers in the Schleswig-Holstein Crisis 1863–64', *English Historical Review*, vol. 78, no. 2 (1963), pp. 263–83.
91. Mosse, *German Question*, p. 147.
92. Bourne, *Foreign Policy*, p. 109.
93. Bourne, *Foreign Policy*, pp. 373–5.
94. Krein, *The Last Palmerston Government*, p. 120.
95. Gooch and H. Temperley, *British Documents, vol. VI*, Salisbury to Iwan-Muller, p. 780.

5
'Floating Downstream'?: Lord Salisbury and British Foreign Policy, 1878–1902

T.G. Otte

'[T]here are few public men about whom less is known.' With this unusual admission opened the first full-scale biography of a man whose active political career spanned nearly half a century, from 1853 to 1902; who had been Prime Minister three times, four times Foreign Secretary, and twice in charge of the India Office; who had presided for two decades over a period of his party's ascendancy at home; and who had conducted Britain's foreign policy virtually uncontrolled, only rarely checked by Cabinet or Parliament.[1] As in life, the historical figure of Lord Salisbury has remained elusive. This was not helped by the fact that, until very recently, Salisbury was not well served by his biographers. Detailed studies on aspects of his career and politics apart, he had been allowed to slip into near oblivion as one of the worthy, but slumbering giants in the Tory Pantheon. In the field of domestic politics this reflected the prevailing historiographical emphasis on the capacity of the Conservatives to adapt to political and social change (though since the 1970s the Conservative Right has rediscovered him as a non-progressive Tory intellectual). Salisbury's status as an international statesman, too, has varied considerably in the judgement of historians, though he has never been the subject of historical controversies like Grey, Neville Chamberlain or Eden. In the immediate aftermath of his retirement he was widely regarded as sound but dull; a short-term fixer when in office; a manager of the expedient rather than a long-term planner. He seemed content to plot 'patiently a series of points on the graph of European relations without any attempt to construct a design he might leave to his successors to follow'. In his oft-quoted simile, foreign policy was 'to float lazily downstream, occasionally putting out a diplomatic boat-hook to avoid collisions'.[2] Indeed, measured against the

Bismarckian standard of international statesmanship, in Sir Robert Ensor's judgement, 'he can scarcely be ranked in the first flight of international statesmen, though his place must be extremely high in the second'.[3] In the later works of Dame Lilian Penson and especially in J.A.S. Grenville's monograph a more positive picture emerged of Salisburian diplomacy.[4] The nature and aptness of his policy, however, continue to be debated, as does his rank as a maker of British foreign policy.

For a long time Lord Salisbury's historical reputation seemed to reflect his outward appearance: he seemed to epitomize the respectable solidity and worthy stuffiness of the Victorian age. Recent research has done much to revise this misleading impression of this rather un-Victorian man.[5] In terms of Britain's foreign relations, his name still tends to be regarded as synonymous with 'isolation', splendid or otherwise, though this understates the subtlety and the many nuances of Salisbury's foreign policy.

When Salisbury was first appointed Foreign Secretary at the end of March 1878 few doubted that he brought substantial experience and robust intellectual equipment to the task. His two spells in charge of Indian affairs had given him a thorough grounding in the imperial dimension of British foreign policy. In the winter of 1876–77 he represented the British government at the ultimately failed conference at Constantinople at the height of the Russo-Turkish war, when the future of the Near East and the peace of Europe hung in the balance. His earlier forays into political journalism had established his credentials as a thoughtful, if sardonic and reactionary, controversialist whose verbal whiplashes secured him an attentive audience.[6] Indeed, this tall, stooping intellectual recluse, who shunned Society and 'Clubland', was not only a consummate practitioner but also a perceptive theoretician of diplomacy. It was here that his chief political interest lay. The Foreign Office and the *minutiae* of international diplomacy, his daughter and biographer wrote, appealed to his 'instinctive reverence for facts'.[7] Undoubtedly the attraction of diplomacy was considerably increased by the fact that it was a branch of politics still relatively shielded from public interference. Having been made to concede much of the plains of politics to the middle classes in the widening of the franchise – moves Salisbury had violently opposed – the summits of diplomacy remained the last preserve of the aristocracy. Still, it would be misleading to interpret Salisbury's often cynical comments as evidence of a 'fundamental defeatism', a 'settled and sardonic belief that things are as they are in the most ironic of possible worlds'; a belief that 'left him with a static view of politics'.[8] Consistency of views ought not to be conflated with inflexibility. Salisbury had opposed Disraeli's extension of the franchise in 1867, but had learnt to accommodate himself to it, albeit wearily. Foreign policy, he remarked, depended on 'the swing of the pendulum at home. It may be taken ... for an axiom that no foreign policy can succeed unless it can be completed within one beat of the pendulum.'[9]

Like his role model, Castlereagh, Salisbury preferred to work unobtrusively: 'A diplomatist's glory is the most ephemeral of all other forms of that transient reward.'[10] He was above all a realist; and foreign policy, in his estimation, was even more an art of the possible than other branches of politics. He held as axiomatic that there were never clear-cut solutions to any given international problem. '[L]ogic is of <u>no</u> use in diplomacy', he observed. Sentimental affinities and moral susceptibilities left him quite cold. He acted upon the understanding that nations were driven by their national interests. He saw little sense in applying to international politics ethical standards, which he deemed exclusively private.[11] When in the late 1890s slave ownership by the Muslim rulers of recently acquired Zanzibar became the subject of much public debate, Salisbury wryly commented that he saw 'no justice in excluding people from the benefit of the eighth commandment because they have not adopted our very modern doctrine upon slavery'.[12] However, such cynicism ought not to be construed into an assumption of Salisbury as a cold-blooded practitioner of *realpolitik* devoid of any moral content. True, unlike Gladstone, Salisbury did not publicize those moral concerns which moved him; and his political priorities clearly lay with British interests abroad. Yet, the Gladstone–Salisbury moral dichotomy, that both their detractors and admirers have built up, is overly simplistic.[13] During the Ottoman massacres in Bulgaria and Armenia Salisbury expressed his hope that the religious and humanitarian impulses of the public coincided with the country's national interest. It is instructive that he maintained friendly relations with Canons Liddon and MacColl, the two most vociferous Anglican agitators at the time of the massacres.[14] At any rate, given the importance of the 'swing of the pendulum at home' it was prudent to be attentive to public moral sentiment. In the interest of bipartisan continuity in foreign policy, too, it had to be taken into account.

Salisbury was not given to moral crusades in aid of oppressed Balkan nationalities, and was scathing of the 'liberal sympathy' for the principle of national self-determination.[15] But he clearly understood that nationalism was a factor of modern international politics. Redrawing political maps and transferring population from one ruler to another, he noted, was a dangerous and potentially futile exercise, for 'these marketable souls would in the end have the deciding voice whether the bargain of which they were the subject should endure or not'.[16] Salisbury conceived of diplomacy as a moderating force. It was not an instrument to pursue ideal solutions, but rather the means by which agreements of limited durability could be arrived at after calm and patient negotiations. Salisbury, in Arthur Marsden's apt phrase, 'went out into the "market place" of international politics determined to get the best bargain possible. He expected to make no gains without paying for them, but he did insist that the price should be a fair one'.[17] A few days into his first tenure of the Foreign Office Salisbury wrote to the ambassador at Constantinople that the idea of Turkish independence and sovereignty had become a fiction: 'the Turkish breakwater ... is now shattered ... . Another dyke may have to be established behind it, which possibly must be constructed from the same material.'[18] This early statement sums up neatly Salisbury's approach to foreign policy. It was saturated with the pessimistic understanding of diplomacy's essentially ephemeral nature. He eschewed grand designs; semi-permanence was the best possible outcome achievable in international politics.

As a pillar of the Victorian political establishment, and even more so as a self-proclaimed disciple of Castlereagh, Salisbury subscribed to the notion of 'the necessity of counterpoise' or balance of power as the main principle of international politics. At any rate, the 'carefully balanced structure [of] ... the European system of nations' was the accepted wider setting of his diplomacy.[19] This wider setting reinforced his instinctive caution. He was not inspired by romantic notions of an imperial mission as Disraeli and Randolph Churchill had been; unlike Rosebery he was not driven by some sense of Anglo-Saxon superiority; and most of all he abhorred the 'Jingo hurricane' so skilfully fanned by Joseph Chamberlain.[20] Ironically, during his ascendancy over British foreign policy vast new territories were added to the British empire. For Salisbury imperial expansion was not an end in itself, but rather the beginning of further problems. Whatever his pessimism in all human affairs, in foreign policy he retained his basic optimism as to British strength. None the less, he was conscious of the military and economic limitations on the country's power. Thus he preferred the 'open door' principle in trade and informal political arrangements to the outright annexation of new territory. A pragmatist, he was inclined to forestall potential rivals, yet at the same time was anxious to conciliate rather than exploit tensions.[21] He was no bluffer; a policy based on hollow foundations, already the young Salisbury had argued, was bound to fail. '[F]ierce notes and pacific measures' were not his style.[22] Reflecting on Salisbury's career his long-time political associate, Sir Michael Hicks Beach, wrote in 1914: 'As to foreign and colonial affairs ... he was a genuine lover of peace, and kept us out of many quarrels which seemed important at the time, but which ... no one would consider worth fighting about now.'[23]

Salisbury clearly found the conditions of the unreformed Foreign Office a conducive environment. He was largely uninterested in the department's administration. In official business, one of his parliamentary private secretaries wrote, he was 'Olympian and aloof'; and Lady Salisbury is reputed once to have said 'that her husband knew no more about the clerks in the Foreign Office than he did about the housemaids at Hatfield, and ... that he did not know his own précis writer by sight'.[24] Indeed, not infrequently he indulged in a farcical 'game of hide-and-seek between chief and staff' in order to evade the latter's intrusions. Salisbury, always loath to delegate tasks, preferred 'working the coach alone'.[25] His decision-making role and the duties he expected his clerks to perform were kept strictly separate. He 'wanted clerks not advisers or experts'. This not only suited his own preference for working alone, it also reflected his understanding of the fundamental principles of the British constitution. Permanent officials were unelected, and could therefore reach no decisions.[26] Salisbury did not completely ignore the Foreign Office machinery. But he expected his officials to respect the limits he had set for them. His Permanent Under-Secretaries Julian Pauncefote, and even more so Philip Currie and Thomas Sanderson appreciated this principle of Salisburian foreign policy, and confined themselves to executing his directives (though his first Permanent Under-Secretary, Lord Tenterden, expected a larger say).[27] The enormous number of red-ink 'S's and his often copious minutes on Foreign Office despatches are an indication of the substantial quantity of material he worked through. His officials, however, were not always kept fully abreast of his decisions or the most recent developments. This is not to suggest that Salisbury consciously tried to conceal any of his transactions. Yet it did not conform to his conception of a clerk's role, no matter how senior, to inform or to consult him *in extenso*.[28] This preference for conducting the most important aspects by way of private communication with British diplomats abroad or foreign representatives in London later incurred him the charge of 'secret diplomacy', most notably in Eyre Crowe's famous memorandum of 1907. Not infrequently, indeed, he confided his views to foreign representatives in London without recording them in writing.[29]

Salisbury's relations with the then still separate diplomatic service were somewhat more complex. The sheer volume of his private correspondence, always written in his own hand, with the heads of mission in the more important capitals, is impressive. Its tone and contents suggest a more equal relationship between the Foreign Secretary and his ambassadors or ministers. Salisbury offered his analyses of current problems and explained, often at great length, his policies. In return he expected the diplomats to supply him with fresh factual information and to offer their interpretations and suggestions as to possible alternative courses. The intention of this somewhat laborious method was to secure the ambassadors' cooperation by rational and consensual means, though Salisbury left them in no doubt that the ultimate decision-making powers lay with him. Salisbury tended to form his conclusions only slowly and was reluctant to be rushed into decisions. Yet once he had formed his conclusions, he would act speedily, as Sanderson noted: 'Remember he is very difficult to move, but he comes down like a bag of bricks when he does move.'[30]

If Salisbury did not know his précis writers by sight, he was certainly very well informed of his ambassadors' political affiliations, even though such affiliations had long ceased to be a significant factor in the appointment of senior diplomats.[31] Similarly, whilst he abdicated much of the responsibility for the day-to-day administration of the Foreign Office to his senior staff, he surveyed continually the performance of the senior diplomats abroad.

Indiscreet comments in the press, lackadaisical execution of their duties, or their private peccadilloes were noted and reprimanded.[32] Although Salisbury accepted the need to win the diplomats' cooperation, he seems to have had little faith in the collective wisdom of the Foreign Office and diplomatic service. 'The Service is hardly good enough', was a frequent complaint of his.[33] In consequence he frequently looked outside the official confines for 'the right man'.

The key to Salisbury's foreign policy lay in the Middle and Near Eastern crisis crescent that stretched from Afghanistan and India's north-western frontier to the Ottoman dominions in the Balkans and north-eastern Africa. Developments here, and their wider repercussions for great power relations, dominated Salisbury's thinking until very nearly the end of his political life. His foreign policy revolved essentially around two twin objectives: to defend India against a Russian invasion or Russian-inspired subversion; and to maintain the independence and, as far as was possible, the integrity of the adjacent, increasingly unstable countries.[34] In the late 1890s, in an oft-quoted speech to the Primrose League, he divided the nations of the world, in the Social Darwinist parlance of the day, into 'the living and the dying'. In the dying nations 'disorganisation and decay are growing almost as fast as organisation and increasing power are advancing in the living nations'.[35]

The 'dying nations' were not a phenomenon of the 1890s alone. It already confronted Salisbury when he was appointed Foreign Secretary for the first time at the end of March 1878. The further decay of the countries bordering on the areas of core strategic interest to Britain and her empire heralded the prospect of a major redistribution of territory in the Near and Middle East. The concomitant shifts in regional influence in Russia's favour would have complicated Britain's European relations, and rendered the defence of India even more difficult. That an Ottoman collapse would very likely, if not inevitably, lead to a general war of the Ottoman succession, a new Crimean War, was further reason for Salisbury to pick his steps cautiously.[36] Still, British foreign policy in the latter stages of the Great Eastern crisis had certain elements of boldness which it would lack during Salisbury's subsequent tenures of the Foreign Office. Of course, during those two years the ultimate control of foreign policy rested in Disraeli's hands – more so than perhaps under his predecessor Derby.[37] Salisbury's readiness to replace Derby, and work with the detested Disraeli was regarded as an indication of unsuspected ambitions ultimately to lead the Conservative Party. Indeed, his earlier connivance with Cairns, the Lord Chancellor, and the Prime Minister in bypassing Derby, and in easing the latter and Colonial Secretary Carnarvon out of office in the early months of 1878 suggests an uncharacteristic duplicity.[38] Yet, with an often ailing Prime Minister not fully in control of his ministers, and with the Cabinet dangerously split on the Balkans question, the alternative would have been the collapse of the ministry and certain diplomatic impotence.

The international situation at Salisbury's assumption of the seals of the Foreign Office was inauspicious, as he explained in bold strokes in his famous circular despatch of 1 April 1878. The preliminary treaty of San Stefano of February had created a greater Bulgaria, 'a strong Slav State ... under the auspices and control of Russia, possessing important harbours upon the shores of the Black Sea and the Archipelago, and conferring upon that Power a preponderating influence over both political and commercial relations in those seas.' Russian influence, in Salisbury's analysis, would spread further under the umbrella of the Orthodox church; the severance of Constantinople from the remainder of Turkey's European provinces would render the Sultan's political control over these areas even more tenuous; and Russia's expansion in central Asia would give her a stranglehold over Persian trade, thus leading to Russian political predominance at Tehran. The geographical areas affected by San Stefano, the Straits of Constantinople, the Suez Canal and the Persian Gulf, were 'of the deepest interest to Great Britain'; and the treaty was a danger 'to English interests and to the permanent peace of Europe'. The key to safeguarding British interests, short of a general war, was the maintenance by international agreement of as much of Ottoman rule in Europe and in Asia as was possible. As regards Turkey-in-Europe, Salisbury was 'anxious that Russia should not be allowed to bring the Slav principality [that is, Bulgaria] down to the Aegean; & that the Straits should be either open to all ships & at all times or under the guardianship of an independent Power'. The Sultan's rule at Constantinople had to be shored up so as to make it both 'politically independent and strategically safe'.[39] However, Salisbury was under no illusions that, given the growth of Balkan nationalism, '[s]ooner or later the greater part of [Turkey's] European Empire <u>must</u> go.' The Balkan provinces should be assigned to Turkey temporarily 'on the grounds on which a patron whose son is not of age presents an old and infirm clergyman to the family living'.[40] To delay this inevitable eventuality was one of Salisbury's main objectives: 'I hope ... to draw a wall across the Peninsula of the Balkans & across Armenia which shall give Turkey respite for twenty or thirty years. If any future remains to the Empire this interval should be made use of.'[41] Historians of the 1878 settlement have argued that the future of the Ottoman empire in Asia was of greater concern to Salisbury than that of Turkey-in-Europe.[42] Yet, Salisbury was too shrewd not to realize that the two questions were inextricably linked. The days of Ottoman rule in Europe might have been numbered, but Salisbury understood that without a firm power base in Asia Turkish rule would collapse sooner rather than later; for 'from Asia it will continue to draw that which is its real strength – the magnificent Mussulman material of its armies'. The key to prolonging the Sultan's rule in the Balkans, then, lay in stabilizing his power in Asia. 'If we can protect the Asiatic Empire from disintegration, & procure a more reasonable frontier in

Europe, there will be a fair chance of the Ottoman Government retaining Constantinople for a considerable period.'[43] Although firm Austrian cooperation and a guarantee of the Ottoman dominions in Europe were not forthcoming, Salisbury was not opposed to the eventual Austrian occupation of Bosnia-Herzegovina. Indeed, he welcomed it as the best means to forestall 'a chain of Slav States from the Euxinus to the Adriatic'.[44] As Vienna's cooperation was not to be had against Russia, Salisbury sought an arrangement with the latter, thus setting a precedent for his future conduct of foreign affairs. In the Salisbury–Shuvalov protocol of 30 May 1878 Russia accepted the limitation of her conquests in north-eastern Turkey. This agreement (then leaked to the *Globe* newspaper and so giving an incentive for the Official Secrets legislation), laid the foundations for the proposed international congress to settle the Turkish question.[45]

It is difficult to establish precisely Salisbury's role in the simultaneous decision to acquire Cyprus from the Sublime Porte. Already at the end of April Disraeli had impressed upon the Queen that 'we must occupy some island or station on the coast of Asia Minor, which will neutralize the presence of Russia in Armenia'.[46] Shortly afterwards Salisbury argued that Russia's now irreversible presence in the Transcaucasus around Kars would increase pressure on Turkey-in-Asia and on Persia; Russia would stir disorder to take advantage of the situation 'to reduce the Porte to impotence, & to turn its provinces into Russian satrapies. The presence of England is the only remedy which can prevent this process of destruction.'[47] The Anglo-Turkish convention of 4 June 1878 was a defensive alliance of sorts, guaranteeing Turkey-in-Asia against further Russian encroachments. In return, the Turkish government agreed to Britain's occupation of Cyprus. British military presence there, Salisbury reasoned, would act as a deterrent against further Russian expansion into Turkey-in-Asia; and it would thus 'strengthen [the] Sultan's authority in Syria and Mesopotamia'.[48] The acquisition of Cyprus was perhaps of greater symbolic than practical value; above all it was meant to rally public opinion if war were to threaten again. Salisbury's perceived duplicity in negotiating the protocol with Shuvalov simultaneously with the Cyprus convention soured relations with Russia and the two Mediterranean powers, Italy and France.[49] None the less, the settlement Disraeli and his Foreign Secretary secured at the Berlin Congress in June–July was a diplomatic success of a kind. It brought 'peace with prestige', and ended the post-Crimean period of 'self-effacement, embarrassment, and ignominy'.[50] It marked Britain's return to European diplomacy.

But the achievements of Berlin, in terms of Britain's international standing, were short-lived. This diminution was by no means exclusively the result of the unsuccessful Gladstone–Granville efforts to revive the Concert of Europe during the Liberal administration of 1880–85. On the contrary, it had already begun before 1880. In so far as the question of Turkey's future was concerned, the Turcophile ambassador at Constantinople rightly argued that the achievements of the Berlin congress were incomplete. Worse still, the 'new nationalities' in the Balkans and their 'dangerous ambitions' afforded 'fresh motives & fresh facilities for Russia to carry on here intrigues with the object of destroying the [Turkish] Empire & possessing herself of the heritage'.[51] Salisbury himself was pessimistic. To maintain, if not to increase, British influence at the Porte was his principal object, 'perhaps the most vital of all'. In Austria he had a natural, if not always reliable, partner in containing Russian influence in Turkey-in-Europe. Yet, he had no illusions about the prospects of Turkish rule – though, ironically, the Sultan and his regime outlived Salisbury by some five years.[52]

Indeed, Salisbury's policy of buttressing Turkey had already begun to unravel soon after the congress. Acting on his axiom that Constantinople was of greater strategic importance than the Suez Canal, he had sought Anglo-French cooperation in north Africa. In private conversations Salisbury and France's chief delegate at the Berlin congress, W.H. Waddington, arrived at an informal understanding. Typically, Salisbury had made no official record of his talks with Waddington. The principal idea of the understanding, however, was that, as compensation for Britain's acquisition of Cyprus, France was given a free hand in Tunis; and that in Egypt the two countries should cooperate.[53] Waddington, who had kept a record of their various conversations was adamant that the Foreign Secretary had given a binding promise, whereas Salisbury claimed that his ideas were of an entirely speculative kind, based on the hypothetical assumption of a complete Ottoman collapse.[54] It is conceivable, as Marsden has argued, that there was a genuine misunderstanding. If there was, Salisbury had proceeded perhaps rashly, but certainly developed his argument clumsily. If he had envisaged a gradual revival of the Anglo-French bond of the 1840s rather than a firm guarantee with immediate effect, then this was at variance with the advice received from Lord Lyons, the British ambassador at Paris.[55] After the premature publicity for the Anglo-Russian protocol and the Anglo-Turkish convention, the Waddington affair threatened further embarrassment; and Salisbury was forced to confirm formally that Britain would not 'view with apprehension or distrust the legitimate and expanding influence of France' in Tunis, though he carefully avoided confirming the earlier 'offer'.[56] This dispatch, and the removal in the following year of Britain's consul at Tunis, amounted to a virtual recognition of French preponderance there. Given the often indiscreet nature of French politics at this time, it is not unlikely that part of the story became more widely known in diplomatic circles; and it may have been this incident that caused Bismarck famously to describe Salisbury as 'ce clergyman laïque, obstiné et maladroit'.[57]

Salisbury's recognition of French ambitions in Tunis did not prevent him, like Bismarck, from encouraging Italy to become involved in Tunis.[58] This episode is instructive of Salisbury's shrewd and calculating grasp of the complex relations between the great powers. Given her exposed coastline

Italy would always have to align herself with a strong naval power. Competition with France in Tunis meant that an Italo-French combination was never likely to emerge as Italy would have to lean towards Britain for diplomatic support and naval protection. This in turn safeguarded Britain's strategically vital Mediterranean sea-lines of communication. Similarly, Franco-Italian rivalry rendered even more impracticable any dormant Italian irredentism at Austria's expense, so keeping undiminished the Hapsburg monarchy's power in the Balkans. The security of Turkey-in-Europe would be enhanced, and Britain's position at Constantinople *vis-à-vis* Russia protected. Moreover, Italian competition in north Africa gave Salisbury some additional leverage over France in Egypt.

Salisbury's Egyptian diplomacy was largely opportunistic, though undoubtedly successfully so. He was able to ward off Waddington's demands for a binding agreement, in the form of an Anglo-French convention on Egypt. The dual control regime over Egypt's messy finances had been in place since 1876. But Salisbury realized that Egyptian affairs might take a turn for the worse, as he explained to Disraeli, 'and it may suit us at some future period to push ahead'. Any binding agreements with France were thus an impediment.[59] Quite clearly, in the event of an Ottoman collapse Salisbury wanted to have a free hand in Egypt. For the moment, the attempts of the native ruler of Egypt, the Khedive Ismail, to bring to an end Anglo-French financial control drew the two countries closer together. Ultimately they succeeded in deposing Ismail in 1879 by putting pressure on his nominal overlord, the Sultan at Constantinople. Turkish action was preferable to unilateral French action, given that in 1879 British troops were tied down in India and Afghanistan. Yet, just as efforts to prop up the Sultan's rule at Constantinople were temporary measures, so was cooperation with France in Egypt. Having agreed with Waddington to exclude other powers from controlling Egypt, the main task of British diplomacy was now to contain French influence on the Nile.[60] The seeds of future Anglo-French discord had been sown; and one might well speculate that, had Salisbury been in power in 1882, his reaction to the Arabi revolt would not have been different from that of Gladstone and Granville.[61]

In central Asia, by contrast, Salisbury's foreign policy was relatively unsuccessful. In India, Lord Lytton, the bellicose Viceroy, brought to its logical conclusion the 'forward policy' formulated by Salisbury when he was at the India Office. The policy aimed at a peaceful penetration of primarily Afghanistan and, though to a lesser degree, Persia. It produced consequences unintended by Salisbury, at a time when he was no longer responsible for Indian affairs, and the Viceroy was able to act more independently of Whitehall.[62] Lytton's more aggressive policy led to the second Afghan war in 1879. Between them, Russian expansionism and Lytton's accelerated 'forward policy' destroyed the concept of Afghanistan as a 'buffer state'. Anything if not consequent in his actions, Salisbury responded to the new situation by pursuing the option of an Anglo-Persian partition of Afghanistan, with the aim of strengthening Persia as a barrier against further Russian expansion into central Asia. What at first glance must appear a volte-face was in fact entirely consistent with Salisbury's policy hitherto. It was at any rate the logical consequence to the disintegration of the Afghan buffer state. Nevertheless the Herat convention of November 1879 was too controversial for the Cabinet's taste, and Salisbury failed to obtain its approval.[63] Indeed, the Afghan imbroglio contributed to the fall of the Disraeli government in 1880.

When the Conservatives returned to office in the summer of 1885, Salisbury combined the premiership with the office of Foreign Secretary. No other British Prime Minister after Salisbury, with the exception of MacDonald's brief and unhappy experiment in 1924, was prepared to shoulder this dual burden. Gladstone, indeed, criticized him for thus removing all control from the Foreign Secretary. Combining the two offices, no doubt, suited Salisbury's inclinations. He also felt compelled to do so in order to keep at a minimum the influence on foreign policy of the pro-Russian Randolph Churchill, his rival for the leadership of the party.[64] But it also reflected his understanding of the late Victorian constitutional arrangements. The premiership, he argued, was 'not an office: it has no bureau, no staff, no pay, no legal power'. It had to be combined with some other office.[65]

The international landscape had changed significantly during the five years of Liberal rule. Bismarck's predominance in European diplomacy, resting on the renewed *Dreikaiserbund* (or Three Emperors' League) with Russia and Austria, was at its zenith. Instead of securing a rapprochement with Russia, Gladstone and Granville had brought Anglo-Russian relations to the brink of war during the Penjdeh crisis; and their Concert of Europe policy, Salisbury commented caustically, 'succeeded in uniting the Continent of Europe – against England'.[66] His second spell at the Foreign Office was something of an interlude, lasting not quite seven months. Lacking a parliamentary majority, and with his Cabinet lacking in unity, Salisbury's freedom of action was curtailed. None the less, act he did; and the brevity of this interlude is no indication of its significance. When leaving office in February 1886, Salisbury looked back on it as 'months of considerable pressure & crisis in our diplomatic affairs'.[67] Salisbury acted speedily, determined to break Britain's dangerous isolation in European affairs. The key, however, lay in Berlin. Without Bismarck's encouragement no Austrian support could be had for containing further Russian expansion in the Balkans; and for as long as Russo-German relations remained close, Russia was free to put pressure on Britain in central Asia. Moreover, the recent colonial rapprochement between Germany and France had highlighted the latent vulnerability of Britain's position in Egypt. The occupation of 1882 had turned the future of Egypt into a sore in Anglo-French relations – one which Bismarck did his utmost to keep festering. Salisbury had fully grasped this. The stability, indeed the durability, of Britain's position in Egypt 'will depend largely on general

European politics, and on the tendencies which animate Germany and France'.[68] The most pressing issue for the moment, however, was the prospect of Russia bearing down on the Zulficar Pass, one of the approaches to the strategically important Afghan city of Herat. If the pass were to fall into Russian hands, whatever was left of the Afghan 'bufferstate' would irrevocably be demolished.[69] Salisbury approached Bismarck, using Philip Currie, his former private secretary, and Bismarck's son Herbert as go-betweens, to enlist the Chancellor's services as mediator in the Afghan question. He also held out the prospect of 'a closer and more intimate alliance' between Britain and Germany, but Bismarck declined the offered role as arbitrator.[70] Ultimately, Bismarck's support in the Afghan question was not necessary. Wary of yet another confrontation with Britain in central Asia, the Russians pulled back, leaving the Zulficar Pass in Afghan hands. That Salisbury seriously entertained the idea of a full diplomatic alliance with Germany seems doubtful. In an earlier letter to Bismarck, which prepared Currie's mission, Salisbury had hinted at limited cooperation in Egypt and Afghanistan. Still, his assurance to Bismarck and the Austrian ambassador, Count Karolyi, that even the return of a Liberal government would not alter the course of British foreign policy is instructive.[71] It was a clear signal on the part of Salisbury that British interests in the geostrategic periphery could not be protected unilaterally, but only by accepting entanglement in Bismarck's web of agreements and understandings. Bismarck, it seems, understood. In a second, specially convened meeting between Currie and himself, albeit after the Russian climbdown over the Zulficar Pass, Bismarck promised support against France in Egypt, though he still carefully refrained from meddling in central Asian disputes. Salisbury's attempt to overcome Britain's diplomatic isolation by leaning towards the German-dominated Triple Alliance, then, was at least partially successful.[72]

Salisbury also had a fair share of that scarcest of political commodities: good fortune. The potential conflict with Russia over Afghanistan had only just been averted, when events in the Balkans began slowly to unravel Bismarck's carefully woven ties between the three Eastern monarchies. In late September the ruler of Bulgaria, Prince Alexander of Battenberg, responded to an uprising in Eastern Roumelia, the Bulgarian-speaking province left under Ottoman rule by the Berlin Congress, with a declaration of union between the two halves of the country.[73] The original purpose of the division of Bulgaria had been to curtail Russian influence in the Balkans and to reduce the danger of a Russian move on the Straits of Constantinople. Salisbury, therefore, initially viewed the creation of a united Bulgaria with apprehension 'for I look upon it as a Russian province in an advanced stage of manufacture'. And a strong Russian military presence in Bulgaria would bring additional pressure to bear on the Sultan at Constantinople.[74] However, Salisbury was resigned to accept the creation of a 'Big Bulgaria'. The weak response by the Porte to the events in its rebellious province had reinforced

Salisbury's pessimistic assessment of Turkey's state of health. She had 'no spark of vitality left'; and with the *Dreikaiserbund* apparently poised to support Battenberg, Britain's options were limited.[75] However matters were not as they appeared. Battenberg, far from being a Russian puppet, had cut the wires that were pulled at St Petersburg, and was anxious to eliminate Russian influence at Sofia. When in the aftermath of the declaration of union it became clear that Russia would oppose Battenberg, Salisbury performed what seemed yet another remarkable volte-face. He was persuaded by White, the British minister *ad interim* at Constantinople, that if Battenberg were allowed to be squashed, Bulgaria's complete Russification would ensue. '[W]e may find ourselves with a Big Bulgaria and a Russian prince', Salisbury now agreed. In consequence Salisbury proposed a personal union between the two Bulgarias.[76] Salisbury had supported Bulgaria's territorial reduction and subsequent division at Berlin in 1878 as the best means of keeping Russia away from the Turkish Straits, based on the assumption that the new Balkan principality would be little more than a Russian satellite. When Battenberg proved the reverse, Salisbury changed course. The means, then, had changed, but not the overall objective of his policy.

In pursuing this new pro-Battenberg course Salisbury took the calculated risk of paralysing the efforts of the ambassadorial conference at Constantinople to solve the smouldering crisis, if not to uphold the Berlin settlement in its original form.[77] The greatest danger of his policy change, however, lay in the implicit encouragement to Serbia and Greece to follow the Bulgarian example, thus precipitating Turkey's final partition. Salisbury's policy was in fact a complicated double game. British naval pressure deterred Greece from attacking Turkey, thus ensuring that any potential conflict could be kept localized. Serbia's attack on Bulgaria in mid-November 1885 relieved Turkey of further pressure. The Bulgarians' crushing victory over the invading Serb army and their subsequent invasion of Serbia then allowed for Austrian intervention between the two warring nations, backed up by Britain. Moreover, the simultaneous first special mission of Sir Henry Drummond-Wolff to Constantinople to restore closer ties with Turkey underlines Salisbury's overall aim of buttressing the Sultan's ramshackle European empire.[78] Admittedly, Salisbury owed much of his success to the Serbian defeat by Bulgaria. But his brinkmanship bore results. Anxious lest further tensions damage the *Dreikaiserbund* irreparably, the three Eastern monarchies accepted Salisbury's original plan of a personal union, which was enshrined in the Turko-Bulgarian agreement of April 1886.

Salisbury's nuanced and calculating diplomacy led Britain out of the dangerous isolation of 1885, and she 're-entered the market place in the Near East'.[79] The successes of 1886 laid the foundations of the further realignment with the Triple Alliance powers in 1887. Moreover, during the brief Liberal intermezzo between February and August 1886, Rosebery confirmed Salisbury's earlier prediction of a bipartisan foreign policy consensus.

The initiative for the Mediterranean agreements came from Italy, though Salisbury undoubtedly welcomed it as step towards strengthening ties with the Triple Alliance.[80] However, Drummond-Wolff's renewed, albeit unsuccessful, mission to Constantinople in 1887 to negotiate Britain's military withdrawal from Egypt on adequate terms was an indication of Salisbury's reluctance to align himself too closely with the German-led group of powers. Thus, he refused to contemplate the original Italian suggestion of a full alliance against France, though he admitted that '"For the present" the enemy is France'.[81] As a result, the first Mediterranean agreement of February 1887 provided for unspecified cooperation against France along the southern shores of the Mediterranean and in support of the *status quo* in south-eastern Europe. The two countries, Salisbury explained to the ambassador at Vienna, 'an island & a peninsula, have very cogent maritime reasons for acting together. We are to a very large extent interested in precisely the same questions; & we have in our fleets the means of giving effect to those interests.'[82] Pointing to the rise of extreme nationalism in France under Boulanger, encouraged by Russia, he justified the limited commitment to Italy entailed in the agreement as the best means of reducing the 'fearful risk, and cost' of diplomatic isolation.[83] Austria's swift adherence to the Anglo-Italian agreement in March 1887, urged on by Bismarck, lent greater significance to it. Britain's two new partners were now tied to the upholding of the *status quo* in the Near East, without incurring specific commitments for Britain. The nature and extent of the envisaged joint measures would be decided upon if and when the need for them arose. Salisbury even obtained a pledge of diplomatic support in Egypt from the Austrian government.[84]

Advantageous though the understandings of the spring of 1887 were, the assumption of a 'free hand' soon proved somewhat illusory. Bismarck was the invisible fourth party to the Mediterranean grouping. Bismarck did not lend his support free of charge, and for the moment he had the advantage over Salisbury. Already in May 1887 Salisbury was forced to yield to German pressure to remove the British consul at Zanzibar as the price for Bismarck's support in the Egyptian question, thus implicitly acknowledging Germany's preponderance along the east coast of Africa: 'It is only Egypt that puts us into this difficulty, for otherwise Bismarck would be of little moment to us. It is heartily to be wished we were delivered from this very inconvenient & somewhat humiliating relation.'[85] Salisbury's wishes remained unfulfilled. The failure in the same month of Drummond-Wolff's draft convention on the eventual evacuation of Egypt preserved German leverage over Britain (though the Anglo-French convention on the Suez Canal of October 1887 somewhat alleviated the situation).[86]

More importantly, in light of the latent enmity between Austria and Italy, Britain had in effect become 'the cement which held the Triple Alliance together'.[87] Thus when in the autumn of 1887 Vienna and Rome pressed Salisbury for an extension of the spring agreements in reaction to the renewed flaring up of the Bulgarian question, he accepted their proposal. Refusal would have encouraged Austria to seek a Balkans settlement with Russia, so reviving the now defunct *Dreikaiserbund* – a prospect Salisbury dreaded as it would have pushed Britain back into the dangerous isolation of 1885. A new agreement, however, offered the opportunity to split the three Eastern powers, and so win greater freedom of action for Britain. In this sense, Salisbury was working towards the same aims as Disraeli had in the late 1870s.[88] The second Mediterranean *accord à trois* of 12 December 1887 committed the three powers to more overt support of the Sultan's regime; it specifically included Turkey-in-Asia, and was poised more against Russia than against France. The net result was the creation of a triple *entente* for the protection of common regional interests.[89]

Salisbury resisted Italo-German efforts in 1888 to convert the Mediterranean *entente* into a more binding instrument. He had no need to do so, for Britain's international position had improved perceptibly. The *Dreikaiserbund* had finally collapsed as a result of the 1887 Bulgarian crisis. Russia, with only the tenuous prospect of possible German support under the Reinsurance Treaty, now refrained from further encroachments upon the Balkans. The effective containment of Russia in the Near East reduced the external pressure on the Sultan's regime.[90] Indeed, Salisbury's failure to extricate Britain from Egypt now provided an incentive to place Britain's position on the Nile on a more secure footing. Ironically, then, the relative success of the Mediterranean *entente* ultimately undermined it, as Egypt began to replace Constantinople as a key strategic interest in the eastern Mediterranean. The passing of the 1889 Naval Defence Act further highlighted Salisbury's attempts to regain a 'free hand' in international affairs by placing greater emphasis on unilateral naval expansion as the best means of safeguarding British interests, rather than on diplomatic compacts. Under the act, Britain's security rested on a future margin of superiority over the combined strength of the next two largest naval powers, the so-called 'Two-Power Standard', without having to rely on Continental partners.[91]

The very real improvement in Britain's diplomatic position also helps to explain the abortive secret approach by Bismarck in early 1889. The sincerity of Bismarck's alliance offer and his motivation have long been the subject of some debate among historians, though it may be taken as a first indication of Bismarck's growing realization that his 'web' of deals and counter-deals was unravelling. Salisbury, of course, was fully aware of Bismarck's long-term aim of binding Britain more closely to the Triple Alliance.[92] When the offer of a defensive alliance came, Salisbury turned it down, pointing to constitutional obstacles. In reality, Salisbury understood only too well that such an alliance would very likely involve Britain in a Franco-German war, whilst German support in the less likely event of an Anglo-Russian clash in central Asia could not be counted upon. Any formalization of Britain's leaning towards the Triple Alliance would have shifted the weights in the Bismarck–Salisbury 'diplomatic duel' again to the former's advantage.[93] An additional factor that made for caution was Salisbury's deep mistrust of the young and volatile Emperor Wilhelm II, whom he thought 'a little off his head'.[94]

Salisbury's cool response to the German approach in 1889, however, did not mean that cooperation with Germany and the Triple Alliance had become superfluous. In the Balkans, he maintained, 'a good understanding with Austria ought to be a cardinal point of English policy'.[95] Furthermore, the increasing strategic importance of Egypt brought eastern Africa, and the upper reaches of the Nile valley more especially, into sharper focus. Baring, Britain's *de facto* ruler of Egypt, warned that '[w]hatever Power holds the Upper Nile Valley, must, by the mere force of its geographical situation, dominate Egypt'.[96] Salisbury saw matters in a similar light. The expansion of German influence in east Africa, and her possible control over the headways of the Nile, would increase her leverage over Britain in Egypt and at Constantinople. An African settlement with Germany was therefore imperative:

> any indefinite postponement of a settlement in Africa would render it very difficult to maintain terms of amity with Germany, and would force us to change our system of alliances in Europe. The alliance of France instead of the alliance of Germany must necessarily involve the early evacuation of Egypt under very unfavourable conditions.[97]

Fortunately for Salisbury Germany's new chancellor Caprivi was quite prepared to trade German influence in east Africa for the North Sea island of Heligoland. The Anglo-German colonial treaty of 1 July 1890 thus shoehorned a potential rival out of the Upper Nile Valley and secured its south-eastern approaches. The delimitation of Italian influence on the Horn of Africa followed soon thereafter. The Heligoland–Zanzibar treaty found its corollary in the Anglo-French agreement of August 1890 which bought off the French threat to the Upper Nile region with concessions in west Africa and in western Sudan.[98] The agreement with France offered a glimpse of future possibilities. For the moment Salisbury remained wedded to the idea of cooperating with the Triple Alliance. A rapprochement with France, he warned his successor on leaving office in August 1892, would involve 'the abandonment of the Triple Alliance by Italy, a reconstruction of the Drei Kaiser Bund and Russia on the Bosphorus'.[99] Salisbury's nuanced diplomacy had led Britain out of the dangerous isolation of the mid-1880s, and gradually enhanced her international position.

That much of this improvement was only temporary became clear during Salisbury's last term of office between 1895 and 1902 (he continued in his dual role of Prime Minister and Foreign Secretary until 1900). Further adjustments were needed to a now rapidly changing international scene. The

Franco-Russian alliance had been progressively tightened since 1891/2; Germany under the young Kaiser showed greater ambition to play a leading role in international affairs; and, out in the wings, the US and Japan began to emerge as new great powers. On taking up office in June 1895, Salisbury was once again faced with a crisis in the Near East. An uprising by Armenian nationalists in the summer of 1894 had been brutally suppressed by Turkish troops. Rosebery's efforts, in conjunction with France and Russia, to force the Sultan to accept reforms which would grant sufficient protection to the Armenian and other Christian populations under Turkish rule bore no fruits.[100] In September 1895 violence erupted again, and lasted throughout the winter of 1895–96. Salisbury himself had become increasingly sceptical about the survival chances of the Sultan's rule. His views were informed as much by his experience of nearly two decades of the Sultan's evasions and reneging on undertakings given, as by Constantinople's reduced strategic importance for Britain. 'I am not at all a bigot to the policy of keeping Russia out of C[onstantino]ple', he admitted to the First Lord of the Admiralty. Indeed, he regarded the burden of maintaining the Ottoman empire as almost intolerable. None the less, Salisbury was reluctant to give up Britain's traditional Near Eastern policy, since 'our fame & prestige are so bound up with it, that when it fails the blow will be tremendous'.[101] Instead he sought the cooperation of the other great powers to bring stability to the Near East. In this, it seems, he preferred joint efforts with Russia. Indeed, during his last term of office Salisbury became increasingly convinced of the need to improve Anglo-Russian relations:

> It may be possible for England and Russia to return to their old relations. But it is an object to be wished for and approached as opportunity offers. [...] We may, without any fault of our own, find ourselves opposed to Russia on this question or that, in consequence of past commitments. All we can do is to try to narrow the chasm that separates us. It is the best chance for something like an equilibrium of Europe.[102]

Instead of Russian support the Armenian crisis produced one of the enigmatic episodes of his stewardship of Britain's diplomatic affairs. Encouraged by his repeated predictions of Turkey's imminent collapse, the German Kaiser proposed in 1895 a scheme for the partition of the Ottoman empire. That Salisbury had made such gloomy hints is beyond doubt. Whether the ambassador, a seasoned diplomat, misunderstood Salisbury's meaning remains unclear.[103] The episode is, however, reminiscent of Salisbury's casual Tunisian 'offer' to Waddington in 1879. At any rate, Salisbury was considerably embarrassed by the German overture which he derided as impracticable.

A naval demonstration with the Mediterranean *entente* powers, by contrast, he argued, would produce 'much effect on the Sultan's mind'.[104] Vienna was responsive and proposed a joint forcing of the Straits with the aim of coercing the Sultan into accepting reform. However, following pressure from his German ally, the Austrian foreign minister soon abandoned the idea.[105] At the same time Salisbury received another set-back when the Cabinet refused to accept his suggestion of pursuing the idea of forcing the Dardanelles, and of giving the ambassador at Constantinople *carte blanche* to call up the navy. Salisbury complained 'that the Navy ha[d] not supported his diplomacy sufficiently'.[106] The Admiralty argued that any such attempt would inevitably produce a Franco-Russian naval combination in the Mediterranean, threatening Britain's strategic lines of communication there. In addition, the Dardanelles had been increasingly fortified, so that the Navy's ability to force them seemed doubtful. But, as his colleagues refused to follow his lead, he had to bow to their decision. It was Salisbury's first real defeat in Cabinet in a matter of diplomacy; and he was forced to pursue 'a policy in which I entirely disbelieve'.[107]

Salisbury's inability to act effectively in response to the Armenian crisis had far-reaching strategic implications. Admiralty assessments of Britain's naval position in the Mediterranean became steadily more pessimistic. In Austria doubts grew about Salisbury's continued commitment to upholding the Near Eastern *status quo*. To force Salisbury to clarify his position, the Austrian government therefore decided not to renew the existing Mediterranean *entente*, and to demand in its place what amounted to a military alliance in defence of Constantinople. This was just the kind of firm undertaking that Salisbury was anxious to avoid. Although he wished to maintain the alignment with Austria, a renewed Austrian approach in early 1897 forced him to refuse the idea of a guarantee of the Straits.[108] In a speech in the House of Lords at the same time, Salisbury conceded that the policy inaugurated by Palmerston of maintaining Turkey against Russia might mean 'that we put all our money upon the wrong horse'. Still, whatever his misgivings, he saw no viable alternatives to this policy.[109] It was the paradox of Salisbury's Turkish policy that, haunted by the spectre of another Crimean War, he chose to shore up 'a rickety sort of Turkish rule' as a temporary measure, whilst fully acknowledging that '[t]here is no vitality left in them'.[110] What appeared to be an admission of error, the '"wrong horse" speech' was nothing but a description of Salisbury's central foreign policy dilemma. The Near Eastern crisis of 1895–96 eroded the basis of the Mediterranean *entente*, and with it Britain's informal link with the Triple Alliance. This alignment now gradually weakened; Austria established a Balkans *entente* with Russia; and Britain entered a period of flux, later termed 'splendid isolation'.[111] The extent to which Britain's international isolation had undermined her ability to take a lead in international matters, and to protect her interests effectively, was demonstrated by the Cretan crisis in 1896–97. His failure to win the Tsar's approval for his scheme of an Anglo-Russian intervention in Turkey in

September 1896, forced Salisbury to fall in with the other powers and jointly occupy Crete.[112] It was his last attempt to play a leading role in the Near East.

Instead, British foreign policy was now increasingly shaped by events in Africa and in the Far East. Here, international attention focused on China, yet another seemingly 'dying nation'. China's defeat in the war with Japan in 1894–95 heightened expectations of her imminent partition amongst the great powers similar to the 'scramble for Africa' in the previous decade. The seizure by Germany of a naval base in northern China in November 1897 seemed to bring this prospect closer. When Russia followed the German lead and occupied another port, Salisbury saw these developments as a threat to Britain's still predominant commercial and political influence in the region. The public, too, demanded vigorous action: '"the public" will require territorial or cartographic consolation in China. It will not be useful, & it will be expensive but as a matter of pure sentiment we shall have to do it.'[113] Salisbury was nevertheless reluctant to embark on a 'policy of grab', and once again worked for an understanding with Russia along the lines of the Near Eastern one he had suggested to Tsar Nicholas II in the autumn of 1896. Once again his approach was rebuffed, and Salisbury decided to acquire a 'cartographic consolation' as a counterpoise to the German and Russian occupations.[114]

The Far Eastern crisis of 1897–98 is instructive on a number counts. Salisbury's initial preference for a Far Eastern understanding with Russia is further illustration of the growing importance he attached to improving relations with St Petersburg. At the same time, discussions in the Cabinet produced divisions within the government about the future course of British diplomacy. A substantial, though not yet decisive, group of ministers had become dissatisfied with Salisbury's assumed 'policy of isolation'. Most notably, Colonial Secretary Joseph Chamberlain demanded forceful action against Russia in China, and advocated Anglo-American-German cooperation.[115] Although Salisbury prevailed over Chamberlain in Cabinet, Chamberlain now took up the issue of an Anglo-German alliance in secret talks with the German ambassador. Salisbury himself was not at all averse to continued cooperation with Germany, provided there was a solid basis of mutual interests. The Anglo-German agreement of August 1898 on the future of the Portuguese colonial empire was a case in point.[116] What his critics regarded as the premier's inactivity, reveals his realistic assessment of the changing circumstances under which British foreign policy had to operate. That unilateral action against Russia in the Near and Far East had become nearly impossible in naval terms was one thing. Equally important was the realization that such action would only lead to France and Russia forging ever closer ties. For Salisbury already kept a weather eye on developments in Africa. With Marchand's French expedition marching to the headways of the Nile, this was no time to antagonize Russia in Asia.[117] The *de facto* collapse of Britain's traditional policy at Constantinople enhanced the strategic importance of Egypt and the Suez thoroughfare. Salisbury's agreements of 1890 had gone some way towards protecting the upper reaches of the Nile Valley. Rosebery's deal with Belgium in 1894 had further shored up British interests there.[118] When the Italian campaign in Abyssinia was routed at Adowa in March 1896, Salisbury responded by sending Kitchener's Egyptian troops into the Sudan, ostensibly to alleviate the pressure on Italy. In light of Salisbury's still continuing efforts to preserve at least the essence of the Mediterranean agreements this made political sense. However, as the Mediterranean *entente* withered away in 1896–97 the continued existence of the Sudanese power vacuum became a source of increasing concern for Salisbury – especially since he feared that in the near future France might establish herself at the headwaters of the Nile.[119] By September 1898 Kitchener had brought most of the Sudan under his control, and in mid-September his superior forces confronted Marchand's small band of men. The stand-off at Fashoda brought Britain and France to the brink of war in October 1898. None the less, Salisbury remained adamant that there could be no compromise with France over the matter:

> I generally insisted ... that the valley of the Nile had belonged, and still belonged, to Egypt and that whatever impediment ... that title might have suffered through the conquest of the Mahdi, had been removed by the victory of the Anglo-Egyptian army [at Omdurman]. There was no pretence therefore for the contention that the region was open to the enterprises or the occupation of a third power.[120]

Salisbury was able to take such a strong line since Russia's preoccupation with the Far East made her support for France in Africa unlikely; and given the strained relations between France and Italy the former had to tread cautiously in the Mediterranean. France had no alternative but to back down. Fashoda was the 'purgative ... necessary before Anglo-French relations could improve'. It secured French recognition of Britain's predominance in the Upper Nile Valley in the Anglo-French agreement of 21 March 1899.[121] Salisbury's policy prior and during the Fashoda crisis illustrates Salisbury's ability to see in context developments taking place in such distant regions as China and north-eastern Africa. His success in keeping Russian attention firmly focused on east Asia, thus disabling Franco-Russian cooperation in Africa, also helps to explain his confidence in Britain's ability to safeguard her interests without the aid of a full alliance. Ultimately, he reckoned that the divisions between the other powers would always outweigh their common animosity towards Britain. Indeed, the year 1899 brought Salisbury closer to the desired rapprochement with Russia. In the so-called Scott–Muraviev agreement of 28 April 1899 the two powers mutually recognized their individual spheres of interest in China. As a result the frenzied scramble of concessions, which had been sparked off by the crisis of 1897–98, gradually died down.[122]

If Salisbury seemed to have stabilized Britain's international position in 1899, events in South Africa nearly dismantled his achievement. The rapid descent into war with the Boer republics, and the catastrophic turn of events at its onset in December 1899 not only demonstrated the parlous state of Britain's army.[123] Russian intrigues aiming at a triple Russo-French-German diplomatic intervention in the conflict in order to force upon Britain a settlement of their choosing threatened international humiliation.[124] Fortunately for Britain these proposals came to nothing. Britain's precarious situation in South Africa, however, reinforced the discontent of a growing group of ministers with Salisbury's policy of eschewing foreign alliances. The situation was further exacerbated when in June 1900 the so-called Boxer Uprising brought the Chinese question back on to the international agenda. With Britain's military and financial resources already fully stretched by the war against the Boers, Salisbury decided against taking a leading part in Chinese affairs. Moreover, in his analysis, the Boxer troubles in the north of China had not affected Britain's main interest in the central area of the Yangtze Valley.[125]

Salisbury's perceived apathy, and Britain's inability to cope with two simultaneous crises in the geostrategic periphery galvanized his internal critics into action. The Secretary of State for India, one of Salisbury's longest-serving ministers, complained that foreign policy under Salisbury had lapsed into 'a hopeless state of flabbiness'; and the First Lord of the Admiralty brought matters to the point: 'absolute isolation is playing the devil'. Very soon the Admiralty concluded that, in view of the steady growth of foreign navies, 'we must look to diplomacy and alliances to help us out'.[126] The powerful combination of ministers responsible for the armed forces and imperial affairs set up an informal committee; and, apparently with the backing of Arthur Balfour, Salisbury's nephew and leader of the Conservatives in the Commons, they forced upon Salisbury their anti-isolationist agenda. Salisbury had to defer to their wishes and negotiate the Anglo-German China agreement of October 1900, which the anti-isolationists hoped would prove to be a first step towards a closer arrangement with Germany.[127] It was his last act as Foreign Secretary. Balfour and the Conservative Chief Whip, Akers-Douglas, moved swiftly to curtail even further Salisbury's influence, and eased him out of the Foreign Office after the general election in October 1900, though he stayed on as Prime Minister until July 1902. It was a curious twist of irony that Salisbury, who had bitterly complained of the drift in British foreign policy in 1877–78, was now seen as the principal reason for Britain's renewed drifting in 1900.[128] It was no less ironic that he who had been the moving force behind the committee of three that eased Derby out of office in 1878, was himself forced to relinquish the Foreign Office by such an informal group of dissatisfied ministers.

Salisbury's somewhat undignified departure from the Foreign Office did not remove his influence over foreign policy altogether. However, the internal balance of power within the government had firmly swung in favour of the anti–isolationists. Salisbury continued to argue against an alliance with Germany as the worst of all possible bargains since Germany would never be of any real help in the event of a conflict with Russia. His observation that there was no real threat to Britain's national security was true, yet he could not deny that imperial interests were now threatened.[129] He was undoubtedly helped by Germany's devious diplomaticking in early 1901 which sabotaged Lansdowne's attempt at a general Anglo-German rapprochement. Salisbury was also critical of Lansdowne's decision to opt for a Japanese alliance, even though the absence of any entangling commitments in Europe emphasized Britain's continued aloofness from the Continent, and stood therefore in direct continuity with his own policy.

Lord Salisbury dominated British foreign policy for much of the closing two decades of the nineteenth century. During this period the international environment in which British diplomacy operated changed rapidly. Salisbury skilfully adapted British diplomacy to these changes. His formative political experience had been the Crimean War and the Palmerston era of Britain's relative preponderance overseas. The latter had already become illusory by the 1870s; and Salisbury (following in Disraeli's footsteps) was realistic enough to understand that British interests and imperial security could only be protected within the European framework of great power relations. This did not mean accepting entangling alliances, even if only temporarily; nor did he envisage Britain's informal alignments with other powers, or groups of powers, to be permanent. On the contrary, the overall objective of Salisbury's diplomacy was to obtain a 'free hand' so as to respond to developments as and when they occurred. Thus, his eschewing of carefully laid plans was one of the strengths of his foreign policy, as it allowed for greater flexibility. His aims were limited, centred on maintaining the *status quo*, and always within the constraints placed upon Britain's naval and military capabilities. But this should not be mistaken for placidity; and Salisbury's boating analogy did not imply a leisurely punting trip on a balmy summer's evening. Salisbury's skilful manoeuvring helped exacerbate the differences between the other powers, and wreck the alliance between the three Eastern monarchies. In so doing he showed great cunning and courage.

Towards the end of his political life Salisbury realized that the country's diplomatic freedom of manoeuvre was shrinking. He desired to revert to the 'old Tory' policy of 'friendship with Russia which existed in 1815'.[130] His perceptive realism, however, had lost something of its earlier constructive edge. He saw perhaps more clearly than his critics the problems facing Britain around 1900. But he seemed to lack the will to tackle them. His isolationist preferences were leavened by a superior intellect; yet it was passive isolationism. The international realities, however, required something more constructive, not least because the other boats on the river had become bigger and faster.

Perhaps it is true that all political careers end in failure. If so, one may regard Salisbury's failings towards the end of his political life as serious enough to find in them confirmation of Salisbury's place on Ensor's ranking list of international statesmen. And yet Salisbury brought to the international diplomacy of the late nineteenth century cool and dispassionate judgement, restraint and flexibility in his pursuit of limited aims, and a constructive realism which helped to ensure international stability and safeguard peacefully Britain's interests in Europe and overseas. Clearly, his place must be in the first flight of foreign policy-makers.

Notes

1. F.D. How, *The Marquis of Salisbury* (London: Isbister & Co, 1902), p. 1.
2. L.M. Penson, 'The Principles and Methods of Lord Salisbury's Foreign Policy', *Cambridge Historical Journal*, vol. v, no. 1 (1935–37), p. 106; Lady G. Cecil, *Life of Robert, Marquis of Salisbury* (4 vols, London: Hodder & Stoughton, 1921–32), vol. ii, p. 13.
3. R.C.K. Ensor, *England, 1870–1914* (Oxford: Clarendon, reprinted 1952), pp. 200–1.
4. L.M. Penson, *Foreign Affairs under the Third Marquis of Salisbury* (London: Athlone Press, 1962); J.A.S. Grenville, *Lord Salisbury and Foreign Policy at the Close of the Nineteenth Century* (London: Athlone Press, 1970).
5. D. Steele, *Lord Salisbury: A Political Biography* (London: UCL Press, 1999) and A. Roberts, *Salisbury: Victorian Titan* (London: Weidenfeld & Nicolson, 1999).
6. M. Pinto-Duschinsky, *The Political Thought of Lord Salisbury, 1854–1868* (London: Archon Books, 1967); cf. M.M. Bevington, *The Saturday Review, 1855–1868: Representative Educated Opinion in Victorian England* (New York: Columbia UP, 1941), p. 337.
7. Cecil, *Salisbury*, vol. ii, p. 13.
8. R. Robinson and J. Gallagher, *Africa and the Victorians: The Official Mind of Imperialism* (London: Macmillan, 2nd edn 1981), p. 256.
9. Salisbury to Curzon, 23 December 1897, Curzon Mss, British Library, Oriental Collection, Mss.Eur.F.112/1B; to Acland (private), 9 April 1896, Acland Mss, Bodleian Library [hereafter Bodl.], Oxford, Ms Acland d.74.
10. Anon. [Lord R. Cecil], 'Lord Castlereagh', *Quarterly Review*, vol. cxi, no. 221 (1862), p. 206; cf. Pinto-Duschinsky, *Political Thought*, pp. 119–21.
11. Salisbury to Lyons (private), 22 May 1878, in Lord Newton, *Lord Lyons: A Record of British Diplomacy* (2 vols, London: Edward Arnold, 1913), vol. ii, p. 141; anon. (ed.), *Essays of the Late Marquess of Salisbury, KG, 1861–1864: Foreign Policy* (London: John Murray, 1905), pp. 9–10.
12. Salisbury to Hicks Beach (private), 8 March 1897, Hicks Beach Mss, Gloucestershire Record Office, Gloucester, PCC/69.
13. Roberts, *Salisbury*, p. 647; H.C.G. Matthew (ed.), *The Gladstone Diaries* (Oxford: OUP, 1987), vol. x, p. cxl.
14. P. Marsh, 'The Conservative Conscience', in *idem*. (ed.), *The Conscience of the Victorian State* (Syracuse, NY: Syracuse UP, 1979), pp. 239–40; Salisbury's corre-

spondence with MacColl can be found in G.W.E. Russell, *Malcolm MacColl: Memoirs and Correspondence* (London: Smith, Elder & Co, 1914).

15. *Essays*, pp. 49–50.
16. Salisbury to Selborne (private), 13 April 1895, Selborne Mss, Bodl., Ms Selborne 5.
17. A. Marsden, *British Diplomacy and Tunis, 1875–1902: A Case Study in Mediterranean Policy* (Edinburgh: Scottish Academic Press, 1971), p. 252.
18. Salisbury to Layard (private), 4 April 1878, Layard Mss, British Library [hereafter BL], Add.Mss.39137.
19. *Essays*, pp. 39 and 41–2.
20. Salisbury to Hicks Beach (private), 14 September 1901, Hicks Beach Mss, PCC/69; also in Lady V. Hicks Beach, *Life of Sir Michael Hicks Beach* (2 vols, London: Macmillan, 1932), vol. ii, pp. 152–3.
21. Grenville, *Lord Salisbury and Foreign Policy*, pp. 19 and 436–7.
22. *Essays*, p. 145.
23. Memo. Hicks Beach (for Lady G. Cecil), January 1914, Hicks Beach Mss, PCC/69.
24. Sir I. Malcolm, *Vacant Thrones* (London: Macmillan, 1931), p. 2; Sir J. Tilley and S. Gaselee, *The Foreign Office* (London: Putnam, 1933), p. 139.
25. Pauncefote to Ponsonby (private), 30 September 1885, Ponsonby Mss, PRO, FO 800/3; Cecil, *Salisbury*, vol. ii, pp. 16–17 and 233–4.
26. Z.S. Steiner, *The Foreign Office and Foreign Policy, 1898–1914* (Cambridge: CUP, 1969), p. 29; N.S. Johnson, 'The Role of the Cabinet in the Making of Foreign Policy, 1885–1895' (unpublished D.Phil. thesis, Oxford, 1970), pp. 98–9.
27. Tilley and Gaselee, *Foreign Office*, p. 126; Penson, 'Principles and Methods', p. 89.
28. Cecil, *Salisbury*, vol. iii, pp. vii and 207; Sir A. Hardinge, *A Diplomatist in Europe* (London: Jonathan Cape, 1927), p. 79.
29. Memo. Crowe, 1 January 1907, in G.P. Gooch and H.W.V. Temperley (eds), *British Documents on the Origins of the War, 1898–1914* (11 vols, London: HMSO, 1928–38), vol. iii, App. A, p. 409 [hereafter *BD*]; H.W.V. Temperley, 'British Secret Diplomacy from Canning to Grey', *Cambridge Historical Journal*, vol. vi, no. 1 (1938), pp. 14–15. For a different view cf. Steiner, *Foreign Office*, p. 29, who claims that his private correspondence was merely supplementary to the official despatches. Closer scrutiny of the archival material for his entire period in office does not furnish evidence for this assertion. Grenville, *Lord Salisbury and Foreign Policy*, p. 28, partially concedes the point, but argues that Salisbury 'was more sinned against than sinning'.
30. Earl of Midleton, *Records and Reactions, 1856–1939* (London: John Murray, 1939), p. 106.
31. Salisbury to Paget (private), 14 December 1882, Paget Mss, BL, Add.Mss.51228. For the background cf. R.A. Jones, *The British Diplomatic Service, 1815–1914* (Gerrards Cross: Colin Smythe, 1983), pp. 43–8.
32. Cf. min. Salisbury, n.d., on tel. White to Salisbury (no. 9, secret), 6 February 1888, PRO, FO 78/4107; Salisbury to Walsham (separate), 12 November 1891, FO 228/1059; min.Salisbury, [c.6 December 1896], Bertie Mss, BL, Add.Mss.63013.
33. Min. Salisbury, [c.22 March 1897], Sanderson Mss, PRO, FO 800/2. The feeling was reciprocated: 'if he hates the service as he is said to do, the service perfectly loathes him', W.E. Goschen to G.J. Goschen, n.d., in C.H.D. Howard (ed.), *The Diary of Sir Edward Goschen* (London: Royal Historical Society, 1980), p. 9.
34. D. Gillard, 'Salisbury', in K.M. Wilson (ed.), *British Foreign Secretaries and Foreign Policy: from Crimean War to First World War* (London: Croom Helm, 1987), p. 124.

35. *The Times* (5 May 1898), p. 7.
36. Salisbury to Northcote (private), 15 December 1877, Iddesleigh Mss, BL, Add.Mss.50019.
37. J.R. Vincent (ed.), *A Selection from the Diaries of Edward Henry Stanley, 15th Earl of Derby (1826–93), between September 1869 and March 1878* (London: Royal Historical Society, 1994), pp. 29–31.
38. Salisbury to Lytton, 19 March 1874, Lytton Mss, HertsRO, O30/43/1; memo. Carnarvon (confidential), September 1879, Carnarvon Mss, BL, Add.Mss.60817; Salisbury to Carnarvon (confidential), 4 January 1878, Carnarvon Mss, PRO, PRO 30/6/13.
39. Salisbury to Paget (private), 17 May 1878, Add.Mss.51228; to Elliot (no. 358), 31 May 1878, FO 7/924; L.M. Penson, 'The Foreign Policy of Lord Salisbury, 1878–80: The Problem of the Ottoman Empire', in A. Coville and H. Temperley (eds), *Studies in Anglo-French History* (Cambridge: CUP, 1935), p. 127.
40. Salisbury to Russell (private), 10 April 1878, in Cecil, *Salisbury*, vol. ii, p. 243.
41. Salisbury to Layard (private), 9 May and 25 June 1878, Add.Mss.39137.
42. Penson, 'Ottoman Empire', pp. 128–9; W.N. Medlicott, *The Congress of Berlin and After: A Diplomatic History of the Near Eastern Settlement, 1878–80* (London: Cass, reprinted 1963), pp. 18–19.
43. Salisbury to Layard (private), 2 May 1878, Add.Mss.39137.
44. Salisbury to Paget (private), 19 June 1878, Add.Mss.51228; M.D. Stojanovič, *The Great Powers and the Balkans, 1875–8* (Cambridge: CUP, reprinted 1968), pp. 244–7.
45. Shuvalov to Gorchakov (*très confidentiel*), 18/30 April 1878, in R.W. Seton-Watson (ed.), 'Unpublished Documents: Russo-British Relations, 1875–8 (II/12), *Slavonic and East European Review*, vol. xxviii, no. 71 (1950), no. 496, pp. 514–5; Tenterden to Salisbury (private), 22 June 1878, Salisbury Mss, Hatfield House, 3M/E/Tenterden.
46. Beaconsfield to Queen Victoria (private), 21 April 1878, in W.F. Monypenny and G.E. Buckle, *The Life of Benjamin Disraeli, Earl of Beaconsfield* (6 vols, London: John Murray, 1920), vol. vi, p. 290.
47. Salisbury to Layard (private), 2 May 1878, Add.Mss.39137; Roberts, *Salisbury*, pp. 191–2.
48. Salisbury to Layard (secret), 10 May 1878, Add.Mss.39137; and tel. (private and most confidential), 25 May 1878, ibid. 39139. He even tried to obtain a Turkish guarantee of unhindered naval access through the Straits in the event of another war in the Near East, tels. Salisbury to Layard (personal and secret), 16 June, and *vice versa*, 22 June 1878, BL, Add.Mss.39137.
49. Loftus to Salisbury (no. 656a, confidential), 20 July 1878, FO 65/1005; Penson, 'Ottoman Empire', p. 132.
50. R. Millman, *Britain and the Eastern Question, 1875–1878* (Oxford: Clarendon, 1979), p. 453.
51. Layard to Elliot (private), 5 and 26 July 1878, Add.Mss.39131.
52. Salisbury to Layard (private), 18 September and 2 October 1878, Add.Mss.39138.
53. Salisbury to Waddington, 6 July 1878 (copy), Tenterden Mss, FO 363/4; to Lyons (no. 492), 7 August 1878, FO 27/2300; Marsden, *British Diplomacy*, pp. 50–9.
54. Lyons to Salisbury (no. 572), 19 July 1878, FO 27/2311; *vice versa* (private), 20 July 1878, in Newton, *Lord Lyons*, vol. ii, pp. 154–5; Waddington to Dufaure (*très confidentiel*), 8 July 1878, in French Foreign Ministry (ed.), *Documents*

Diplomatique Français (Paris: Imprimerie Nationale, 1930), 1st ser., vol. ii, no. 325 [hereafter *DDF*].

55. Lyons to Salisbury (private), 4 June 1878, in Newton, *Lord Lyons*, vol. ii, pp. 145–7; Marsden, *British Diplomacy*, p. 58.

56. Salisbury to Lyons (no. 493), 7 August 1878, FO 27/2300; d'Harcourt to Waddington (no. 72), 24 July 1878, and *vice versa* (*confidentiel*), 25 July 1878, *DDF*, 1st ser., vol. ii, nos. 324–5.

57. De Saint-Vallier to Waddington (no. 2, *confidentiel*), 5 January 1879, in *DDF*, 1st ser., vol. ii, no. 369, p. 413.

58. Salisbury to Paget (private), 18 February 1879, BL, Add.Mss.51228; Depretis to Menabrea (no. 507), 18 January 1879, in Italian Foreign Ministry (ed.), *I Documenti Diplomatici Italiani* (Rome: Istituto Poligrafico, 1986), 2nd ser., vol. xi, no. 222 [hereafter *DDI*].

59. Salisbury to Beaconsfield (private), 5 September 1878, Disraeli Mss, Bodl., Dep. Hughenden 92/3.

60. Salisbury to Vivian, 3 May 1878, in Cecil, *Salisbury*, vol. ii, p. 330.

61. C.J. Lowe, *Reluctant Imperialists: British Foreign Policy, 1878–1902* (New York: Macmillan, 1969), p. 43.

62. M. Cowling, 'Lytton, the Cabinet, and the Russians, August to November 1878', *English Historical Review*, vol. lxxxv, no. 1 (1961), pp. 59–79.

63. The text of the abortive 'Herat convention' is in tel. Thomson to Salisbury (no. 60), 29 October 1879, FO 60/423; cf. A.P. Thornton, 'British Policy in Persia, 1858–90 (I)', *English Historical Review*, vol. lxix, no. 3 (1954), pp. 569–72.

64. Salisbury to Northcote (confidential), 16 June 1885, Add.Mss. 50020; cf. Johnson, 'Role of the Cabinet', pp. 51–4. For Gladstone's criticism cf. J.P. Mackintosh, *The British Cabinet* (London: Methuen, 2nd edn 1968), p. 396.

65. Salisbury to Curzon (private), 15 April 1898, Mss.Eur.F.112/1B; to Cadogan (private), 7 February 1888, Cadogan Mss, House fo Lords Record Office, CAD/323.

66. Cecil, *Salisbury*, vol. iii, p. 136; Salisbury to Cairns (private), 3 March 1885, Cairns Mss, PRO, PRO 30/51/6.

67. Salisbury to White (private), 5 February 1886, White Mss, PRO, FO 364/8.

68. Salisbury to Baring (private), 15 September 1885, Cromer Mss, PRO, FO 633/7; Marquess of Zetland, *Lord Cromer* (London: Hodder & Stoughton, 1932), pp. 127–8.

69. Col. Ridgeway to Salisbury (nos.70 and 73, 8 and 12 August 1885, FO 65/1248; D.R. Gillard, 'Salisbury and the Indian Defence Problem, 1885–1902', in K. Bourne and D.C. Watt (eds), *Studies in International History* (London: Longmans, 1967), pp. 246–7.

70. Currie to Salisbury (private), 4 and 10 August 1885, 3M/E/Currie; R.L. Greaves, *Persia and the Defence of India, 1884–1892* (London: Routledge, 1959), pp. 239–41.

71. Salisbury to Bismarck, 2 July 1885, and *vice versa*, 8 July 1885, in J. Lepsius et al. (eds), *Grosse Politik der Europäischen Kabinette* (40 vols, Berlin: Deutsche Verlagsanstalt, 1924), vol. iv, nos.782–3 [herafter *GP*].

72. Memo. Currie, 28–9 September 1885, 3M/E/Currie. By contrast, K.Bourne, *The Foreign Policy of Victorian England, 1830–1902* (Oxford: Clarendon, 1970), p. 145, regards Salisbury's efforts as 'a complete failure'.

73. Lascelles to Salisbury (private), 5 October 1885, Lascelles Mss, PRO, FO 800/7; W.N. Medlicott, 'The Powers and the Unification of Bulgaria, 1885 (I)', *English Historical Review*, vol. liv, no. 1 (1939), pp. 67–8.

74. Salisbury to Paget (private), 24 September 1887, Add.Mss.51228.
75. Salisbury to White (private), 24 September 1885, FO 364/8; to Grosvenor (no. 355), 22 September 1885, FO 65/1215.
76. White to Salisbury (no. 392), 25 September 1885, FO 78/2753; Salisbury to Queen Victoria, 28 September 1885, in G.E. Buckle (ed.), *The Letters of Queen Victoria* (3 vols, London: John Murray, 1928), 2nd ser., vol. iii, pp. 694–5 [herafter QVL].
77. White to Salisbury (nos.485 and 489, confidential), 8 and 9 Nov.1885, FO 78/3754; C.L. Smith, *The Embassy of Sir William White at Constantinople, 1886–1891* (Oxford: OUP, 1957), pp. 29–31.
78. Smith, *William White*, pp. 32–4; A. Ramm, *Sir Robert Morier: Envoy and Ambassador in the Age of Imperialism, 1876–1893* (Oxford: Clarendon, 1973), pp. 211–13; M.P. Hornik, 'The Special Mission of Sir Henry Drummond-Wolff to Constantinople, 1885–7', *English Historical Review*, vol. v, no. 4 (1940), pp. 600–7.
79. Lowe, *Reluctant Imperialists*, p. 103.
80. Salisbury to Lumley (no. 10A, very secret), 17 January 1887, FO 45/572; Di Robilant to Corti (*personale*), 26 January 1887, *DDI*, 2nd ser., vol. xx, no. 456.
81. Salisbury to Paget (private), 9 February 1887, Add.Mss. 51229; to White (private), 10 August 1887, FO 364/8; Hornik, 'Special Mission', pp. 612–0.
82. Salisbury to Paget (private), 23 February 1887, Add.Mss. 51229; W.N. Medlicott, 'The Mediterranean Agreement of 1887', *Slavonic Review*, vol. v, no. 13 (1926), pp. 71–4.
83. Salisbury to Queen Victoria, 10 February 1887, PRO, CAB 41/20/31; C.J. Lowe, *Salisbury and the Mediterranean, 1886–1896* (London: Routledge & Kegan Paul, 1965), pp. 16–17.
84. Salisbury to Paget (no. 39, secret), 26 February 1887, FO 7/1113; and (no. 52), 16 March 1887, FO 7/1114; Lumley to Salisbury (no. 80, secret), 15 March 1887, FO 45/574; Lowe, *Mediterranean*, p. 18.
85. Salisbury to Scott (private and confidential), 4 May 1887, Scott Mss, BL, Add.Mss.52295; to Baring (private), 25 February 1887, Cromer Mss, PRO, FO 601/7; E. de Groot, 'Great Britain and Germany in Zanzibar: Consul Holmewood's Papers , 1885–1887', *Journal of Modern History*, vol. xxv, no. 2 (1953), pp. 135–6.
86. Hornik, 'Special Mission', pp. 616–17; F.A.K. Yasamee, *Ottoman Diplomacy: Adülhamid II and the Great Powers, 1878–1888* (Istanbul: Isis Press, 1996), pp. 141–52.
87. Lowe, *Mediterranean*, p. 18; cf. Salisbury to Kennedy (private), 17 February 1888, in A.L. Kennedy, *Salisbury, 1830–1903: Portrait of a Statesman* (London: John Murray, 1953), pp. 360–3.
88. Salisbury to Pauncefote (secret), 10 October 1887, 3M/E/Pauncefote; F.H. Hinsley, 'Bismarck, Salisbury and the Mediterranean Agreements of 1887', *Historical Journal*, vol. i, no. 1 (1958), p. 78. Medlicott is undoubtedly right in arguing that Salisbury's policy increased, at the least in the short term, Russia's dependence on Bismarck, cf. 'Bismarck and the Three Emperors Alliance, 1881–1887', *Transactions of the Royal Historical Society*, 4th ser, vol .xxvii, (1945), pp. 66–7. For the view that Salisbury's and Disraeli's policies were quite distinct, cf. J. Charmley, *Splendid Isolation?: British Foreign Policy, 1874–1914* (London: Hodder & Stoughton, 1999), pp. 195–6.
89. For the texts cf. *BD* viii, ch.1; note Salisbury to Catalani, 25 November 1887, *DDI*, 2nd ser, xxi, no. 350. A.J.P. Taylor's contention that the second agreement

amounted to 'an alliance ... for the defence of Bulgaria and Asia Minor', is a characteristic overstatement of the facts, cf. *The Struggle for Mastery in Europe, 1848–1918* (Oxford: OUP, 8th edn 1988), p. 321.

90. Scott to Salisbury (personal and confidential), 31 March 1888, Add.Mss.52295; Salisbury to O'Conor (private), 10 August 1887, O'Conor Mss, Churchill College Archive Centre, OCON 5/5/2.

91. J.T. Sumida, *In Defence of Naval Supremacy: Finance, Technology and British Naval Policy, 1889–1914* (London: Routledge, 1990), pp. 13–18.

92. Salisbury to Baring (private), 25 February 1887, Cromer Mss, FO 633/7; memo. Currie, 26 March 1889, 3M/E/Currie.

93. P. Kluke, 'Bismarck und Salisbury: Ein diplomatisches Duell', *Historische Zeitschrift*, vol. clxxv, no. 2 (1953), pp. 285–306.

94. Salisbury to Paget (private), 16 October 1888, Add.Mss.51229; cf. my '"The Madness of Kaiser Bill": The British Foreign Policy Elite and the Last German Emperor, 1885–1914' (forthcoming).

95. Salisbury to Paget (private), 24 August 1890, Add.Mss.51229.

96. Baring to Salisbury (secret), 15 December 1889, FO 78/4243.

97. Salisbury to Queen Victoria, 10 June 1890, in *QVL* 3rd ser., vol. i, p. 613. Salisbury's commitment to an Upper Nile Valley strategy remains vigorously disputed. I do not agree with John Darwin's contention that Salisbury entered into the Heligoland–Zanzibar deal out of a mixture of entirely opportunistic reasons and an inability to resist a fabricated (proconsular) case for intervention in east Africa, cf. 'Imperialism and the Victorians: The Dynamics of Territorial Expansion', *English Historical Review*, vol. cxii, no. 3 (1997), pp. 637–40.

98. G.N. Sanderson, 'The Anglo-German Agreement of 1890 and the Upper Nile', *English Historical Review*, vol. lxxviii, no. 1 (1963), pp. 49–72; A.S. Kanya-Forstner, 'French African Policy and the Anglo-French Agreement of 5 August 1890', *Historical Journal*, vol. xii, no. 4 (1969), pp. 628–50. For a different view cf. D.R. Gillard, 'Salisbury's African Policy and the Heligoland Offer of 1890', *English Historical Review*, vol. lxxxv, no. 3 (1960), pp. 631–53.

99. Salisbury to Malet (private), 16 August 1892, Malet Mss, FO 343/3; and to Currie, 18 August 1892, in Cecil, *Salisbury*, vol. iv, p. 404. This letter was clearly meant for Rosebery's consumption, cf. Lowe, *Mediterranean*, p. 90.

100. Currie to Salisbury (private), 27 June 1895, 3M/A/135/6; R. Douglas, 'Britain and the Armenian Question, 1894–7', *Historical Journal*, vol. xix, no. 1 (1976), pp. 113–32.

101. Salisbury to Goschen (private), 3 December 1895, 3M/E/Goschen (1895–96).

102. Salisbury to Iwan-Muller (confidential), 31 August 1896, *BD*, vi, appendix IV; to Lascelles (private), 27 July 1895, FO 800/16.

103. Tel. Hatzfeldt to *Auswärtiges Amt* (no. 2, *geheim*), 7 August 1895, *GP*, x, no. 2385; memo. Swaine (secret), 30 August 1895, FO 64/1351; cf. Grenville, *Foreign Policy*, pp. 31–7.

104. Salisbury to Goschen (private), 1 October 1895, 3M/E/Goschen; C.J. Lowe, 'Anglo-Italian Differences over East Africa, and their Effects on the Mediterranean Entente', *English Historical Review*, vol. lxxxi, no. 2 (1966), pp. 329–30.

105. Monson to Salisbury (no. 343, confidential), 22 November 1895, FO 7/1229; Salisbury to Queen Victoria, 5 December 1895, 3M/A/84/3; J.A.S. Grenville, 'Goluchowski, Salisbury, and the Mediterranean Agreements, 1895–7', in *Slavonic and East European Review*, vol. xxxvi, no. 87 (1958), pp. 353–5.

106. Goschen to Lansdowne (private), 22 November 1895, Lansdowne Mss, BL, Lans(5)45; Salisbury to Hicks Beach (private), 2 January 1896, PCC/69; P.T. Marsh, 'Lord Salisbury and the Ottoman Massacres', *Journal of British Studies*, vol. xi, no. 2 (1972), pp. 77–80.

107. Salisbury to Goschen (private), 19 December 1895, 3M/E/Goschen; memo. Chermside, 'Dardanelles Defences', 18 September 1895, 3M/A/135/50; Steele, *Salisbury*, p. 322.

108. Salisbury to Rumbold (no. 6, very confidential), 20 January 1897, *BD*, ix, appendix II, pp. 775–6; Grenville, 'Mediterranean Agreements', pp. 363–6.

109. *Hansard (House of Lords)*, 4th ser., vol. xlv, cols.28–9 (19 January 1897); W.N. Medlicott, 'Lord Salisbury and Turkey', *History*, vol. xii, no. 3 (1927), p. 247.

110. Min. Salisbury, n.d., on memo. Tenterden, 29 December 1878, FO 363/5; Salisbury to White (private), 24 September 1885, FO 364/8; to Balfour, 16 December 1895, Balfour Mss, BL, Add.Mss.49690.

111. C.H.D. Howard, *Splendid Isolation: A Study of Ideas* (London: Macmillan, 1967), pp. 9–10.

112. Memo. Salisbury, 27/29 September 1896, PRO, CAB 37/42/35; K. Neilson, *Britain and the Last Tsar: British Policy and Russia, 1894–1917* (Oxford: Clarendon, 1995), pp. 171–2.

113. Salisbury to Chamberlain (private), 30 December 1897, Chamberlain Mss, Birmingham University Library, JC 5/67/88; cf. my 'Great Britain, German, and the Far Eastern Crisis of 1897–8', *English Historical Review*, vol. cx, no. 439 (1995), pp. 1157–79.

114. Salisbury to O'Conor (no. 7, secret), 17 January 1898, *BD*, i, no. 5; Neilson, *Last Tsar*, pp. 186–95.

115. Chamberlain to Balfour (private), 3 February 1898, Add.Mss.49773; *The Times* (14 May 1898), p. 12; cf. my 'A Question of Leadership: Lord Salisbury, the Unionist Cabinet, and Foreign Policy-Making, 1895–1900', *Contemporary British History*, vol xiv, no. 4 (2000), pp. 10–13.

116. Min. Salisbury, [c.10–14 August 1898], OCON 6/1/20; Salisbury to Balfour, 9 April 1898, Add.Mss.49690. For the text of the convention cf. *BD*, i, no. 90.

117. Salisbury to Monson (private), 12 February 1897, Monson Mss, Bodl., Ms.Eng.hist.c.594; L.M. Penson, 'The New Course in British Foreign Policy, 1892–1902', in I.R. Christie (ed.), *Essays in Modern History* (London: Macmillan, 1968), pp. 320–1.

118. M.P. Hornik, 'The Anglo-Belgian Agreement of 12 May 1894', *English Historical Review*, vol. lvii, no. 2 (1942), pp. 233–42; A.J.P. Taylor, 'Prelude to Fashoda: The Question of the Upper Nile, 1894–5', *English Historical Review*, vol. lxv, no. 1 (1950), pp. 52–80.

119. Salisbury to Cromer (private), 29 October 1897, FO 630/7; to Sanderson (private), 2 November 1896, FO 800/1.

120. Salisbury to Monson (no. 393), 12 October 1898 (copy), Ms.Eng. hist.c.594; cf. P.M. Holt, *The Mahdist State in the Sudan, 1881–1898* (Oxford: Clarendon, 1970), pp. 223–42.

121. J.D. Hargreave, 'Entente Manquée: Anglo-French Relations, 1895–6', *Cambridge Historical Journal*, vol. xi., no. 1 (1953), p. 92. For the text of the agreement, cf. *BD*, i, no. 245.

122. Scott to Salisbury (no. 127), 29 April 1899, FO 65/1578; E.W. Edwards, *British Diplomacy and Finance in China, 1895–1914* (Oxford: Clarendon, 1987), pp. 47–9.

123. Salisbury's role in the origins of the conflict remain disputed, with A.N. Porter arguing the case for Salisbury's fundamental agreement with Chamberlain, cf. 'Lord Salisbury, Mr Chamberlain, and South Africa, 1895–9', *Journal of Imperial and Commonwealth History*, vol. i, no. 1 (1972), pp. 3–26; whereas Chamberlain's most recent biographer places greater emphasis on 'Joe's' machinations, P.T. Marsh, *Joseph Chamberlain: Entrepreneur in Politics* (New Haven, CT: Yale UP, 1994), pp. 372–447.

124. Grenville, *Lord Salisbury and Foreign Policy*, pp. 270–4 and 287–90; note Urusov, 6 March 1900, *DDF*, 1st ser, xvi, no. 93; tel. Bülow to Radolin (no. 41), 3 March 1900, *GP*, xv, no. 4472.

125. Tels, Salisbury to MacDonald (no. 58 and 64), 22 May and 7 June 1900, FO 17/1419; cf. my '"Heaven knows where we shall finally drift": Lord Salisbury, the Cabinet, Isolation, and the Boxer Rebellion', forthcoming in K. Neilson and G. Kennedy (eds), *The Butterfly's Wings: Incidents in International Relations, 1750–1950* (New York: Praeger, 2001).

126. Hamilton to Curzon (private), 6 June 1900, Hamilton Mss, BLOC, Mss.Eur.C.126/2; Goschen to Chamberlain (private), 2 September 1900, in J. Amery (cont. J.L. Garvin), *The Life of Joseph Chamberlain* (4 vols, London: Macmillan, 1932–51) vol. iv, pp. 138–9; Kerr to Bridge, 26 November 1901, as quoted in I.H. Nish, *The Anglo-Japanese Alliance, 1894–1907* (Westport, CT: Greenwood Press, reprinted 1976), p. 184; memo. Selborne, 'British naval policy in the Far East', 4 September 1901, CAB 37/58/81.

127. Salisbury to Brodrick (private), 8 October 1900, Midelton Mss, PRO, PRO 30/67/5; Lansdowne to Lascelles (private), 17 November 1900, FO 800/17.

128. Salisbury to Northcote (private), 15 December 1877, Add.Mss.50017.

129. Memo. Salisbury, 29 May 1901, *BD*, ii, no. 86.

130. Salisbury to MacColl, 6 September 1901, in Russell, *MacColl*, pp. 282–3.

6
'Control the Whirlwind': Sir Edward Grey as Foreign Secretary, 1906–16

Keith Neilson

The day before he resigned as Foreign Secretary, Sir Edward Grey wrote a retrospective analysis of his time in office to his old friend, the former Prime Minister, Lord Rosebery. 'As I look back & reflect', Grey noted, 'I cannot but think that tremendous forces have been at work in the world & that individuals have been helpless to arrest them. We could take an honourable part but we could not control the whirlwind'.[1] Whether Grey, or anyone, could have controlled events that led to the First World War is a moot point (and one which will be discussed below), but Grey's 11 years in office saw him make considerable efforts to ensure that Britain did not reap the whirlwind.

Grey and his foreign policy remain controversial. Some have claimed that his incurable Germanophobia led him to pursue a course that tied British policy to France and Russia, to the detriment of Britain's own interests.[2] Others have maintained that he was intellectually not up to the job and that he should have remained immersed in his favourite pursuits of bird-watching and fishing.[3] More balanced accounts have stressed the context – both domestic and foreign – of Grey's decision-making in order to show the influences that acted upon him and how they affected the range of choices that he could make.[4]

It is the contention here that Grey's foreign policy before the outbreak of war (during the war it was necessarily different, as discussed below) can be best understood by taking a different approach, one that focuses on Britain's strategic foreign policy, that is to say, how Grey attempted to maintain Britain's global interests with, particularly, the naval and military means at his disposal. Given that Britain was the world's predominant naval power but only a minor military power, this meant that Grey pursued two distinct policies. With respect to the British empire, Grey attempted to isolate it from European complications so that the Royal Navy would be sufficient to safeguard the British position without recourse to military action. With respect to Europe, Grey attempted, by all reasonable means (including arms control), to maintain the peace so that Britain would not be forced to choose between giving her (necessarily limited) military support to either of the contending – Franco-Russian and Austro-German – power blocs. In theory, these were two separate policies. However, given that Germany, France and Russia in particular had imperial aspirations that impinged on British interests, in practice Grey's policies were intertwined. That entwining provided the dynamic for pre-war Liberal policy.

Grey became Foreign Secretary on 11 December 1905 in the midst of a major European crisis over German attempts to contest the French position in Morocco. But, just as significantly, the European balance of power established by the formation of the Franco-Russian alliance in 1894 was wobbling due to the defeat of Russia in the Russo-Japanese War.[5] This meant that the nature of the newly created Anglo-French *entente* would be tested, as the French, in the absence of Russian help, sought British support. This meant that, upon enquiries from the French as to Britain's position, Grey had to make an immediate declaration of intent.[6] His reply reflected the cautious nature of his policy, and its essential continuity with that of his predecessor, Lord Lansdowne:

> Diplomatic support we are pledged to give and are giving. A promise in advance committing this country to take part in a Continental war is another matter and a very serious one: it is very difficult for any British Govt to give an engagement of that kind. It changes the entente into an alliance and alliances, especially continental alliances are not in accordance with our tradition.[7]

While Grey felt that, should a Franco-German war break out, 'we cannot stand aside, but must take part with France', he refused to commit the government in advance of circumstances. As he informed the First Lord of the Admiralty, '[w]e haven't *promised* [France] any help, but it is quite right that our Naval and Military Authorities should discuss the question ... with the French'.[8]

This was tied tightly to Grey's evaluation of the European situation. On 22 December 1905, the Foreign Secretary had written to Sir Cecil Spring Rice, the British *chargé d'affaires* in Russia.[9] Grey asked Spring Rice for the latter's opinion about the outcome of the revolutionary activities wracking that country. He then noted: 'I hope the struggle won't last too long. I want to see Russia re-established in the councils of Europe & I hope on better terms with us than she has yet been.' The first part of this quotation illustrates Grey's concern that Russia's temporary weakness had upset the European equilibrium. The second part pointed towards Grey's desire to conclude a colonial, 'Asiatic', agreement with Russia.[10] This was not new. Both

Lansdowne and Salisbury, when the latter was Foreign Secretary, had attempted to get such an accord, and Grey himself, while in the opposition, had called for such a move.[11]

Here, Russian weakness worked in Grey's favour. Needing time to recover, the Russians were willing to deal, and Grey, supported by the Secretary of State for India, John Morley, was able to negotiate a settlement, despite the opposition to a Russian agreement within his own party.[12] The result was the Anglo-Russian convention of 31 August 1907, which eliminated the long-standing 'Asiatic' colonial frictions between the two countries. Simultaneously, Grey was trying to fine-tune the Anglo-Japanese alliance in order to provide some assistance for the defence of India from Tokyo should the Anglo-Russian convention collapse.[13] While the Japanese proved elusive, it was evident that the Foreign Secretary remained committed to separating his European and imperial commitments.

Grey's first years in office also brought the issue of arms limitation to the fore.[14] Grey's push for this at the Second Hague Peace Conference was both sincere and self-interested. Lower expenditure on armaments would provide the budgetary leeway to pursue Liberal social policies and appease the strong pacifist Radical wing of the party (to whom the government had been 'promising the moon'), but at the same time would ensure British naval superiority – and hence the safety of the empire – and deflect at least some of the Unionist criticism that would come from lowered naval spending.[15] But, if Grey could not get other states – here, primarily Germany – to agree to arms limitation, he was certainly not about either to throw away Britain's own naval supremacy or adopt naval laws of war that would negate that strength. Thus, when Berlin rejected any talk of arms limitation at The Hague, Grey also refused to yield the British position concerning belligerent rights at the subsequent London Conference, held from December 1908 to February 1909.[16]

The same refusal to give up concrete strengths in exchange for theoretical or frangible concessions affected Anglo-German relations with respect to the naval race and colonial issues.[17] Grey had called for improved Anglo-German relations before taking office, but the Moroccan crisis and the German rejection of arms control made any warming of relations difficult. None the less, Grey was willing to listen to German proposals for colonial cooperation, particularly with respect to railway building in the Middle East. While Grey preferred to undertake such activities in cooperation with St Petersburg, in the spring of 1906 he made it clear that this should not be done 'to create difficulties with Germany'.[18] Despite later concerns about imperial defence, when the Germans raised the issue again in 1909, Grey was open to the idea.[19]

However, by this time, the Anglo-German naval race, with all its implications for the European balance and the security of the British empire (not to mention its domestic impact), had taken centre stage.[20] Grey preferred negotiations with Berlin, but was unwilling to be pressured into any settlement disadvantageous to Britain. This meant that any Anglo-German agreement was difficult to achieve since, when, in mid-1909, the Germans offered a comprehensive settlement – dealing with the naval race and some outstanding colonial issues including the Baghdad line – it included the proviso that Britain would remain neutral in any European war, while the German building programme would only be reduced in tempo.[21] This was an unacceptable offer for a variety of reasons.

First, it needs to be seen in the context of the diplomatic events of the previous year. In 1908–09, two intertwined crises – the Bosnian and the Casablancan – had suggested that Germany would take advantage of St Petersburg's continuing military weakness to bully Russia and her French ally.[22] In the Bosnian crisis, Grey wished, as far as possible, to support the Russians, both for the sake of nurturing the newly formed Anglo-Russian convention and because he opposed Austria-Hungary's tactics (as backed by Germany). As he told the British ambassador in Russia, Sir Arthur Nicolson, Britain should not 'cold-shoulder Izvolsky' over the Balkans.[23] Equally, in the Moroccan episode, Grey had decided to throw Britain's support behind France as a means of checking Germany's advances.[24] When these two crises were combined with Wilhelm II's erratic behaviour, typified by the so-called *Daily Telegraph* interview, Grey could not but be suspicious both of German motives and German consistency of policy.[25]

Second, in the imperial context, the German proposal offered little. If the Baghdad railway issue were settled *à deux*, between Germany and Britain, then France, and particularly Russia, would be offended.[26] When Grey insisted that the latter two countries should be involved in any railway talks, the Germans declined, furthering Grey's suspicions of the ultimate purpose behind their offer.[27] Problems with Russia over Persia were to be particularly deprecated, as Grey's critics within the Liberal Party were especially unhappy about Anglo-Russian cooperation in that state.[28] But, perhaps even more importantly, a German presence in the region would provide endless opportunities for Berlin to fish in troubled waters.

Thus, the German offer of a comprehensive settlement had nothing to recommend it. In Europe, a British promise of neutrality would have shattered the rough equilibrium among the loose groupings of the great powers, and would have deprived Britain of her freedom of action. Further, France and, particularly, Russia would have felt less constrained by their colonial settlements and the British imperial position would not have been improved. Finally, while a German settlement – with even a partial naval-building holiday – might have satisfied some of Grey's Radical critics, it would have shattered the cross-bench support for Grey's foreign policy.

Grey's rejection of the German offer did not bring an end to the Foreign Secretary's attempt to find some sort of accommodation with Berlin. When Russia and Germany flirted with *rapprochement* at Potsdam in November 1910, Grey told the British ambassador at St Petersburg, Sir George Buchanan, that 'I am delighted that Russia should be on the best terms with Germany, so long as that is not allowed to make a breach between her and us.'[29] And, in fact, in March 1911, the British put forward a proposal to the Germans calling for a reduction in armaments.[30] But, despite the fact that in the Cabinet there were 'several members who desire to come to what they term a "friendly understanding" with Germany at almost any cost', Grey ensured that the offer was couched in terms that did not imply any weakening of the British agreements with Russia and France.[31]

Despite Grey's professed intention to maintain the *status quo*, it was clear that the European situation was far from settled. Franco-Russian relations had declined after the French had offered little support to Russia in the Bosnian crisis, while the Potsdam meetings made it clear that better relations between St Petersburg and Berlin were not impossible.[32] In such circumstances, Grey's offering of an olive branch to Germany distressed many of his advisers, who believed that this presaged an end to the Triple Entente and opposed it.[33] As Nicolson, now the Permanent Under-Secretary at the Foreign Office wrote on 19 April: 'I look forward to a troublesome time during the next few months; but so far as my voice is heard, it will always be in favour of a firm maintenance of our understanding with France and Russia.'[34]

It was in such circumstances that the Agadir crisis occurred.[35] Grey's response was to propose to the Germans the calling of a conference, 'with an intimation that, in the event of their refusal, we should take steps to assert and protect British interests'.[36] With the Cabinet divided and the French offering Germany colonial concessions, no initiative was made.[37] However, for William Tyrrell, Grey's private secretary at the Foreign Office, the issue was clear: 'It is depressing', he wrote to Hardinge,

> to find that, after six years' experience of Germany, the inclination here is still to believe that she can be placated by small concessions and even large cessions of territory in tropical Africa. What she wants is the hegemony of Europe.[38]

It was, he concluded, 'a vital interest for us to support her [France] on this occasion in the same way in which the Germans supported the Austrian policy of 1908 in Bosnia'.

None the less, Grey was determined to promise only support for a conference, despite a welcome swing towards a firmer policy from David Lloyd George, the Chancellor of the Exchequer and a leading light in Radical circles.[39] Grey was afraid that to give *carte blanche* to the French would encourage an obstructive policy by them, one likely to lead to war. However, it should not be thought that Grey favoured giving in to the German demands. While the Director of Military Operations, Sir Henry Wilson, derided Grey's knowledge of the military balance in Europe, the Foreign Secretary based his policy on ensuring that, if Britain were to intervene on the side of France in a war with Germany, 'the point was whether our intervention would make the difference between defeat and victory'.[40] Part of Grey's concern was based on the lukewarm support that the Russians offered to the French, although by September 1911, this was dispelled.[41] In any circumstances, Grey was unwilling to 'create consternation' by forbidding 'our military experts to converse with the French'.[42]

There was a domestic price to pay. Grey's critics within the Liberal Party were incensed by the Anglo-French staff talks, which they viewed as compromising the Cabinet's freedom of action in European affairs.[43] As the Liberal-leaning editor of the *Edinburgh Review* put it: 'My own fear is lest we should become a *mere* ally of France, or of France and Russia, and should some day find ourselves paying the piper without having ourselves called the tune.'[44] The unhappiness with Grey's foreign policy among his own party was exacerbated by the actions of Russia in Persia.[45] The result was a 'serious crisis' in the Cabinet, but Grey held firm.[46] In a speech in the House of Commons on 27 November 1911, the Foreign Secretary defended his policies in uncompromising terms.[47] While Grey did not (and, perhaps, could never) satisfy his critics, his position was clear: Britain would not abandon her agreements with France and Russia, would support them against German bullying but would not commit herself, in advance, in all circumstances, to give such support.[48] Such a balanced approach could not appeal to the Radicals, whose policy, as one member of the diplomatic service put it, was 'to quarrel with our friends of the time being in order to get on good terms with one's enemies for the time being, to whom in order to induce them to smile, we must make every conceivable sacrifice. This being their idea of a really well balanced foreign policy, their present attitude doesn't surprise us in the least.'[49]

Grey was only too aware of the impact that such feelings had on his foreign policy. Early in 1912, he discussed the rumour that Russia and Austria-Hungary might patch up the relations between them, relations which had been frigid since the Bosnian crisis. His explanation of why he favoured such an occurrence explains his difficulties in shaping an even-handed policy of balance:

What makes me work for a working understanding between Russia and Austria is that a war between them would be very inconvenient. I do not think that we could take part in it, and intervene on the Russian side in a Balkan War; and yet our absenteeism would prove a danger to the maintenance of the present grouping of European Powers .... On the whole, it seems to me that, unless France and we were prepared to go to war on behalf of Russia, the danger of upsetting the present grouping of the Powers would be far greater if Russia became involved in a war with Austria than if she came to a working agreement with that country. Of course, I cannot actively promote an agreement between Russia and

Austria against the wishes of France .... An agreement is more likely to come about if we do not mix ourselves in the matter .... [50]

While believing that Britain's ability to influence the policy of others was necessarily limited, Grey was willing, much to the dismay of his permanent officials past and present, to placate his critics by sending a mission headed by Lord Haldane, the Secretary of State for War, to Berlin to discuss restrictions on naval building.[51] Equally, the Foreign Secretary was willing, this time at the risk of incurring disfavour from the opposition, to open colonial discussions with Berlin.[52]

These overtures to Berlin had failed by the spring of 1912, foundering once more on the German insistence that any agreement on naval matters was contingent on a promise of British neutrality in a European war. But this did not mean that Grey was willing to tie himself more closely to Russia and France.[53] A proposal by the French that Britain should join in a Franco-Russian naval agreement was rejected by Grey. The Foreign Secretary was also very careful to ensure that he maintained his support within the Liberal Party. As he noted on a memorandum discussing the proposed naval talks: 'The Cabinet has now the same knowledge of what has taken place that the Prime Minister & I have.'[54]

As Grey continued to attempt to maintain as great a degree of latitude as possible for Britain in European affairs, so, too, did he attempt to keep the empire isolated from them. This was illustrated best in 1911, when Grey discussed the extension of the Anglo-Japanese treaty at the Imperial Conference held in London.[55] Grey stressed that Britain's power was based on the Royal Navy, and pointed out that the Anglo-Japanese alliance – in which Japan had been 'good allies' – was the keystone of the defence of the British empire in the Far East. Without the support of the Imperial Japanese Navy, and, indeed, with it as a potential enemy, there would be a 'tremendous and undesirable change ... in the strategical situation'. While Grey kept from the Imperial representatives the fact that the Admiralty was considering reducing the Royal Navy's presence in the Far East, this does not diminish the fact that naval power, and the need to keep Imperial affairs separate from those European, was the basis upon which British policy was built.[56]

Significant, too, was the fact that Grey's main subsidiary concern about the extension of the Anglo-Japanese alliance was to ensure that it could not lead to a conflict with the US, with whom a General Arbitration Treaty agreement was being worked out simultaneously.[57] Here, Grey was following well-established lines. Canada was clearly the most vulnerable spot in the empire, and the British had long since decided that it could not be defended against a hostile America.[58] And, while the US possessed a substantial fleet, the British had no intention of considering it in any interpretation of the two-power standard that determined British naval strength before 1914. As Reginald McKenna, the First Lord of the Admiralty, told the Imperial

Conference on 29 May 1911: 'it was perfectly obvious that we have not to consider the United States Navy as possibly hostile'.[59] The US was a regional power of consequence, and Grey was intent on ensuring – as the solutions to the Venezuelan and Alaskan boundary crises had indicated before he came to office – that it remained so.

By the autumn of 1912, with Anglo-German relations improved, Grey's major outstanding problem seemed to be Persia.[60] However, the outbreak of the First Balkan War in October faced him with a new crisis.[61] Grey immediately attempted to work with the Germans to find a solution.[62] This was important, for this seemed to be the best way to ensure that Russia and Austria-Hungary did not become hostile towards one another and create all the problems, noted above, that Grey had said might result from a Balkan war. This hope was strengthened by the fact that Grey had met with the Russian foreign minister, Sergei Sazonov, at Balmoral in September, and the latter had been 'very emphatic about putting strong pressure on the Balkan States to keep the peace'.[63] While Sazonov had second thoughts – due to Russian public opinion – about such a policy once war began and the French were concerned about being 'dragged along' by Russia, Grey stuck to his even-handed policy.[64]

This was not easy. Passions over the Balkan imbroglio flared in both Vienna and St Petersburg.[65] By the beginning of December, there was talk of war, a possibility made more likely when the Germans promised support for Austria-Hungary in a conflict with Russia. Grey was not to be intimidated. He informed the Germans that St Petersburg would not give way, and Haldane warned that Britain would not likely remain neutral.[66] The result was German anger, but, despite this, a conference of ambassadors came into session on 17 December. The success of the conference cemented Grey's position. As Nicolson told Hardinge, 'there is little doubt that Grey has very much increased his own prestige ... He is carrying on these Ambassadorial meetings very skilfully and firmly, and has shown gifts which I confess I did not think he possessed.'[67]

Indeed, Grey's diplomacy in the first third of 1913 was at its zenith. The London conference was heading towards a settlement, relations with Germany were improving thanks to colonial settlements brokered by Britain involving the Portuguese colonies, and Grey's Cabinet colleagues were applauding 'the skill & success with which he is piloting the European ship through troubled waters'.[68] Even Grey was pleased. 'It seems almost too much to expect', he wrote from a fishing holiday in Scotland, 'to expect that everything including both Balkan crisis & salmon fishing should go well simultaneously, but it does not seem impossible'.[69]

Grey's pleasure was not mirrored by some of his officials. For Nicolson, Grey's balanced approach to European affairs was the wrong one.[70] The Permanent Under-Secretary would have preferred an alliance with France, and found solace only in 'the great recovery which Russia has made and the enormous powerful State which she has become in every sense of the word'.[71] In fact, there were fears that Grey had fallen too much under the influence of Tyrrell, who was purported to have argued that the British position was so strong that 'we can now snap our fingers both at the Triple Alliance and at France and Russia, upon the latter of whom he has gone back in the most astonishing way'.[72] From India, Hardinge shared this concern, noting that Grey was 'temperamentally ... quite ready to listen to German blandishments'.[73]

While Tyrrell advocated no realignment of the powers, he was strongly opposed to the 'cynical selfishness' of Russian policy in Asia, and believed – due to the reluctance of Berlin to push an aggressive policy in the Balkans and the slowing down of German naval building – that the 'German menace' was temporarily in abeyance.[74] Thus he advocated taking a stronger line with Russia, particularly in Asia. This put him at loggerheads with Nicolson, whose influence with Grey was thought to be waning.[75]

Tyrrell's advice was attractive to Grey. Maintaining the Anglo-Russian convention was always difficult, given the ideological gap between the states, and Russia's actions in Persia and minor incidents between London and St Petersburg did not make things easier for Grey.[76] However, before any serious discussion with Russia about, in particular, Persia could take place, the Second Balkan War broke out. Grey's policy here was consistent. He preferred 'to preserve Ottoman rule in Asia', contending that it was the 'only safe policy'.[77] At the same time, Grey attempted to tie up many of the loose ends in the Ottoman empire that had the potential to cause difficulties for Britain's relations with the European powers.[78] British commercial interests in the Middle East were protected by railway settlements with Germany and the Ottoman empire, although these tended to irritate the Russians, who feared that their own commercial position would be jeopardized. Similarly, St Petersburg was infuriated by the appointment of Liman von Sanders as both the commander of the German military mission in Turkey and the Turkish First Army Corps. Grey was unwilling to support Russia in this regard – 'unless Russia is prepared to make it a *casus belli* and I do not believe it is worth that' – further emphasizing the policy that Tyrrell had advocated and Grey's own desire to maintain a balance.[79]

Thus, at the beginning of 1914, Grey's policy remained constant and consistent. He made the nature of his efforts clear to one of his colleagues, who had chided the Foreign Secretary for the use of the phrase 'Triple Entente':

The best course I think is to let things go on as they are without any new declaration of policy. The alternatives are either a policy of complete isolation in Europe, or a policy of definite alliance with one or the other group of European Powers.

My own desire has been to avoid bringing the choice between these two alternatives to an issue; and I think we have been fortunate in being able to go on so long as we are.[80]

How was this avoidance of alternatives to be carried out? In the remaining months of peace, what threatened Grey's delicate balance was Russia and, particularly, the clash of British and Russian sensibilities over Persia.[81]

Grey found galling Sazonov's continued complaints about Britain's objections to a linking of the Indian and Russian railway lines.[82] Grey did not want to block Russia from maintaining her position in Persia, but was unwilling, for strategic reasons, to link the two lines. In addition, he found Russian actions in Persia generally to be anti-British and designed to increase Russia's dominance there. 'We wish Persia to be a neutral buffer State', Grey told the British ambassador to Russia, Sir George Buchanan, 'they are willing to partition it'.[83] Grey was willing to consider this in the context of a complete revision of the Anglo-Russian convention – including a cession of the neutral zone of Persia to Britain, but feared that London had 'nothing to give' in return. Grey's attempt to isolate any imperial complications from the European context was thus in danger of foundering.

Nor was he willing to patch this over by means of making any steps towards alliance. In a long, despairing letter to Buchanan on 7 April 1914, Nicolson outlined the state of British foreign policy.[84] While the Russians were pushing for a closer Anglo-Russian relationship, the Permanent Under-Secretary noted that there 'is very little hope that the [British] Government will feel itself in a position to go any distance on that road'. As to Anglo-French relations, the military and naval discussions about cooperation were so 'undecided' that they had 'little real practical value'. In fact, Nicolson lamented, 'I am afraid that should war break out on the continent the likelihood of our despatching any expeditionary force is extremely remote'. With the 'present welter' in domestic affairs, it was 'hopeless to expect that the Cabinet will seriously consider any new departure in our foreign policy'. Even joint Franco-Russian pressure was unlikely to move British policy. 'I do not know for how much longer', Nicolson wrote later in the month, 'we shall be able to follow our present policy of dancing on a tight rope and not be compelled to take up some definite line or other.'[85] Not even the importunities visited upon Grey during his trip to Paris in April could move the Foreign Secretary towards considering an Anglo-Russian alliance.[86]

What was clear, though, was the need for a revision of the Anglo-Russian convention. This began on 10 June, and proceeded until it was overtaken in late July by the events that led to war.[87] This was clearly going to be a difficult matter, as it would involve not only the usual negotiations with Russia, but also complicated discussions with the government of India and considerations of Anglo-Chinese relations with regard to Tibet, where a bilateral settlement between Britain and Lhassa had, in Nicolson's words, the potential to 'blow the 1907 [Anglo-Russian] Convention to pieces'.[88] Grey's desire to dance on a tightrope and to keep his European and imperial policies separate was faced with a difficult balancing act.

Grey, however, was determined to try. His actions during the July crisis were entirely consistent with the policy that he had followed since coming to office.[89] From the assassination at Sarajevo until the last few days of July, Grey attempted to work with the Germans, in the fashion of his action during the First Balkan War, to ensure that the crisis remained a localized affair. Once it became apparent that this was not possible, Grey could no longer remain on his tightrope. Here was the difficulty with practising a policy designed to preserve peace by means of balance. Once one grouping of the powers had decided to risk war, Grey was faced with the unpalatable alternatives of staying neutral – with risks that will be discussed below – or committing Britain to a war whose nature and outcome were uncertain. That he chose the latter was not surprising, although both his allies and his closest professional advisers were uncertain to the very end both that he would do so and that he could convince his Cabinet colleagues to agree.

Once Britain had declared war, Grey's policy necessarily changed. Britain was now part of a coalition, and Grey's first goal was to ensure, as far as possible, that the alliance functioned smoothly. His second aim was both to find new allies from among the neutrals and to ensure that relations with the other neutrals remained smooth. Finally, Grey attempted to keep, as he had before the war, the empire separate from European events. All of these tasks were difficult, particularly as they often had to be pursued in tandem with Britain's allies.

This latter constraint was quickly apparent with respect to the attempt to create a 'Balkan bloc' in support of the Entente. Here, while Grey supported the idea, the bulk of the running was done by Sazonov, as British influence in the region was necessarily less than that of St Petersburg.[90] Nor was Grey instrumental in the signing on 5 September of the Pact of London, which prevented any of the Entente from signing a separate peace.[91] Grey was more influential in the attempts to confine the struggle to Europe. In the Far East, the Foreign Secretary endeavoured to persuade Japan to play a limited role, but was powerless to prevent the Japanese from taking advantage of the war to advance in China.[92] In the Near East, Grey preferred to keep the Ottoman empire neutral, thus ensuring British interests in the area, keeping communications to the Far East open and preventing any Moslem unrest in the British empire from being fomented by the declaration of a *Jihad*.[93] However, once the Porte had entered the war, Grey was willing to guarantee Russia Constantinople in any post-war settlement as a means of ensuring that Russia focused her military effort on Germany rather than on Austria-Hungary and territorial gains in the Balkans.[94] But, he was unwilling to deal with the contentious question of Persia, until the latter became tied up with the complex negotiations involving Italy's entrance into the war. At that time, Italy was given substantial gains in both the Balkans and Asiatic Turkey; Russia was formally promised Constantinople; Britain, France and Russia partitioned much of the Ottoman empire, while London and St Petersburg agreed to divide Persia between them. In these decisions, Grey's voice was significant, but military concerns about the defence of the empire were paramount.[95]

Grey also found that keeping imperial matters separate from European ones was difficult with respect to France. When the British initiated the Dardanelles campaign in 1915, this stirred French suspicions that London intended to use the war as an opportunity to steal a march in the Near and Middle East.[96] This profoundly complicated Anglo-French relations, particularly with respect to the Dardanelles and Salonikan campaigns. Here, Grey could only do his best to ensure that frictions were kept to a minimum, often, as was the case with the decision not to evacuate Salonika, at the expense of what the British perceived to be the best course of action.

In the effort to attract new members to the Allied side, Grey's ability to influence events was limited. As he told Rosebery, the 'criticism on diplomatic failure during the war is mostly based on the false assumption that diplomacy in war can supply the want of military success'.[97] Italy's and Roumania's entrances into the war on the Allied side were due to their calculation that the Entente was likely to win and could promise more to Italy than could the central powers.[98] On the other hand, the Ottoman empire and Bulgaria joined the central powers because they thought that the latter was more likely to be triumphant and could promise them a greater share of the spoils than could the Entente.[99]

Relations with the neutrals were also complicated, particularly with respect to the British blockade.[100] The British determination to prevent war material from reaching the central powers inevitably put them in opposition to the US, which clung to the idea of the freedom of the seas.[101] This meant that Grey had to move carefully, weighing the need to acquire money and supplies from the US against the need to enforce the blockade as tightly as possible.[102] When this was combined with President Wilson's efforts to mediate peace, it meant that Anglo-American relations required careful handling. Occasionally, as in the case of Sweden, blockade policy and inter-Allied relations became entwined, causing endless complications.[103] Generally, Grey delegated such work – which he termed 'a mess of questions of contraband & kindred subjects that don't exist in time of peace and are a disagreeable brood spawned by war' – to others, particularly Sir Eyre Crowe, who became head of the new Contraband Department created at the Foreign Office to deal with the issue.[104]

Much of this reflected the fact that, during the war, the role of the Foreign Office was diminished.[105] When he returned as Permanent Under-Secretary in 1916, Hardinge found the Foreign Office 'a very different place' than before the war, with an independent Ministry of Blockade – which 'undoubtedly at times ... overlaps the political side of the question' – operating in parallel within the Office.[106] Such a diminution of the Foreign Office's ambit was also caused by the greater influence both of the Service departments and of the new ministries spawned by the exigencies of war. Grey's authority remained high, but his health was poor, and he had to resort to occasional breaks in which he did nothing but sleep and eat bread and milk.[107] By the time that he resigned in December 1916, Grey had endured enough of the 'continuous storm & trouble' of his years in office.[108]

There have been a number of criticisms levelled at Grey over the years that need to be addressed. Many of them do not stand up in the light of recent research. For example, the idea that Grey was secretive and did not keep the Cabinet informed of the military talks with France in 1906 and afterwards has been shown to be false.[109] A belief that Grey was somehow dominated by the Radical wing of the Liberals or by his permanent officials cannot be sustained. For example, Grey's policy with regard to the Congo, often credited to E.D. Morel – one of the leading Radicals and the head of the Congo Reform Association – was influenced more by the reports of Grey's own agents than by anything done by Morel, a fact that Morel himself recognized.[110] Nor did Grey adopt the policy of his Radical critics after Agadir, as A.J.P. Taylor maintained.[111] Both before and after 1911, Grey attempted to follow his policy of balance. And, as shown above, if Grey had been under the influence of his advisers, then the tightrope would have been abandoned for a tightly bound alliance with France and Russia. Equally, the savage attack on Grey launched by David Lloyd George in his memoirs – that Grey had led his innocent colleagues into war and, during the war, had been unhelpful in its prosecution – reflects more Lloyd George's concern with his own place in history than reality.[112] It is also impossible to accept the idea that Grey stumbled into being Foreign Secretary and had little knowledge of or guiding principles concerning foreign affairs. Grey's concern about and attempts to shape British policy after the First World War points to the fact that he had well-developed ideas about what constituted the proper conduct and direction of foreign relations.[113]

Finally, we come to Grey's responsibility for the outbreak of war. Could a different foreign policy – say a British formal adherence to one of the European blocs or British isolation (splendid or otherwise) – have either prevented the First World War or saved Britain from its consequences? This leads us to a consideration of the roots of Grey's policy. Grey belonged to that group of men who came to power around the turn of the century for whom a policy of isolation and detachment was temperamentally unsuitable.[114] For these 'Edwardians', Germany seemed to be the threat to European stability, something that Grey experienced first-hand during the Uganda crisis when he was Parliamentary Under-Secretary for Foreign Affairs.[115] While Grey is generally considered to be a 'Liberal-Imperialist', this needs some qualification.[116] Grey's attitude towards the British empire was not that of men like Curzon, who favoured expansion, but one of consolidation and protection of the *status quo*. As he wrote in 1912, 'if there is one thing more than another that I have striven to secure during the last seven years it is that we should not incur any increase of Imperial liabilities'.[117]

For Grey, the British empire, whose strength was to prove so important to Britain during the First World War, needed to be isolated from Europe. Nothing had made this clearer before he came to office than the Far East. In 1897–98 there had been a Far Eastern crisis that threatened the British position in China, triggered by the German acquisition of Kiaochow.[118] That crisis had in turn sparked the Boxer rebellion, which, combined with the stark revelation of Britain's isolation, had led to the ousting of Salisbury as Foreign Secretary and his replacement by one of the Edwardians, Lord Lansdowne.[119] The Anglo-Japanese alliance, as conceived by Lansdowne, was designed to be a regional pact, aimed at controlling Russian expansion, a position endorsed by Grey.[120] His attitude with regard to the Anglo-Russian convention was similar: the convention promised to stabilize the empire and save substantial amounts on imperial defence by reducing the Russian threat to India. This was strategic foreign policy at its best, using foreign policy to maximize Britain's ability to defend her interests.

In Europe, Grey tried to maintain a balanced policy because he believed that a commitment to either side would not promote peace.[121] If he had joined Britain to the Franco-Russian alliance, this would have increased German fears about encirclement. If he had accepted the numerous German offers of alliance, they would have carried with them a requirement for British neutrality in a European war. This was unacceptable, because to do this was to acquiesce in a possible German domination of the Continent, with both immediate and future perils for the British position.[122] Further, to do so would incur the wrath of France and Russia. The latter, in particular, was well-positioned to threaten Britain's empire, something that the other strand of Grey's policy had been designed to prevent. This latter does not mean that Britain went to war in 1914 to defend the British empire against Russia, as has been contended, but it does show how Britain's European and Asiatic policies were related.[123] Grey's twin policies in the end proved insufficient to prevent the whirlwind, but there is little doubt that they in no way sowed it. The impetus for war came from Vienna and Berlin, not from London.

Notes

1. Grey to Rosebery, private letter, 10 December 1916, Rosebery Papers, MS 10028, N[ational] L[ibrary of] S[cotland].
2. Most recently in Niall Ferguson, *The Pity of War* (London: Allen Lane, 1998), pp. 55–81. Ferguson's argument follows Keith Wilson, *The Policy of the Entente:*

Essays on the Determinants of British Foreign Policy, 1904–1914 (Cambridge: Cambridge University Press, 1985), esp. pp. 85–99 and *idem*, 'Grey' in Keith Wilson (ed.), *British Foreign Secretaries and Foreign Policy: From Crimean War to First World War* (London: Croom Helm, 1987), pp. 172–97.

3. These schools are discussed in the best biography of Grey, Keith Robbins, *Sir Edward Grey: A Biography of Lord Grey of Fallodon* (London: Cassel, 1971), pp. xiii–xv, 369–72. Ferguson manages to combine his condemnations of Grey's supposed Germanophobia with a disparagement of the Foreign Secretary's fondness for fishing; *Pity of War*, pp. 59–60.

4. Here, the pre-eminent work is that of Zara Steiner; see *The Foreign Office and Foreign Policy 1898–1914* (Cambridge: Cambridge University Press, 1969), pp. 83–171 and *passim*; *idem*, 'The Foreign Office under Sir Edward Grey, 1905–1914', in F.H. Hinsley (ed.), *British Foreign Policy under Sir Edward Grey* (Cambridge: Cambridge University Press, 1977), pp. 22–69 and *idem*, *Britain and the Origins of the First World War* (London: Macmillan, 1977). For a recent evaluation of Grey's policy with respect to Russia, see Keith Neilson, *Britain and the Last Tsar. British Policy and Russia, 1894–1917* (Oxford: Clarendon Press, 1995), pp. 11–15; 267–372.

5. Neilson, *Britain and the Last Tsar*, pp. 238–64; David G. Herrmann, *The Arming of Europe and the Making of the First World War* (Princeton: Princeton University Press, 1996), pp. 40–58.

6. Robbins, *Grey*, pp. 145–7.

7. Grey to Bertie, letter, 15 January 1906, P[ublic] R[ecord] O[ffice, Kew], Grey Papers, F[oreign] O[ffice], 800/49.

8. Grey to Tweedmouth, letter, 16 January 1906, PRO, Grey Papers, FO 800/87.

9. Grey to Spring Rice, private letter, 22 December 1905, PRO, Spring Rice Papers, FO 800/241.

10. Grey to Spring Rice, letter, 19 February 1906, PRO, Spring Rice Papers, FO 800/241.

11. Neilson, *Britain and the Last Tsar*, pp. 197–204, 227–37, 268–70; Grey to Brodrick, letter, 11 March 1899, PRO, Midleton Papers, PRO 30/67/4; Selborne to Curzon, conf. letter, 23 March 1899, B[ritish] L[ibrary], Curzon Papers, MSS Eur 111/229.

12. On the transformation of Russian foreign policy, see B.J. Williams, 'The Revolution of 1905 and Russian Foreign Policy', in C. Abramsky, *Essays in Honour of E.H. Carr* (London: Macmillan, 1974), pp. 101–25; A.V. Ignatiev, *Vneshnaia politika Rossii v 1905–7 gg.* (Moscow, 1986).

13. Ian Nish, *The Anglo-Japanese Alliance: The Diplomacy of Two Island Empires 1894–1907* (London: Athlone Press, 2nd edn, 1985), pp. 353–8; Neilson, *Britain and the Last Tsar*, p. 134; Keith Wilson, 'The Anglo-Japanese Alliance of August 1905 and the Defending of India: A Case of the Worst Scenario', *Journal of Imperial and Commonwealth History*, 21, 2(1993), pp. 334–56.

14. Andre T. Sidorowicz, 'The British Government, the Hague Peace Conference of 1907, and the Armaments Question', in B.J.C. McKercher (ed.), *Arms Limitation and Disarmament: Restraints on War, 1899–1939* (Westport, Connecticut: Praeger, 1992), pp. 1–21; David Stevenson, *Armaments and the Coming of War: Europe 1904–1914* (Oxford: Oxford University Press, 1996), pp. 105–11.

15. Chirol to Nicolson, private letter, 19 March 1907, PRO, Nicolson Papers, FO 800/339; A.J.A. Morris, *Radicalism Against War 1906–1914: The Advocacy of Peace and Retrenchment* (Totowa, New Jersey: Rowman and Littlefield, 1972), pp. 97–121; for the relationship between Grey and the Unionists, R.H. Williams,

'Arthur James Balfour, Sir John Fisher and the Politics of Naval Reform 1904–1910', *Historical Research*, 60, 141 (1987), pp. 80–99 and *idem, Defending the Empire: The Conservative Party and British Defence Policy 1899–1915* (New Haven and London: Yale University Press, 1991), pp. 77ff.

16. Keith Neilson, '"The British Empire Floats on the British Navy": British Naval Policy, Belligerent Rights, and Disarmament, 1902–1909', in McKercher (ed.), *Arms Limitation*, pp. 21–41; more widely, John W. Coogan, *The End of Neutrality. The United States, Britain, and Maritime Rights 1899–1915* (Ithaca, New York: Cornell University Press, 1981).

17. Paul Kennedy, *The Rise of the Anglo-German Antagonism, 1860–1914* (London: Allen & Unwin, 1980), pp. 413–31; D.W. Sweet, 'Great Britain and Germany, 1905–1911', in Hinsley (ed.), *British Foreign Policy*, pp. 216–35.

18. Grey to Nicolson disp. 237, 23 May 1906, FO 371/125/17967. The idea of Anglo-German cooperation in the building of the railway had long roots. In 1903, Lansdowne had favoured doing so, but had failed to carry his Cabinet with him; see R.M. Francis, 'The British Withdrawal from the Baghdad Railway Project in April 1903', *Historical Journal*, 16 (1973), pp. 168–78 and Avner Cohen, 'Joseph Chamberlain, Lord Lansdowne and British Foreign Policy 1901–1903: From Collaboration to Confrontation', *Australian Journal of Politics and History*, 43, 2 (1997).

19. Minutes of the 92nd meeting of the C[ommittee of] I[mperial] D[efence], 26 July 1906, PRO, Cab[inet Office] 2/2; 'Report [of the Baghdad Railway Committee]', R.P. Maxwell, R. Ritchie, W.H. Clark, W. Tyrrell, A. Parker, 26 March 1907, Cab 37/87/36.

20. Arthur J. Marder, *From the Dreadnought to Scapa Flow. The Royal Navy in the Fisher Era.* vol. I, *The Road to War, 1904–1914* (London: Oxford University Press, 1961), pp. 105–85 remains the classic account; see also, Phillips Payson O'Brien, *British and American Naval Power. Politics and Policy, 1900–1936* (Westport, Connecticut: Praeger, 1998), pp. 73–98.

21. Sweet, 'Great Britain and Germany, 1905–11', pp. 227–33.

22. F.R. Bridge, 'Izvolsky, Aehrenthal, and the End of the Austro-Russian Entente, 1906–8', *Mitteilungen des Österreichischen Staatsarchivs*, 29 (1976), pp. 315–62 and *idem, Great Britain and Austria-Hungary 1906–14* (London: Routledge, 1972), pp. 80–91; G.E. Silberstein, 'Germany, France and the Casablanca Incident 1908–9: An Investigation of a Forgotten Crisis', *Canadian Journal of History*, 11 (1976), pp. 331–4; E.W. Edwards, 'The Franco-German Agreement in Morocco', *English Historical Review*, 78 (1963), pp. 483–513.

23. Grey to Nicolson, private letter, 27 October 1908, PRO, Grey Papers, FO 800/73. For further evidence of Grey's support for Russia, see Grey to Nicolson, private letter, 2 February 1909, ibid. The reference is to Alexander Izvolsky, the Russian foreign minister.

24. See Esher's journal entry, 12 November 1908, C[hurchill] C[ollege] A[rchives] C[entre, Cambridge], Esher Papers, ESHR 2/11.

25. T.G. Otte, '"An Altogether Unfortunate Affair": Great Britain and the *Daily Telegraph* Affair', *Diplomacy & Statecraft*, 5, 2 (1994), pp. 296–333.

26. Neilson, *Britain and the Last Tsar*, pp. 310–12.

27. Grey to O'Beirne [British *chargé d'affaires*, St Petersburg], private letter, 9 July 1909, PRO, Grey Papers, FO 800/73.

28. D. McLean, 'English Radicals, Russia, and the Fate of Persia 1907–13', *English Historical Review*, 93 (1978), pp. 338–42.

29. Grey to Buchanan, private letter, 7 January 1911, PRO, Grey Papers, FO 800/74.

30. Asquith to the King, letter, 9 March 1911, Bodleian [Library, Oxford], Asquith Papers, I/6; Nicolson to Buchanan, private letter, 14 March 1911, PRO, Nicolson Papers, FO 800/347.

31. Nicolson to Hardinge, private letter, 2 March 1911, C[ambridge] U[niversity] L[ibrary, Cambridge], Hardinge Papers, vol. 92.

32. See J.F.V. Keiger, *France and the Origins of the First World War* (London: Macmillan, 1983), pp. 42, 88–9; D.C.B. Lieven, *Russia and the Origins of the First World War* (London: Macmillan, 1983), p. 38; I.I. Astafev, *Russko-germanskie diplomaticheskie otnosheniia 1905–1911 gg. (ot portsmutskogo mira do potsdamskogo soglasheniia)* (Moscow: Izdatel'sto moskovskogo universiteta, 1972), pp. 219–48.

33. Nicolson to Lowther (British ambassador, Constantinople), private letter, 6 February 1911, PRO, Lowther Papers, FO 800/193; Nicolson to Goschen (British ambassador, Berlin), private letter, 28 February 1911, PRO, Nicolson Papers, FO 800/347; Hardinge (British Viceroy, India) to Bertie (British ambassador, Paris), private letter, 5 April 1911, PRO, Bertie Papers, FO 800/180. I use the term 'Triple Entente' advisedly as a shorthand for the grouping of Britain, France and Russia, not implying that there was any alliance between them.

34. Nicolson to Hardinge, private letter, 19 April 1911, CUL, Hardinge Papers, vol. 92.

35. On the Agadir crisis and British policy, see J.-C. Alain, *Agadir 1911: Une crise impérialiste en Europe pour la conquête de Maroc* (Paris: Publications universitaires française, 1972); K.A. Hamilton, *Bertie of Thame: Edwardian Ambassador* (London: Royal Historical Society/Boydell Press, 1990), pp. 214–47; and M.L. Dockrill, 'British Policy during the Agadir Crisis of 1911', in Hinsley (ed.), *Grey*, pp. 271–87 and Thomas Otte, 'The Elusive Balance. British Foreign Policy and the French Entente before the First World War', in Alan Sharp and Glyn Stone (eds), *Anglo-French Relations in the Twentieth Century: Rivalry and Cooperation* (London and New York: Routledge, 2000), pp. 23–6.

36. Asquith to the King, reporting on the Cabinet, 19 July 1911, Bodleian, Asquith Papers I/6. For Grey's difficulties within the Cabinet, see Samuel R. Williamson, Jr., *The Politics of Grand Strategy: Britain and France Prepare for War, 1904–1914* (paperback edition, London and Atlantic Highlands, NJ: The Ashfield Press, 1990), pp. 143–53.

37. Asquith to the King, reporting on the Cabinet, 22 July 1911, ibid.

38. Tyrrell to Hardinge, private letter, 21 July 1911, Hardinge Papers, vol. 92.

39. Williamson, *The Politics of Grand Strategy*, pp. 157–9; B.B. Gilbert, 'Pacifist to Interventionist: David Lloyd George in 1911 and 1914: Was Belgium an Issue?', *Historical Journal*, 28, 4 (1985), pp. 863–84.

40. Minutes of the 114th meeting of the CID, 23 August 1914, Cab 2/2. Wilson diary entry, 9 August 1911, I[mperial] W[ar] M[useum], Wilson Papers.

41. Nicolson to Buchanan (British ambassador, St Petersburg), private letter, 12 September 1911, PRO, Nicolson Papers, FO 800/350; Bertie (British ambassador, Paris) to Nicolson, private letter, 19 September 1911, ibid.

42. Grey to Asquith, private letter, 8 September 1911, PRO, Grey Papers, FO 800/100; Otte, 'The Elusive Balance', pp. 24–5.

43. Asquith to the King reporting on the Cabinet, 2 and 16 November 1911, both Bodleian, Asquith Papers I/6.

44. Arthur Elliot to Cromer, letter, 14 November 1911, PRO, Cromer Papers, FO 633/20.

45. Neilson, *Britain and the Last Tsar*, pp. 320–5; John A. Murray, 'Foreign Policy Debated: Sir Edward Grey and His Critics, 1911–1912', in L.P. Wallace and W.C. Askew (eds), *Power, Public Opinion, and Diplomacy* (Freeport, New York: Books for Libraries Press, 1959), pp. 140–71.

46. Esher journal entry, 24 November 1911, CCAC, Esher Papers, ESHR 2/12.

47. *Parliamentary Debates*, 27 November 1911, 5th series, 23, 152–65.

48. A.J.A. Morris, *The Scaremongers: The Advocacy of War and Rearmament 1896–1914* (London: Routledge & Kegan Paul, 1984), pp. 302–6.

49. Esme Howard (British Consul-General, Berne) to his brother, Stafford, private letter, 1 February 1912, Cumbria County Record Office, Carlisle, Howard Papers, DHW 4/Family/13.

50. Grey to Bertie, private letter, 9 January 1912, PRO, Grey Papers, FO 800/53.

51. Asquith to the King, reporting on the Cabinet, 3 February 1912, Bodleian, Asquith Papers, I/6; Goschen diary entry, 5 February 1912, in C.H.D. Howard (ed.), *The Diaries of Edward Goschen 1900–1914* (London: Royal Historical Society, 1980), pp. 259–60; Chirol to Hardinge, private letter, 15 February 1912, CUL, Hardinge Papers, vol. 92; Bertie to Nicolson, personal letter, 11 February 1912, PRO, Nicolson Papers, FO 800/353; Hardinge to Nicolson, private letter, 12 March 1912, FO 800/354. On the Haldane mission, Stevenson, *Armaments and the Coming of War*, pp. 205–9.

52. Nicolson to Grey, memorandum, 22 May 1912, PRO, Grey Papers, FO 800/94. On the colonial talks, see R.T.B. Langhorne, 'Great Britain and Germany, 1911–1914', in Hinsley (ed.), *British Foreign Policy*, pp. 308–14.

53. The rest of this paragraph is based on Neilson, *Britain and the Last Tsar*, pp. 325–6; Keith Neilson, '"Greatly Exaggerated": The Myth of the Decline of Great Britain Before 1914', *International History Review*, 13, 4(1991), pp. 702–4.

54. Grey's minute (5 May 1912) on Nicolson's confidential memorandum (4 May 1912), PRO, Grey Papers, FO 800/94.

55. Minutes of the 111th meeting of the CID, 26 May 1911, PRO, Cab 2/2; P. Lowe, 'The British Empire and the Anglo-Japanese Alliance 1911–1915', *History*, 44 (1969), pp. 212–16; Ian Nish, *Alliance in Decline: A Study in Anglo-Japanese Relations* (London: Athlone, 1972), pp. 46, 54–9; *idem*, 'Great Britain, Japan and North-east Asia, 1905–1911', in Hinsley (ed.), *British Foreign Policy*, pp. 362–7; for a harsher view, see Robert Joseph Gowen, 'British Legerdemain at the 1911 Imperial Conference: The Dominions, Defense Planning, and the Renewal of the Anglo-Japanese Alliance', *Journal of Modern History*, 52 (1980), pp. 385–413.

56. Nicholas Lambert, 'Economy or Empire? The Fleet Unit Concept and the Quest for Collective Security in the Pacific, 1909–1914', in Keith Neilson and Greg Kennedy (eds), *Far-Flung Lines: Essays on Imperial Defence in Honour of Donald Mackenzie Schurman* (London: Frank Cass, 1996), pp. 55–84.

57. Generally, see P.A.R. Calvert, 'Great Britain and the New World, 1905–1914', in Hinsley (ed.), *British Foreign Policy*, pp. 382–94.

58. Samuel F. Wells, Jr., 'British Strategic Withdrawal from the Western Hemisphere, 1904–1906', *Canadian Historical Journal*, 49 (1968), pp. 335–56.

59. Minutes of the 112th meeting of the CID, 29 May 1911, PRO, Cab 2/2.

60. Neilson, *Britain and the Last Tsar*, pp. 326–8.

61. Robbins, *Grey*, pp. 264–9; R.J. Crampton, 'The Balkans, 1909–1914', in Hinsley (ed.), *British Foreign Policy*, pp. 256–70.

62. See R.J. Crampton, *The Hollow Detente: Anglo-German Relations in the Balkans 1911–1914* (London: George Prior, 1979), pp. 55–74.

63. Grey to Buchanan, private letter, 8 October 1912, PRO, Grey Papers, FO 800/74.
64. Grey to Buchanan, private letter, 21 October 1912, ibid.; Bertie to Grey, private letter, 7 November 1912, PRO, Grey Papers, FO 800/53.
65. Outlined in Neilson, *Britain and the Last Tsar*, pp. 329–30.
66. See K. Wilson, 'The British *Démarche* of 3 and 4 December 1912: H.A. Gwynne's Note on Britain, Russia and the First Balkan War', *Slavonic and East European Review*, 62 (1984), pp. 552–9. I do not accept Wilson's interpretation of the actions of Grey and Haldane.
67. Nicolson to Hardinge, private letter, 9 January 1913, CUL, Hardinge Papers, vol. 92.
68. Not everyone was pleased with the Portuguese settlement; Nicolson termed it 'one of the most cynical pieces of diplomacy that has ever occurred', ibid. For the praise, see Asquith to the King outlining the Cabinet, 9 January 1913, Bodleian, Asquith Papers, I/7.
69. Grey to Nicolson, private letter, 16 April 1913, PRO, Nicolson Papers, FO 800/365.
70. Nicolson to Goschen, private letter, 11 March 1913, PRO, Nicolson Papers, FO 800/364.
71. For the British appreciation of Russia's recovery, see Keith Neilson, 'Watching the "Steamroller": British Observers and the Russian Army before 1914', *Journal of Strategic Studies*, 8 (1985), pp. 199–217.
72. Chirol to Hardinge, private letter, 10 April 1913, CUL, Hardinge Papers, vol. 93 and same to same, private letter, 20 June 1913, *ibid*. For Tyrrell and his influence, see Edward T. Corp, 'Sir William Tyrrell: The *Éminence Grise* of the British Foreign Office, 1912–1915', *Historical Journal*, 25, 3 (1982), pp. 697–708; Steiner, *Foreign Office*, pp. 118–21.
73. Hardinge to Chirol, private letter, 30 April 1913, CUL, Hardinge Papers, vol. 93.
74. Chirol to Hardinge, private letter, 18 April 1913, CUL, Hardinge Papers, vol. 93.
75. Hardinge to Chirol, private letter, 8 May 1913, ibid. For Nicolson's long-term support of Russia, see Keith Neilson, '"My Beloved Russians": Sir Arthur Nicolson and Russia, 1906–1916', *International History Review*, 9, 4 (1987), pp. 521–54.
76. Neilson, *Britain and the Last Tsar*, pp. 84–109, idem, '"Incidents" and Foreign Policy: A Case Study', *Diplomacy & Statecraft*, 9, 1 (1998), pp. 53–88; Michael Hughes, *Diplomacy Before the Russian Revolution. Britain, Russia and the Old Diplomacy, 1894–1917* (Basingstoke, Hampshire: Macmillan, 2000), pp. 20–61.
77. Asquith to the King, reporting Grey's view in Cabinet, 9 July 1913, Bodleian, Asquith Papers, I/7.
78. The following is based on Neilson, *Britain and the Last Tsar*, pp. 333–4.
79. Grey's remarks on a minute by Sir Eyre Crowe, 29 December 1913, in H. Temperley and G.P. Gooch (eds), *British Documents on the Origins of the War, 1898–1914* (11 vols in 13; London: HMSO, 1926–38), X, pt. 1, document 452. That he pursued such a policy with one eye firmly on the Cabinet, see Grey to L. Harcourt (Secretary of State for Colonies), letter, 11 January 1914, PRO, Grey Papers, FO 800/91.
80. Grey to L. Harcourt, private letter, 10 January 1914, ibid.
81. What follows, except where otherwise noted, is based on Neilson, *Britain and the Last Tsar*, pp. 334–40.
82. Grey to Buchanan, private letter, 11 February 1914, PRO, Grey Papers, FO 800/74.
83. Grey to Buchanan, private letter, 18 March 1914, ibid.

84. Nicolson to Buchanan, private letter, 7 April 1914, PRO, Nicolson Papers, FO 800/373.
85. Nicolson to Buchanan, private letter, 21 April 1914, ibid. For a similar view, see Goschen to Nicolson, private letter, 24 April 1914, PRO, Nicolson Papers, FO 800/374.
86. Untitled memorandum by Bertie, 27 April 1914, BL, Bertie Papers, Add MSS 63032; Grey to Bertie, secret disp. 249, 1 May 1914, FO 371/2092/19288; Grey to Buchanan, private letter, 7 May 1914, PRO, Grey Papers, FO 800/74.
87. Neilson, *Britain and the Last Tsar*, pp. 337–8.
88. Hardinge to Chirol, private letter, 11 June 1914, CUL, Hardinge Papers, vol. 93; Nicolson to Buchanan, private letter, 30 June 1914, PRO, Nicolson Papers, FO 800/374; E.W. Edwards, 'China and Japan, 1911–1914', in Hinsley (ed.), *British Foreign Policy*, pp. 376–81.
89. The best account remains Steiner, *Britain and the Origins*, pp. 242–57 and Steiner and M.G. Ekstein, 'The Sarajevo Crisis', in Hinsley (ed.), *British Foreign Policy*, pp. 397–410; but cf. Wilson, *Policy of the Entente*, pp. 74–84, 95–9 and 115–20. Wilson is very good on the political pressures on Grey, see his 'Britain' in K. Wilson (ed.), *Decisions for War, 1914* (London: UCL Press, 1995), pp. 175–208.
90. Asquith to the King, reporting on the Cabinet, 20 August 1914, Bodleian, Asquith Papers, I/7; C.J. Smith, Jr., *The Russian Struggle for Power, 1914–17* (reprinted, New York: Greenwood, 1969), pp. 21–42.
91. David Stevenson, *The First World War and International Politics* (Oxford: Clarendon, 1988), p. 110.
92. Ian Nish, 'Japan and China', in Hinsley (ed.), *British Foreign Policy*, pp. 452–65.
93. Marian Kent, 'Asiatic Turkey, 1914–1916', in Hinsley (ed.), *British Foreign Policy*, pp. 436–51; Neilson, *Britain and the Last Tsar*, pp. 357–62 upon which the rest of this paragraph, except where otherwise noted, is based.
94. Keith Neilson, *Strategy and Supply: The Anglo-Russian Alliance 1914–17* (London: Allen & Unwin, 1984), pp. 49–51; Bertie to Grey, private and confidential letter, not sent, PRO, Bertie Papers, FO 800/177; untitled memorandum by Bertie, 18 December 1914, BL, Bertie Papers, Add MSS 63035.
95. Keith Neilson, '"For Diplomatic, Economic, Strategic and Telegraphic Reasons": British Imperial Defence, the Middle East and India, 1914–1918', in Neilson and Kennedy (eds), *Far-Flung Lines*, pp. 103–23; John Fisher, *Curzon and British Imperialism in the Middle East 1916–19* (London: Cass, 1999), pp. 1–41.
96. George H. Cassar, *The French and the Dardanelles. A Study of Failure in the Conduct of War* (London: Allen & Unwin, 1971); David Dutton, *The Politics of Diplomacy: Britain and France in the Balkans in the First World War* (London and New York: I.B. Taurus, 1998).
97. Grey to Rosebery, private letter, 10 December 1916, NLS, Rosebery Papers, MS 10028.
98. W.A. Renzi, *In the Shadow of the Sword: Italy's Neutrality and Entrance into the Great War, 1914–15* (New York: 1987); Stevenson, *First World War*, pp. 61–4.
99. Stevenson, *First World War*, pp. 59–61.
100. A. Marsden, 'The Blockade' in Hinsley (ed.), *British Foreign Policy*, pp. 466–88.
101. The problems of blockade are in Coogan, *End of Neutrality*; Greg C. Kennedy, 'Strategy and Supply in the North Atlantic Triangle, 1914–1918', in B.J.C. McKercher and L. Aronsen, (eds), *The North Atlantic Triangle in a Changing World. Anglo-American-Canadian Relations, 1902–1956* (Toronto: University of Toronto Press, 1996), pp. 48–80; Marian C. Siney, *The Allied Blockade of Germany 1914–16*

(Ann Arbor, Michigan: University of Michigan Press, 1957), and A.C. Bell, *History of the Blockade of Germany and the Countries Associated with Her in the Great War, Austria-Hungary, Bulgaria and Turkey, 1914–1918* (London: HMSO, 1937; re-issued, 1961).

102. On the British needs from the United States and abroad generally, see Kathleen Burk, *Britain, America and the Sinews of War 1914–1918* (London: Allen & Unwin, 1985); Neilson, *Strategy and Supply, passim*, and Avner Offer, *The First World War: An Agrarian Interpretation* (Oxford: Clarendon, 1989). On Anglo-American relations generally, see C.M. Mason, 'Anglo-American relations: Mediation and "Permanent Peace"', in Hinsley (ed.), *British Foreign Policy*, pp. 466–87.

103. K. Neilson and B.J.C. McKercher, '"The Triumph of Unarmed Force": Sweden and the Allied Blockade of Germany 1914–17', *Journal of Strategic Studies*, 7 (1984), pp. 178–99.

104. Grey to Rosebery, private letter, 7 February 1915, NLS, Rosebery Papers, MS 10028; Sibyl Crowe and Edward Corp, *Our Ablest Public Servant. Sir Eyre Crowe GCB, GCMG, KCMG 1864–1925* (Braunton, Devon: Merlin Books, 1993), pp. 274–302.

105. Zara Steiner, 'The Foreign Office and the War', in Hinsley (ed.), *British Foreign Policy*, pp. 516–31; R. Warman, 'The Erosion of Foreign Office Influence in the Making of Foreign Policy', *Historical Journal*, 15 (1972), pp. 133–59.

106. Hardinge to Errington, letter, 27 June 1916, CUL, Hardinge Papers, vol. 22.

107. For example, see Grey to Haldane, private letter, 25 December 1914, NLS, Haldane Papers, MS 5910 and Grey to Crewe (substituting for Grey at the FO), private letter, CUL, Crewe Papers, C/17.

108. Grey to Rosebery, private letter, 10 December 1916, NLS, Rosebery Papers, MS 10028.

109. John W. Coogan and Peter F. Coogan, 'The British Cabinet and the Anglo-French Staff Talks, 1904–1914: Who Knew What and When Did He Know It?', *Journal of British Studies*, 24 (1985), pp. 110–31.

110. John B. Osborne, 'Wilfred G. Thesiger, Sir Edward Grey, and the British Campaign to Reform the Congo, 1905–9', *Journal of Imperial and Commonwealth History*, 27, 1 (1999), pp. 59–80; Morel to Cromer, private letter, 14 February 1908, PRO, Cromer Papers, FO 633/18.

111. A.J.P. Taylor, *The Troublemakers: Dissent over Foreign Policy 1792–1939* (paperback edn, Harmondsworth: Penguin, 1985), p. 125.

112. Nicely summarized and commented upon in Michael G. Fry, *Lloyd George and Foreign Policy*, Vol. I: *The Education of a Statesman: 1890–1916* (Montreal and London: McGill-Queen's University Press, 1977), pp. 68–70.

113. See the informative Joseph Charles Heim, 'Liberalism and the Establishment of Collective Security in British Foreign Policy', *Transactions of the Royal Historical Society*, sixth series, V (1995), pp. 91–110.

114. See the discussion in Neilson, *Britain and the Last Tsar*, pp. 48–50.

115. On the incident, see Gordon Martel, *Imperial Diplomacy. Rosebery and the Failure of Foreign Policy* (Montreal and Kingston: McGill-Queen's University Press, 1986), pp. 80–7.

116. The following is informed by Keith Robbins, 'Sir Edward Grey and the British Empire', *Journal of Imperial and Commonwealth History*, 1, 2 (1973), pp. 213–22.

117. Grey to C.P. Scott (editor, *Manchester Guardian*), private letter, 21 September 1912, PRO, Grey Papers, FO 800/111.

118. T.G. Otte, 'Great Britain, Germany, and the Far-Eastern Crisis of 1897–8', *English Historical Review*, 90, 439 (1995), pp. 1157–79.
119. Neilson, *Britain and the Last Tsar*, pp. 203–37.
120. See Lansdowne to Balfour, private letter, 12 December 1901, BL, Balfour Papers, Add MSS 49727; L. Mallet (Lansdowne's précis writer) to Sandars (Balfour's private secretary), private letter, 21 March 1905, Bodleian, Sandars Papers, MS Eng hist. c 749.
121. The argument made by Keith Wilson, 'The Making and Putative Implementation of a British Foreign Policy of Gesture, December 1905 to August 1914: The Anglo-French Entente Revisited', *Canadian Journal of History*, 31 (1996), that Grey maintained the Anglo-French Entente at the risk of war ('For the Liberal Imperialists, war with Germany was preferable to isolation.', p. 254) seems a perverse interpretation of Grey's policy and one that misunderstands the motivations behind it.
122. Clearly outlined in D. French, *British Strategy and War Aims: 1914–1916* (London: Unwin & Allen, 1986), pp. 21–3.
123. Keith Wilson, 'Imperial interests in the British Decision for War, 1914: The Defence of India in Central Asia', *Review of International Studies*, 10 (1984), pp. 189–203.

7
Austen Chamberlain

Richard S. Grayson

I am much more of an 'Européen' than most of my countrymen, for I have a clearer perception than they of the inextricable way in which our interests are bound up with every possibility of the European situation.

Austen Chamberlain to William Tyrrell, 19 September 1927[1]

Austen Chamberlain's reputation is one of those great oddities of historiography. He is known primarily for what he did not do, for whom he was not, and for the qualities he did not have. Thus we know much of the man who was the only leader of the Conservative Party in the twentieth century (prior to William Hague) never to be Prime Minister. We are also familiar with him as the other Chamberlain, neither Neville nor Joe. And the fact that we know this information above all else is explained by his lack of ambition for top jobs. All we need to know of Austen seems to have been told by the altogether wittier and more momentous Winston Churchill and his 1935 epithet: 'Poor man, he always plays the game and never wins it.'[2]

Yet Austen's career was far from devoid of achievement. He may not have been Prime Minister, but he did at least lead his party – something that the likes of great Conservatives from R.A. Butler to Michael Heseltine and Kenneth Clarke would envy. And he held a succession of senior Cabinet positions. In particular, he was longer in office than any other Foreign Secretary of the inter-war years, in the second Baldwin government of November 1924 to June 1929. He was certainly no mere time server in this post, being one of the most active Foreign Secretaries of the era, negotiating not only the Locarno Agreements, but subsequently playing a major role in European diplomacy and the League of Nations.

That he had to deal with significant challenges is undoubted. Far from being a period of calm, the mid to late 1920s were eventful in international history. As for significant treaties, we can look to the Locarno agreements of

1925, and the Kellogg–Briand pact of 1928; in imperial affairs, there were further moves towards Egyptian independence and the eventful Imperial Conference of 1926. There were also flashpoints a plenty, especially in China, where the civil war led to the despatch of 13 000 British troops to Shanghai in 1927. War with Turkey over Mosul in northern Iraq briefly threatened, and was, perhaps, only narrowly avoided. And in the League of Nations, disarmament and the League's developing authority had high profiles.

Of greatest interest to Chamberlain among these problems was Europe, specifically Western Europe. It is argued here that Chamberlain's foreign policy was a cogent attempt to tackle the problems of inter-war Europe, especially the questions left open or unanswered by the peace treaties. It was based on a clear view that British interests depended upon a stable and secure Western Europe, and that Britain was influential enough to play a major role in European diplomacy to bring this about. As such, Chamberlain deserves a prominent place in the pantheon of twentieth-century British foreign policy-makers.

This essay will examine first, the mindset with which Chamberlain approached these problems; second, the nature of the diplomatic machinery in place; and third, how he tackled the numerous extra-European difficulties that he faced. It then focuses on the core aspects of Chamberlain's policy: Western Europe and the League of Nations.

Chamberlain and the Foreign Office

It has often been said (now and by contemporaries) that Chamberlain's policy was profoundly influenced by his love of French culture, and a personal hostility to the German way of doing things. Soon after leaving Cambridge in 1885, he had travelled around France and Germany. His fondness for all things French is contrasted with his opinions of Germany and a passage from a letter he wrote home in 1887: 'I fear my generation of Germans, and those a little younger will be far more high-handed and will presume far more on the victories of '66 and '70 than those who won them.'[3]

What impact did this have on his policy? First, one should note that Chamberlain's fears of Germany were proved justified, both in his generation and another. As Woody Allen is often quoted as saying, 'Just because you're paranoid, it doesn't mean nobody is out to get you.' But key to an understanding of Chamberlain's views in his formative years is not his hostility towards Germany, or his love of French culture. Rather, it is that he saw the problems France might cause. In the same letter enunciating his fear of Germany, he added that some there were 'as bad as the French military school'.[4] For Austen, a preference between the two countries certainly existed; but it was far more about holiday destinations and culture, than suitability as allies. There was also a substantial gap, in experience and development, between the travelling student of 1887 and the man who became Foreign Secretary 37 years later.

The main impact on his politics by that time was the extent to which he had become convinced in the early 1920s that Britain's main interests lay in securing European stability. He supported Keynes' plans for the financial reconstruction of Europe, and accepted the arguments of *The Economic Consequences of the Peace*. In June 1920, when Britain's future relations with France and Belgium were on the agenda, Chamberlain argued strongly that Britain should make a pact with both, in order to show the world (and its own people) the circumstances in which Britain would fight.[5] He was already standing out: although nobody in the Cabinet thought Britain did not have interests in Europe, Chamberlain was committed to that tradition of opinion which argued for active involvement there.

The other major impact on Chamberlain's mindset might be expected to have been his strong support for the family cause: tariff reform. But in fact, when it proved such an unpopular cause in the December 1923 general election, the realist in Chamberlain came to the fore. He successfully proposed that the Conservative Party reaffirm its long-term commitment to tariffs, but state that, since the public was opposed to them at present, they would not be put forward.[6] When one looks later for the influence of Joseph Chamberlain on his eldest son's foreign policy, and finds it lacking, one must return to this dropping of tariffs in February 1924. Later, when commercial matters demanded his attention, he made no attempt to resist the free trade orthodoxy of the Foreign Office. Furthermore, for Austen, imperial unity never had the emotional appeal it held for his father. Rather than an ideal in itself, it was an element of tariff reform, and does not appear to have had any existence outside the scheme. With the dropping of tariff reform, he had no clear idea either of how to bring about imperial unity, or that it was a burning issue at all. Faced with the necessities of European diplomacy, the idea was cast aside.

Arriving at the Foreign Office in November 1924, Chamberlain took over a department that had changed much since the Great War – in the light of great public hostility (notably through the Union of Democratic Control) towards 'secret diplomacy'. The war-time structure had been dismantled and replaced with six new departments: Eastern, Western, Central, Northern, American and Far Eastern. The Foreign Office and diplomatic service had been amalgamated to improve efficiency and standards through interchanging staff. A more efficient system for registering documents received was introduced, providing policy-makers with more information than ever before. And finally, not through conscious change by the Foreign Office but more as a reflection of broader social changes, the social and educational backgrounds of staff altered over 1919–29. There were at least six recruits from state grammar schools, and the number of Old Etonians decreased – they had represented 67 per cent of entrants in 1909–14, but only 24 per cent in 1929.[7]

The reforms did little to create a 'new' diplomacy. But, there is no doubt the Foreign Office inherited by Chamberlain in November 1924 was more efficient than before the war. Chamberlain's main point of contact with the system was via the four senior staff members: a Permanent Under-Secretary, and three assistant under-secretaries. In 1924, the Permanent Under-Secretary was Eyre Crowe. On his death in 1925, he was succeeded by one of the three assistants, William Tyrrell. When he left to become Ambassador to Paris in 1928, he was replaced by Ronald Lindsay, who moved from the Berlin embassy.[8]

The policy-making sections of the Chamberlain Foreign Office were the seven political departments, each dealing with a specific geographical area, though the Western Department also covered the League and general matters. These departments reported to the Foreign Secretary via under-secretaries. In departments, reports from abroad were interpreted by clerks, and policy options were formulated through minutes and memoranda. Differences of opinion between clerks were dealt with by a minute from the department head, covering the pros and cons of each view. Information was then relayed to the Foreign Secretary via the Permanent Under-Secretary, his Deputy and two assistants. The Foreign Secretary could take a variety of actions: endorse the views received, decide between conflicting views, ask for further information, or offer his own suggestions. As we shall see, Chamberlain did all at different times.

There was much more to the resources at Chamberlain's disposal than the Foreign Office – mainly the embassies, consulates and legations abroad. At the end of 1924, there were nine embassies: the most important were those in the capitals of the great powers – France, Germany, Italy, Japan and the US. Embassies were also found in Belgium, Brazil, Spain and Portugal, while the legation in Argentina received embassy status in 1927. Each embassy acted not only as the contact point between London and foreign capitals. They also spent much time entertaining, and coordinated the activities of local offices. The French and German embassies were a little separate from the rest. Certainly they had the closest contact with Chamberlain, although it is fair to say, too, that he often bypassed them by dealing with Briand and Stresemann direct, or occasionally via the French and German embassies in London.

It was not only the Foreign Office that had a role in foreign policy with the British government machine. The Colonial Office was the department with which the Foreign Office had most contact. This was followed, although by no means closely, by the service departments, the India Office and the Board of Trade. Of course, the highest profile matters concerning more than one department were often resolved in Cabinet by ministers; but many areas were dealt with by civil servants, either by exchanging letters and minutes, or through inter-departmental meetings, sometimes described as conferences. The latter were most important when treaties were negotiated. Meanwhile, the Treasury had an influence via inter-departmental conferences, and especially via the Chancellor, Winston Churchill, in Cabinet.

Following the end of the Great War, the Dominions became increasingly assertive in foreign affairs. Thus, in 1924 the position of the empire in the making of foreign policy was in a state of flux, and it remained so until at least the Statute of Westminster in 1931, a period covered by some excellent studies.[9] In the 1924–29 period, forms of consultation were agreed, but Chamberlain essentially wanted to prevent the Dominions from restricting his freedom of action, and the Dominions were not an important part of the diplomatic machine, and nor did they wish to be.

Many of the most important foreign policy debates took place in Cabinet, and foreign affairs accounted for much Cabinet time.[10] Here, in terms of experience in the House of Commons, Chamberlain was the most senior member, having served longer than any of his colleagues still in the Commons, although Churchill had had a longer ministerial career. However, he did not represent any particular section of the Conservative Party, so his position came from his personal reputation and his office. Nevertheless, he had been found important enough by Baldwin to be brought into the Cabinet in a senior position. Baldwin himself, in accordance with his general style, gave Chamberlain a free hand. The extent of Cabinet influence on policy varied according to the issue; but when necessary, and sometimes with Baldwin's support, Chamberlain was able to fight off strong attempts at interference by colleagues such as Churchill.

Non-European policy

Chamberlain was at his least creative, and most reliant on the foreign policy machine, when it came to non-European affairs. Throughout his term of office, Chamberlain faced several crises in this field. In Egypt, he was one of many British politicians managing a gradual reduction of British influence. With regard to Mosul in northern Iraq, he was one of several ministers involved in maintaining the province as part of Iraq, while avoiding war with rival claimant, Turkey. Anglo-American relations took some time too, especially with protracted negotiations over naval disarmament. These issues have been covered in detail elsewhere,[11] and rather than take a cursory glance at each, this essay examines Chamberlain's China policy, to illustrate the varying nature of his control on and interest in non-European affairs.

Britain was involved in China through a long-term trade presence and a commitment made at the Washington Conference in 1922 to give China control of its own tariffs, which were controlled by the 'Powers' in China, principally, Britain, the US, France and Japan. This was complicated by the Chinese civil war. As a result, in 1924–29 Britain appeased the Chinese, making concessions both to maintain Britain's vital interests, and to undermine the Communists.

Chamberlain's main role was as a crisis-manager. For example, at the end of May 1925, after the killing of seven Chinese demonstrators by the British police in Shanghai, a wave of anti-British strikes and boycotts broke out across southern China and Hong Kong. These involved organized attempts to prevent Chinese handling or purchasing of British goods. As the Foreign Office discussed how to respond, Chamberlain led the way, setting clear guidelines and taking part in drafting communications to Shanghai; he felt as able as his staff to formulate a response to the riots. However, the policy he advocated was one of leaving most matters to the local consuls: 'We can give those on the spot only the broadest directions – & our confidence & support.' Later, he showed he had a particular approach in his mind when he noted, 'Our proper (& most difficult) duty is to steer a course between refusal to do anything because of the strikes, riots, murders & yielding or appearing to yield because of the same events.' Thus, he adopted the advice of George Moss (of the Far Eastern Department) that the Peking government should be told Britain would negotiate on treaty revision when order was restored.[12]

Despite being primarily a crisis-manager, Chamberlain did make one specific contribution to Britain's China policy: he was a keen advocate of international cooperation. Publicly, he laid greater emphasis than any of his advisers had done on the necessity of international cooperation. He was perhaps influenced by the Chiefs of Staff, who said, 'it is essential to realise that offensive action on a large scale is not possible in China for the British Empire acting alone. China is a vast country offering no decisive military objective.' But Chamberlain made the idea his own and consistently argued that only international action, with Japan as the leading participant, could have any significant effect. This case had to be made against background noise from Cabinet colleagues that independent action might be necessary.[13]

On long-term China policy, Chamberlain was guided in part by Britain's Peking legation. When a tariff conference met towards the end of 1925, Chamberlain insisted that not only details, but also decisions over practicality be left to the legation. The conference eventually ground to a halt, but it had been a clear sign of Chamberlain trusting the man-on-the-spot rather than the Foreign Office.[14]

With the failure of the tariff conference, new long-term policies were needed. Here, the Foreign Office had the upper hand, as Chamberlain left them in charge of discussing how to grant tariff autonomy to the Chinese. Essentially, the Foreign Office decided that unilaterally doing so would be the best option. Amery was prompted to write to Baldwin, on 18 September 1926:

To be quite frank I cannot help feeling that Austen is so preoccupied with the League and all these tiresome and trivial European issues (for in the long run they are mostly trivial for our point of view), and his talks with Briand, Stresemann and the rest of them that he is inclined to leave the extra European things to the Department which on this particular matter is hopelessly weak.[15]

The Cabinet, with some apprehension, backed the unilateral option. It was a policy developed almost entirely by the Foreign Office.

The Cabinet did not let this position go unchallenged however. In 1927, the Cabinet asserted itself in a way it had not done previously on Chinese matters, and in February Chamberlain lost a major dispute. This arose from a mob attack, probably Communist-led, on the British concession at Hankow, during which a local decision was made for the British force to withdraw. At first this looked erroneous, but it was soon felt to have averted much bloodshed.[16] Now, however, many feared that when Nationalist troops reached Shanghai, there would be similar problems. Since all agreed Shanghai was the most important British interest in China, plans were made to protect it, with 13 000 troops, along with tanks and aeroplanes.

But even though troops had been sent, the Cabinet had not firmly stated they should be landed at Shanghai; this caused a Cabinet controversy in which Chamberlain was defeated. The Foreign Office felt none should be landed until absolutely necessary, as their presence would anger the Chinese.[17] Amery spoke against Chamberlain, saying Britain should not bow to threats, and he felt he was carrying the Cabinet; but Balfour constructed a compromise whereby the troops would stop at Hong Kong under the guise of allowing time to consult the Japanese. This proposal defeated a suggestion from Amery that one brigade land, although only by Baldwin's casting vote. Balfour's plan then defeated Chamberlain's own proposal by one vote. It was a major defeat for Chamberlain. As his brother noted, 'he couldn't find one single member of the Cabinet to approve what he wanted to do'.[18]

Perhaps because of this, Chamberlain later took a more hawkish position on Chinese affairs, opposing the Foreign Office by urging the use of troops later in 1927–29, as Nationalist influence spread throughout China. Nevertheless, the core of Britain's China policy in 1924–29 was initiated by the Foreign Office, even if Chamberlain had proved to be a hands-on, and sometimes effective, crisis-manager.

Locarno

If Chamberlain's control varied outside Europe, he never loosened his grip on Continental policy. His European policy had two stages: first, he aimed to calm French fears about being attacked by Germany. This process reached its fruition at Locarno. But his policy did not stop there. It had a second stage – having calmed France, Chamberlain aimed to further stabilize Europe by persuading the French to make concessions on what he perceived to be legitimate German concerns on matters such as troop evacuation. This depended upon a significant diplomatic involvement in Europe – far more

that the first thought of Castlereagh after 1815 was to restore the Concert of Europe, & that the more ambitious peacemakers of Versailles, when they framed the Covenant, still left a gap which only a new Concert of Europe can fill. For this reason amongst others ... I should rejoice to see Germany join the League & take her seat at the Council.[65]

In November 1926, on his installation as Rector of the University of Glasgow, Chamberlain developed this: he spoke of the special position of the great powers in the League, and was adamant that nothing could be achieved if the great powers were divided into two camps.[66] In effect, he was arguing that Britain, France, Germany, Italy and Japan should take on the leadership of the League, whilst at the same time recognizing the necessity of involving other nations. This is also clear from a minute written two months before, in which Chamberlain declined German proposals to pre-arrange the Assembly's agenda on the grounds that 'the League is an assembly of equals. There may be some who are first among their equals ... but we, Great Powers within the League ... know that if we do not recognise the equality of all powers, the Assembly will not recognise the primacy of the Great Powers.'[67]

There was certainly much gradualism in Chamberlain's views. In 1927, he wrote that he wanted the League to 'develop slowly and naturally, to avoid radical changes and ambitious attempts to recast its constitution, to pray that it may not have to face a great crisis until it is much more firmly established'.[68] Significantly, Chamberlain was opposed to American entry, showing he had clearly thought about what would strengthen the League, and what would not. He wrote, 'I am by no means persuaded that, in the present stage of their constitutional development, the accession of the United States to the League would be of advantage to the latter.' This was because the Senate would insist on examining every piece of League business in which American representatives were involved. It would tie American Council members so much that their presence at Geneva would throw the League into confusion.[69] All this suggests Chamberlain saw limits on the League, and saw the great powers as most important within it. But it also shows Chamberlain believed it *could* be developed and *wanted* to do so. His view of the League, then, may be summarized as 'hopeful pessimism' but certainly not 'hostility'.

Chamberlain initially had no plan for involving the League extensively in policy. But he became impressed by the work of its committees, its handling of the Greco-Bulgarian dispute in October 1925, and its work in the Mosul crisis in 1926.[70] Meanwhile, Locarno had given the League a higher profile as Germany was to become a member. When Germany thus joined in September 1926 (after some controversy[71]), the prestige of the League was much increased, and a new Concert was established. But what did this mean? Primarily, Chamberlain saw the Concert as a way of making the League work; in no way did it replace the League. Because of this, it is argued here that the importance of the so-called Geneva tea-parties has, in the context of the League, been overestimated by Jacobson and Walters.

As for the details of the tea-parties, that the meetings were held in Geneva, and often took place at tea-time is not in question; but much else is. When we look at the meetings it is clear that many issues, which could have been discussed if the Locarnites were seeking to manage business themselves, were not. These include prominent items such as matters relating to Danzig (March, June, September and December 1927), the Memel Convention (June 1927), minorities in Greece and Albania (June 1928), and the system to be used for electing non-permanent Council members (December 1926). Tea-parties also never discussed a request from Chamberlain, supported by the League's Secretary-General, Eric Drummond,[72] to reduce the number of Council sessions from five to four per year,[73] to enable foreign ministers to attend regularly. It was originally proposed in March 1927, and finally agreed to in November 1929, after Chamberlain had left office. Throughout, no discussions were held privately.

So what was discussed at the tea-parties? After German entry to the League, the first took place in December 1926, attended by Chamberlain, Briand, Stresemann, and the representatives of Belgium, Italy and Japan.[74] The inclusion of Italy and Belgium was because of their role as Locarnites; and although it could be argued that Japan was there as a great power, it also had a role in the implementation of Versailles, which was to be discussed. These December 1926 meetings reveal that the participants were not usurping the Council's authority or arranging League business amongst themselves. In fact, they discussed only military control in Germany. This was an issue concerning only those at the tea-party, and it is difficult to imagine how it could have been solved more easily in high-profile discussion at the Council table.

Following this, Chamberlain used the meetings to foster good relations and understanding between the leaders of the Locarno powers. For example, he spoke of how a meeting of himself, Briand, Stresemann and Mussolini might stop the latter feeling as isolated as he was said to feel from European affairs.[75] But this did not undermine the League; rather, it was part of an attempt to bring Mussolini more into it, perhaps to avoid a repeat of the Corfu occupation in 1923. Chamberlain seemed to be succeeding when Mussolini sent a senior adviser to work for the League's secretariat, and pledged to pursue a 'League policy'.[76]

The controversy between Italy and Yugoslavia also sheds light on the tea-parties. Walters cites it as a clear example of the Locarnites preventing the Council from discussing matters which might embarrass them. In this instance, Italy had accused Yugoslavia of preparing for war against Albania, and had made representations to the Locarnites without indicating what they should do. Germany had suggested, tentatively, that the Council might consider the matter, but Mussolini was set firm against any such idea.

Chamberlain had long taken the view that, '*it is essential* that we should keep Italy, a growing power, in sympathy with our policy & in cooperation with us. This may be vital in the future either to maintain peace in Europe or to restrain or guide Italy outside Europe.'[77] As part of this general appeasement, Chamberlain believed it was important not to make Mussolini hostile to the League. On this particular occasion he also believed the League could inflame the situation by 'still further exciting public opinion and giving rise to a fresh crop of rumours'. Meanwhile, Briand took the view that there was no clear way in which the League could intervene. Both were probably right, and Stresemann agreed. After a flurry of communications between ambassadors and foreign ministers, it was decided there should be no reference to the League. Walters' argument is that the Council could have considered the Italian accusations, but that, to save Mussolini's face, the Locarnites rallied around and prevented this from taking place. However, it is unclear how the League could have helped; and the episode is more significant as an example of Chamberlain's belief that a referral to the League could in some cases worsen a situation by entrenching the positions of those in dispute. In the event, Italy and Yugoslavia agreed to discuss the matter and the situation was calmed.[78] The League might only have got in the way, and might not have made any capital for itself.

At the June 1927 Council, there were two 'tea-parties'. Chamberlain, Stresemann, Briand, Vandervelde (Belgium), Scialoja (Italy) and Ishii (Japan) met, after Stresemann asked for a meeting to discuss the effects of Britain's recent diplomatic breach with the Soviets. This was the principal item of discussion, and one that could not have come before the League without raising the stakes. However, they also considered a further Yugoslav–Albanian dispute, which had arisen out of the Albanian arrest of a Yugoslav, Vúko Juraskovitch, on charges of espionage. Yugoslavia sent a strong note of protest, and diplomatic relations were broken off on 4 June. It was agreed at the meeting that whilst France could try to influence Yugoslavia, Italy could do the same in Albania; Stresemann later said he would instruct the German ministers in both countries to act with their French and Italian colleagues.[79]

All this was aimed at calming matters which were not yet serious enough for the Council, rather than undermining the League; as Briand was later to say in public, 'I consider it desirable to deal outside the League of Nations with such international differences as can be settled by the normal processes of diplomacy before they constitute any real danger to peace.'[80] This approach was successful, as Juraskovitch was released in July, and diplomatic relations were resumed in August.[81] Soviet threats to Poland were also discussed at this tea-party, and Stresemann promised to make representations to Moscow. Once again, though, this was a matter that could not be brought before the Council easily. Nor could the Franco-German matters discussed later in the same session.[82] None of this can indicate Chamberlain's hostility to the League. In fact, it shows a real concern for gradual development of that organization.

Conclusion

Chamberlain arrived at the Foreign Office in 1924 with an awkward position in the Conservative Party, as a failed leader who nevertheless had a senior position. Because of this, his return to the fold necessitated high office, and he wielded strong influence in the Cabinet on many issues. Except for difficult moments in 1924–25, he was totally in command of Western European issues, and was able to pursue a policy of first calming France through a guarantee of French security at Locarno, and then calming Germany. This he did through assisting Stresemann to further his limited aims on troop reductions and reparations, especially by successfully pressurizing Briand into making concessions. Of Chamberlain's judgement of Stresemann's intentions, which remain an open question, one must add that, as now, nobody in Europe in the 1920s knew exactly what they were, and it is quite possible Chamberlain was correct. All of this represented a strong Continental commitment by Britain to a European diplomatic role. In no sense can it be said that Chamberlain's active approach to European policy in 1925 was not matched by a similar record in 1926–29. Aside from this strong commitment, the other main feature of Chamberlain's policy was to develop the League of Nations, partly through a revived Concert of Europe, which was able to strengthen the League in its weaker moments.

As the longest-serving inter-war Foreign Secretary, Chamberlain emerges well from comparison with his predecessors and successors. Ramsay MacDonald was successful over the French evacuation of the Ruhr and the Dawes Plan, but his plan for security, the Geneva Protocol, was fraught with difficulty, and he did not have to deal with the challenges that faced Chamberlain outside Europe. Some saw Curzon as a disaster because of his effect on Anglo-French relations. Meanwhile, none of the Foreign Secretaries in the 1930s, except for Halifax in 1939,[83] were to be as influential as Chamberlain, and although faced with graver problems, they arranged nothing to rival Locarno.

How Chamberlain would have fared in the 1930s is an interesting point for speculation. But, his actual record as Foreign Secretary must go a long way to rescuing his reputation, despite his lack of success as a domestic politician. Many facile comparisons have been made between Austen and his father, one of Britain's most talented politicians; unsurprisingly, the comparison has always been unfavourable to Austen. Yet, as Neville Chamberlain had pointed out, a more appropriate comparison would be to assess Austen by the standards of a Grey or a Salisbury.[84] Judged in this way, Chamberlain's record in 1924–29 at least matches their tenures at the Foreign Office. Locarno alone is a significant factor in Chamberlain's favour. This interpretation of Chamberlain's worth does not overlook his failings in domestic politics; but it does suggest that his attributes were more suited to foreign affairs, and that his understanding of the issues was considerable. Both enabled him to achieve significant successes.

The picture of Chamberlain in 1924–29 is of a Foreign Secretary who successfully managed to commit Britain to a European diplomatic role, believing the greatest threat to peace lay there. He also played a large part in the League of Nations, and had views on how to develop it. In all of this, he was accused by colleagues like Amery of neglecting British interests in the rest of the world. It is difficult to see how this was so, for he always took a lead when crises developed, while allowing the experts to plan more complicated matters.

Amery's hostility to Chamberlain's *Weltanschauung* was based on the Colonial Secretary's consistent stand in the 1920s against a European role for Britain. It is a debate that remains at the heart of British politics today. In particular, this has implications for the historiography of the Conservative Party. It is now more widely recognized that factionalism within the Conservative Party is deeply rooted in attitudes to Britain's place in the world. When I first wrote on Austen Chamberlain, that debate looked unresolved as far as the Conservative Party's internal politics were concerned. Five years on, it seems that Amery would be a happy man if he could see his party.

Austen Chamberlain would be less pleased at the extent to which his tradition has been left behind by the Conservative Party. As John Charmley has persuasively argued, it is profoundly mistaken to see commitment to an active role in European diplomacy as *the* traditional Conservative policy, let alone the traditional British policy.[85] Nevertheless, it is undeniable that it is *a* tradition that has been strong and vibrant throughout Liberal, Conservative and social democratic politics in Britain. Periodically, as in 1924–29, it has had a decisive impact on the policy of the nation. That makes Austen Chamberlain all the more important in the story of Britain's relationship with Europe.

Notes

1. Austen Chamberlain to William Tyrrell, 19 September 1927, Austen Chamberlain Mss, P[ublic] R[ecord] O[ffice], FO 800/261/330–41.
2. Churchill to Clementine Churchill, in Martin Gilbert (ed.), *Winston S. Churchill, Volume V, Companion Part II: The Wilderness Years, 1929–1935* (London: Heinemann, 1981), p. 1363.
3. Richard S. Grayson, *Austen Chamberlain and the Commitment to Europe: British Foreign Policy, 1924–29* (London: Frank Cass, 1997), pp. 2–3 and 32.
4. Austen Chamberlain, *Down the Years* (London: Cassell, 1935), p. 44.
5. Grayson, pp. 4–5.
6. Grayson, pp. 7–8.
7. Zara Steiner and M.L. Dockrill, 'The Foreign Office Reforms, 1919–1921', *Historical Journal*, vol. XVII, no. 1 (1974), pp. 131–56.

8. For staff biographies, see, G.E.P. Hertslet (ed.), *The Foreign Office List and Diplomatic and Consular Year Book* (London: Harrison, 1925 *et seq.*).
9. See Grayson, p. 30, n. 60.
10. An approximate count shows that 408 of 1850 (22 per cent) Cabinet papers covered foreign affairs. In 1924–26, this figure was 179 of 1050 (17 per cent); in 1927–29, 229 of 800 (29 per cent).
11. See Grayson, Chapter 8 on Mosul and Egypt, Chapter 6 on the US.
12. Grayson, p. 176.
13. Grayson, p. 177.
14. Grayson, pp. 179–81.
15. Leo Amery to Stanley Baldwin, 18 September 1926, Baldwin Mss, Cambridge University Library, Baldwin 115, ff. 120–3.
16. Consul General Goffe to Foreign Office, 3 January 1927 and Austen Chamberlain to Miles Lampson, 6 January 1927, PRO, Foreign Office Papers, Foreign Office 371/12430, F 67 and 96/67/10.
17. Foreign Office Memorandum, 22 January 1927, PRO, Foreign Office 371/12450, F 656/156/10.
18. Minutes of meeting of 4 February 1927, CC 7(27), PRO, Cabinet Papers, CAB 23/54. *Amery Diaries* pp. 494–5; Neville Chamberlain to Hilda Chamberlain, 5 February 1927, Chamberlain Mss, Birmingham University Library, NC 18/1/561.
19. Austen Chamberlain minute, 4 January 1925, W.N. Medlicott and Douglas Dakin (eds), *Documents on British Foreign Policy*, First Series, Vol. XXVII, (1986), no. 180.
20. F.G. Stambrook, '"Das Kind": Lord D'Abernon and the Origins of the Locarno Pact', *Central European History*, Vol. 1 (1968), p. 253; Neville Chamberlain diary, 22 October 1925, Chamberlain Mss, Birmingham University Library, NC 2/21; Viscount D'Abernon to Lady D'Abernon, 2 December 1925, D'Abernon Mss, British Library, Add. MS 48936, ff. 204–5.
21. Viscount D'Abernon to Austen Chamberlain, 20 and 23 January and 10 February 1925; Viscount Crewe to Austen Chamberlain, 13 February 1925, W.N. Medlicott and D. Dakin (eds), *Documents on British Foreign Policy, 1919–1939*, (*DBFP*), first series, vol. 27 (London: HMSO, 1986), I, XXVII, nos 189, 194, 197 and 198.
22. Austen Chamberlain to Viscount Crewe, 16 February 1925, *DBFP*, 1, XXVII, no. 200.
23. Central Department Memorandum, 9 March 1925, PRO, Foreign Office 371/10756, C 3539/3539/18.
24. Austen Chamberlain note, 20 January 1925, *DBFP*, I, XXVII, no. 188.
25. Erik Goldstein, 'The Evolution of British Diplomatic Strategy for the Locarno Pact, 1924–1925', in Michael Dockrill and Brian McKercher (eds), *Diplomacy and World Power: Studies in British Foreign Policy, 1890–1950*, (Cambridge: CUP, 1996), p. 118.
26. Stephen Roskill, *Hankey: Man of Secrets, Vol. II, 1919–1931*, (London: Collins, 1972), p. 396.
27. Austen Chamberlain to D'Abernon, 2 April and 7 May 1925, *DBFP*, I, XXVII, nos 283 and 313.
28. Austen Chamberlain to Viscount Crewe, 2 April 1925, Chamberlain Mss, PRO, Foreign Office 800/257/483.
29. A.J. Balfour to Austen Chamberlain, 16 October 1925, Chamberlain Mss, Birmingham University Library, AC 37/24.
30. Georges Suarez, *Briand, sa vie, son œuvre, avec son journal, VI: L'artisan de la paix, 1923–32*, (Paris: Plon, 1952), p. 134; Anthony Adamthwaite, *Grandeur and Misery: France's Bid for Power in Europe, 1914–1940*, (London: Arnold, 1995), pp. 121–2.

31. *Hansard*, 5th Series, 188, col. 420.
32. Viscount Cecil to Marquess of Salisbury, 8 November 1925, Cecil Mss, British Library, Add. MSS 51085, ff. 69–70.
33. Austen Chamberlain to Ida Chamberlain, 31 October 1925, Chamberlain Mss, Birmingham University Library, AC 5/1/367.
34. Sally Marks, *The Illusion of Peace: International Relations in Europe, 1918–1933* (London: Macmillan, 1976), p. 74; Jon Jacobson, *Locarno Diplomacy: Germany and the West, 1925–1929* (Princeton: Princeton University Press, 1972), p. 373.
35. Austen Chamberlain to Crewe, 2 April 1925, Chamberlain Mss, PRO, Foreign Office 800/257/483.
36. Jacobson, *Locarno Diplomacy*, pp. 119–23; *The Times*, 19 May 1927, p. 14.
37. Martin Gilbert, *The Roots of Appeasement* (London: Weidenfeld & Nicolson, 1966), p. 119.
38. Goldstein, p. 135.
39. Austen Chamberlain to Viscount Crewe, 16 August 1926, W.N. Medlicott and Douglas Dakin (eds), *Documents on British Foreign Policy*, Series IA, Vol. II, (1968), no. 15 3.
40. For detailed discussion of the merits of Chamberlain's approach to Stresemann, see Grayson, pp. 117–20.
41. Grayson, pp. 118–19.
42. Austen Chamberlain to Viscount D'Abernon, 2 February 1926; Austen Chamberlain to Viscount Crewe, 31 March 1926; Austen Chamberlain to Viscount D'Abernon, 23 April 1926, W.N. Medlicott and Douglas Dakin, (eds), *Documents on British Foreign Policy*, Series IA, Volume I, (1966), nos 236, 386 and 455.
43. Austen Chamberlain to Viscount D'Abernon, 28 July 1926, *DBFP*, IA, II, no. 107.
44. Austen Chamberlain to Briand, 29 July 1926, Chamberlain Mss, PRO, Foreign Office 800/259/668–678.
45. Grayson, pp. 120–2.
46. Austen Chamberlain minute, 18 November 1926, PRO, Foreign Office 371/11292, C 12088/436/18.
47. Austen Chamberlain to William Tyrrell, 3 December 1926, *DBFP*, IA, II, no. 318.
48. Notes of meetings, 6, 10, 11 and 12 December 1926, *DBFP*, IA, II, nos 333, 345, 352, 353 and 355.
49. Austen Chamberlain to Ronald Lindsay, 12 January 1927, *DBFP*, IA, II, nos. 392 and 395.
50. Austen Chamberlain to Ronald Lindsay, 19 January 1927, Chamberlain Mss, Birmingham University Library, AC 54/333.
51. J.V. Perowne minute, 30 April 1929, W.N. Medlicott and Douglas Dakin (eds), *Documents on British Foreign Policy*, Series IA, Vol. V, (1973), no. 131 and n. 8.
52. Grayson, p. 130.
53. C. Howard-Smith minute, 29 July 1927, PRO, Foreign Office 371/12148, C 6402/2050/18.
54. Austen Chamberlain minute, 6 August 1927, PRO, Foreign Office 371/12148, C 6512/2050/18.
55. Viscount Crewe to Austen Chamberlain, 10 August 1927, PRO, Foreign Office 371/12149, C 6776/2050/18.
56. Grayson, p. 131.
57. Austen Chamberlain note of conversation with Briand, 13 October 1927; Austen Chamberlain to Ronald Grahame, 6 February 1928; Eric Phipps to Orme Sargent, 19 March 1928, W.N. Medlicott and Douglas Dakin (eds), *Documents on British Foreign Policy*, Series IA, Vol. IV, (1971), nos 20, 129 and 164.

58. Ronald Lindsay to Austen Chamberlain, 19 May 1928; Austen Chamberlain to Viscount Crewe, 30 May 1928; Austen Chamberlain to Harold Nicolson, 4 July 1928, *DBFP*, IA, V, nos 31, 42 and 79.

59. Austen Chamberlain to Horace Rumbold, 1 January 1929, *DBFP* Series IA, Vol. VI, (1975), no. 16.

60. Austen Chamberlain to Horace Rumbold, 24 January 1929, Chamberlain Mss, PRO, Foreign Office 800/263/234–236.

61. Josiah Stamp to Winston Churchill, 28 April 1929, PRO, Foreign Office 371/13594, C 3310/1/18.

62. Austen Chamberlain minute, 8 May 1929, PRO, Foreign Office 371/13594, C 3330/1/18.

63. F.P. Walters, *A History of the League of Nations* (Oxford: OUP, 1952, 1960 edn), pp. 339–40.

64. Jacobson, *Locarno Diplomacy* pp. 69–70; Jon Jacobson, 'The Conduct of Locarno Diplomacy', *Review of Politics*, vol. 34 (1972), pp. 67–81. Walters, *History of the League*, pp. 341–3.

65. Austen Chamberlain minute, 21 February 1925, PRO, Foreign Office 371/11064, W 1252/9/98.

66. Austen Chamberlain, *Peace in Our Time: Addresses on Europe and the Empire* (London: Philip Allan, 1928), p. 163.

67. Austen Chamberlain minute, 26 August 1926, PRO, Foreign Office 371/11898, W 8109/223/98.

68. Austen Chamberlain to F.S. Oliver, 17 January 1927, Chamberlain Mss, Birmingham University Library, AC 54/408.

69. Austen Chamberlain to Esme Howard, 25 January 1927, Chamberlain Mss, PRO, Foreign Office 800/260/131–133.

70. Grayson, pp. 82–6.

71. Grayson, pp. 86–94.

72. Eric Drummond to Austen Chamberlain, 19 and 28 March 1927, Chamberlain Mss, PRO, Foreign Office 800/260/324 and 347.

73. The Council met in March, June, September and December, with its work either side of the Assembly in September, counting as two sessions.

74. Notes of meetings, 6, 10, 11 and 12 December 1926, *DBFP*, IA, II, nos 333, 345, 352, 353 and 355.

75. Austen Chamberlain to Viscount Crewe, 7 January 1927, Chamberlain Mss, PRO, Foreign Office 800/260/57–58.

76. Austen Chamberlain to William Tyrrell, 12 September 1927, *DBFP*, IA, IV, no. 5.

77. Austen Chamberlain minute, 7 October 1926, *DBFP*, IA, II, no. 243.

78. Grayson, p. 99.

79. Grayson, pp. 99–100.

80. *The Times*, 10 August 1927, p. 10.

81. M. Epstein (ed.), *Annual Register, 1927* (London: Longman Green, 1928), p. 191.

82. Grayson, pp. 100–1.

83. John Charmley, *Chamberlain and the Lost Peace* (London: Hodder & Stoughton, 1989), pp. 163–75.

84. Robert Self (ed.), *The Austen Chamberlain Diary Letters: The Correspondence of Sir Austen Chamberlain with his Sisters, Hilda and Ida, 1916–1937* (Cambridge: CUP, 1995), p. 10.

85. John Charmley, *Splendid Isolation?: Britain and the Balance of Power, 1874–1914* (London: Hodder & Stoughton, 1999), pp. 1–7.

8
'Rat in Power': Neville Chamberlain and the Creation of British Foreign Policy, 1931–39

Greg Kennedy

> And shame and agony descend upon us
> Blacker than a 'London particular',
> Black as Chamberlain's own heart and void
> Of all comfort as his skull of a creditable brain
> The meanest man who ever sneaked into high political place ...
> Even littler
> Than Hitler!
> The rat in power![1]

The story of Neville Chamberlain, Britain's Prime Minister from 1937 to 1940, and his views and ideas about the conduct of Great Britain's strategic foreign policy in the 1930s have been the subjects of much scholarly debate.[2] Much of the scholarship has unfortunately used the red herring of appeasement as the yardstick by which to measure his performance. In its inter-war manifestation and as a medium for the appreciation of the performance of a British Prime Minister, appeasement is an intellectually bereft and unsophisticated concept. Chamberlain's ideas on how to manage Britain's strategic foreign policy and that policy's relationship to Britain's defence planning was no more an issue of appeasement than it had been for any previous Prime Minister.[3] Chamberlain's direction of Anglo-Italian relations; the resignation of Anthony Eden as Foreign Secretary; and Britain's need to deal with the strategic perils raised by Adolf Hitler's Germany were problems of national security, of which appeasement was only a part of the policy-making process.[4]

Historical judgements, starting with the 'guilty men' charges of the late 1930s, have moved forward through the revisionist and now the post-revisionist explanations for Chamberlain's actions.[5] The main objective has been to try to ascertain whether Neville Chamberlain really knew what he was doing in his attempts to run, influence and guide British strategic foreign policy, particularly in the period from 1937 to 1940. To make that judgement, his personality, prejudices, intentions, knowledge of issues, training and experience, as well as convictions as a political figure, have all been elaborated upon and dissected.[6]

The aim of this chapter is to provide a survey of Chamberlain's performance in those criteria during certain key events, not only as Prime Minister, but also as an important member of Cabinet for the entire period from 1931 to 1939, bringing back into play the ideas of morality and personality.[7] By this method we can gain an appreciation of how Chamberlain's early experiences at the Treasury affected his foreign policy decisions later on in his career. Equally, we can gain an insight into his style of decision-making in matters pertaining to strategic foreign policy, including his tendency to interfere in matters outside his own area of expertise; his violent prejudices; his narrow and dogmatic style of decision making; his supreme belief in the correctness of his own view once it was formulated; and his willingness to act without sufficient evidence. It is also important, in terms of taking the longer view of Chamberlain's involvement in policy making, to see how he allowed others under his authority to influence that process. Here, what latitude and support Chamberlain gave to the vision of men such as Warren Fisher and Frederick Leith Ross also helps to paint a clearer picture of the vision that the Chancellor/Prime Minister Chamberlain held.

Also, and perhaps more importantly, this discussion will analyse just how well Neville Chamberlain did, or did not, understand Great Britain's strategic foreign policy position and its imperial defence needs. In short, using the model put forward by David French of the important elements traditionally thought of as critical in the process of safeguarding Britain's imperial interests, did Neville Chamberlain have a solid understanding of what those requirements were?[8] Using French's wider criteria is important because Chamberlain has been traditionally portrayed as a Chancellor of the Exchequer, and later a Prime Minister, who above all else was concerned with the protection of Great Britain's economic strength. As a result, Chamberlain is supported by some economic historians as a prudent and thoughtful statesman.[9] However, economic strength was only one of the pillars of traditional British imperial defence. The fiscal and economic strength of the empire depended upon a powerful and dominant Royal Navy, able to protect that imperial trade and commerce, upon which British fiscal strength depended. And lastly, Great Britain's history as a great power spoke of the need for alliances if it were successfully to meet the challenge of protecting a global empire. So, it is important to have a clear understanding of whether or not Neville Chamberlain understood these other two elements sufficiently in his considerations on strategic foreign relations, and more importantly, how the courses of action that he put forward and defended affected the ability of those other two pillars to support that policy.[10]

Therefore, with the naval question and alliance issue in mind, it is important to note that, while the discussion has ranged far and wide over Chamberlain's personal life, his views of the European situation in the 1930s, and, to some extent, even his knowledge, or, more aptly, lack of knowledge, about matters concerning Britain's relations with nations such as the USSR and Japan, there remains a singularly large gap in much of that analysis: Chamberlain's views of and relationship with the US and its representatives.[11] Those studies that do address this particular facet of inter-war Anglo-American relations focus their attention almost entirely on Chamberlain's view of Franklin D. Roosevelt himself and the discourse between those two men, missing the more important aspect of the development of not only individual, but institutional, mental maps of that relationship.[12] Chamberlain's mental map of Franklin Roosevelt's US came into existence in 1933, when he was Chancellor of the Exchequer. From that point on, Anglo-American relations, in Chamberlain's eyes, did not resemble 'a special relationship', a reality that had already once helped Britain win a major modern war and that was seen by many other British policy-makers as being the key to Britain's survival as a first-rank, global power. The Chancellor of the Exchequer obviously had earlier assessments and appreciations of the US which he brought with him to dealing with Roosevelt's administration.[13] However, given the vast differences of style and direction between the previous American governments and Roosevelt's, 1933 was the pivotal year in the formulation of Chamberlain's views of the US.

Neville Chamberlain's initial attitude toward Franklin Roosevelt and the New Deal America was not at all favourable. In order to understand why he took such an early negative outlook towards FDR and the US, it is important to remember the ambitious and arrogant nature of Chamberlain, a man who recognized the limited time left for him to make his mark on history and to endeavour to become Britain's Prime Minister. Driven by an ego second to none and a constant desire to be at the centre of any policy-making process, Chamberlain rose to the position of Chancellor of the Exchequer in 1931. This put him in a position of great authority within Cabinet and the British policy-making elite. By January of 1932, the press of time was playing on his mind; he confided to his sister Hilda that 'I feel that this is going to be a very momentous year for me. Probably it will be the turning point or perhaps I should rather say the critical point in my political career. If I don't make a success of it I shall slowly drop back. There's some luck about it, but most depends on myself, and I am not down hearted.'[14] That view of the future led Chamberlain to develop two very important concepts of how he would operate in pursuit of his goal. The first was to tolerate no interference in his plans; an approach that soon led to a direct confrontation between the Treasury and the Foreign Office over which would control and direct Britain's foreign policy. Second, but related to the first point, Chamberlain was willing to manipulate all committees, budgetary processes, and other bodies designed to create policy by whatever means required, be that personal intervention, promise of promotion or the threat of the withholding of funds, in order to obtain his desired end.[15] He also believed that, with a weak Foreign Secretary such as Sir John Simon, matters concerning foreign affairs would always work their way around to his (Chamberlain's) point of view. Unfortunately, as one nation rarely has the ability to direct the policy or actions of another, Chamberlain's style of direction and agenda manipulation was often unsuccessful and unproductive, resulting in an inability to win Cabinet debates and bureaucratic battles in order to influence the strategic foreign policy-making process. As a result of this lack of success, he became frustrated and annoyed with things that did not go the way he envisioned.[16] The US and its position on economic issues affecting Britain, such as war debts and reparations, as well as world economics in general, and matters related to naval disarmament, proved most problematic for him.

Chamberlain's intentions regarding the payment of war debts and reparations to the US were to dodge the matter for as long as possible and, in the end, pay the Americans nothing.[17] In early January 1932, believing that no permanent settlement was possible, he suggested asking the United States for a short extension of the existing moratorium on repayment, while trying to arrange a postponement of any economic or monetary conference until Britain's position improved.[18] He believed that the US, as well as the Foreign Office, supported his proposed plan for a reduced repayment scheme with no linkage between the issue of reparations and war debts.[19] He, along with other key officials at the Treasury – Warren Fisher and Frederick Leith Ross – believed themselves superior to and had a contempt for their American counterparts, particularly those officials appointed to the American Treasury by the new Roosevelt government.[20] All three men believed that the American officials were unable to grasp the finer points of high finance and could be easily manipulated or deceived.[21] So, in spite of the increasingly uneasy state of affairs in the Far East, where American support against Japanese expansionism would have been welcome (an issue over which Chamberlain disagreed with the Foreign Office vehemently[22]), Chamberlain entrenched himself in a position that was sure to antagonize the new American government.[23]

Worried that Prime Minister Ramsay MacDonald was at times prone to be too well disposed towards the Americans, Chamberlain contended that,

> He [MacDonald] fears that the Americans will force us into Repudiation. I don't think they can unless we choose and so far as I am concerned I have made it my plan that I don't choose. We may be forced to postpone

payment and of course I don't like that, but postponement is very different from Repudiation ...[24]

Ignorant of the domestic forces at play in the American electoral process, Chamberlain convinced himself that Hoover and Stimson would be pressured into agreeing to an Anglo-French plan for settlement, with the threat of cancellation if that plan were not accepted being the trump card. He could not believe that the Americans would reject the proposal in the face of the pressure mounted by a combined Anglo-European bloc.[25] Chamberlain was also convinced there was support on the American side of the house for his plan. Without any apparent good reason, he was of the opinion that Norman Davis, head of the American delegation to Geneva, both agreed with him and was telling others in the American administration so. He and the British Treasury were gratified to think that Davis would perform such a service for him because

> If we could so arrange that it was not necessary to call upon the Americans to make any decision now it might be possible to keep Repns. War Debts off the party platforms. Then in Nov. Mr. Hoover might say we can't settle this question finally between now and Dec.15 (when the next payments become due) but we shall not expect any payment then and we can sit down and talk comfortably after that. This is not only gratifying because it is exactly the way I have said things should be handled with America all along, but also because it helps to keep R.M. himself firmly in the path of cancellation which I have sometimes feared he might leave under pressure from the Yanks.[26]

All talk of war debts was to be discouraged by any British representative going to the US, in the hope that such a refusal to discuss the matter would keep it from becoming a point of contention in the fall elections. The archival record is clear: this was a classic case of a Chamberlain delusion, a delusion for which there was no evidence or basis of support. No matter, Chamberlain and the Treasury remained confident that after the election, so long as the American public did not take the debt issue between their teeth, the US government could be made to see that the resumption of payments was not necessary.[27]

Not suprisingly, any hope that the war debts issue could be kept from becoming a political target in the US during and after the election was short-lived. By early December 1932, it was becoming obvious to British observers of America that, in the wake of the Roosevelt victory over Hoover, any promise of a renegotiation of the war debt issue made by Stimson would not be honoured by the new US government. Britain was in danger of being cast in the role of delinquent debtor, a role that would do its own economy and the general world economy no good.[28] Chamberlain was furious with the change of events that cast his carefully laid plans into the dustbin. He accused the new American government, American officials in general, and, indeed, all prominent American men of not having 'a scrap of moral courage' and declared that '(they have no leaders)'.[29] The Roosevelt administration's refusal to align itself with his vision of how the situation should be handled now threatened to place Great Britain in the same position as the smaller European nations who had earlier reneged on their loans, and had been chastised for it by the British government. However, if Britain now paid up, after the long, hard efforts to try and produce a situation that offered some relief from the payment system, a perception of weakness and subservience to the US would be created. Frustrated at his lack of being able to produce an effective solution to the problem; vexed by what he saw was the slow-witted inability of others to see his brilliance, Chamberlain railed at the Americans and dreamed of being able to throw the payment issue in their face:

> I think it really requires more courage to refuse to pay than to pay; but at present that is the course I am inclined to. I should repudiate; I should expressly admit the obligation but at the last moment I should inform the Yanks that my conscience would not allow me to take a step which I was convinced would upset the world and throw back all chance of recovery for an indefinite period.[30]

The reality of the situation was, however, that the British had only two choices: to pay or to default.

A decision to pay was arrived at by the national government. Although many besides Chamberlain did not like the prospect of having to climb down from their previous position and make another payment on 15 December, the majority of the Cabinet believed the time was not ripe to repudiate the repayment system.[31] Chamberlain, however, remained bitter towards the US for having forced him to retreat from his original position of trying to exempt Britain from future payments. It was his strong conviction that America, like France, had to have its public and official opinion educated to the 'realities' of why such repayment was a danger to the world. The Americans were just a bit slower on the uptake than the French, he conceded, 'But the longer they go without payment the more easy will it be for them to accept the prospect that there never will be any payment.'[32] However, once he had been forced to change his policy, it was not hard for Chamberlain to convince himself that making the payment was actually the best thing that could have happened. He explained his willingness to submit to a complete reversal of his vision by claiming that Stanley Baldwin, former Prime Minister and now Lord President of the Council, had made a convincing case for accepting the payment plan.[33] However he coated the pill, the swallowing was still bitter.[34] This first contact with the new American administration left an acrid taste in Chamberlain's mouth about dealing with the US in general, and it was a taste he was not soon to be rid of.[35] It was also a demonstration of the manner by which he assessed a nation and its international aspirations. Using sketchy, incomplete information, personal prejudices based on either his personal feelings toward individual representatives, a willingness to abide by national stereotypes, and a constant belief in his rightness and an unwillingness to consider any other options or contrary opinions from other sources, was the hallmark of Chamberlain's style of policy making and management.

In the immediate aftermath of the failed World Economic Conference and the failure to reach a solution on debt repayment with the US, Britain's strategic foreign policy-making elite was presented with a difficult problem. In the face of the growing Japanese aggression in the Far East, who was the more reliable ally? Should Great Britain appease Japan and arrive at some sort of power-sharing arrangement with Tokyo over the fate of China? Or, should Great Britain respect the predictable American protests over such actions and work instead to create some sort of Anglo-American front in the Far East?[36] Inextricably tied to that equation was the question of what size of navy should Great Britain maintain. In November 1933, Neville Chamberlain's experiences of working with, or rather against, American interests were fresh in his mind when he and his Treasury entered into the Committee of Imperial Defence debate that dealt with these matters.

The Chancellor's point of view did not coincide with that of either the Foreign Office or the Admiralty, even though he had nothing but anecdotal evidence, hearsay and half-formed personal views from which to form his opinion. The two institutions in opposition to him were basing their policy proposals on expert reports, intelligence assessments from multiple sources, and eyewitness experiences that were sophisticated and comprehensive. This material was then put into a global perspective and processed in a proper systemic fashion. While neither the Royal Navy nor Foreign Office were overly enamoured of the US, they were, however, cognisant of the need not to provoke America unnecessarily into either a greater naval-building race or retaliatory actions because of overly friendly British overtures to the Japanese.[37] Furthermore, both the Admiralty and the Foreign Office believed that alienating the US to 'buy off' the Japanese, would, in the long run, be a far worse risk to take economically, diplomatically and defensively, although the Royal Navy acknowledged the short-term gains that closer relations with Japan could bring. But those gains were minimal and unstable. The US was the only nation that could, in the face of Japan's aggression, realistically be expected to have parallel but not identical attitudes and interests in the Far East. The Foreign Office and Admiralty were both very concerned about the message that any overtures for a closer relationship to Japan would send, not only to the Japanese (as a signal for the division of China by the two island nations) but also to other aggressor states (who would conclude that Britain had abandoned the League and collective security and was now ready to condone and profit from those aggressive actions).[38] Foreign Office and Admiralty officials saw clearly the dangerous path that such a precedent would establish for the future of Britain's ability to find security with traditional allies such as France and the US. Both departments proposed and fought for a more robust rearmament programme that could assist a strategic foreign policy aimed at a firm and resolved resistance to any further Japanese aggression. That military strength would be a useful lever for a policy that coincided with or played off the realities of the intentions and actions of the USSR and America, both seen as counterweights to Japanese expansion in the Far East.[39] The Foreign Office and Admiralty had launched subtle, far-reaching initiatives to woo their American counterparts and were having success in creating, at a sub-official level, a special relationship.[40] Chamberlain's policy of buying-off the Japanese in the Far East was ill-thought out and simply reflected the continuation of his anti-American sentiments, as well as a lack of understanding of the complicated, interconnected nature of relations between the USSR, Japan, the US and Great Britain in the global balance of power.[41]

As had been the case with the World Economic Conference, Chamberlain did not want British policy to be shaped primarily by considerations of what would be approved by the US. While he did not think there was any chance of Britain going to war with the US in the foreseeable future, Chamberlain wanted to avoid the perception of British favouritism towards any American proposals for disarmament, because that would poison the chance for the future betterment of Anglo-Japanese relations. He reiterated his belief that the breaking of the long-standing alliance with Japan in 1922, in order to create the Washington Treaty system and accommodate American concerns, had been wrong. Equally, it was certainly wrong now to continue to give good relations with the US a higher priority than having cordial relations with Japan.[42] He agreed to the creation of a special sub-committee, the Defence Requirements Sub-Committee (DRC), that would prepare recommendations for Cabinet as to how Britain could prepare to meet its 'worst deficiencies' for defending the empire. He agreed, however, implicitly with the intention that the Treasury representative on that committee, Sir Warren Fisher, would make Chamberlain and the Treasury's anti-American position the dominant one.

The story of the DRC has been well told, if not always accurately, in a number of places.[43] It is not required for the purposes of this study that a complete recounting of the workings of that group be provided. Only two points are critical. The first is the attitude displayed by Warren Fisher during the committee's debates. Reflecting and espousing Chamberlain's views and attitudes, Fisher opined that Britain's defence planning had to show that it was not a 'backboneless nation' required to bow down to the US. He also reinforced the Chancellor's belief that the worst aspect of British defence deficiencies was Great Britain's entanglement with the Americans.[44] The Treasury believed that the entanglement with the Americans had prevented British diplomacy being able to establish better Anglo-Japanese relations. In a paper prepared by the Treasury for the DRC, Fisher put forth the department's view as to how Great Britain should proceed to deal with the Americans in any naval talks:

> it is essential in my view to get clear of our 'entangling' agreement with the USA who should be left to circle the globe with ships if they want, to gratify their vanity by singing 'Rule Columbia, Columbia rules the waves,' and to wait and see for how many years the politically all-powerful Middle West will continue to acquiesce in paying a fantastic bill related to not real requirement but primarily to indulge the braggadocio of Yahoodom.[45]

His attitude reflected his superior's almost exactly on the matter: 'I have *no* doubt we could easily make an agreement with them [the Japanese] if the U.S.A. were out of the picture. It is the Americans who are the difficulty and I don't know how we can get over it.'[46]

The resulting debate in the committee over the place of America in Britain's plans for defence rejected Chamberlain's and the Treasury's views on matters. They were thwarted by a Foreign Office/Admiralty coalition, supported by the Cabinet Secretary, Sir Maurice Hankey, all of whom appreciated the narrowness of the Treasury view and the need to maintain good relations with America. The Admiralty and Foreign Office, in the face of Chamberlain's attempts to move rapidly towards appeasing Japan, had held firm. The US, and possibly France, would not be alienated by any rush to divide China and allow Japan a free hand in Asia. However, Chamberlain gained some satisfaction in his refusal to acknowledge or allow a large naval rearmament programme to begin. In the discussions over the funding of the defence programme put forward by the DRC, the Treasury stuck to its pro-Japan beliefs and argued still that a two-ocean navy was not necessary. The funds required to help the Royal Navy acquire the necessary strength to support Britain's strategic position and foreign policy in the Far East were denied by Chamberlain.[47] Chamberlain never realized that his refusal to allow the DRC to progress as the experts had suggested practically ensured that Great Britain would have to rely more heavily on America's support in the Far East, particularly after the failure of the 1935 London Naval Conference and the resulting naval arms race.

From the time of the DRC onwards, until his becoming Prime Minister in 1937, Chamberlain was at odds with both the Foreign Office and the Admiralty. He was also clearly confused by the events swirling around the international arena, not only globally, but in particular in Europe. He viewed the Foreign Office as a department of do-nothings and the Navy officials as narrow and largely ignorant men. What is more, in his arrogance, he did not care that such was the case and was determined instead to make himself the focal point in the creation of Britain's foreign policy.[48] His views, objectives and methods, however, were vaguely defined and fluctuated on key strategic foreign policy issues. He was not sure whether Britain's interests would be best served by a Locarno-type system of pacts or a system of alliances, two very different propositions. Also, despite denying money for rearmament as put forward by the DRC, in his own mind he envisioned himself as a great supporter of the rearming of Great Britain.[49] At the end of May 1935, wooed by reassurances from Hitler that Germany intended no harm to anyone, Chamberlain believed there existed a *détente* that would allow for a slowing down of Britain's 'panicky and wasteful' air rearmament to fit his own conditions.[50]

It was the diplomatic and foreign policy front that gave him the most trouble. Mussolini's Abyssinian campaign would simply not go away. What was more, it threatened not only relations between Italy and Britain, an alignment that Chamberlain thought could be a stabilizing arrangement, but also soured relations between Great Britain and France.[51] Indeed, by the summer of 1935, Chamberlain was no longer capable of dealing with the 'new' Europe. He had deluded himself, as he had in the case of the American response to the debt issue, into believing what he wanted to believe about Mussolini and Italy's policy. Supportive of the energy and imagination of the new Foreign Secretary, Sam Hoare, whom Chamberlain liked and saw as being a forceful, competent change after the obstructionist Simon, the Chancellor of the Exchequer had already envisioned British proposals for a settlement of the Abyssinian affair being successful. He was crushed when that pre-ordained outcome did not develop:

> The Abyssinian affair goes from bad to worse and it seems more than ever unlikely that Laval will consent to anything that might embroil him with Mussolini. Yet if the latter goes on he will torpedo the League and the small states in Europe will just race one another to Berlin. Our offer has had a very bad reception and our stock had had a perceptible jar. ... At present I am bankrupt of fresh ideas and see no way out of our dilemma.[52]

By the end of 1935, the weight of events, both foreign and domestic, were beginning to take their toll on Chamberlain. He feared that Mussolini might attack Britain in the Mediterranean and that Hitler's Germany would take full advantage. The pressures of an election were upon him. And he feared the reaction of the British public when the figures for the new spending for defence were given out in Parliament. He hoped that the defence spending would shock the British people into giving him a clear indication of what his safest course to take politically would be. Chamberlain feared the effects that new defence spending would have on his political future and thus his dreams of being Prime Minister. But, he attempted to shrug off the possibility of any negative outcomes to his sister Ida with forced indifference:

Oh dear! Oh dear! Who'd be a Chancellor of the Exchequer in such times and why don't I retire now with the laurels of my four years successful finance instead of stopping on to be cursed and kicked by and an ungrateful B.[ritish] P.[ublic]? I suppose the answer is that I know no one that I would trust to hold the balance between rigid orthodoxy and a fatal disregard of sound principles and the rights of posterity, and, perhaps, when I come to think of it, I don't really care much what they say of me now so long as I am satisfied myself that I am doing what is right. For it isn't as if I had ambitions which might be ruined by present unpopularity. I believe S.[tanley]B.[aldwin] will stay on for the duration & by the next election I shall be 70 and shant care much I daresay for the strenuous life of leader even if some one else hasn't overtaken me before then.[53]

Chamberlain's gloomy predictions over his future turned out to be no more accurate than his myriad insights into Britain's defence and foreign policy direction. However, one bright ray of sunlight shone out of Chamberlain's interference in foreign and defence affairs as Chancellor of the Exchequer. He saw in Anthony Eden a man with whom he agreed on many points and with whom he felt he could work, or more aptly, whom he could control.[54] Both men rejected a balance of power approach to Britain's foreign policy, but neither was clear in what should replace it. Chamberlain moved more and more throughout 1936 towards the concept of a cheap defence option, based on air power, to support Britain's strategic position, while at the same time meeting the legitimate grievances of the dictators in order to create some sort of 'relationship'.[55] He fluctuated between wanting to draw nearer the French, whom he feared would put Britain in the lead on European collective security matters, the use of sanctions to punish aggressor states, and wanting to find a workable alliance structure that would check both Germany and Italy, in some re-creation of a Bismarckian web. His views and concrete procedures for attaining these conditions were never clearly defined or well thought out. In fact, they resembled nothing more than his own instinctive or 'gut' reaction in favour of avoiding war at all costs. There seemed to be no other rationale or agenda, and thus there was no concept or clarification of a long-term vision or policy for the able governance of Great Britain's imperial position and foreign strategic policy.

Eden's ascent to the position of Foreign Secretary in 1935, with his views of and experience with collective security,[56] accompanied by Chamberlain's rise to Prime Minister in 1937, should have, in Chamberlain's opinion, signalled the creation of a cooperative and unified foreign policy-making team.[57] Such was not the case. By February 1938, Eden had resigned as Foreign Secretary. The reason for his resignation was clear. He refused to condone Chamberlain's continued failure to appreciate the complex nature and demands of Britain's strategic foreign policy, particularly the requirement not needlessly to alienate the US and thereby weaken Britain's strategic position in the Far East.[58] What the episode showed, as far as revealing the Chamberlain form of policy making, was the stubborn and unsubstantiated style of governance that Chamberlain continued to practise even as Prime Minister.

The continued efforts of the Foreign Office and Admiralty to create closer trust between themselves and their American counterparts were beginning to pay dividends.[59] However, the new Prime Minister's anti-American sentiments and thoughtless disregard for America's being an important part of Britain's strategic foreign policy-making equation threatened the very fabric of that budding relationship.[60] The focal point of the difference of opinion towards the conduct of Britain's policy centred around the aftermath of the Abyssinian crisis. Chamberlain's actions, Eden's reaction to Italy and the idea of appeasing Mussolini by offering *de jure* recognition of the Italian conquest of Abyssinia, are well chronicled elsewhere.[61] What emerged from those series of events, however, was a clear indication that Chamberlain had now reversed his positive appreciation for Eden's talents and insights because the Foreign Secretary disagreed with the Prime Minister's views. Also, the Foreign Office, a continual thorn in Chamberlain's paw, was as usual in opposition to his plans. That tension was a result of the fact that while Foreign Secretary, Eden had been educated by the Foreign Office to the fact that Britain's imperial defence policy was based on a balance of power policy and that there were critical links between events in the Far East and events in Europe. Unlike Chamberlain, Eden now saw how that interrelationship occurred and was not as Euro-focused as the Prime Minister. Eden acknowledged and accepted that reality. Chamberlain did not, and instead continued to look for any sign that the Italians and Germans were willing to be 'civilized' about their expansion in Europe.[62] In particular, and in the face of his own doubts and evidence presented to him by colleagues and other governmental departments,[63] he convinced himself that his efforts were making progress towards finding some solution to appeasing Italy and Germany. In short, he saw himself as being not only the Prime Minister, but also the Foreign Secretary:

> My interview with Grandi seems to have made a very good impression in Italy and I see they have now 'revealed' that I sent a personal letter to Mussolini. I make it appear that it was a spontaneous idea arising out of the conversation but of course I had made up my mind to do it beforehand. But I thought it would make a better impression if Grandi could report that I had sat down and written it in his presence without consultation with anyone else and I hear that Grandi himself was delighted and report that Italy and England had been divorced for two

years but were now going to be remarried! I believe the double policy of rearmament and better relations with Germany & Italy will carry us safely through the danger period if only the F.O. will play up. I see indications that they are inclined to be jealous, but though it is natural that they should be annoyed at Press headlines about the 'Chamberlain touch' instead of the 'Eden touch' there is no desire on my part to take credit away from the F.O. ...[64]

That magnanimous attitude lasted only as long as Eden did not openly or directly challenge Chamberlain's interference and could work around the Prime Minister's agenda. Chamberlain's real attitude, more and more, was that he saw himself as the central creator and instigator of British foreign policy, a domain that was his and his alone. That policy also, he believed, was to change the face of Europe. The Prime Minister was giddy with the power and authority he now commanded, and was in a position to disregard other views and opinions with even greater abandon than he had before as the Chancellor of the Exchequer.[65] In truth, his dislike for the continued questioning of his direction of Britain's strategic foreign policy by the Foreign Office, and their resistance to his micro-management style of management, had, if possible, increased his dislike of that department.

I am not too happy about the F.O. who seem to me to have no imagination & no courage. I must say A[thony] E[den] is awfully good in accepting my suggestions without grumbling but it is wearing to have always to begin at the beginning again & sometimes even to re-write their despatches for them. I am terribly afraid that we should let the Anglo-Italian situation slip back to where it was before I intervened. The F.O. persist in seeing Musso. only as sort of a Machiavelli putting on a false mask of friendship in order to further nefarious ambitions. If we treat him like that we shall get nowhere with him and we shall have to pay for our mistrust by appallingly costly defences in the Mediterranean.[66]

In such circumstances the Foreign Secretary and Foreign Office could not condone Chamberlain's appeasement policy. They were forced to challenge the Prime Minister, in order to try to get him to cease considering only European matters and to recognize the global nature of Britain's strategic position and the negative ramifications his appeasement of Italy could have.

Eden agreed that appeasement was a legitimate foreign policy tactic, but was not convinced that the ends would justify the means in the Italian case. On the other hand, he did not see appeasement as the only solution. The creation of strong, viable alliances was as important as appeasement. Thus, Eden believed that if Roosevelt's initiatives towards making a common stand against aggressor states were snubbed by Chamberlain; if the Americans were made to believe that they could not trust the British on such issues, even if that issue were not directly involved with the Far Eastern situation, then the sense of trust and cooperation that had been established between the two nations at many levels on Far Eastern matters, would immediately be shattered. If cooperation concerning and coordination in Far Eastern matters were destroyed, then there would certainly be little hope for drawing the Americans into any closer cooperation in the European theatre.[67] The gap between Eden and Chamberlain in their views of Britain's global foreign policy can be seen by considering a particular case.

When commenting on a meeting held on 18 December 1937 at All Souls College Oxford, to debate Great Britain's foreign policy choices, Eden had stated that Anglo-American cooperation in the Far East was a vital part of Britain's total strategic foreign policy. He held that belief firmly and did not make such utterances for public opinion or media consumption in order to influence American views. His position was reflective of the consensus reached by that gathering. The latter came to the conclusion that, while America could not be counted on for immediate assistance in any conflict, when it did weigh into the fray, that action, just as in 1917, would be decisive. Overall, the advice from the gathering to Britain's foreign policy makers was that, if Britain led, American would follow in the Far East. That would make closer relations over European issues more possible as well. America, however, could not and would not, because of domestic political pitfalls, promise anything in advance. Nevertheless:

> It was felt that this risk was worth taking because: (a) It would settle the Japanese question. (b) More importantly, it would provide us with an affirmation of strength as regards Germany and the Berlin-Tokyo Axis. (c) It might encourage Germany to exchange Japanese friendship for Russian friendship. (d) It would be comparatively acceptable to our own opinion since London would not be bombed. (e) It would unite us with America.[68]

Eden took that message to Chamberlain at the end of 1937, telling the Prime Minister that, although 1938 was going to be a difficult year for British diplomacy, one bright spot was cooperation with the US. The Foreign Secretary was certain that real progress was being made, even if it were at times slow and difficult. His approach to the Americans in the new year would be to '... do everything we can privately to encourage the Americans'.[69] Chamberlain assured Eden that he understood the importance of the Americans, but in reality the Prime Minister was still deeply suspicious of Roosevelt and the US in general, refusing to change his mind at all about their real worth. He continued to think of England standing alone. The ability or capacity to use alliances to help Great Britain's cause was a concept that eluded Chamberlain's thinking and so appeasement was the only viable option:

Now in the present state of European affairs with the two dictators in a thoroughly nasty temper we simply cannot afford to quarrel with Japan and I very much fear therefore that after a lot of ballyhoo the Americans will somehow fade out & avoid it ... .[70]

Typically, in classic Chamberlain fashion, by January 1938 he had flip-flopped on how he felt about the US and confided to the Foreign Secretary that he was now considering asking the Americans to use their navy in conjunction with the Royal Navy to provide a show of force against the Japanese.[71] Unable to comprehend the situation in the Far East and how to approach the Americans, the Prime Minister was an unstable presence who would blow hot and cold on Anglo-American relations, confusing attempts on both sides of the Atlantic to create confidence and stability in that relationship.[72]

It is clear, then, why it was that Eden felt betrayed when Chamberlain insisted on playing the Italian cards his own way, ignoring Roosevelt's warnings not to make a deal with them over Abyssinia lest that alienate American public opinion from Britain.[73] For Eden, if Chamberlain's appeasement of Italy erased the growing coordination of Anglo-American policy and sentiment; if the American mental map of British foreign policy were torn asunder, then Britain would find itself facing Japan, Italy and, quite possibly Germany, alone.[74] That had been the situation which every British Foreign Secretary from 1932 onwards had desperately tried to avoid. Eden was unwilling to allow such steps as Chamberlain proposed to go ahead without consequence, and so, on 20 February, resigned.[75] Edward Halifax replaced Eden as Foreign Secretary.

Halifax's time in office began in the same way as Eden's with regard to his relationship with Chamberlain. The Prime Minister thought Halifax a capable man, whose ideas on how to approach and deal with the dictators matched his own.[76] However, it was not long until he, too, had moved away from Chamberlain's views of appeasement and supported the Foreign Office fully in its attempts to make the Prime Minister realize the dangers that his continued running after Hitler was creating.[77] The cause of that diversion of opinion and views remained the same as it had been during Eden's time at the Foreign Office. Chamberlain refused to deviate from his chosen path, this time even in the face of arguments put forward and supported by such staunch and reliable a former colleague as Halifax. More telling is the fact that not once, after two Foreign Secretaries had changed their views on Britain's strategic foreign policy to one at odds with his in the space of less than a year and a half, did Chamberlain pause to consider that perhaps his own position might need some reconsideration. Instead, that single-minded myopia led to Chamberlain's greatest act of arrogance and appeasement, Munich.

The British Prime Minister never once considered that during the events leading up to and including September 1938, that he was not the central figure. Chamberlain had no empathy and, thus, no ability to gauge with any chance of accuracy the real motives and drives behind German aims.[78] Instead, he viewed the options available to him through the same prism he had utilized for the previous five years: avoiding war through a *rapprochement* with Germany. He took the counsel of those who told him what he wanted to hear. He continued to ignore and malign the Foreign Office and Service Chiefs in committees. And, he refused to see the defection of members of his own party away from his position as a serious sign of his failing leadership. Instead, he fobbed such occurrences off as the actions of weaker and less capable men.[79] His Plan Z, a secret meeting with Hitler to use the 'Chamberlain touch' to arrive at some agreement, worried even Halifax and other members of Cabinet. Still, Chamberlain remained immune to the advice of other informed and more knowledgeable colleagues.[80] He was, however, no longer in a position that allowed him to command the course of events. Fearing the outbreak of a European war more than anything else; fearing Britain's lack of military preparedness, a condition that his own policies had helped create over the last five years; and not understanding the subtle timings involved in such diplomatic manoeuvrings, Britain's Prime Minister found himself in a position that he had chastised others for: running after other powers in an attempt to get a deal, any deal.[81] To Chamberlain there was no moral issue at stake, no greater commitment to mankind to consider. His goal was to use appeasement to provide time either for Britain to rearm to an adequate level, or to allow the aggressor states to come to the end of their demands and begin to take a more 'conventional' role in European affairs. Neither option came to fruition.

How, then, can one judge Neville Chamberlain as a 'maker' of Great Britain's strategic foreign policy? Not too favourably is the answer. His personal style of decision making and governance displayed all the signs of an arrogant, narrow, vindictive man. His style suited the opposition he faced, not so much within the ranks of British government, but outside it. A petty dictator in his own right, Chamberlain was as much a man who relied on his own views of the world and interpretation of events around him as Hitler, Mussolini or Stalin. Unable to eliminate those who sought to offer a differing opinion, Chamberlain ignored, banished, financially or politically crippled, maligned, defamed, or marginalized not only his opposition, but those bodies and institutions whose job it was to direct and create Britain's foreign policy. Indeed, his attitude and actions ensured an unnecessarily longer period of poisoned Anglo-American relations, especially at the highest level of Treasury to Treasury and, then, Prime Minister to President, than should have been the case. As a result of his style of governing and politics, Chamberlain helped prevent any pre-war formal Anglo-American security arrangement. Without such a pact there was little hope of impressing the aggressor nations, and certainly no ability to put a formal alignment to good use as a deterrent in the Far East.

Chamberlain was certainly guilty, but he was not alone, in his belief that war was to be avoided at all costs. There was a clear trend – an unsubstantiated religious fervour – amongst the post-First World War British policy-makers, particularly those whose job it was to defend the empire after 1930, that war and any variation of use of force was to be abhorred. Certainly, when compared to the comprehensive and sophisticated global views of British foreign policy makers of the pre-First World War era, most of those of the inter-war pale in ability, intellect and knowledge in dealing with the problems that faced them. Of course, a sane and civilized people would have recognized that to use force is an undesirable choice. But that faith in appeasement could not be allowed to blind those responsible to the possibility that, in certain circumstances, the use of appropriate force was not only justified, but morally necessary. But, that style of blind belief governed Chamberlain, as it did others, so that a logical, rational assessment of the situation was almost an impossibility for him. In that regard, appeasement was the *only* option he could conceive.[82]

On the merits of his performance in the three critical areas of economics, alliance building and naval rearmament the evidence points clearly to a man who succeeded in achieving success in only one of those areas. His story reinforces the central importance to historians of the need to understand the significance of individuals within that strategic foreign policy-making process. His fiscal policies as Chancellor and as Prime Minister ensured that one pillar of the triad was prepared to defend Britain's global position. Ironically, in his eyes, the main adversary to Britain's dominance in the economic arena was the growing economic and fiscal strength of the US. Economic solvency was achieved at the expense of the preparation of the armed forces. Great Britain's military weakness, created in the 1920s and extended in the 1930s, certainly allowed Italy and Japan to create a mental image of Britain being unwilling and unable to defend its own or the League's ideals and territories. Chamberlain, as both Chancellor of the Exchequer and as Prime Minister, did not address the defence issue adequately. Instead, he opted for defence on the cheap with an air force that was severely limited in its capability and reach. The main pillar of imperial defence, the Royal Navy, was continually restricted through budgetary means and not afforded the money required to rebuild itself in order to be able to fight a two-ocean war and defend the empire. Without an adequate navy or an effective alliance system that gave weight to Great Britain's foreign policy, Chamberlain's sporadic and reactive policies were unable, in either Europe or the Far East, to deter the aggressor states. In sum, he was indeed guilty of being incapable of comprehending or defending the needs of Britain and the empire. His policies, attitudes and actions worsened Britain's position within the global balance of power that was the reality of international relations after 1932. Thus, he must be judged as the worst of Britain's inter-war strategic foreign policy-makers.

Notes

1. A poem by Hugh MacDiarmid as quoted in the article '"Littler than Hitler": Hugh MacDiarmid's unknown attack on Chamberlain' by Margery P. McCulloch, *Times Literary Supplement* (17 March 2000), p. 15.
2. Some of the more recent and scholarly works on the topic of Neville Chamberlain and his role in British foreign/strategic policy-making are: Frank McDonough, *Neville Chamberlain, Appeasement and the British Road to War* (New York: St Martins Press, 1998); Michael L. Roi, *Alternative to Appeasement* (Westport, CT: Greenwood Press, 1997); R.A.C. Parker, *Chamberlain and Appeasement: British Policy and the Coming of the Second World War* (London: Macmillan, 1993); John Charmley *Chamberlain and the Lost Peace* (London: Macmillan, 1989).
3. The worst of the apologists and instigators of this concept of appeasement and particularly Chamberlain's role is A.J.P. Taylor's, *Origins of the Second World War* (Harmondsworth: Penguin, 1964). See also: D.C. Watt, 'The historiography of appeasement', in A. Sked and C. Cook (eds), *Crisis and Controversy* (London: Macmillan, 1976); W.J. Mommsen and L. Kettenacker, *The Fascist Challenge and the Policy of Appeasement* (London: Unwin Hyman, 1983).
4. W.N. Medlicott, *Britain and Germany: The Search for Agreement, 1930–1937*, (London: Longman, 1969); Gaines Post Jr., *Dilemmas of Appeasement, British Deterrence and Defense, 1934–1937* (Ithaca, NY: NY State UP, 1993); Larry W. Fuchser, *Neville Chamberlain and Appeasement: A Study in the Politics of History* (New York: St Martins Press, 1982); David Dilks, '"We must Hope for the Best and Prepare for the Worst": The Prime Minister, the Cabinet and Hitler's Germany, 1937–1939', *Proceedings of the British Academy*, 73 (1987); Ritchie Ovendale, *Appeasement and the English Speaking World: Britain, the United States, the Dominions and the Policy of 'Appeasement', 1937–1939* (Cardiff: University of Wales Press, 1975); William Scott, 'Neville Chamberlain and Munich: Two Aspects of Power,' in Leonard Krieger and Fritz Stern (eds), *The Responsibility of Power: Historical Essays in Honor of Hajo Holborn* (New York: Macmillan, 1967); Paul M. Kennedy, '"Appeasement" and British Defence Policy in the Inter-War Years', *British Journal of International Studies*, 4 (1978); William R. Rock, *British Appeasement in the 1930s* (London: Edward Arnold, 1977); Lawrence R. Pratt, *East of Malta, West of Suez: Britain's Mediterranean Crisis, 1936–1939* (London: CUP, 1975); Peijian Shen, *The Age of Appeasement: The Evolution of British Foreign Policy in the 1930s* (Stroud: Sutton Publishing, 1999); John Ruggiero, *Neville Chamberlain and British Rearmament: Pride, Prejudice, and Politics* (Westport, CT: Greenwood, 1999).
5. For a quick survey of some of the more recent material, see Wesley Wark, 'Review Article: Appeasement Revisited', *International History Review*, 3 (1995). For a thorough review of the literature see the appropriate sections of Sidney Aster's, *British Foreign Policy, 1918–1945*, revised edn, (Wilmington, DE, 1991).
6. John Vincent, 'Chamberlain, the Liberals and the Outbreak of War, 1939', *The English Historical Review*, CXIII, (1998) pp. 367–83; Clement Leibovitz, *The Chamberlain-Hitler Deal* (Edmonton, Alberta: University fo Alberta Press, 1993); R.A.C. Parker, 'Economics, Rearmament, and Foreign Policy: The United Kingdom before 1939 – A Preliminary Study', *Journal of Contemporary History*, x (1975), pp. 637–47; Wesley Wark, 'The Air Defence Gap: British Air Doctrine and Intelligence Warnings in the 1930s', in Horst Boog (ed.), *Airpower in World War Two* (Oxford: Berg, 1992), pp. 511–26; Bruce Strang, 'Two Unequal Tempers: Sir

George Ogilvie-Forbes, Sir Nevile Henderson and British Foreign Policy, 1938–39', *Diplomacy and Statecraft*, 5, (1994), pp. 107–37.

7. The best account of Chamberlain's role in Britain's pre-war policy making in this vein is, Sidney Aster, '"Guilty Men": The Case of Neville Chamberlain', in Patrick Finney (ed.), *The Origins of the Second World War* (London: Routledge, 1997), pp. 62–78.

8. David French, *The British Way in Warfare, 1688–2000*, (London, 1990).

9. G. Peden, *British Rearmament and the Treasury, 1932–1939* (Edinburgh: Scottish Academic Press, 1979); R. Shay, *British Rearmament in the Thirties: Politics and Profits* (Princeton: Princeton University Press, 1977); B.J.C. McKercher, *Transition of Power: Britain's Loss of Global Pre-eminence to the United States, 1930–1945* (Cambridge: CUP, 1999), pp. 216–48; Gaines Post Jr., *Dilemmas of Appeasement*, pp. 65–6. Michael Howard, 'British Military Preparations for the Second World War', in David Dilks (ed.), *Retreat from Power: Studies in Britain's Foreign Policy of the Twentieth Century*, vol. 1, 1906–1939, (London: Macmillan, 1981), pp. 106–7.

10. Works which illustrate that larger context are: Robert Mallet, 'The Anglo-Italian War Trade Negotiations, Contraband Control and the Failure to Appease Mussolini, 1939–40', *Diplomacy and Statecraft*, 8, (1997), pp. 137–67; Reynolds M. Salerno, 'The French Navy and the Appeasement of Italy, 1937–9', *The English Historical Review*, CXII, (1997), pp. 66–105; and a review article by Michael Jabara Carley, 'Generals, Statesmen, and International Politics in Europe, 1898–1945', *Canadian Journal of History*, XXX, (1995), pp. 289–321.

11. On Chamberlain's view of the US and Roosevelt see: William R. Rock, *Chamberlain and Roosevelt: British Foreign Policy and the United States, 1937–1940*, (Columbus, OH: Ohio UP, 1988); D.C. Watt, 'Roosevelt and Neville Chamberlain: Two Appeasers', *International Journal*, 28 (1973), pp. 185–204. Some insights into his views of Russia can be gleaned from Keith Neilson's, 'A Cautionary Tale: The Metro-Vickers Incident of 1933', in the forthcoming Greg Kennedy and Keith Neilson (eds), *Incidents and International Relations: Personalities, Perceptions, and Power* (New York: Praeger-Greenwood Publishers).

12. The issue of mental maps and their place in strategic foreign policy-making is best dealt with in: T.G. Otte, 'Introduction: Personalities and Impersonal Forces in History', in T.G. Otte and Constantine A. Pagedas (eds), *Personalities, War and Diplomacy: Essay in International History* (London: Frank Cass, 1997), pp. 1–14; Keith Neilson, *Britain and the Last Tsar: British Policy and Russia, 1894–1917* (Oxford: Clarendon Press, 1995), pp. xi–xii and pp. 3–50; D.C. Watt, 'The Nature of the Foreign-Policy Making Elite in Britain', in D.C. Watt (ed.), *Personalities and Policies: Studies in the Formulation of British Foreign Policy in the Twentieth Century* (London: Longman, 1965), pp. 1–15; Zara Steiner, *The Foreign Office and Foreign Policy, 1898–1914* (Cambridge: CUP, 1969); idem, 'Elitism and Foreign Policy: The Foreign Office Before the Great War', in B.J.C. McKercher and David J. Moss (eds), *Shadow and Substance in British Foreign Policy, 1895–1939* (Edmonton: University of Alberta Press, 1984), pp. 19–56; A.K. Henrikson, 'The Geographical "Mental Maps" of American Foreign Policy Makers', *International Political Science Review*, 1 (1980), pp. 496–530.

13. A work that attempts a somewhat similar task, though not centred specifically on Chamberlain, is: Erik Goldstein, 'The British Official Mind and the United States, 1919–42', in Otte and Pagedas (eds), *Personalities, War and Diplomacy*, pp. 66–80.

14. Neville Chamberlain to Hilda Chamberlain, 3 January 1932, Neville Chamberlain Papers Birmingham University Library, NC 18/1/766.

15. See David Reynolds, *The Creation of the Anglo-American Alliance, 1937–41: A Study in Competitive Co-operation* (London: Europa, 1981), pp. 1–34; Greg Kennedy, *Imperial Crossroads: The Influence of the Far East on Anglo-American Relations, 1932–1939* (London: Frank Cass Publishing, forthcoming).

16. Aster, 'Guilty Men', p. 76; Parker, *Chamberlain and Appeasement*, p. 43.

17. For the full background a story of Britain's war debt problem see: R. Middleton, *Towards a Managed Economy: Keynes, the Treasury and the Fiscal Debate of the 1930s* (London: Macmillan, 1985); I. Drummond, *The Floating Pound and the Sterling Area, 1931–1939* (Cambridge: CUP, 1981); Diane Kunz, *The Battle for Britain's Gold Standard in 1931* (London: Hodder and Stoughton, 1987); P. Williamson, *National Crisis and National Government: British Politics, the Economy, and Empire, 1926–1932* (Cambridge: CUP, 1992); *idem*, 'The World Economic Conference 1933: The Failure of British Internationalism', *Journal of European Economic History*, 20 (1991), pp. 489–527.

18. Letter from N. Chamberlain to Hilda, 14 January 1932, NC 18/1/767.

19. Letter from N. Chamberlain to Hilda, 13 February 1932, NC 18/1/770.

20. Leith Ross memorandum, 5 February 1932, Treasury Archives, P[ublic] R[ecord] O[ffice], Kew, T172/1381.

21. Note from Leith Ross to Chamberlain and minute by Fisher, 27 May 1932, T 172/1815, 1933 World Economic Conference.

22. See Kennedy, *Imperial Crossroads*.

23. This context is best established by: Christopher Thorne, 'The Shanghai Crisis of 1932: The Basis of British Policy', *The American Historical Review*, 75 (1970), pp. 1616–39.

24. Letter from N. Chamberlain to Hilda, 11 June 1932, NC 18/1/786.

25. Letter from N. Chamberlain to Ida, 20 June 1932, NC 18/1/788.

26. Ibid.

27. Note from Leith Ross to Warren Fisher and Chancellor of Exchequer, 12 September 1932, T188/58.

28. Dispatches from Sir Ronald Lindsay (British Ambassador to the United States) to Sir John Simon (Foreign Secretary), 4 and 13 December, 1932, *Documents on British Foreign Policy*, 2nd ser. vol. ii (London: HMSO, 1956).

29. Letter from N. Chamberlain to Hilda, 26 November 1932, NC 18/1/807.

30. Ibid.

31. Letter from D. Fergusson to Chancellor of the Exchequer, 27 November 1932, T172/1507; note from Fisher and Sir Robert Vansittart, Permanent Under-Secretary at the Foreign Office to Chamberlain, 28 November 1932, ibid.

32. Letter from N. Chamberlain to Ida, 4 December 1932, NC 18/1/808.

33. Ibid.

34. For the story surrounding the British preparations and discussions with the United States about the war debt issue between February and 15 June, 1933, see the sizeable volume of correspondence found in the minutes and papers generated by the eleven meetings of the Cabinet body known as the British War Debts to United States of America Committee, PRO, Kew, CAB[inet] 27/548.

35. Letter from N. Chamberlain to Ida, 17 December 1932, NC 18/1/180.

36. Greg Kennedy, '1935: A Snapshot of British Imperial Defence in the Far East', in Greg Kennedy and Keith Neison (eds), *Far Flung Lines: Essays in Honour of Donald M. Schurman* (London: Frank Cass, 1997), pp. 190–217.

37. Minutes of the 261st Meeting of the Committee of Imperial Defence (CID), 9 November 1933, CAB 2/6.

38. Record of meeting between Eden, Lord Stanhope, Orme Sargent, Rex Leeper and Ralph Wigram, 30 April 1934, Foreign Office 371/18524/W4214/1/98; letter from N. Chamberlain to Ramsay MacDonald, 8 March 1934, PREM (Prime Minister's Office)1/175; 'Report of the Defence Requirements Committee – Subjects for Cabinet Consideration', 12 March 1934, CP-70(34), CAB 24/248; Cabinet 9(34), 14 March 1934, CAB 23/78; Chamberlain minute, 15 January 1934, T 161/624/S.36130/34; 1 Mtg, NCM(35), 16 April 1934, CAB 29/147; Chatfield to Dreyer, 2 February 1934, Chatfield Papers, CHT 4/4, National Maritime Museum; Chatfield to Warren Fisher, 4 June 1934, CHT 3/1; 'Note by First Lord of the Admiralty', NCM(35)10, 18 May 1934, CAB 29/148.

39. The author is grateful to the insights of Keith Neilson on British-Russian-Japanese relations in the Far East, who is presently finishing a manuscript on Anglo-Russian relations in the inter-war.

40. Greg Kennedy, *Imperial Crossroads*, Ch.1.

41. Plans Division memo, 'DC(M)(32) 120-General Comments', 20 June 1934, ADM[iralty] 116/3436; 'Note by the Chancellor of the Exchequer on the Report of the Defence Requirements Committee', 20 June 1934, DC(M)(32) 120, CAB25/511; Hankey to Vansittart, 31 May 1934, CAB 21/388.

42. Minutes of 261st Meeting CID, 9 November 1933, CAB 2/6.

43. Morrisey, C. and M.A. Ramsey, '"Giving the Lead in the Right Direction": Sir Robert Vansittart and the Defence Requirements Sub-Committee', *Diplomacy and Statecraft*, 6 (1995), pp. 39–60; D.C. Watt, 'Sir Warren Fisher and British Rearmament against Germany', in D.C. Watt, *Personalities and Policies* (London, 1965), pp. 100–16; Wesley K. Wark, *The Ultimate Enemy* (Ithaca: Cornell UP, 1985), pp. 27–32; B.J.C. McKercher, 'Old Diplomacy and New: The Foreign Office and Foreign Policy, 1919–1939', in Michael Dockrill and B.J.C. McKercher (eds), *Diplomacy and World Power: Studies in British Foreign Policy, 1890–1950* (Cambridge: CUP, 1995), pp. 79–115.

44. See, minutes of the 3rd Meeting of the DRC, 4 December 1933, CAB 16/109; minutes of 19th Meeting of DRC, 'Note by Sir Warren Fisher', 17 February 1934; letter from Fisher to Hankey, Cabinet Registered Files, 17 February 1934, CAB 21/434.

45. Minutes of 12th Meeting of DRC, 'Note by Sir Warren Fisher', 30 January 1934, CAB 16/109.

46. Chamberlain to Ida, 27 October 1934, NC 18/1/893.

47. 'Note by the Chancellor of the Exchequer on the Report of the Defence Requirements Committee', 20 June 1934; Shen, *The Age of Appeasement*, pp. 30–1; Parker, *Chamberlain and Appeasement*, pp. 36–46.

48. Chamberlain to Hilda, 27 August 1934, NC 18/1/885; Chamberlain to Hilda, 3 November 1934, NC 18/1/894; Chamberlain to Hilda, 17 November 1934, NC 18/1/896; Chamberlain to Ida, 30 October 1937, NC 18/1/1026.

49. Chamberlain to Hilda, 9 March 1935, NC 18/1/908; Chamberlain to Ida, 16 March 1935, NC 18/1/909.

50. Chamberlain to Hilda, 26 May 1935, NC 18/1/919.

51. Chamberlain to Hilda, 12 May 1935, NC 18/1/915; Chamberlain to Hilda, 26 May 1935, NC 18/1/919; Chamberlain to Hilda, 22 June 1935, NC 18/1/923; Chamberlain to Hilda, 14 July 1935, NC 18/1/925.

52. Chamberlain to Ida, 6 July 1935, NC 18/1/924.

53. Chamberlain to Ida, 8 December 1935, NC 18/1/941. See also, Chamberlain to Hilda, 15 December 1935, NC 18/1/942.

54. Parker, *Chamberlain and Appeasement*, pp. 93–123; William R. Rock, *British Appeasement in the 1930s* (London: Edward Arnold, 1977), pp. 4–6; William C. Mills, 'The Nyon Conference: Neville Chamberlain, Anthony Eden, and the Appeasement of Italy in 1937', *The International History Review*, xv (1993), pp. 1–22; Chamberlain to Hilda, 9 March 1935, NC 18/1/908; Chamberlain to Ida, 16 March, NC 18/1/909; Chamberlain to Hilda, 26 May 1935, NC 18/1/919; Chamberlain to Hilda, 1 September 1935, NC 18/1/930; Chamberlain to Hilda, 21 March 1936, NC 18/1/952.

55. Gilbert, *The Roots of Appeasement* (London: Weidenfeld and Nicolson, 1966), pp. 155–7; David Reynolds, *The Creation of the Anglo-American Alliance, 1937–1941: A Study in Competitive Cooperation* (Chapel Hill: University of North Carolina Press, 1982), pp. 7–10; David Dilks, '"We Must hope for the Best and Prepare for the Worst": The Prime Minister, the Cabinet and Hitler's Germany, 1937–1939', *Proceedings of the British Academy*, 73 (1987), pp. 309–52; R.A.C. Parker, 'Economics, Rearmament and Foreign Policy'; Warren Fisher to Chamberlain, 15 September 1936, NC 7/11/29/19; Chamberlain to Hilda, 9 February 1936, NC 18/1/949.

56. A.R. Peters, *Anthony Eden at the Foreign Office, 1931–1938* (New York: St Martins Press, 1986); Sydney Aster, *Anthony Eden*, (London, 1976); Earl of Avon, *Facing the Dictators* (London: Cassell, 1962); Chamberlain to Hilda, 21 March 1936, NC 18/1/952.

57. Chamberlain to Hilda, 4 April 1936, NC 18/1/955; Chamberlain to Hilda, 2 May 1936, NC 18/1/959; Mills, 'The Nyon Conference', pp. 1–3.

58. Ovendale, *'Appeasement' and the English Speaking World*, pp. 66–116; F[oreign] O[ffice] memo, 24 March 1938, Foreign Office 371/21526/A2127/64/45; despatch from Foreign Office to Lindsay [British Ambassador to USA], February 22 1938, Foreign Office 371/21547/A1409/64/45.

59. The following is based on Ch. 6 of Kennedy, *Imperial Crossroads*.

60. Chamberlain to Ida, 28 September 1936, NC 18/1/978; Chamberlain to Ida, 8 February 1937, NC 18/1/993; Chamberlain to Ida, 4 July 1937, NC 18/1/1010.

61. See, R. Ovendale, *'Appeasement' and the English Speaking World*; N.Rose, 'The Resignation of Anthony Eden', *The Historical Journal*, 25 (1982); D.C. Watt, *How War Came. The Immediate Origins of the Second World War, 1938–1939* (London: Heinemann, 1989), pp. 47–110.

62. Chamberlain to Ida, 4 July 1937, NC 1010; Chamberlain to Ida, 24 July 1937, NC 18/1/1013.

63. See Aster, 'Guilty Men'.

64. Chamberlain to Hilda, 1 August 1937, 18/1/1014.

65. Chamberlain to Ida, 8 August 1937, 18/1/1015; Chamberlain to Hilda, 21 November 1937, NC 18/1/1029; Chamberlain to Hilda, 5 December 1937, NC 18/1/1030a

66. Chamberlain to Hilda, 12 September 1937, NC 18/1/1020; Chamberlain to Hilda, 6 November 1937, NC 18/1/1027; Chamberlain to Ida, 14 November 1937, NC 18/1/1028. The Foreign Office was right in their appreciation. For Italian designs and Mussolini's intentions see: R.B. Mallet, *The Italian Navy and Fascist Expansion, 1935–1940* (London: Macmillan, 1998); *idem*, 'The Anglo-Italian War Trade Negotiations, Contraband and the Failure to Appease Mussolini, 1939–40'; *idem*, 'Fascist Foreign Policy and Official Italian Views of Anthony Eden', *Historical Journal*, 43 (2000), pp. 157–88; *idem*, 'Multilateral Strategy and Diplomacy: the Anglo-German Naval Agreement and the Mediterranean Crisis, 1935–36', *Journal of Strategic Studies*, 17 (1994), pp. 56–63.

67. Eden to the King, memo 'The Far East', undated November 1937, Eden MSS, Foreign Office 954/6, PRO.
68. Record of meeting at All Souls College, 18 December 1937, Eden MSS, Foreign Office 954/7.
69. Eden to Chamberlain, 31 December 1937, Eden MSS, Foreign Office 954/7; Eden to Chamberlain, 9 February 1938, NC 7/11/31/100.
70. Chamberlain to Hilda, 9 October 1937, NC 18/1/1023.
71. Reynolds, *The Creation of the Anglo-American Alliance*, p. 297, note 29; Cadogan to Eden, 12 January 1938, Eden MSS, Foreign Office 954/6.
72. The conclusion is based on Kennedy, *Imperial Crossroads*, which deals in detail with all of these issues.
73. FDR to Chamberlain, 17 January 1938, *Foreign Relations of the United States Diplomatic Papers (FRUS)*, 'General', vol. 1, pp. 120–2; Foreign Office minute by Ashton Gwatkin, 21 January 1938, F[oreign] O[office] 371/21490/A556/1/45; ibid, minute by J. Balfour, 31 January 1938; memo of conversation between Cordell Hull [US Secretary of State] and Sir Ronald Lindsay [British Ambassador to the US], 20 January 1938, *FRUS*, 'The Far East', vol. III, pp. 312–13.
74. David Dilks (ed.), *The Diaries of Sir Alexander Cadogan, 1938–1939* (London: Cassell, 1971), pp. 35–55.
75. A full account of the American influences on Eden and his resignation are found in the extensive files of Foreign Office memo. 24 March 1938, Foreign Office 371/21526/A2127/64/45 and dispatch from Lindsay to Foreign Office, 22 February 1938, Foreign Office 371/21547/A1409/1409.
76. D.C. Watt, 'Chamberlain's Ambassadors', in Dockrill and McKercher (eds), *Diplomacy and World Power*, pp. 145–7; Chamberlain to Hilda, 13 March 1938, NC 18/1/1041; Chamberlain to Ida, 20 March 1938, NC 18/1/1042.
77. Watt, 'Chamberlain's Ambassadors', p. 146; Parker, *Chamberlain and Appeasement*, p. 124–55.
78. The literature on Munich is far too large and extensive to include here. A collection that provides the necessary bibliography and is a full study in its own right of Munich is Igor Lukes and Erik Goldstein (eds), *The Munich Crisis, 1938: Prelude to World War II* (London: Frank Cass, 1999), originally appeared as a special edn of *Diplomacy and Statecraft*, 10 (1999). For our purposes the most relevant chapter is, Erik Goldstein, 'Neville Chamberlain, the British Official Mind and the Munich Crisis', pp. 276–92.
79. Chamberlain to Ida, 9 October 1938, NC 18/1/1071; Chamberlain to Hilda, 15 October 1938, 1072.
80. Chamberlain to Ida, 3 September 1938, NC 18/1/1066; Chamberlain to Hilda, 6 September 1938, NC 18/1/1067; Chamberlain to Hilda, 25 June 1938, NC 18/1/1057. No attempt has been made here to discuss his personal dealing with the Japanese Ambassador to Great Britain, Yoshida, a liaison that created a dual-tracked Far Eastern foreign policy and confused Foreign Office and Royal Navy attempts to make a more stable Far Eastern environment.
81. On the running after other powers, see Chamberlain to Hilda, 9 March 1935, NC 18/1/908. On his assessment of the situation, his acceptance of the Canning method of foreign policy direction, and his fear of Britain's weak military, see Chamberlain to Ida, 11 September 1938, NC 18/1/1068.
82. Aster, 'Guilty Men', pp. 74–6.

9
Ernest Bevin: Reluctant Cold Warrior

Sean Greenwood

Ernest Bevin has never been without his detractors, though his stock as Foreign Secretary between 1945 and 1951 remains generally high. In 1946 his Private Secretary, with evident approbation, compared Bevin's forthright assertion of British interests with Palmerston.[1] Forty years on, his grasp of detail in foreign affairs was likened to Lord Curzon's. He is, it has been said, 'head and shoulders above all Britain's other Foreign Secretaries in the post-war era' and 'one of the greatest Foreign Secretaries this country ever had'.[2] Evaluations of Bevin's reputation turn principally on his part in creating an anti-Soviet military alliance. In the received view, this resulted from a prescient judgement of Soviet ambitions followed up with purposeful and successful efforts to persuade the US to commit themselves to the defence of Western Europe. In the eyes of Bevin's admirers his failures, such as over Palestine and as a European integrationist, are cancelled out by NATO. Critics of his policies and to whom a correlation between Bevin and his predecessors from a high imperial age is apposite but damning also tend to concentrate on Bevin's Cold Warrior reputation.[3] These find in him a predisposition to combativeness towards the USSR, and too ready a dependency on the US. Not entirely logically, these defects are read as symptomatic of his refusal to reassess Britain's place in a changed world. The theme of this essay is that Bevin's esteem is well-founded but for rather different reasons than often expressed across these two divides.

In the first place, there is no clear evidence that Bevin in 1945 was inclined either by temperament or by experience to seek confrontation with the Soviet Union. On the contrary, in October 1945 he asserted to the French Foreign Minister that 'he was opposed in principle to the formation of "fronts" and "blocs"' and, around the same time, implied as much to both Stalin and his Foreign Minister, Molotov.[4] Frequent recourse is made to the supposed equation between his antipathy to Communist infiltrators into the trades unions in the 1920s and 1930s and his attitude to the Soviet Union in the

1940s. This, however, is misleading and owes much to the lack of precise information on his views on post-war Soviet ambitions (or the role of the US in peacetime, for that matter) before 1945 which forces us to judge him by his actions once in office. His pugnacious style and robust language tend to cloud matters further. But Bevin did not anticipate having to take sides in an ideologically fractured world and privately, among his advisers, his tone was more considered, his elucidation of his objectives often more cautious and his wish to evade either a wholesale breakdown with the Soviet Union or an exclusive partnership with the US more clear. Second, though he may be criticized for a lack of vision in his refusal to participate in schemes for economic integration for Western Europe in 1950 (and there were sound enough reasons why he should adopt this stance),[5] economic cooperation in Western Europe (as well as economic development in the Middle East and south-east Asia) were central to his objectives as Foreign Secretary. But, of course, Bevin did help construct an anti-Soviet bloc in 1949 and did reject British participation in the Schuman Plan a year later. Perhaps the best way to throw light on what may at first sight appear to be contradictions is to split Bevin's conduct of Britain's foreign policy into two distinct periods. The first of these, from 1945 to around the middle of 1948, saw his thinking at its most creative. Yet it was also the most exasperating in terms of positive outcomes. Between that point and giving up the Foreign Office in 1951 not only were Bevin's energies depleted, but a rather different set of priorities may be seen to emerge which demonstrated his final acceptance of factors which he had earlier been reluctant to recognize; Britain's long-term economic weakness, the institutionalization of East–West tension and the need of American support to counter both of these. The latter period is the one on which Bevin's reputation as Foreign Secretary rests, though to confuse what emerged during that time as representing the outcome of long-held objectives – despite Bevin's later assertions that this was so – is to distort the historical record.

The summer of 1945 saw the new Foreign Secretary animated by an assured and inventive dynamic which envisaged a radical shift in the conduct of Britain's foreign policy. His imprint is chiefly discernible in two initiatives taken with noteworthy speed shortly after returning from his duties at the Potsdam Conference. One concerned the future of Western Europe, the other Britain's place in the Middle East. A little over six months later his attention turned to a similar proposal for south-east Asia. The first two in particular were fuelled by the characteristic brashness of a self-made man at the height of his powers who accepted as givens that the edifice of British world power, if at the moment dilapidated after recent exertions, remained essentially sound and that he was the man to undertake the restoration. That this would require an entirely new approach within a state system which now had at its core two recently peripheral powers whose strength could eclipse Britain's own he fully accepted. Perhaps because he was reluctantly thrust into the arena of foreign affairs – though there is a sliver of evidence that he did, in fact, have ambitions to be Foreign Secretary – he found himself reaching back to ideas consistent with his social democratic convictions to link the stark issue of preserving British authority with the more reflective question of how a civilized state system should improve the lot of all.[6] 'I cannot help feeling', he had written to his predecessor at the end of 1942, 'that so far we have been thinking too much in terms of political groupings, derived from the old balance of power ... I am deeply concerned to get a different approach to post-war organisation – an approach which recognises that while man as a political animal tends to look backwards, as an economic animal he is forced, whether he likes it or not, to look forward.'[7] It was this kind of thinking which encouraged his early promotion of new international groupings in Western Europe, the Middle East and in south-east Asia which would recast the foundations of British power, lay the basis for international cooperation and improve the living standards of the masses across the globe.

Less than a fortnight after returning from Potsdam, Bevin outlined his long-term policy towards Europe. This involved constructing what he called a 'Western Union' which he described as 'workable understandings' between Britain and those countries on the 'Mediterranean and Atlantic fringes of Europe' and especially those surrounding Germany. The heart of this arrangement was to be an Anglo-French accord. It would have a commercial and economic emphasis as well as the political one of keeping Germany in check and would be kick-started by the industrial resources of the Ruhr which would be removed from German control and run by an international consortium.[8] What has been called his 'grand design', was to be deferred and reshaped by opposition from the economic ministries and in response to the uncertain international climate. Yet it remained a central objective of the Foreign Secretary over the next three years. Bevin's thoughts chimed in with those of his advisers who saw political advantage in such an arrangement allowing Britain to gain weight in the counsels of the Big Three and 'restore to us ... the former status of top dog which we have now lost to the USA and USSR'.[9] Bevin would not have demurred and the retention of British authority throughout the world was a mainspring of all his policies. But, as a socialist, he was also concerned with the economic betterment of the masses, and his informal education, as he frequently put it, 'plucked from the 'edgerows of experience' had convinced him of the connection between peace and economic prosperity on the wider international stage. This is clear from his occasional public statements on foreign affairs in the 1920s and 1930s and as a member of the War Cabinet after 1940 he frequently badgered the then Foreign Secretary, Anthony Eden, on the need for an economic foundation to post-war international relations. In the spring of 1944, for instance, he was urging Eden to set up a Mediterranean-based customs union to include Italy, Austria, Greece, Albania and Yugoslavia. In order to 'meet Russian fears' this would not be a political federation and, for the same reason, would not include Czechoslovakia and Poland, though he hoped that the future prosperity of the customs union would encourage these two to join later.[10]

Similar considerations inspired his approach to the Middle East. Again, the swiftness with which he laid out his policy and the consistency with which he was to hold on to it are remarkable. To those officials directly concerned with the region Bevin emphasized from the start his desire to eradicate old-style imperialist exploitation and develop a partnership with the Arabs which would modernize the economies of the region and increase the prosperity of ordinary people. The ideas which made up what one authority has termed Bevin's Middle Eastern 'grand design', 'flowed exuberantly from the tradition of "enlightened" British imperialism'.[11] Here too, his thinking meshed with his advisers in the Eastern Department of the Foreign Office who saw the promotion of social and economic progress as the only way to avoid an anti-capitalist revolution. 'The untrammelled and outrageous exploitation of the workers by the capitalists throughout the Middle East area', one official had remarked in November 1943, 'makes anyone from Europe astonished that the whole working class is not Communist, or at least actively revolutionary'.[12] This was an important concern at a conference on the Middle East which Bevin chaired between 5 and 17 September, 1945. 'We should', he decided, 'broaden the base on which British influence rests and to this end should develop an economic and social policy that would make for the prosperity and contentment of the area as a whole'. Social and economic reform would sap the strength of appeals for revolution as well as producing the economic benefits for Britain of increased markets and continued access to oil. The principal outcome of the conference was the creation of the British Middle East Office intended to coordinate programmes for social and economic improvement across the whole region. It was taken for granted that the Middle East would remain the hub of Britain's global possessions.[13] 'Philanthropy and naked self-interest were thus nicely blended and the whole influenced by a wonderfully optimistic sense of the future prospects of the Middle East as a British sphere of influence.'[14] When in November 1945 the linchpin of this hub, Egypt, requested a revision of the 1936 Anglo-Egyptian treaty upon which the legitimacy for Britain's military presence in the country rested Bevin was prepared to comply. The central issues were the withdrawal to the Suez Canal Zone of those British troops which had spread throughout the country to meet the threat of the Axis and Britain's right to return in time of conflict to protect Egypt (and British installations). Renegotiation of the treaty fitted in with Bevin's instinct to operate on the basis of a partnership rather than as an occupying power and he was prepared to offer British withdrawal from Cairo and Alexandria as it seemed more likely to lead to Egyptian acceptance of a permanent British presence in Suez.[15] A public announcement of the government's decision to withdraw was made by the Prime Minister, Clement Attlee, on 7 May 1946. Even so,

Bevin exhibited some uncertainty. Though the evacuation was 'against our better judgement', he was prepared to proceed because it was 'in pursuance of our undertaking to treat Egypt as an Ally and an equal'.[16] Defending the decision in the House of Commons he was more upbeat. 'Here is a new age', he asserted, 'and we are trying to meet it with advice on education, social services, health, training and all the rest of it'. Once Egypt had tasted these fruits, friendship between the British and the Arabs would cover the whole of the Middle East.[17]

Bevin's intention in November 1945 was to hold another conference to investigate a similar coordination of policies in the Far East. It was not, however, until April 1946 that, at a conference of Commonwealth Prime Ministers, Bevin was able to replicate for south-east Asia his intentions in the Middle East, that is, the need to raise the living standards of the peoples of the region. The delay was significant. At one level it reflected the then subordinate position of the Far East in the hierarchy of British interests. He was also thwarted by his swelling commitments as Foreign Secretary. Most of these concerned intricate issues surrounding Britain's principal interests in Europe and the Middle East. Increasingly, these involved deepening tension with the Soviet Union and this evolution helped to slow down, to shape and eventually to alter the developmental thrust of Bevin's policies. Though, for instance, he spoke at the Prime Ministers' Conference of assisting the economic development of south-east Asia in order to raise the standard of living in that part of the world, his major concern had become the defence of the area and economic development principally as a means to entice Australia and New Zealand into sharing the burden of finance and manpower by the prospect of expanded markets and access to raw materials.[18] '"If the British Empire is liquidated", he told the Prime Ministers, '"it will be liquidated by you!" Australia had withdrawn all her troops from the Far East, New Zealand had only 7,000 men there, and they didn't contribute a penny. Yet they expected [him] to stand up to the Russians and the Americans on their behalf.'[19]

This shift of emphasis was something of a straw in the wind and provides a glimpse too of the impact of the deteriorating international climate since the summer of 1945. By 1946 Bevin had little to show for his efforts. Indeed, his principal biographer has observed that had Bevin retired or died at the end of that year he would have been remembered for a catalogue of failures.[20] Palestine provided the most conspicuous example, not least because shortly after taking office he had publicly stated his intention to 'stake my political future on solving the problem'.[21] This rash assertion reflected a typical over-confidence and that

> he he had not yet fully grasped the intractable nature of the Palestine problem. He believed that men of common sense investigating the problem would quickly conclude that a small territory such as Palestine

could not possibly provide a solution to the Jewish refugee problem and that in any event his skill as a negotiator would see him through.[22]

President Truman's request in August 1945 that 100 000 Jewish refugees from Nazi persecution be admitted to Palestine, if acquiesced and let in, would, Bevin considered, wreck his hopes of a settlement and therefore of buttressing British power in the Middle East via cooperation with the Arab states. Palestine also held the possibility – if the process of treaty revision with Egypt came unstuck, which it did at the end of 1946 – as the fulcrum of the defence of the Middle East and as an alternative to the Suez base. Moreover, Bevin shared the reflex, unthinking anti-Semitism common to his generation (Truman also made jibes at the expense of the Jews – though he chose less public places to express them) and this was inflamed by the implacable and violent fanaticism of extremist Zionists.[23] He also suspected a link between Jewish immigrants and Communism.[24] The President made it quite clear that he needed the Jewish vote. On this, American policy remained consistent, as it did on refusal to permit Jewish immigration to the US, or a joint mandate with Britain in Palestine or troops to police the likely violent response from the Arabs in Palestine if increased Jewish immigration took place. For his part, Bevin was not unsympathetic to the recent traumatic experience of the Jews but saw European assimilation as the solution to the refugee problem. He believed, too, that the case of the Palestinian Arabs was being obscured by the higher profile of the Zionists and their advocates and feared that agreement on the 100 000 would be tacit approval for unlimited immigration. Instead he pressed for a conjointly governed binational state in Palestine and hoped to educate the Americans through diplomatic dialogue, joint committees and conferences into sharing responsibility for attempts to find a solution which would not involve the use of force. But the Americans proved immune to this. Instead, Truman's public statements became more overtly pro-Zionist. On 4 October 1946 he endorsed the support of a Jewish state in Palestine. Faced with escalating violence from extremists, Bevin had decided by the end of the year to turn over British responsibilities in Palestine to the United Nations. A contemporary who was not well-disposed towards Bevin nevertheless commented that 'the villains of the piece are the Americans who have abused us all along in order to please the Jews in New York'.[25]

Bevin's fortunes were clearly in a trough at the end of 1946 – though they were yet to reach their nadir. In November whilst attending a meeting of the Council of Foreign Ministers (CFM) in New York he was hissed and booed in public by New Yorkers because of British actions in Palestine. At home, a group on the left of the Labour Party criticized his policies in the House of Commons as too anti-Soviet and too accommodating to the Americans. In fact, his position on relations with the great powers was quite in keeping with Labour Party thinking. A paper on the post-war settlement which had been circulated by the International Sub-committee of the National Executive Committee of the Labour Party in March 1944 had stressed the importance of continuing 'the closest possible Anglo-American-Russian cooperation' as a 'solid nucleus of a World Organisation'.[26] Bevin's 'line' as Foreign Secretary, in the view of an unsympathetic onlooker, was likely to be 'the appeasement policy of Russia' and in his first Commons speech in his new post, Bevin reiterated that the government's foreign policy 'rests in the main on agreement and cooperation between the Great Powers that have emerged from this war'.[27] An unpromising first encounter at the Potsdam Conference in the summer of 1945 and possessive Soviet behaviour in Eastern Europe, which disturbed Attlee as well as Bevin, did not deflect the Labour government's approach. 'We believe', Attlee wrote at the end of August, 'that the only road to safety lies in the maintenance of trust and understanding between the Great Powers which will give some opportunity for the successful establishment and functioning of the World Organisation on which our hopes for the future are based.'[28]

Bevin would not have disagreed with Attlee's prescription for future peace, but 14 months later fulfilling it was presenting him with serious difficulties. The first post-war meeting of the major powers at the London CFM in October 1945 had concluded disharmoneously. Bevin interpreted the Soviet claim for bases in Turkey and a part of the ex-Italian empire in north Africa as a challenge to Britain's position in the eastern Mediterranean – the hinge of Britain's world authority. The particular circumstance on which the conference broke down, whether France should be permitted full participation in all the proceedings of the peace treaties, added to Bevin's suspicions. At the start of the CFM Molotov agreed to French involvement but he later rescinded his approval. This was quite correctly deciphered as an attempt to promote British collusion in offending French *amour propre* and to prevent the construction of a Western bloc. It was recognized that Molotov had 'had his head washed from the Kremlin' where, recent documents reveal, Stalin was convinced that 'Churchill and his pupils from the Labour Party are the organisers of a British-American-French bloc against the USSR' and over which 'a policy of tenacity and steadfastness should be our guide'.[29] Bevin was convinced, moreover, that what the Russians really wanted from Africa was not bases but uranium. Privately, Molotov suggested that if Soviet possession of one of the Italian colonies was out of the question, he would be prepared instead to have the Belgian Congo which was 'where all the radio-active stuff is mined'.[30] Three months further on, the first meeting of the Security Council of the United Nations, also held in London, descended into Anglo-Soviet recriminations over competing objectives in Greece, the Middle East and south-east Asia. In March 1946 antagonism over Soviet activity in Iran escalated into the first significant international crisis since the end of the war. Bevin's wary approach to the next CFM in Paris was 'like the opening moves of a game of chess or rather poker' and to some the continued discord suggested that 'below the surface of friction and frustration the lines of the future are forming and the world is already beginning to divide into two camps'.[31] Even so, towards the end of a strenuous year, in September 1946, Bevin still sought to account for Soviet behaviour on the grounds that they 'were going through a bad time internally' and Stalin's suspicious reaction to Churchill's Fulton speech. Yet he had to admit that 'he didn't know why the Russians were so difficult'.[32]

The Labour Left believed they had the answer. To them it was Bevin who was the problem. Stalin, of course, thought so too. Speaking to the British Ambassador in Moscow early in 1946 he said 'rather sadly' that he did not understand Bevin's attitude or that of his government. Bevin 'did not treat the Russians as allies' and recent false accusations that the Soviet Union had territorial ambitions had been '"rough" and had given offense to him and to public opinion in Russia'. All Stalin wanted, he explained, 'was to be trusted and to be treated as an ally. He was not getting such treatment.' Stalin complained that at the Moscow CFM at the end of 1945, the Foreign Secretary 'had not been "natural" about Turkey' and his approach 'had offended him' but 'he had been "patient" and let it pass. Nevertheless, he had not liked it ...' Stalin confided to the Ambassador that 'he felt unhappy about our general relationship and much wished that it could be put on a better basis, but so long as the "principal spokesmen" of His Majesty's Government expressed themselves in public as [Bevin] had done, he did not see much chance of this.'[33]

Leaving aside some scepticism that the sensitivities of the Generalissimo could be so easily injured, Bevin was not without responsibility for the turn-down in relations with the Russians. His presentation of the British case over the previous 18 months had noticeably lacked subtlety. A lifetime of trade union negotiations and of bludgeoning union and political colleagues had not prepared him for the more deft requirements of diplomatic intercourse. The Stalin he saw at Potsdam, he dismissed as 'a man with too much on his mind' and therefore 'weak' and he naively equated dealing with Stalin and Truman with his past experience of negotiating shipping disputes with Russian or American sea captains; 'Oh yes', he had decided, 'I can handle them.'[34] But at one point the London CFM almost came to a premature conclusion when Bevin compared Molotov's procedural methods to Hitler's. Forced to apologize in order to avoid the risk of breaking up the proceedings Bevin, according to the American Ambassador to the USSR, was 'crestfallen', 'depressed' and 'humiliated'. One British participant noted that Bevin 'does not speak well. He rambles and repeats himself'.[35] From the vantage point of his post as Ambassador in Washington, Lord Halifax wondered whether Bevin's predecessor, Anthony Eden, might not have handled the Russians more adroitly.[36] Eden himself , observing from a distance, considered Bevin 'had become hysterical' and on two occasions in 1946 the Foreign Secretary did seem temporarily out of his depth. After the resignation of General de

Gaulle as provisional President of France on 20 January he was alarmed that this would precipitate a Communist coup leading to 'civil war within the year' after which 'the Channel ports will virtually be in Russian hands'. Two months later he was again 'in a strung up state' over the possibility of war with the Russians over Iran.[37]

Yet Bevin's critics were wrong to see his policies driven by antipathy to the Soviet Union. Notwithstanding his inexperience, naivety and bluster Bevin's instincts fitted in with the Labour government's general line of trying to work with the Russians where they did not interfere with British interests. But breaking through what the Chancellor of the Exchequer, Hugh Dalton, called 'this queer transparent wall which seems to separate us' was no easy matter.[38] Bevin had recognized from the first that his ambition to construct a politico-economic 'Western Union' as a basis for enhanced British authority was likely to give rise to apprehensions both in Moscow and Washington. Out of consideration for these, especially the former, he was inclined, against the advice of his experts, to proceed slowly in order to educate the Russians to the view that what he had in mind implied continued East–West collaboration rather than a challenge. At the end of 1946 his aim remained to develop an informal foundation for British power which would allow continued independence of either the USSR or the US. In any case the Americans were proving unreliable and unsupportive and this tied in with his preference that Britain should stand on her own.[39] Bevin, for instance, went to the Paris CFM instructed to oppose both the Russian and American proposals for the future of the Italian colonies. He was keen to do so. The British government, he told an official, 'were fed up. "Russia said this and America says that. Where do we come in who did the fighting there?"'.[40] But, for the time being at least, the Americans held the financial cards and this added another set of frictions. As Hugh Dalton noted, 'the abrupt stoppage of Lend-Lease followed by these long negotiations [for a US loan] in Washington, in which Halifax and [John Maynard] Keynes go on explaining but meet nothing but a row of poker faces across the table are not encouraging'.[41] Eden privately commented that 'at the election Labour had claimed that they could get on better with Russia. They had not. In the US the whole position was being reversed'.[42] Bevin's confidence over how this could be managed was less bright than it had been in the summer of 1945. Then he had approached his new responsibilities 'bursting with ideas', his 'magnificent mind' throwing out 'too many ideas', and much of the frustration of his first months in office was in learning the limits of the weakest member of a great power triumvirate and, therefore, separating what was desirable from what was practicable.[43] Dalton observed in March 1946 that 'in these last weeks [Bevin] has seemed sometimes much less self-confident and self-sufficient than he used to be. Sometimes, indeed, he has seemed to be clinging for support to me and one or two other colleagues. He finds himself facing bigger difficulties than he ever expected.'[44] Returning with Bevin from the New York CFM on the *Queen*

Elizabeth his Private Secretary noted in his diary the intensity of the Foreign Secretary's workload – the peace treaties, Germany, Egypt, Palestine, Iran and Greece – which at times made 'the poor S. of S. ... almost unmanageable'. Not surprisingly, the more so given his proclivity for strong drink ('when you went to see him at the FO', one visitor noted, 'he had a bottle in the bottom drawer of his desk') and cigarettes, his health began to give way. From the summer of 1946 until reluctant retirement his term of office was increasingly punctuated by signs of physical decay and stays in hospital.[45]

In the winter of 1945/46 Bevin's thoughts, as did others, turned to what he saw as a world separating out into rigid spheres of influence. At a meeting of Foreign Ministers of the Big Three in Moscow at the end of 1945 he spoke to James Byrnes, the American Secretary of State, of a world 'drifting into the position of "three Monroes"' – the existing American 'Monroe', a developing Soviet sphere, and leaving Britain 'between the two with the western world all divided up'. It was not a prospect he relished and his preference was to avoid so precise a partition by working through the United Nations, pursuing Big Three cooperation and continuing for the time being to avoid setting up an explicit regional group with Britain's European neighbours. He was conscious, however, that in their own interests the British might eventually have to

> rely on our right to maintain the security of the British Commonwealth on the same terms as others are maintaining theirs, and to develop, within the conception of the United Nations, good relations with our near neighbours in the same way as the United States have developed their relations on the continent of America.[46]

In line with this thinking, inter-departmental groups investigated the possibilities of a customs union with the West European states and in March 1947 a treaty was signed at Dunkirk with France – the key partner in any 'Western Union'. Resistance came from the Treasury and Board of Trade whose arguments were reinforced by the power shortages brought on by the extraordinary winter of early 1947 and the convertibility crisis of the following summer. Domestically, there was mild alarm over a possible drift to Communism and more widespread talk of coalition government.[47] Coincidentally Bevin announced his intention to withdraw support from the increasingly intractable political situation in Greece – though he did not anticipate Truman's publicly strident response. Retreat here was thus added to withdrawal in India, Egypt and Palestine. One critic condemned the 'barrenness of the results' of Bevin's foreign policy adding tartly, 'the only thing to his credit is his alliance with a France more decadent than it was in 1940'.[48]

A crucial battleground of two of the emergent 'three Monroes', Bevin believed, was likely to be Germany where 'every sort of political trick will be resorted to in order to control or eliminate this eventual reservoir of power'. Particularly vital was the Ruhr, the heartland of German industry and the forge of 'Prussian' militarism. Bevin had already embraced the notion of the coalmines and steel mills of the Ruhr being made to work for the benefit of a 'Western Union' with an enthusiasm which was to impact upon his whole attitude towards Germany. 'He hoped', he said, 'that the Ruhr might become a unifying instrument owing to the system of trade exchanges which might be set up between it and other countries in Europe.'[49] This vision, however, did not include the USSR and an anti-German strategy was also, from the start, anti-Russian. Though it took some time for Bevin to work out his ideas he was always wary of an international control which would 'encourage the Soviet Government to stake out claims in the Ruhr' which he saw as a strictly West European enterprise.[50] But, as his officials were warning at the end of 1945, Stalin, who had been led to believe at the end of the war that the Ruhr would be operated by 'the Allies', was unlikely to accept any scheme which excluded them altogether.[51] By the spring of 1946 the Ruhr issue had merged with a more general deterioration in Four Power policy in Germany which amplified Bevin's determination to keep the Russians out. By this time, his German policy

> faced the fact that Europe was now being divided into two spheres of influence and it would give us an opportunity to prove that we could build up in western Germany, under a democratic system, an efficient industrial organisation which challenged comparison with that which is being created under a different system in east Germany.[52]

This was a change in direction of profound proportions and broke a cardinal principle of Labour thinking on post-war international relations. On his return from Potsdam, for example, Attlee had warned that any hint of an attempt to resuscitate or deal leniently with the Germans would only harden the Soviet attitude in Eastern Europe and cut across the principle that 'the maintenance of Allied unity is of paramount importance'.[53] Bevin was temperamentally inclined to be tough on Germany and, even as British occupation policy began to change, his instinct remained that the Germans might, after all, be the ones most likely to disturb the peace. Being hard on the Germans, however, proved to be more complex than the British had anticipated. At the first United Nations meeting in January 1946, Bevin tried to ease Russian fears of a revived Germany being used against them by telling the Soviet representative, Andrei Vyshinsky, that the British government was not prepared to spend a penny to keep Germany going. 'At the same time', he admitted to the French a little later, 'he could not believe that it would be practicable to hold Germany down on the basis of absolute starvation. Such a policy would produce a militant reaction in a few years time.'[54] Of more immediate moment, not to give the Germans economic respite involved self-inflicted damage to Britain which was having to divert dollars and wheat imports to prevent collapse in their zone of occupation. Friction emerged from opposing positions on the industrial resource the Germans would need for their economic survival before they began to make reparation payments. Understandably, the British were increasingly inclined to favour a higher industrial capability for the Germans in order to rid themselves of a burden. Equally understandably, the Soviet Union, which had suffered more material damage than any other victorious power, argued for a lower volume for German industry to allow for a greater surplus from which reparation could be taken. The tension was magnified by suspicions on each side that economic arguments disguised political objectives. As Bevin put it, 'it is difficult to see what the Russians are after by adopting this attitude unless it were to make the standard of living in West Germany so low that Communist influence would rapidly spread over it'.[55] Advice from his experts on how to face up to this was mixed, though the consequences of a Western consolidation were clearly stated:

> If we decide to build up our own zone, or the three Western zones together we should have to realise that the Russians would react by intensifying the absorption of their zone into the Russian system and we should be establishing a definite frontier line between Russia and the West on the Russian zonal boundary instead of having Germany as a kind of glacis between the two systems but adhering wholly to neither.[56]

Nevertheless, though with some trepidation, Bevin shaped British policy over the rest of 1946 towards the likelihood of a divided Germany.

Bevin's uncertainty over what to do in Germany is quite apparent, especially his irresolution over fusing the British and American zones in mid-1946, suggesting that his intention was not an irrevocable breach with the Soviets over Germany but rather a desire to stake out what he considered to be the boundaries of essential British interests and so lay the ground for a consequent *modus vivendi*. If, in doing so, he stimulated Russian suspicions that the West was bent upon reviving German strength Stalin, on the evidence of Soviet and Soviet bloc files, was unable to decide whether he wanted a divided or a united (and communised) Germany. Bevin's eventual decision to work for the former simply beat the Soviets to the punch.[57] Over the Ruhr, however, Bevin was consistently firm and his insistence on prohibiting Soviet participation well before the emergence of more general controversies sowed the dragon's teeth of inevitable confrontation with Moscow. Yet, even here, one must take account of the fact that Bevin was operating on two levels. On the first was his determination to take the Ruhr from Germany yet not give access to Russia. This reflected a not unreasonable uncertainty as to where the next threat to world peace emanated. The past suggested Germany, the future was inevitably cloudy. Meanwhile, the

Ruhr should play its part in his wider schemes for the resuscitation of Britain and Western Europe without dependence on the two states who were to become the dominant superpowers.

Dissension over Germany coloured the Moscow CFM during March and April of 1947. Bevin wrote home to Attlee that he was 'fed up with the long stay here. There are such little or no results'. There is, he noted, 'courtesy, there are no high words being used, no tempers, but all of it is cool, calculated and between the two big boys looks to me to be pretty determined'. 'For us as Britishers', he wrote, 'in between the two of them, our task is very difficult.'[58] On his return to London he told officials in early May that given that Russian power was pre-eminent in Eastern Europe and American in the west of the globe, it was time for Britain to begin to develop its own sphere in Western Europe.[59] A month later the American Secretary of State, George Marshall, in an understated speech at Harvard seemed to hint at a new financial approach to Europe. Bevin's recognition of its import and his energy in shaping the inference into the reality of what became the Marshall Plan has commonly been regarded as the Foreign Secretary's 'finest hour'.[60] Such a judgement largely depends on whether we see him pushing the West Europeans into the safety of the stockade which Washington now appeared to be erecting. Yet, the British economic setback of the dreadful winter of 1947 was traumatic rather than structural and, as the more serious prospect of convertibility approached, Bevin seemed to view the haemorrhage of dollars with equanimity. 'The US will see us through', he told his private secretary, '... leave it to me and Lew Douglas [the American Ambassador to Britain]'.[61] This reflects his initial hope that the Marshall proposals would allow London to be the channel of aid to the Europeans, so giving the British an illusion of preferential status. As he soon discovered, it was a quite unrealistic expectation and there was no chance of Douglas, or any other American, putting a case for individual treatment for the UK. But what continued to attract him was the integrationist thrust of the Marshall speech which held implications for a 'Western Union' as a third way between the two emerging superpowers. In September Bevin was insisting to Attlee that

> I am sure we must free ourselves of financial dependence on the United States of America as soon as possible. We shall never be able to pull our weight in foreign affairs until we do so ... Hence the importance not only of closer trade relations with the Commonwealth and Empire but also of an intensified effort for development within them. To take one example, if we could develop the Wankie coal field in Southern Rhodesia, we could sell coal to the Argentine which would help us indirectly to get food for the United Kingdom.[62]

Here was a further elaboration of the 'grand design' for cooperation between the states of Western Europe which he had outlined in August 1945.

But so far it had made little progress. As we have seen, this was in part because it might summon opposition from Washington and Moscow. There was also obstruction from the Treasury and Board of Trade that neither Britain nor her European neighbours were in strong enough positions to embark upon novel schemes of economic collaboration. The latter pushed Bevin towards collaboration which would embrace the colonial dependencies of the Western Europeans. Disengagement in India, Palestine, Greece and Egypt also focused Bevin's attention on the possibilities of cooperation in sub-Saharan Africa. By this time, too, a small Cabinet committee – which included Bevin – had decided to authorize the manufacture of a British atom bomb and it was in central Africa that most of the world's supply of uranium existed. And, once more, he was revisiting ideas of the pooling of European colonial resources which he had first mooted nearly ten years ago. He declared to the French Prime Minister in September 1947 that since becoming Foreign Secretary,

> one of [his] principal objectives had been to strengthen good relations between the two countries. With their populations of 47 million and 40 million respectively and with their vast colonial possessions they could, if they acted together, be as powerful as either the Soviet Union or the United States … In addition to their populations they possessed between them supplies of raw materials greater than those of any other country.

His impression was that the French believed, as he did, that the division of Europe was now 'inevitable' and it was necessary to organize Western Europe into a 'coherent unity'. The Marshall Plan provided 'an opportunity of making the first step in this direction by endeavouring to form a customs union'.[63]

The Marshall Plan, of course, accentuated European divisions and Bevin was to play his part in this process. When the Marshall proposals emerged, Bevin 'on his own initiative' decided to go to Paris to consider them with the French. In 'a discussion in a corner with the French PM and Bidault' it 'became apparent that they are determined to give the Russians a chance of coming in. We do not disagree. Except that we are determined to go ahead without the Russians if they frustrate or stall us'.[64] On 2 July Molotov walked out of the ensuing deliberations over a clash between Anglo-French insistence in sticking to the explicit American directive that the Europeans should come up with a joint scheme and the Soviet desire for individual submissions. As noted, Bevin was as eager as Molotov to be in receipt of particular American aid but the aspirations of both were dashed. Nevertheless, the Marshall Plan's approval for European integration (coupled with worsening relations with the Soviets) meant that he could now bring into the open his plans for West European cooperation which he had harboured since the summer of 1945. In Cabinet in January 1948 he proposed 'to mobilise the resources of Africa' in support of a Western

European union and that, 'if some such union could be created, including not only the countries of Western Europe but their Colonial possessions in Africa and the East, this would form a *bloc* which, both in population and productive capacity, could stand on an equality with the western hemisphere and Soviet *blocs*.' 'It is', he asserted,

> for us as Europeans, and not the Americans, to give the lead in spiritual, moral and political sphere [sic] to all the democratic elements in Western Europe which are anti-Communist and, at the same time, genuinely progressive and reformist, believing in freedom, planning and social justice – what one might call the 'Third Force'.

Material support for this would have to come via Marshall Aid. At the same time, the Western Europeans 'despise the spiritual values of America' and if a Western European system were organized and backed by the resources of the Commonwealth and America 'it should be possible to develop our own power and influence to equal that of the United States of America and the USSR'. The emphasis, as one informed outsider recognized when these ideas were made public in a Commons speech on 22 January, was not so much on defence but 'stood for an economic and, if possible, political union of western Europe'.[65] The military weakness of the Europeans in the face of an apparent threat from the Soviet Union was a consideration and American defensive support seen to be important. But Bevin was also 'definitely of the opinion that we ought to aim at a joint multi-lateral economic, social and defensive treaty without any previous guarantee of American backing'.[66]

The outcome of this thinking, the Brussels Treaty, which was signed between Britain, France and the Benelux states on 17 March 1948, was the high-water mark of Bevin's attempt to organize what he called 'the middle of the planet' as a counterpart to the US and USSR. Of the Treaty's ten clauses the first three asserted the collective aspirations of the signatories in economic, social and cultural policies. The acceding states were to be known collectively as 'Western Union', harking back to the ideas Bevin had first put to his officials less than three years before. Yet within a year Bevin had decided that tighter economic links with the Europeans were inimical to British interests and had guided the UK and its principal European partners into a defensive alliance with the US. The reasons for this quite rapid change of direction are varied. In common with others, Bevin had assumed that the financial and economic dysfunction caused by the war would soon pass. Both Dalton and Keynes had encouraged this optimism during the first year of the Labour government.[67] But the convertibility crisis of 1947 was followed two years later by a 30 per cent devaluation of sterling. The shift of emphasis of the 'grand design' from Europe to colonial cooperation, merely added another set of problems – shortage of consumer goods to entice indigenous workers to increase productivity, the reluctance of these workers to change their means of production and an inadequate economic infrastructure. This was most evident in Africa. Moreover, in November 1948 the Treasury argued that unless the sterling area began to pay its way in a world where dollars were in short supply 'the United Kingdom itself will be unable to provide the overseas capital investment upon which the Colonial territories must rely if their economic development is to be accelerated'.[68] In the Middle East, too, the necessary funds and resources were thin on the ground and there was difficulty in recruiting personnel with the relevant economic expertise. The relinquishing of the Palestine mandate and the declaration of the state of Israel in 1948 was, according to the head of the Middle East Office, inimical to fostering economic and social change among the Arabs because 'their hearts will not be in development while they are all the time looking over their shoulders at the Israeli frontier'. Furthermore, the British found that a partnership to ease the lot of the masses boiled down to collaborating with the forces of reaction whilst burgeoning nationalist opinion detected no distinction between Bevin's form of association and what had existed before.[69] In south-east Asia, too, the colonial slant of 'Western Union' aroused indigenous suspicions of the Europeans ganging up to exploit them. Insurrection in Malaya in the summer of 1948 – which Stalin was widely judged to be behind – and the Communist victory in China in 1949 edged development policy in the area, further in the direction of containing Communism. Initiatives towards south-east Asia continued to have an ethical impetus and Bevin's personal involvement in the Colombo Plan, inaugurated in January 1950 to provide direct aid to the area, indicates his continuing interest in them. Yet the Colombo scheme, as well as being predicated on economic development to resist the spread of Communism in south-east Asia, expected the bulk of the cost to come from America – 'on the basis', as Bevin put it, 'that the United Kingdom provided experience and the United States provided finance'.[70]

Not surprisingly, the particular schemes which Bevin came up with in the context of his broader objectives – a 'new triangle of trade' between east Africa, India and Australia; a trans-African highway from Lagos to Mombasa – 'proved on investigation to be unworkable'.[71] It may be doubted, though, whether economic difficulties alone would have staunched Bevin's creativity. Constantly shadowing his aim to build a renewed foundation for British authority, however, was the gloomy prospect of a breakdown in international cooperation. The Treaty of Dunkirk, for instance, had been inspired by fears of Communist influence in France and the Brussels Treaty was induced by the Stalinist coup in Czechoslovakia. This deteriorating international scene reached new depths in the summer of 1948 with the onset of the Berlin blockade. Bevin saw this menacing crisis, which his German policy had helped to bring on, as 'an issue of will' which could lead to a *modus vivendi* with the Soviets if only the West stood firm. At the same time, it revealed the military weakness of the Western Europeans and accentuated the defensive benefits of a 'Western Union'. The Americans, too, were now more fearful of Soviet expansionism and, in early 1949, were willing to put their name to Western European defence. Yet even as the negotiations for the North Atlantic Treaty were being finalized the Cabinet was urged that 'we should use US aid to gain time, but our ultimate aim should be to attain a position in which the countries of Western Europe would be independent both of the US and the Soviet Union'.[72] Only a year on and this last vestige of Bevin's previous aims had vanished under the impact of an obviously politically ruptured world. In May 1950 a Cabinet paper from Bevin accepted that

> in all matters of foreign policy and defence policy there could be no doubt that our interests would best be served by the closest co-operation with the United States and Canada. It was clear that, even with the support of the Commonwealth, Western Europe was not strong enough to contend with the military dangers confronting it from the East ... and for the original conception of Western Union we must now begin to substitute the wider conception of the Atlantic community.[73]

With the collapse of his 'grand designs' for Europe and the Middle East and the developing strains of the Cold War Bevin's foreign policy now began to fit the image which received wisdom has allotted it. Recently an ardent supporter of cooperative developments in Western Europe he became, with almost equal fervour, a sceptic of integrationist proposals emerging from the Continent. The Americans, whom he had originally hoped to keep at arm's length, were transformed into indispensable partners against a predatory Soviet Union. Most of his colleagues had undergone similar conversions. Few, for instance, in the summer of 1950 doubted that Stalin was behind North Korea's invasion of the South. Indeed, Soviet archives indicate that this was the case. More to the point, they also suggest that Bevin's refusal since 1945 to concede to pressure was the proper course and that the Soviet threat was no exaggeration. Though Stalin wished to preserve the war-time alliance with the West he also believed that ideological contradictions meant that cooperation could not last. In the meantime, his 'Bolshevik style' of diplomacy involved '"knocking at all doors" in search of possible gains, frequent use of brinkmanship and wedging tactics, brutal pressure and persistence'.[74] It may be that Bevin's policies, especially in Germany, induced a hostile response from Stalin sooner rather than later though the evidence suggests that, so long as Stalin was alive, it could not have been put off indefinitely. It is to Bevin's credit that he closed avenues of Soviet penetration whilst preserving the hope that some permanent stability might emerge. And if, in hindsight, his rearguard action to preserve Britain's role in a world in flux appears futile this was far from obvious at the time and, given the imaginativeness with which he engaged the campaign, his stature is the greater for the attempt. The creation of an American alliance through NATO was an important achievement in that it closed the door to the Soviets in the West and was ultimately to contribute to victory in the Cold War – but it had played no part in his original intentions.

Inevitably, falling in with the Americans had a price and in his anxiety to ensure that their commitment to NATO survived Bevin soon developed a deep disinclination to annoy Washington. He succumbed to pressure from Washington to increase defence spending – though in this he was supported by Attlee, the Treasury and the Chiefs of Staff. But Bevin had clearly changed his tack towards the Americans. Kenneth Younger, who was Minister of State at the start of the Korean War and who deputized for Bevin when he was hospitalized, put the Foreign Secretary firmly in the '"don't be rude to the Americans" school'. In January 1951 Younger, fearful that the Americans were building themselves up for a limited war against China, urged the government, with the Commonwealth, 'to speak more brutally about it' to Washington. Bevin 'obviously disliked' the suggestion and in front of Attlee 'wailed almost tearfully that this was the end of the US/UK alliance'. In his diaries, the Minister of State expressed his 'total lack of confidence in Ernie. I know he would simply like to follow Acheson [the American Secretary of State] quietly, because he has as good as said so in an Office meeting. He also said that if we didn't go with the Americans on this "we would be letting the Americans down"'.[75] Younger was right. The British had leverage but after NATO Bevin was averse to using it and submission to regular American threats that they would abandon support for the defence of Europe ignored America's own interest in not doing so. He was not alone in this. In the Cabinet as a whole there was 'great reluctance to be tough with the Americans' and many in the Foreign Office adopted the same line. Even Aneurin Bevan, Minister of Health and an outspoken critic of surrender to American imperialism, privately argued that over Korea 'we could do nothing but support the Americans: "When you are in a world-wide alliance, you cannot retreat from it on a single issue"'.[76] When the chips were down Younger, too, balked at a major breach with Washington.[77] There was at least some excuse for Bevin's inertia. By this time he was barely functioning. In Younger's view, Bevin's judgement was 'very good indeed' when not in pain but he operated for little more than two hours a day and 'was so heavily drugged every night that he didn't really come properly out of the drugs until about 11.30 the next morning'. 'He just manages to get through his essential work, but he has no energy left for anything more.'[78]

Bevin's analogue in dealing with the Americans should have been Western European integration. Here US pressure for the UK to participate in the Schuman Plan and a European Army was resisted. Though he now favoured the concept of European unity as a way of countering the 'present material and moral weakness' of the Western European states and for the preservation of democracy, after careful examination of its implications, Britain's own participation in closer economic integration with the Europeans was firmly rejected.[79] If, from our vantage point, this seems misguided it was unquestionably in harmony with majority thinking in Britain. The same might be said of each stage of Bevin's foreign policy. Few were prepared to contemplate a new war with the Soviet Union. On the other hand, a comprehensive retreat from British responsibilities in the early post-war years would have been regarded as a policy of scuttle and surrender. Furthermore, Attlee's well-known preference at the end of 1946 for a British withdrawal from the Middle East implied a vacuum which, Bevin, the Foreign Office and the Chiefs of Staff insisted, Stalin would have filled. And the Soviet archives suggest that they were right. An attempt to inject a humanitarian configuration to British colonialism without detriment to Britain's material or strategic world position also squared with the moderate socialism for which an overwhelming majority had voted in 1945.[80] So too did the rejection of spheres of influence or power blocs in the conduct of world affairs. Bevin was sensitive to each of these. If this passed unnoticed by the left wing of his party he was himself largely to blame. It was not that he concealed his views from the Left but rather that he didn't much care about their opinions – so long has they left him to conduct his policies unhindered. A Foreign Affairs Group, intended to manage opinion within the parliamentary Labour Party, was 'a disaster', mainly because of Bevin's 'contempt' for it. As a colleague recollected, Bevin 'was not a Parliamentarian; ... He didn't give a damn for MPs and didn't know quite why they were there. He never made the slightest effort to get himself accepted.'[81] Continuity in foreign policy is not necessarily a pejorative, though in the hands of some of Bevin's critics it is intended to be. But continuity was not the essence of Bevin's plan. In any case, continuity of what? Churchill's war-time hope for continuing cooperation with the Soviets after the war; or his suspicion of Stalin which came to predominate the five months before victory? Bevin's association with Eden after 1945 is well documented though he was not a captive of his predecessor's thinking.[82] Eden was, in any case, an advocate of working with the Soviets in 1945. So too were most of Bevin's professional advisers and when their view hardened in 1946 he was slow to follow. If anything Bevin was closer to Churchill's earlier position though with a vision of Britain playing an equal role to the emerging superpowers that Churchill's fondness for a 'special relationship' with the US did not allow. Though he failed in the objectives which he set himself in 1945, the vision of what he had hoped to achieve remained with him until the end. Two years after NATO and when his life was almost over he expressed to a member of his Private Office rare, introspective doubts about whether or not he had been successful.

> 'If only I had had a bit longer ... If only', he went on, 'I'd had time to make the Atlantic Pac[t] ... into something large, into a wider organism, with a budget and other things for the whole area' – he was talking more in his

old ways now, great, vague but visionary ideas. He sat with his hands lying lifeless on their sides on the desk ... He went on: 'And given time, I think I would have been able to settle Egypt. I am just on the verge. When we began six years ago nobody knew all the changes that would happen in the Far East ... I could have done a lot in Asia.'[83]

Notes

1. Pierson Dixon Diary, 1 February 1946.
2. Wm. Roger Louis, *The British Empire in the Middle East, 1945–51* (Oxford: Clarendon Press, 1984), p. 3. Frank Roberts, another of Bevin's Private Secretaries, provides some of these appraisals in 'Ernest Bevin as Foreign Secretary', R. Ovendale (ed.), *The Foreign Policy of the British Labour Governments, 1945–51* (Leicester: Leicester University Press, 1984), p. 21; A. Shlaim, P. Jones and K. Sainsbury, *British Foreign Secretaries Since 1945* (Newton Abbot: David & Charles, 1977), p. 69.
3. P. Weiler, *British Labour and the Cold War* (Stanford, CA.: Stanford University Press, 1988), pp. 191–4; P. Weiler, *Ernest Bevin*, (Manchester: Manchester University Press, 1993), pp. 144–87; J. Saville, *The Politics of Continuity: British Foreign Policy and the Labour Government, 1945–46* (London: Verso, 1993), *passim*.
4. P[ublic] R[ecord] O[ffice], FO 371,49070, Z12033/13/17; PRO, CAB 129(3), CP(45)218.
5. See S. Greenwood, *Britain and European Integration Since the Second World War* (Manchester: Manchester University Press, 1996), pp. 36–7.
6. K. Young (ed.), *The Diaries of Sir Robert Bruce Lockhart, 1939–65* (London: Macmillan, 1980). Diary entry, 14 July 1945, p. 468.
7. Bevin to Eden, 8 December 1942. Cited in A. Bullock, *The Life and Times of Ernest Bevin, Vol 2* (London: Heinemann, 1967), p. 205.
8. PRO, FO 371, 49069, Z9595/13/17; 45731, UE3683,3689/3683/53.
9. PRO, FO 371, 49069, Z9196/13/17, minute by Hebblethwaite, 10 August 1945.
10. PRO, FO 371, 38832, C7449/164/3, record of conversation between Bevin and Eden, 31 May 1944.
11. Wm. Roger Louis, *British Empire*, p. 46.
12. PRO, FO 371, 39988, minute by Hankey, 29 November 1943. Cited in Wm. Roger Louis, *British Empire*, pp. 47–8.
13. PRO, CAB 129/2, CP(45)174, 17 September 1945; CAB 128/1, CM 38(45)6, 4 October 1945.
14. W.K. Wark, 'Development Diplomacy: Sir John Troutbeck and the British Middle East Office, 1947–50', in J. Zametica (ed.), *British Officials and British Foreign Policy, 1945–50* (Leicester: Leicester University Press, 1990), p. 233.
15. PRO, CAB 131/1, DO(46)8, 18 March 1946. Cited in Wm. Roger Louis, *British Empire*, p. 233.
16. Wm. Roger Louis, *British Empire*, p. 236.
17. House of Commons Debates, 24 May 1946, cols 779–90.
18. T. Remme, *Britain and Regional Cooperation in South-East Asia, 1945–49* (London: Routledge, 1995), pp. 23 and 57–9.
19. Oliver Harvey Diary (British Library), 29 April 1946.
20. A. Bullock, *Ernest Bevin: Foreign Secretary, 1945–1951* (London: Heinemann, 1983), p. 345.

21. House of Commons Debates, 13 November 1945, col. 1934.
22. Wm. Roger Louis, *British Empire*, p. 390.
23. See, C. Mayhew, *Time to Explain* (London: Hutchinson, 1987), pp. 118–20.
24. Wm. Roger Louis, *British Empire*, pp. 42–3.
25. S. Ball (ed.), *The Headlam Diaries, 1935–51* (Cambridge: Cambridge University Press, 1999), 10 December 1947, p. 536.
26. Bevin Papers (Churchill College, Cambridge), BEVN 2/12.
27. S. Ball (ed.), *Headlam Diaries*, 2 August 1945, p. 472; House of Commons Debates, 513, 20 August 1945.
28. J. Van der Poel (ed.), *Selections from the Smuts Papers, Vol. VII, August 1945–October 1950*, (Cambridge: Cambridge University Press, 1973), Attlee to Smuts, 31 August 1945, p. 6.
29. Dalton Diary (London School of Economics), 5 October 1945; V.O. Pechatnov, *Foreign Policy Correspondence Between Stalin and Molotov, September, 1945-December, 1946* (Washington DC: Woodrow Wilson Centre, 1999); Cold War International History Project (CWIHP), Working Paper 26, pp. 11 and 14.
30. Dalton Diary, 5 October 1945.
31. Oliver Harvey Diary, 25 April 1946; Van der Poel (ed.), *Smuts Papers, Vol. VII*, Smuts to J. H. Hofmeyer, 29 August 1946, p. 73.
32. Hugh Dalton, *High Tide and After, 1945–1960* (London: Muller, 1962), pp. 155–6.
33. Inverchapel Papers (Bodleian Library, Oxford), Sir Archibald Clark-Kerr to Bevin, 29 January 1946.
34. N. Henderson, *The Private Office* (London: Weidenfeld & Nicolson, 1984), p. 22.
35. W.A. Harriman and E. Abel, *Special Envoy to Churchill and Stalin, 1941–46* (London: Hutchinson, 1976), p. 507; Duff Cooper, *Old Men Forget* (London: Hart-Davis, 1953), p. 363.
36. Halifax Diary (University of York), A7.8.17, 1 October 1945.
37. Young (ed.), *Diaries of Sir Robert Bruce Lockhart* diary entry, 10 March 1946, pp. 526 and 531; PRO, FO 371, 59956, Z697/21/17. Undated Bevin minute on FO memorandum dated 21 January 1946; Dalton Diary, 22 March 1946.
38. Dalton Diary, 16 May 1945.
39. Van der Poel (ed.), *Smuts Papers*, Attlee to Smuts, 31 August 1945; Halifax Diary, 2 August 1945; Harvey Diary, 13 August 1945.
40. Harvey Diary, 29 April 1946.
41. Dalton Diary, 5 October 1945.
42. K. Young (ed.), *The Diaries of Sir Robert Bruce Lockhart*. Diary entry, 16 February 1946, p. 526.
43. Piers Dixon, *Double Diploma: The Life of Sir Pierson Dixon* (London: Hutchinson, 1968), diary entries 8 August 1945 and 9 October 1945, pp. 178 and 196.
44. Dalton Diary, 22 March 1946. The last sentence of this quotation is not in the original diary but included, as though it was, in Dalton's third volume of memoirs, *High Tide and After*, p. 105.
45. Young (ed.) *Diaries of Sir Robert Bruce Lockhart* diary entry 12 March 1947, p. 588.
46. *Foreign Relations of the United States*, 1945 (II), pp. 585 and 629; S. Greenwood, *The Alternative Alliance: Anglo-French Relations Before the Coming of NATO, 1944–48* (London: Minerva, 1996), pp. 103–4; R. Edmonds, *Setting the Mould: the United States and Britain, 1945–50* (Oxford: Clarendon Press, 1986), pp. 27–8.
47. S. Ball (ed.), *Headlam Diaries*, 17 April 1947, p. 500; Dixon Diary, 21 February 1947.
48. K. Young (ed.), *Diaries of Sir Robert Bruce Lockhart*, 8 August 1947, p. 619.
49. PRO, FO 371, 55402, C4777/14/18, 15 April 1946.

50. PRO, FO 371, 46989, C6583/5317/18; 46723, C6134/22/18, Bevin to Bidault, 16 September 1945; 48929, Z13223/188/4, Bevin to Spaak, 26 November 1945.
51. PRO, FO 181/990/2, report of a meeting in the Kremlin, 17 October 1944.
52. PRO, CAB 129(8), CP(46)139, 15 April 1946; CAB 128(5), CM(46)36, 17 April 1946.
53. J. Van der Poel (ed.), *Smuts Papers*, Attlee to Smuts, 31 August 1945, pp. 6–7.
54. PRO, FO 371, 59971, Z1080/65/17, Bevin to Bidault, 1 February 1946.
55. PRO, FO 371, 55402, C4633/14/18, Bevin to Netherlands Prime Minister, 13 April 1946.
56. PRO, FO 371, 55400, C2311/14/18, Strang minute, 27 February 1946; C3648/130/18, Roberts memorandum, 20 February 1946; C2968/2/18, Burrows minute, 22 March 1946.
57. W. Loth, 'Stalin's Plans for Post-War Germany', in F. Gori and S. Pons (eds), *The Soviet Union and Europe in the Cold War, 1943–53* (London: Macmillan, 1996).
58. Sargent Papers, PRO, FO 800, 272, Cfc/47/4, Bevin to Attlee, 16 April 1947.
59. J.W. Young, *Britain, France and the Unity of Europe, 1945–51* (Leicester: Leicester University Press, 1984), p. 60; G. Warner, 'The Labour Governments and the Unity of Western Europe, 1945–51', in R. Ovendale (ed.), *The Foreign Policy of the British Labour Governments, 1945–51* (Leicester: Leicester University Press, 1984), p. 63.
60. A. Danchev, *Oliver Franks: Founding Father* (Oxford: Clarendon Press, 1993), p. 58. Also, Edmonds, *Setting the Mould*, p. 161; K.O. Morgan, *Labour In Power, 1945–51* (Oxford: Oxford University Press, 1985), p. 270.
61. Pierson Dixon Diary, 27 July 1947.
62. PRO, FO 800/444, ff 29–31, 16 September, 1947.
63. Bullock, *Life and Times of Ernest Bevin,Vol.1*, p. 623; PRO, FO 371, 67673, Z8461, Z8579, Z9053/G, report of conversations between Bevin and Paul Ramadier, 22 September 1947. For Bevin's thinking at this point, see: S. Greenwood, *Alternative Alliance*, Ch. 13; M.J. Hogan, *The Marshall Plan*, pp. 46–53; J. Kent, *British Imperial Strategy and the Origins of the Cold War, 1944–49* (Leicester: Leceister University Press, 1993), *passim*; Warner, 'Labour Governments', pp. 62–6; J.W. Young, *Britain, France and Unity*, Ch. 7.
64. Dixon Diary, 17 June 1947.
65. S. Ball (ed.), *Headlam Diaries*, 22 January 1948, p. 539. See also 2 April 1948, p. 555.
66. PRO, CAB 128/12, CM 2(48)5, 8 January 1948; CAB 129, CP(48)8, 4 January 1948; CP(48)6, 4 January 1948; Warner, 'The Labour Governments', pp. 66–7.
67. Dalton Diary, 22 March, 1946; Halifax Diary, 5 March 1946. As late as 6 March 1947 Dixon referred to Britain's 'temporary weakness', Dixon Diary.
68. PRO, CAB 134/219, EPC(48)92, 1 November 1948.
69. Sir John Troutbeck to Attlee, 29 December 1949. Cited in Wark, 'Development Diplomacy', p. 240; Wm. Roger Louis, *British Empire*, p. 18–19.
70. Cited in Remme, *Britain and Regional Cooperation*, p. 205. See also p. 212.
71. R. Hyam (ed.), *British Documents on the End of Empire, Series A, Vol. 2, Part 1* (London: HMSO, 1992), p. 1.
72. Kent, *British Imperial Strategy*, p. 70. See also S. Greenwood, *Britain and the Cold War, 1945–51* (London: Macmillan, 2000), pp. 67–72.
73. PRO, CAB 128/17, CM 29(50)3, 8 May 1950.
74. E. Bajanov, 'Assessing the Politics of the Korean War, 1949–51', *Cold War International History Project (CWIHP)*, Bulletin, Winter 1995/6; V.O. Pechatnov, *CWIHP*, Working Papers 13 and 26.
75. Younger Diary, 7 January 1951. I am most grateful to Professor Geoffrey Warner for allowing me to examine the Younger Papers.

76. Kenneth Younger Diary, 5 August 1950. This comment by Younger seems to have been added to the diaries four years later.
77. Kenneth Younger Diary, 7 January 1951.
78. Kenneth Younger Transcript, (Nuffield College, Oxford), pp. 22 and 24; Younger Diary, 29 May 1950.
79. PRO, CAB 129/40, CP(50)120, 2 June 1950; CAB 129/42, CP(50)236, 19 October 1950; Warner, 'Labour Governments'.
80. J. Saville, *Politics of Continuity*, p. 21.
81. Morgan, *Labour In Power*, pp. 60–1; Younger Transcript, p. 43.
82. See, K. Young (ed.), *Diaries of Sir Robert Bruce Lockhart*, 25/7 August 1945, p. 498.
83. N. Henderson, *Private Office*, p. 51.

10
Anthony Eden

David Dutton

Arguably, Anthony Eden was the most important single figure in the making of British foreign policy between the mid-1930s and the mid-1950s. During that time he served for three periods as Foreign Secretary – a total of something like ten years and three months. His own ill-fated premiership, when he continued to maintain a strong personal control over foreign policy, especially after Harold Macmillan his first appointment as Foreign Secretary had been replaced by the more malleable Selwyn Lloyd, adds a further 21 months to this total. During the most extended period within these two decades when he was not in charge, covered by the Labour government of 1945–51, the country pursued an essentially bipartisan foreign policy of which Eden largely approved. Indeed, he kept in close touch with Labour's Foreign Secretary, Ernest Bevin, and was regularly consulted by him on the major issues of the day.[1]

It might seem fanciful to seek any pattern of overriding goals over such an extended period, and one in which the problems facing the country and Britain's own intrinsic position in the world changed dramatically. The years of Eden's ascendancy witnessed the challenge of the European dictators, the trauma of global war, the initial phase of the Cold War, the beginnings of decolonization and the first steps towards European integration. At the same time, Britain's relative power and authority in world affairs diminished apace. Moreover, it was at one time usual to criticize Eden, particularly in relation to his final period as Foreign Secretary, on precisely this score – that he had no long-term vision; that he was too wrapped up in the minutiae of diplomacy to grasp the bigger issue; that he was a tactician but no strategist. Thus, according to Avi Shlaim:

He lacked the attributes of realism, breadth of vision and the capacity to think ahead which mark the true statesman ... Eden's conservative outlook, his uncritical acceptance of orthodox assumptions, his intuitive and pragmatic approach to events, his pre-occupation with day to day problems as opposed to overall strategy and his aversion to planning all predisposed him towards continuing along the traditional lines of British foreign policy and militated against any fundamental reappraisal of Britain's role in the world, let alone any bold and imaginative departures.[2]

The charge is easily made. It was certainly Eden's great strength to master the particular issue of the day and to apply this mastery in detailed diplomatic negotiations where his charm, his patience and his powers of persuasion were at a premium. Towards his staff and subordinates he was often short-tempered, petulant and rude – though usually quick to apologize. But he almost invariably managed to keep such characteristics hidden in the actual conduct of international negotiations. Foreigners saw a diplomat in complete control of his emotions. Eden's forte was to seek out the ground for compromise and conciliation where none seemed to exist. A European observer noted the way he could 'change the atmosphere of a conference from deep pessimism and general distrust to mild optimism and willingness to cooperate.'[3] His skills were often concealed by the apparent manner and habits of a dilettante. But this was deceptive. Eden's capacity for sheer hard work has been equalled by few Foreign Secretaries this century. Perhaps none was as conscientious with his diplomatic boxes. Hastings Ismay wrote as one who was converted by first-hand experience to a more appreciative attitude towards Eden's qualities:

> I had always liked and admired him, but I had hitherto been inclined to think that he was one of fortune's darlings ... and that his meteoric success had been primarily due to charm of manner and a lucky flair for diplomacy. I now saw how wrong I had been. His hours of work were phenomenal ... Nothing was too much trouble and he never went to a meeting without making sure that he had every aspect of the problem at his finger tips.[4]

So there was perhaps more perspiration than inspiration in Eden's approach to his work. He would probably not have regarded himself as an intellectual, though he was a far more cultured and well-read man than some of his contemporaries seemed to realize.[5] But if Eden was not naturally given to long-term planning and elaborate *tours d'horizon*, it is worth noting that one man's notion of vision may strike another as little more than idle speculation. Richard Crossman, who certainly was an intellectual, found Eden's practical, no-nonsense approach refreshing: 'Eden opened the ... debate with an extremely adroit performance – not the appalling tour of the horizon to which Ernest Bevin and Herbert Morrison subjected us, but a well-composed, well-delivered speech on a few outstanding topics.'[6] At the same time, the accusation levied against Eden that he lacked the capacity to look beyond the short-term often boils down on closer examination to the proposition that he lacked the particular vision of those who brought this charge, both among his contemporaries and later commentators. In particular, it became usual from the mid-1960s onwards to suggest that it was Eden's lack of foresight which prevented British participation in the early stages of the European movement at a time, it has been claimed, when the leadership of that movement was there for the taking. As Anthony Nutting recalled, Eden

> did not see the importance of Europe, either in economic terms or political terms, I think largely because Eden was essentially a tactician in politics, in foreign policy. He was not a strategist. He did not see the broad picture, of a Europe revived such as exists today; of Western Europe with Germany as a great industrial and economic giant as it is today. He could not see this.[7]

By 1986 Roy Jenkins, writing with the authority of his period as President of the European Commission behind him, could sum up the received wisdom on the price paid for Eden's short-sightedness. He 'more than anyone else was responsible for allowing Europe to be made without us in the crucial years from 1951 to 1956'.[8]

Busy Foreign Secretaries can be forgiven if they do not find time to speculate too often about goals and ambitions for the longer term, especially when the world in which they operate is visibly and rapidly changing around them. This was especially so in Eden's case during the latter part of the Second World War when his ministerial burdens became almost unendurable. In addition to his existing responsibilities, he took over from Stafford Cripps in November 1942 the not inconsiderable task of leading the House of Commons. Thereafter the diaries of his civil servants are liberally spiced with complaints about his inability to give enough attention to the daily concerns of the Foreign Office, let alone longer-term considerations. In such a situation, suggested Oliver Harvey, foreign affairs were left 'to the fag end of the day or to hasty moments snatched between parliamentary business. He cannot give them first attention or adequate reflection.'[9] Yet Eden was perfectly capable of long-term planning when time allowed. In the first days of the war, when he occupied the less demanding position of Dominions Secretary, he raised the question of the country's war aims. Few at this stage could have had the opportunity, or indeed the inclination, to think beyond the immediate task of countering Hitler's aggression. But Eden's 'vision' was particularly interesting in view of his later reputation as an anti-European. The 'only possible solution', he concluded, was 'some form of European federation'. This would comprise a European defence scheme, a European customs union and a common currency. It was necessary to show to the British people and foreigners alike that the country was 'fighting for something more worthwhile than our imperial interests, or even the creation of the world as we knew it two months ago'.[10] Such a readiness to look beyond the immediate horizon was not always welcomed by Eden's later master in Downing Street, Winston Churchill, whose capacity for the 'visionary' has been endlessly applauded. When in January 1945 Eden sent the Prime Minister a memorandum on the probable German reaction to defeat, Churchill urged him to circulate it to the Cabinet. But 'I will read it when I can. We have not defeated them yet.'[11] Churchill had made the same point more memorably just over two years earlier. When Eden left a Foreign Office paper proposing a Four-Power Plan for running the world after the war at Chequers for the Prime Minister's perusal, it prompted the latter's celebrated rebuff: 'I hope that these speculative studies will be entrusted to those on whose hands time hangs heavy, and that we shall not overlook Mrs. Glass's Cookery Book recipe for Jugged Hare – "First catch your hare."'[12]

Anthony Eden was born in 1897, the year of Queen Victoria's Diamond Jubilee. It is of course easy to describe all British politicians born before the turn of the century as 'Victorians', with the clear implication that their minds reflected the self-confidence of the nineteenth century when the Pax Britannica seemed beyond serious challenge and that they were, as a consequence, ill-equipped to cope with the changing circumstances of the new century. But 1897 was also the year in which Kipling published *Recessional* with its warnings against the comfortable complacency of an age that was now passing. At much the same time a debate was beginning inside the British government as to whether the country could any longer afford the luxury of Splendid Isolation. In fact the whole of Eden's public career was concerned with the problem – although he would not have liked the phrase – of managing a process of relative decline. Through the 1930s, 1940s and 1950s Britain was confronted not only by a succession of over-mighty enemies but also by a series of allies, in turn reluctant and overbearing but all understandably unwilling to play the precise role Britain had in mind for them. Those charged with responsibility for the country's external affairs in these years had to chart a difficult course through a minefield occupied by friend and foe alike. Eden enjoyed neither the luxury of some of his predecessors in being the most powerful player on the international stage nor the antithetical virtue of comparative irrelevance experienced by many of those who came after him. Britain's responsibilities in the world remained vast in Eden's day, but few of the key variables of the international order were now within her absolute control. Eden's performance as a maker of British foreign policy deserves to be judged on the record of three distinct periods in office but, if there is a consistent theme running through his long career, it is the importance of sharing the burdens of Britain's still extensive world role with her allies.

Eden first established his credentials as a significant figure in British politics as a committed internationalist. As he reminded his audience in a television broadcast at the very end of his career, 'I've been a League of Nations man and a United Nations man, and I'm still the same man with the same convictions, the same devotion to peace. I couldn't be other, even if I wished.'[13] This image had stuck long before Eden spoke these words. Indeed, it was one of the reasons why the Suez crisis of 1956, which left Britain isolated and condemned by the vast majority of world opinion, did so much damage to him both at the time and in terms of his subsequent historical reputation. But it was circumstance as much as conviction which first created the close association of Eden and the League in the public mind. He was appointed Parliamentary Under-Secretary at the Foreign Office on the formation of the national government in August 1931. There he served successively under two Liberal lawyers, the Marquess of Reading and Sir John Simon. By the end of 1932 Simon had become increasingly concerned by his workload and the accompanying exercise in shuttle diplomacy between London and Geneva. As a result, in the course of 1933 Eden was allowed to take over more and more of the Foreign Secretary's responsibilities in so far as they concerned the League of Nations. Upon Simon's replacement by Sir Samuel Hoare in June 1935 Eden entered the Cabinet as Minister for League of Nations Affairs. By the time, therefore, that Eden himself became Foreign Secretary six months later his image as a 'League of Nations man' was well established. Not surprisingly the *Spectator* suggested that 'to the average League supporter he symbolizes not merely British policy but the ideal League policy'.[14]

But it is easily overlooked that Eden's mentor in foreign affairs was Austen Chamberlain, whose Parliamentary Private Secretary Eden had been between July 1926 and May 1929. Chamberlain's most celebrated achievement as Foreign Secretary had been to secure the signature of the Locarno Treaties of 1925, one of whose practical effects had been to limit British commitments in continental Europe to clearly specified areas of national interest.[15] This inevitably brought him into conflict with the universality of the League and prompted conflict with that body's more ardent enthusiasts such as Lord Robert Cecil. As Cecil put it, Chamberlain 'thought of [the League] as just one cog in the diplomatic machine, to be used or not at the discretion of the Cabinet. I regarded it as the essential international organ for the maintenance of peace.'[16] As Chamberlain's Parliamentary Private Secretary Eden was obliged by convention largely to keep his own counsel in regard to the key foreign policy issues of the late 1920s. Such evidence as we have, however, suggests that his views did not differ significantly from those of the Foreign Secretary. Eden manifested a realistic rather than an idealistic attitude towards the League's potentialities. Its greatest value, he believed, would be to create an opportunity for international statesmen to meet one another and exchange opinions. The greatest threat to the League came from idealists who carried 'their heads in the clouds and their brains in their slippers'.[17] In a Commons speech in November 1927 Eden expressed his preference for a policy which would later be described as 'limited liability'. Referring to the Labour Party's enthusiasm for the Geneva Protocol of 1924, which Chamberlain and the Conservative government had declined to ratify, he pointed out that under this proposed agreement Britain would have had to take on increased obligations 'in applying sanctions to any recalcitrant member of the League'. A most serious obligation would fall upon Britain because of her geographical position and the very existence of the Royal Navy. 'The powers which this House enjoys would be in a great measure surrendered. We would be bound beforehand to definite action in certain eventualities. That is a course which I do not think this House or the country will take.' He could understand why smaller nations favoured the Protocol. They 'get all the advantages and this country has to bear the greater share of the burdens'.[18]

This same hard-headed approach was apparent when Eden, as the number two minister in the Foreign Office, was confronted by the first major challenge to the League's authority following the Japanese invasion of Manchuria in September 1931. This meant accepting that Britain was in no position to risk involvement in a major confrontation on the other side of the world. Even economic sanctions against Japan were likely to inflict damage upon Britain at a time when the national economy was already in serious difficulties. 'We with vital interest at stake', Eden insisted, 'must continue to moderate the zeal of those with none.'[19] He was quick to throw cold water on any proposal for the economic coercion of Japan. 'Collective offensive action, which sanctions imply – even if desirable – is, we know, unobtainable.'[20] Eden may have adopted a more League-orientated stance during the period when his specific ministerial responsibilities demanded it, but by the time that he himself became Foreign Secretary a healthy scepticism had returned. The supposed internationalist had reverted to a conventional exponent of traditional Foreign Office thinking on Britain's national self-interest. Early in 1936 Major Henry Pownall, Military Assistant Secretary to the Committee of Imperial Defence, noted that Eden had been 'talking to Hankey about "Collective Security". At last the light is dawning! Eden notes that the thing is an illusion. It has failed in the "perfect case" of Italy [over its invasion of Abyssinia], it will never work for a German crisis.'[21] On 22 April 1936 Eden told the Cabinet of his doubts whether the League could prevent a German *putsch* against Austria and was soon agreeing with Neville Chamberlain that the time had come to strip the international body of its power to impose sanctions. This would have left the League as little more than 'a moral force and focus', with responsibility for the maintenance of peace transferred to a system of regional pacts, an idea to which Eden would return in his final period as Foreign Secretary.[22] On 29 April he suggested to the Cabinet that three fundamental questions needed answering. What future did the League have after its humiliation over

Abyssinia; what future was there for sanctions; and what policy should be followed towards Germany. A committee to consider the future direction of British policy met the following day and heard the Foreign Secretary maintain that collective security was likely to be less rather than more successful in the future.[23]

Against this background it seems difficult to argue that any annoyance displayed by Eden at Chamberlain's pre-emptive speech on 10 June, suggesting the lifting of sanctions against Italy, reflected anything more than pique at the way in which his Cabinet colleague had gone about the matter. Rather like Austen Chamberlain a decade before, Eden now sought to define the limits of British obligations on the Continent. In an important speech to his constituents in November he insisted that Britain would only take military action in self-defence, in defence of the empire and in fulfilment of specific treaty obligations. 'Nations cannot be expected to incur automatic military obligations save for areas where their vital interests are concerned.'[24]

Eden's eventual resignation from Neville Chamberlain's government in February 1938 was a defining moment in his whole career. Over the years which followed he squeezed every possible advantage out of the reputation as an 'anti-appeaser' with which this decision had endowed him. But his own evaluation of this episode has not been universally accepted. Historians have now written extensively on the reasons for his resignation and it seems unlikely that many more fresh insights wait to be uncovered.[25] In brief, it seems clear that as regards policy towards Germany there were no fundamental differences of principle between the Foreign Secretary and his Prime Minister. Eden had never set his face against the possibility of a negotiated settlement with Adolf Hitler. If the real distinction of the anti-appeasers was their recognition that the intrinsic nature of the Nazi regime was such as to rule out treating it according to the traditional conventions of diplomatic conduct, then Eden has few claims for membership of this exclusive club. By contrast, the idea of making any further concessions to Mussolini had come to stick in his throat, at least in the absence of some reciprocal gesture on the part of the Duce. He rejected Chamberlain's contention that the opportunity had to be seized in early 1938 to improve Anglo-Italian relations in order to disturb the Rome–Berlin axis and place Britain in a stronger position for future negotiations with Germany. This important but relatively narrow policy difference was compounded by an increasing irritation on Eden's part (which, outside his own circle, he found it difficult to articulate) at Chamberlain's growing interference in the work of the Foreign Office and, in particular, his unconventional methods of doing so.

Of more interest in the present context, however, is Eden's attitude towards Britain's allies, actual and potential, at this time. Few disagreed with the proposition that in Germany, Italy and Japan the country faced an array of possible enemies which singly and, more frighteningly, collectively posed grave dangers to British national interests. But Eden took a conspicuously more optimistic view than many of his colleagues, Chamberlain in particular, of the country's overall predicament once friendly states were brought into the equation. During 1936 he had become anxious that the US should play a more active role in European affairs. An agreement with America could be invaluable in easing Britain's mounting strategic dilemma. It would, of course, be difficult to attain. Eden faced a bitter legacy of almost two decades of mutual suspicion and occasional antagonism in Anglo-American relations, compounded in recent times by the enshrinement of the principle of neutrality in American legislation. Talks with the American ambassador, Judge Bingham, at the beginning of 1937, however, encouraged him to believe that President Roosevelt was himself dissatisfied with the existing neutrality legislation and looking for a suitable opportunity to amend it.[26] Speaking in Aberdeen in March Eden declared that partnership with the US was a 'great stabilising factor, the influence and authority of which was of evident advantage to mankind'. American help could be of particular value in policing the western Pacific, thereby allowing Britain to concentrate her own naval resources against Italy in the Mediterranean and it was for such an arrangement that Eden strove for much of 1937, though largely without success. Not surprisingly, Eden welcomed Roosevelt's famous 'quarantine' speech on 5 October as an indication that the US might be moving towards a more active involvement in world affairs. He was concerned not to rebuff any sign that America was emerging from its isolation: 'any suggestion that we are lukewarm in the matter of joint action might fatally impair the good will of President Roosevelt ... .'[27] Such thinking makes sense of Eden's enthusiasm for Roosevelt's so-called peace initiative in January 1938 and his pained reaction when Chamberlain appeared to pour cold water on the same scheme. This episode might in itself have been sufficient to prompt Eden's resignation but for the difficulty of explaining his case over a matter which, on the President's insistence, had been kept confidential.

But it was not only in relation to the US that Eden took a positive view of the potential alignment of friendly powers. His attitude towards the French was also more optimistic than that of the Prime Minister. Eden had not favoured a joint Anglo-French response when German troops remilitarized the Rhineland in March 1936, though he did suggest opening military conversations to coordinate possible future action. As the international scene grew ever more threatening, Eden became increasingly concerned to maintain close and supportive relations with the French government. The conclusion he drew from the Nyon Conference of September 1937 was that 'the really important political fact is that we have emphasized that co-operation between Britain and France can be so effective, and that the two Western democracies can still play a decisive part in European affairs'.[28] Eden and Chamberlain were in clear disagreement on the question of France at a meeting of the Committee of Imperial Defence on 2 December 1937.[29] Eden took comfort from the fact that the French navy was stronger than it had been in 1914 and 'relative to the German navy, very much stronger'.[30] He also believed that the French army was 'absolutely sound'.[31]

By the spring of 1939, by which time he had ceased to have any direct responsibility for British foreign policy, Eden had become convinced of the importance of an alliance with the Soviet Union if Britain's new obligations to Eastern Europe were to have any meaning. He was critical of the dilatory manner in which the Cabinet approached the whole question and condemned Britain's conduct of the Anglo-Soviet negotiations as lacking 'boldness and imagination'. The proposal for a tripartite pact with France and Russia should, he believed, have been seized with open hands.[32] Eden recognized the weakness of the British bargaining position and the fact that this would necessitate concessions. 'I think that in the end we shall give Russia all she is asking for', he conceded. 'There is no doubt that we could have got better terms ... had we not been so hesitant in the early stages.'[33] Struck by the government's reluctance to entrust these delicate negotiations to a figure of Cabinet rank, he offered his own services in June to head the British delegation. Chamberlain, suspicious of his motives, declined this offer.

Writing in 1947 Eden summed up his approach to the foreign policy problems of the 1930s with, it must be admitted, somewhat greater clarity than he had shown at the time:

> This peril [of three potential enemies] could not be [removed] by trying to buy off any one of them. The result of any such effort must be to underline our weakness and bring our three potential enemies closer together. The correct way was to do all in our power to improve our relations with the United States of America and with our Allies and thus increase the respect of the dictators for ourselves. Only on such a basis was successful negotiation really possible.[34]

The obstacles in the way of the sort of Grand Alliance which Eden seemed to envisage were, of course, enormous. But the concept does at least serve to differentiate his policies from those of the national government and to emphasize his keen awareness of the vital importance of allies if Britain were to have any chance of prevailing in a future war.

By the time that Anthony Eden resumed responsibility for British foreign policy in December 1940, when the sudden death of the British ambassador in the US offered Churchill the opportunity to shunt Lord Halifax to the Washington embassy, Britain's finest hour in the Second World War had already passed. Though Britain still stood largely alone (apart from the empire) in the struggle against Nazi Germany and Fascist Italy, the process had already begun which would turn what began as a European conflict into one of truly global proportions. This had inevitable and obvious consequences for those charged with the direction of Britain's foreign relations. The War Cabinet had concluded in May 1940 that, in the event of France falling, prospects of final victory were largely dependent on increasingly active American cooperation.[35] By June 1941 the Soviet Union was a belligerent and in the following December, after the Japanese attack on Pearl Harbor, the US had also joined the fray. The formation of the Grand Alliance made it probable, certain perhaps, that Britain would achieve her military objectives; yet those in the realm of foreign policy became, paradoxically, more elusive. Eden wrote that 'the aim of British policy must be, first, that we should continue to exercise the functions and responsibilities of a world power'.[36] It was an aspiration from which few contemporaries would have dissented. But Eden's task was no longer, as it had been a few years earlier, to woo new allies to share burdens beyond Britain's capacity to bear. Those allies were in place. He now had to strive for a balance between the benefits available from the military potential of the US and the Soviet Union and the danger that these two powers might squeeze out Britain's interests and influence from the settlement which would come at the end of the war.

As Foreign Secretary in war-time, Eden had to work within parameters defined by Churchill. This was something which, in the last resort, he had to accept. It was especially the case in relation to the priority which the Prime Minister insisted on giving to Anglo-American relations and as regards Churchill's determination to keep this aspect of British diplomacy primarily within his own hands. But this did not mean that the Foreign Secretary accepted Churchill's vision of the Special Relationship without qualification, nor did it stop him trying to modify it when the need arose. Notwithstanding his attitude in the 1930s, Eden came to believe that too close an association with the US would compromise British autonomy and endanger the country's national interests. He was able to view the Anglo-American relationship without the emotional element which was intrinsic to Churchill's conception and was far readier to see the US, as he saw the Soviet Union, as a potential post-war rival. His misgivings were magnified by growing doubts about Roosevelt's competence in diplomatic matters. Eden's memoirs are not renowned for their lightness of touch, but a passage conveying his scarcely veiled disdain for the President's abilities merits quotation:

> Roosevelt was familiar with the history and geography of Europe. Perhaps his hobby of stamp-collecting had helped him to this knowledge, but the academic yet sweeping opinions which he built upon it were alarming in their cheerful fecklessness.[37]

Looking to the post-war world Eden hoped that Britain would be able to balance her partnership with the US with a strong position in Western Europe, buttressed by a revived France, and if possible through continuing partnership with the Soviet Union. Where the situation demanded it, Eden was prepared to wage a war of attrition against both Roosevelt and Churchill to ensure that his own views prevailed. In doing this he showed a greater awareness of the need to plan for the longer-term than some of his critics have allowed. The question of relations with General de Gaulle and the Free French movement is probably the outstanding example of his clarity of thought.

Eden came to see the restoration of a strong France, even though this might take many years to secure, as a primary British war-aim. France was, he once said, a 'geographical necessity'.[38] To have any chance of revival France needed leadership and Eden quickly reached the conclusion that de Gaulle, whatever his failings – which were many – was the only one who could provide it. Between 1941 and the end of the war he proved to be the General's doughtiest champion in the higher reaches of the Allied war directorate.[39] Matters came to a head in May 1943 when Churchill visited Washington without his Foreign Secretary. Roosevelt subjected the Prime Minister to a barrage of complaints about de Gaulle's intolerable behaviour, but Churchill probably needed little prompting to telegraph London to suggest that the time had come to eliminate the General as a political force. Eden braced the War Cabinet to resist its absent leader and at least secured a postponement of any decision. Over the following weeks relations between Eden and Churchill steadily worsened to a point of crisis. Far from giving way, however, the Foreign Secretary raised the stakes by suggesting that it was now necessary to recognize de Gaulle's National Committee and to get the Americans to do the same. At one point Churchill suggested that he and his Foreign Secretary, by now moreover his designated successor, might be 'coming to a break'.[40] But it was Eden who prevailed. By late July Churchill had adopted the policy of recognizing de Gaulle's Committee as his own. The culmination of Eden's strategy came at the Yalta Conference in February 1945 when he and Churchill succeeded in endowing post-war France with the trappings of great power status – permanent membership of the United Nations Security Council and a zone of occupation in defeated Germany.

In an ideal world Eden would have liked to place Britain's dealings with the Soviet Union on the same footing as those with the US. In practice this was never possible, but he saw no reason for giving Stalin unnecessary grounds for complaint. He recognized that the Soviet contribution to the defeat of Germany would be vital and that Britain could not turn a blind eye to Soviet ambitions for the post-war world. The elimination of Hitler would leave Russian forces entrenched further westwards than they had been in 1941 and a victorious Soviet Union would inevitably demand more generous frontiers than she had held before the Nazi attack. Eden believed that these circumstances compelled Britain to seek political arrangements with the Soviet government. He aimed to strike a balance between satisfying Soviet ambitions, in the interests of war-time and, it was to be hoped, post-war cooperation, and doing his best to preserve the independence and strength of the states of Eastern Europe. Granted the disposition of available power and the way the war developed he was bound to be more successful in his first objective than his second. 'It must be borne in mind', he wrote in January 1942, 'that we shall not be able to affect the issue [of the political configuration of Eastern Europe] at the end of the war by anything we do or say or refuse to say.'[41] His realistic approach towards Soviet aspirations was evident in his visit to Moscow in December 1941, in negotiations for an Anglo-Soviet Treaty in 1942 and in the Moscow Foreign Ministers Conference of October 1943. Often Eden did not have a strong hand to play, but his diplomatic skill was a major factor in winning over the Russians to at least a tolerable rapport with their British allies of convenience. His attitude towards the Soviet Union inevitably hardened as the war progressed and evidence mounted of Soviet bad faith. In January 1942 he had written: 'It is very difficult to know what [Stalin's] real motives are but I believe him to be genuinely concerned for the future security of his country ... I do not believe that at the moment he is greatly interested in international Communism.'[42] By the closing stages of the conflict he was not so sure. But his contemporary comments give no evidence of a fixed belief that the Soviet Union, as the leader of an ideological crusade, was an impossible partner for Britain in the post-war world. As the war ended Eden still hoped, though without total conviction, that it would be possible for Britain, the US and the Soviet Union to continue their collaboration into the years of peace through the mechanism of the new United Nations Organization which he had played a considerable part in bringing into being and about which he had submitted his first Cabinet paper in January 1943.[43]

Much happened in the following six years to remove whatever doubts Eden and most other observers had about the realities of Soviet foreign policy. By the time that he resumed office as Foreign Secretary in Churchill's peacetime administration in October 1951 the Cold War was a reality and Britain's position within that conflict as the leading European ally of the US was firmly established. But this did not imply a total community of interest with the US any more than it had during the Second World War. Though Eden, like other British policy-makers showed a natural tendency to equate British interests with wider 'Western' ones, this was not necessarily how politicians on the other side of the Atlantic viewed the situation.

  Britain remained a great power in 1951, even though the key measure in this assessment was increasingly commitments and obligations rather than resources. In an important Foreign Office memorandum drawn up at the end of the Second World War and enthusiastically endorsed by Eden there had been few signs of a readiness to accept a diminished role in world affairs. 'Stocktaking after VE-Day' had suggested that 'we shall have to take risks and even live beyond our political means at times'. But British aims would not be secured in isolation:

we must base our foreign policy on the principle of cooperation between the three World Powers. In order to strengthen our position in this combination we ought to enrol the Dominions and especially France, not to mention the lesser Western European Powers, as collaborators with us in this tripartite system.[44]

But what had been difficult enough in the war years would prove an even greater task in the atomic age dominated by the superpowers, one of them now a declared enemy, when Britain was falling ever more rapidly behind her war-time allies.

In this delicate act of reconciling still extensive aims, interests and ambitions with ever diminishing resources – 'the maintenance of status without power'[45] – historians have come to recognize a consistent strategy from the war years into the 1950s in which Eden was a key player. Styled by David Reynolds 'the policy of power by proxy', it meant using the resources of other countries and particularly the US to secure British interests.[46] The aim, as the Foreign Office had put it in 1944, was 'to make use of American power for purposes which we regard as good'.[47] Eden spelt out this idea in more detail in an important report on 'British Overseas Obligations' presented to the Cabinet in June 1952:

> Our present policy is in fact directed towards the construction of international defence organisations for the Middle East and South-East Asia in which the United States and other Commonwealth countries would participate. Our aim should be to persuade the United States to assume the real burdens in such organisations, while retaining for ourselves as much political control – and hence prestige and world influence – as we can.[48]

Eden's thinking on regional and worldwide organizations stressed not their internationalism but their potential role as instruments of British foreign policy, as in all probability it had always done from the 1920s onwards. As he had told the Cabinet in 1942, 'we can only hope to play our part either as a European Power or as a World Power if we ourselves form part of a wider organization'.[49]

British interests spanned the globe in the early 1950s, but Eden's major concerns focused on the Far East where, in addition to the international trouble-spots in Korea and Indo-China, Britain faced its own particular difficulties in dealing with Communist insurgency in Malaya; the Middle East where the importance of oil to the economies of the Western world was becoming ever more apparent and where British influence at that date still outstripped that of the US; and Europe where the embryonic Coal and Steel Community and early discussions of a European Army suggested that the tide of federalism was gaining momentum. In all of this Eden faced considerable difficulty converting the US to the British point of view. His problems were exacerbated by poor personal relations with successive American Secretaries of State, Dean Acheson (which he tended to play down when he wrote his memoirs) and John Foster Dulles (which he was inclined, if anything, to exaggerate). It soon became apparent to the Foreign Secretary that Britain had much less bargaining power than even in the latter days of the war. It was impossible, noted his Private Secretary, 'not to be conscious that we are playing second fiddle'.[50] His first contact with the American administration in January 1952 left Eden

> forcibly struck – indeed horrified at the way we are treated by the Americans today. They are polite; listen to what we have to say, but make (on most issues) their own decisions. Till we can recover our financial and economic independence, this is bound to continue.[51]

As the months went on his exasperation with the US only increased. At one tense moment during the Geneva Conference of 1954 he gave vent to his feelings: 'All the Americans want to do is replace the French and run Indo-China themselves. They want to replace us in Egypt too. They want to run the world.'[52] Eden never quite grasped that Americans no longer wanted the sort of Special Relationship with Britain which he (and Churchill) took for granted. America valued the British alliance – but not to the exclusion of all her other international relationships. Yet, notwithstanding the enormous obstacles which he faced, Eden's final Foreign Secretaryship was marked by a succession of conspicuous achievements, a tribute to his by now well-honed diplomatic skills, sheer good sense and sound judgement. The problem was that many of these successes, as at Geneva, were achieved at the expense of the US, at least in terms of that country's injured pride. Eden had a dangerously shallow reservoir of American goodwill upon which to draw. When in 1956 he needed it most, the supply had dried up completely.

The charge so frequently levied against Eden of anti-Europeanism is no longer tenable.[53] Eden fully recognized the importance of close cooperation between the states of Western Europe and pursued a more consistent and credible policy than his later critics, many of whom only discovered the strength of their European convictions with hindsight. But he did rule out from the beginning – as did just about every other leading figure in the two main British political parties at this date – participation in a federal union. With a clarity which still seems striking as the uneasy partnership between Britain and the European community continues in a new century, he spelt out his view: 'What we must not do ... is to join any organisation without a full understanding of its implications and then find ourselves being swept further than we intended ... . Better clarity now than recrimination a few years hence.'[54] Recent research has shown that Eden was far more supportive of the European Defence Community than was the outgoing Labour government.[55] He saw it as the only practical means to secure the permanent integration of the West German state into the Western system of defence and he was willing to make major concessions to secure its success providing these fell short of the full pooling of British sovereignty. Only in mid-1954, after repeated French delays in ratifying the treaty, did Eden give up in despair and turn to alternative proposals. These bore fruit with the setting up of the Western European Union in 1955, very much Eden's creation and the starting point for a revamped North Atlantic Treaty Organization including West German membership. Where Eden, in common with most of his contemporaries, did miscalculate was over the speed with which the federalists would recover from the setback of 1954 and recapture the agenda of European integration.

As regards south-east Asia Eden was concerned at the implications of Britain's exclusion from the Anzus pact signed in 1951. To restore the British position his long-term goal was the creation of a sort of NATO for the Far East. This would serve to protect British interests in outposts such as Malaya and Hong Kong while providing a restraining mechanism in relation to the US. Eden believed that American policy in this area had become heavy-handed and unsophisticated. Policy towards the People's Republic of China epitomized this trend. In contrast to America's confrontational attitude towards the Chinese Communists, Britain was keen to avoid unnecessary provocation in the hope of moving gradually towards normal diplomatic and trading relations.[56] Not the least of Eden's achievements at the Geneva Conference in 1954 was to bring about a settlement which, whatever its imperfections, averted the possibility of a Third World War, an eventuality which Eden regarded as a real danger and for which American diplomacy would have borne a heavy responsibility. But the problems of Indo-China illustrated the narrow but important distinctions between British and American policy. A meeting between Eden and Dulles on 11/12 April 1954 left the American Secretary of State convinced that Eden had misled him. A communiqué issued on 13 April suggested that the two countries were ready to take part in examining the possibility of collective defence in south-east Asia. What Eden envisaged was a NATO-style body which might be organized some time in the future, depending on what came out of the Geneva Conference. By contrast, Dulles was thinking in terms of an immediate mechanism to internationalize the Franco-Vietnamese conflict before the conference even began.

In the Middle East Eden was less successful. It is too easy to suggest a clear distinction between British policy in this area based on national self-interest and an American strategy which gave priority to the requirements of the wider Cold War. While Britain's dependence on Middle-Eastern oil inevitably added an extra dimension to her attitude to a country such as Iran, both Britain and the US viewed the Cold War as a confused amalgam of national self-interest and supposedly disinterested opposition to Communist expansion. As Eden wrote of south-east Asia, though the sentiments were equally applicable to the Middle East: 'We are no less aware of the dangers of communist expansion ... than they are', but 'we have and are entitled to have our own ideas on how best this can be [contained].'[57] As part of his reappraisal of Britain's over-extended commitments Eden concluded that her interests in the Middle East could best be protected by new agreements with the Arab states rather than by trying to prop up the traditional pillars of imperial strength. His favoured option was for multilateral defence pacts which would avoid the imperialistic associations of existing treaties. Again, however, there existed narrow but important distinctions between British and American policy. By the beginning of 1955 Eden's hopes seemed ready to bear fruit. Following a Turkish initiative a Turco-Iraqi pact was signed in February. Britain acceded to it in April at which time it became known as the Baghdad Pact. As the pact seemed to represent the partial fulfilment of Dulles's notion of a Northern Tier of states to act as a defensive bulwark against Soviet aggression in the Middle East, it was reasonable to hope that British and American policies were for once entirely compatible. But the attitude of the US quickly changed. Dulles increasingly saw the pact as likely to antagonize the Egyptian dictator, Colonel Nasser, whom the Americans had singled out as the key player in the area and the one Arab leader capable of carrying unpopular decisions such as making peace with Israel. In addition Dulles doubted whether Britain could shake off the imperialistic connotations of her policy as readily as Eden seemed to suppose. This breach in Anglo-American understanding had not been closed by the time of the Suez crisis of 1956.

Suez is now the subject of a vast literature in its own right. Against the background of Eden's career to date it remains difficult to present it as other than an aberration. It suggests that the experience of the previous 20 years had been in vain. Britain, admittedly in conjunction with France and, secretly, with Israel, attempted to go it alone in a major foreign policy initiative in defiance not only of the two superpowers but also of the vast majority of the rest of world opinion. Eden has been accused of the worst sort of gunboat diplomacy, carried out a hundred years too late.[58] There may, of course, be a simple explanation in terms of the collapse of his health, though this is difficult to square with the fact that other key figures in the government went along with the policy readily enough. It is possible that the crisis revealed that a man with proven diplomatic skills did not necessarily possess the talents of executive direction needed in a Prime Minister. Yet this is surely not enough to explain an apparently complete collapse of judgement. Perhaps Suez represented for Eden, in his exaggeration of the threat posed by Nasser (again, an assessment in which he was by no means alone), one of those moments of supreme national importance when, as he had always believed, the country might have to go it alone.

But most accounts have probably given insufficient weight to the way in which Eden did at least try to take the Americans with him through the evolving crisis. As he later reflected, 'we leant over backwards to keep in line with U.S. – Users Club was classic example. We did not like it. It was U.S. project. We would have preferred to go direct to U.N. We endorsed it.'[59] Even when Eden did decide to abandon American cooperation, he did so on the mistaken assumption, encouraged by poor advice from Chancellor of the Exchequer Harold Macmillan in particular, that the Americans could in the last resort be relied upon not to make too much fuss. If anything, Eden had placed excessive confidence in the US. He had no reason to believe that the Americans would welcome military action. But his catastrophic miscalculation was over the scale and intensity of American opposition. The very fact that, once British military action was suspended, he expected to resume normal relations with the US as if nothing had happened, expecting Eisenhower to invite him to Washington for talks, was indicative of the extent of his misjudgement. Not easily given to self-criticism, Eden did once admit, 'I certainly made mistakes. One of these was my judgement of what the United States Government's reaction would be to the Anglo-French intervention.'[60]

Many have argued that Suez was by no means Eden's only mistake. Both in the war years and after he seemed to have an illusory expectation of what Britain could still achieve in world affairs. He knew that the world had moved on and yet had difficulty reconciling himself to diminished British influence.[61] As he had stated in 1952, 'once the prestige of a country has started to slide, there is no knowing where it will stop'.[62] At the opening of the twenty-first century it is easy to argue that such unrealistic aspirations worked to the country's long-term disadvantage. 'Only abdication as a great power', judges one critic, 'would have released sufficient resources to arrest economic decline.'[63] But if Britain's status as a world power was an illusion, it was one which was widely shared across the political spectrum throughout Eden's career and beyond it. Judged within the parameters of what was politically possible, Eden's performance over more than two decades was, on the whole, a positive one. If he could not bring himself to abandon the traditions of world power which he inherited and to which many of those who came after him were equally committed, he did at least usually recognize that Britain needed friends and allies to have any hope of securing her diplomatic objectives. His strategic vision bears comparison with that of any other major player in the field of twentieth-century British foreign policy.

Notes

1. P. Dixon, *Double Diploma: The Life of Sir Pierson Dixon, Don and Diplomat* (London: Hutchinson, 1968), p. 179.
2. A. Shlaim, P. Jones and K. Sainsbury, *British Foreign Secretaries since 1945* (Newton Abbot: David and Charles, 1977), pp. 108–9.
3. G. Hagglof, *Diplomat: Memoirs of a Swedish Envoy in London, Paris, Berlin, Moscow and Washington* (London: The Bodley Head, 1972), p. 79.
4. Lord Ismay, *Memoirs* (New York: Viking Press, 1960), p. 327.

5. See, for example, A. Horne, *Macmillan 1894–1956* (London: Macmillan, 1988), p. 376.
6. J. Morgan (ed.), *The Backbench Diaries of Richard Crossman* (London: Hamish Hamilton, 1981), p. 37.
7. M. Charlton, *The Price of Victory* (London: BBC, 1983), pp. 140–1.
8. *Observer*, 12 October 1986.
9. J. Harvey (ed.), *The War Diaries of Oliver Harvey 1941–1945* (London: Collins, 1978), p. 210.
10. Eden to Halifax, September 1939, Avon Mss, AP7/11/23V.
11. Churchill minute on Eden to Churchill, 3 January 1945, Avon Mss, AP 20/13/4.
12. Churchill to Eden 18 October 1942, Avon Mss, FO 954/7.
13. BBC broadcast, 3 November 1956.
14. *Spectator*, 18 October 1935.
15. D. Dutton, *Austen Chamberlain: Gentleman in Politics* (Bolton: Ross Anderson, 1985), pp. 249–53; J. Jacobson, *Locarno Diplomacy: Germany and the West 1925–1929* (Princeton, NJ: Princeton University Press, 1972), p. 379.
16. Viscount Cecil, *All the Way* (London: Hodder and Stoughton, 1949), p. 190.
17. House of Commons Debates, 5th series, vol. 193, cols 1105–9.
18. Ibid., vol. 235, cols 697–8.
19. *Documents on British Foreign Policy*, 2nd series, vol. 10, no. 545.
20. C. Thorne, *The Limits of Foreign Policy: The West, the League and the Far Eastern Crisis of 1931–1933* (London: Hamish Hamilton, 1972), p. 241.
21. B. Bond (ed.), *Chief of Staff: The Diaries of Lieutenant-General Sir Henry Pownall, 1933–1940* (London: Leo Cooper, 1972), p. 110.
22. Eden diary 27 April 1936, Avon Mss, AP 20/1/16; N. Chamberlain diary 27 April 1936, Chamberlain Mss, NC 2/23A.
23. Cabinet 29 April 1936, P[ublic] R[ecord] O[ffice], CC (36)31, CAB 23/84; FP(36)1, CAB 27/622.
24. *The Times*, 21 November 1936.
25. D. Dutton, *Anthony Eden: A Life and Reputation* (London: Arnold, 1997), pp. 82–111; A. Peters, *Anthony Eden at the Foreign Office 1931–1938* (Aldershot: Gower, 1986), pp. 321–51; R. Douglas, 'Chamberlain and Eden, 1937–38', *Journal of Contemporary History*, vol. 13, no. 1 (1978), pp. 97–116; N. Rose, 'The Resignation of Anthony Eden', *Historical Journal*, vol. 25, no. 4 (1982), pp. 911–31.
26. S. Roskill, *Naval Policy Between the Wars: The Period of Reluctant Rearmament 1930–1939* (London: Collins, 1976), p. 360.
27. M. Murfett, *Fool-Proof Relations: The Search for Anglo-American Naval Cooperation During the Chamberlain Years 1937–1940* (Singapore: Singapore University Press, 1984), p. 82.
28. W. Churchill, *The Gathering Storm* (London: Cassell, 1948), p. 192.
29. 303rd meeting of Committee of Imperial Defence, PRO, CAB 2/7.
30. Eden to Chamberlain 9 September 1937, Avon Mss, AP 20/5/10.
31. Eden to Chamberlain 31 January 1938, PRO, PREM 1/276.
32. J. Harvey (ed.), *The Diplomatic Diaries of Oliver Harvey 1937–1940* (London: Collins, 1970), p. 289.
33. Eden to Cranborne 27 June 1939, Avon Mss, AP 14/2/27A.
34. Eden to Churchill 8 October 1947, Avon Mss, AP 19/4/5.
35. P.M.H. Bell, *A Certain Eventuality: Britain and the Fall of France* (Farnborough: Saxon House, 1974), pp. 50–1.
36. Memorandum 8 November 1942, PRO, WP (42)516, CAB 66/30.

37. Earl of Avon, *The Reckoning* (London: Cassell, 1965), p. 374.
38. Lord Moran, *Winston Churchill: The Struggle for Survival 1940–1965* (London: Constable, 1966), p. 501.
39. C. Giuliani, 'Eden, de Gaulle and the Free French: un bienfait inscrit dans la mémoire?' in D. Dutton (ed.), *Statecraft and Diplomacy in the Twentieth Century* (Liverpool: Liverpool University Press, 1995), pp. 111–34.
40. Eden diary 13 July 1943, Avon Mss, AP 20/1/23.
41. C. Ponting, *Churchill* (London: Sinclair Stevenson, 1994), p. 569.
42. Eden to Halifax 22 January 1942, Halifax Mss, A4.410.4.15.
43. Avon, *Reckoning*, pp. 366–7.
44. *Documents on British Policy Overseas*, 1st series, vol. 1, no. 102.
45. K. Ruane, 'Refusing to Pay the Price: British Foreign Policy and the Pursuit of Victory in Vietnam, 1952–4', *English Historical Review*, vol. cx, no. 435 (1995), p. 92.
46. D. Reynolds, *Britannia Overruled: British Policy and World Power in the Twentieth Century* (London: Longman, 1991), p. 178.
47. Ibid.
48. Paper by Eden 18 June 1952, PRO, C(52)202, CAB 129/53.
49. Cabinet 8 November 1942, PRO, WP (42)516, CAB 66/30.
50. E. Shuckburgh, *Descent to Suez: Diaries 1951–56* (London: Weidenfeld and Nicolson, 1986), p. 32.
51. Horne, *Macmillan*, p. 347.
52. Shuckburgh, *Descent*, p. 187.
53. Dutton, *Eden*, pp. 290–302; J. Young, 'Churchill's "No" to Europe: The Rejection of the European Union by Churchill's Post War Government', *Historical Journal*, vol. 28, no. 4 (1985), pp. 923–37.
54. Draft speech, Avon Mss, AP 20/50/108.
55. S. Mawby, 'From Distrust to Despair: Britain and the European Army, 1950–1954', *European History Quarterly*, vol. 28, no. 4 (1998), pp. 487–513. See also K. Ruane, *The Rise and Fall of the European Defence Community* (London: Macmillan, 2000).
56. K. Ruane, 'Anthony Eden, British Diplomacy and the Origins of the Geneva Conference of 1954', *Historical Journal*, vol. 37, no. 1 (1994), pp. 156–7.
57. K. Ruane, '"Containing America": Aspects of British Foreign Policy and the Cold War in South-East Asia, 1951–54', *Diplomacy and Statecraft*, vol. 7, no. 1 (1996), p. 169.
58. See, for example, A. Nutting, *No End of a Lesson: The Story of Suez* (London: Constable, 1967).
59. Notes in Eden's 1957 diary, Avon Mss, AP 20/2/5.
60. Note by Eden for talk with Kenneth Harris, October 1972, Avon Mss, AP 33/7.
61. S. Greenwood, *Britain and the Cold War 1945–91* (London: Macmillan, 2000), p. 135.
62. Ibid., p. 105.
63. A. Adamthwaite in J. Young (ed.), *The Foreign Policy of Churchill's Peacetime Administration, 1951–1955* (Leicester: Leicester University Press, 1988), p. 10.

11
'A Rear Guard Action': Harold Macmillan and the Making of British Foreign Policy, 1957–63

Nigel J. Ashton

In an otherwise unremarkable meeting on the afternoon of 22 October 1962, Prime Minister Harold Macmillan let slip a particularly glum assessment of the task of making British foreign policy by the early 1960s. 'Our whole position in the world', he commented, 'was in the nature of a rear guard action.'[1] The meeting had been called to discuss the implications of the civil strife which had broken out in Yemen for the British position in the Gulf. Mulling over the possible dangers, Macmillan's comment was provoked by the consensus reached in the meeting that 'if we were driven out of Aden, our loss of prestige would be such as to render it impossible for us to stay in the Gulf under any circumstances'. The most important feature of the task of framing British policy here as in other parts of the world, Macmillan seemed to be admitting, was to conduct an orderly retreat, and not to be seen to have been compelled to change course under pressure of events. If the latter perception of British foreign policy became common currency, then the resulting loss of prestige, and exposure of British weakness, might lead to an unseemly rout, with commitments being shed like the baggage of a retreating army.

The glumness of Macmillan's appraisal of the prospects for British foreign policy by the winter of 1962/63 stands in contrast to the hopes he had entertained in the early years of his premiership. Although Macmillan had taken office in January 1957 in the most inauspicious of circumstances, with British prestige at a low ebb in the wake of the Suez fiasco, it appears that his sights for the framing of British foreign policy at this stage were set rather higher than the orderly retreat at which he aimed by the final year of his premiership. Whilst the Macmillan of 1957 believed that Britain would have to adjust to a period of change in her international role and position he did not believe that this would necessarily result in the loss of Britain's great power status. The strategy he quickly determined to deploy to adjust to changing circumstances involved three main planks: the re-creation of a close Anglo-American alliance; the maintenance of the British independent nuclear deterrent; and the development of the British role as leader of the Commonwealth. If successful, these policies would help mask British decline, and possibly even give the nation a new and extended lease of life as a great power. Interestingly, in view of later developments, in Macmillan's grand strategy at this stage the European dimension occupied a relatively low priority. This is ironic to the extent that the greatest departure in the making of British foreign policy for which the Macmillan premiership would subsequently be remembered was the application to join the European Economic Community, unveiled at the end of July 1961.

That Macmillan initially should have given the Anglo-American 'special' relationship a high priority in the framing of his foreign policy was perhaps not surprising. Both his family background and his formative experiences in political office inclined him towards the Atlantic alliance. His American mother, Helen or 'Nellie' Macmillan, proved a formidable driving force behind his early political career. Having staked out the ambition for her son to become Prime Minister, she was not about to let Harold's youthful delicacy of health and bookishness of character prove obstacles to her determined pursuit of his political advancement. Much of the personal drive and ruthlessness which Macmillan later deployed to get to the top in politics was instilled in him by his American mother.[2] The veneer of detachment and languor which he cultivated to conceal his ambition was more the product of his English public school and Oxford education.

As regards formative influences, it has become something of an historical cliché to say that for those of Macmillan's generation who fought in the Great War, the experience of the trenches left an indelible mark on their character. And yet, for Harold himself, this observation is well worth both repeating and emphasizing. Even in the limited context of this study of Macmillan's making of foreign policy as Prime Minister, one often finds the experience of the trenches bubbling to the surface. For instance, on 15 September 1961, the day that the Kennedy administration resumed underground testing of hydrogen bombs, Macmillan reflected in his diary that: '45 years ago, today, I was taking part in the September 15th attack by the Brigade of Guards in the Battle of the Somme. This was the first time that tanks were used. I was severely wounded – for the third time – and spent most [of] the last two years of the war in hospital.'[3] Lurking in the back of Macmillan's mind as Prime Minister, was an instinctive abhorrence of war, and a desire to do what he could, whether in the form of his pursuit of *détente*, or a nuclear test ban treaty, to forestall its outbreak. Lest this sound too rosy or sympathetic an assessment of Macmillan's motives for those who see only cynical domestic political calculation behind these policies,[4] let me hasten to qualify the statement by admitting that this instinctive abhorrence of war was not the only, or even always the most important, factor in framing Macmillan's actions. However, to deny its presence, and its periodic influence over his statecraft, is to neglect one of the subtleties of what Anthony Sampson rightly called a 'study in ambiguity'.[5]

For instance, in the wake of his December 1961 talks with President John F. Kennedy at Bermuda, Macmillan returned home to a Christmas of glum reflection on the prospects of the likely US resumption of atmospheric nuclear testing. Convinced of the dangers of a nuclear arms race, and the dire prospects for humanity of nuclear war, Macmillan drafted an eloquent plea to the President to negotiate a ban on nuclear testing with the Soviet Union. 'It would really seem to any ordinary person who reflects calmly upon it', he wrote, that humanity is setting out on a path at once so fantastic and so retrograde, so sophisticated and so barbarous, as to be almost incredible.' Warning of the long-term dangers of nuclear proliferation, he observed that: 'If all this capacity for destruction is spread about the world in the hands of all kinds of different characters – dictators, reactionaries, revolutionaries, madmen – then sooner or later, and certainly I think by the end of this century, either by folly or insanity, the great crime will be committed.'[6] To be sure, there was a domestic political dimension to the problem of atmospheric test resumption in the shape of the President's request to use the British territory of Christmas Island in the South Pacific for the test series, but there were deeper roots to Macmillan's appeal than simply eloquence in pursuit of political calculation.

If Macmillan's Great War experiences had instilled in him an instinctive abhorrence of war, the lessons he drew from his political career during the 1920s and 1930s were of a rather different character. Regarded as something of a maverick on both domestic social, and international political issues, Macmillan nevertheless staked out a clear position against the appeasement policies of the Baldwin and Chamberlain governments. He was, for instance, one of only two Conservative MPs to vote against the government over its handling of the Abyssinian crisis after the foreign affairs debate of 23 June 1936.[7] During the same period, Macmillan moved into Churchill's orbit, although it is fair to say that he remained one of the outer bodies in the Churchillian constellation. Churchill seems never to have been entirely at ease with him,[8] a sentiment which was reflected in the initially modest pace of Macmillan's political advancement once Churchill became Prime Minister in May 1940.

Although on the face of things contradictory, Macmillan's stand against appeasement during the 1930s was in fact reconcilable with an underlying abhorrence of war. His differences with Chamberlain were not over the *end* of averting war, but rather over the *means* by which this could best be achieved. The notion of the need to stand up to dictators, and the lessons of the failure of the policy of appeasement, were to be applied out of context by Macmillan, and others of his generation, during the Suez crisis of 1956. Interestingly, the descriptions of the Egyptian leader, Gamal Abdel Nasser, as a sort of Arab Mussolini or Hitler, which were common currency during the crisis, lingered in Macmillan's mind long after the dust of the Suez crisis itself had settled. As late as the end of February 1963, Macmillan annotated a despatch from the British Ambassador in Cairo, Harold Beeley, on the subject of 'Nasserism', with the words: 'for Nasser read Hitler and it's all very familiar.'[9]

Turning our minds back to the progress of Macmillan's early political career, though, by the time the Second World War broke out, Macmillan's assembled political baggage included a driving personal ambition, an abhorrence of war, a belief in the need to stand up to dictators, and a personal admiration for Winston Churchill. During the war itself, after holding minor positions in the Ministry of Supply and the Colonial Office, Macmillan secured the post that was to be the key to his future political advancement in November 1942, that of Minister Resident with the Allied forces in Algiers. Here Macmillan forged close relations with the American Commander of the Allied forces, Dwight D. Eisenhower. He also developed, as Richard Crossman memorably recalled, a conception of the British as the 'Greeks', quietly running the American 'Roman' empire.[10] Once he assumed the premiership, this somewhat Machiavellian notion of attempting surreptitiously to turn American power towards British ends was to be a key feature of his foreign policy.

In addition to developing his own ideas as to how American power might be manipulated, Macmillan was enormously impressed by what he witnessed of Churchill's statecraft during the Casablanca Conference of January 1943, probably the high-water mark of British war-time influence over US strategy. Recording his impressions of the Churchill–Roosevelt meetings in his diary, Macmillan noted that 'I christened the two personalities the Emperor of the East and the Emperor of the West, and indeed it was rather like a meeting of the later period of the Roman Empire.'[11] For Macmillan, their meetings were 'remarkable and romantic episodes', during which the great affairs of state were resolved by the two Emperors late at night, with the aid of a great deal of alcohol.[12] During his own premiership, a hankering after what Churchill himself dubbed meetings at the summit, was to mark Macmillan's conduct of foreign policy. Indeed, this mode of political operation dovetailed nicely with Macmillan's belief in his own ability to act as a British 'Greek' adviser to any American 'Roman' President. Unfortunately, this strategy was to prove flawed, not least in respect of the degree to which it underestimated the political sophistication of both of the American Presidents with whom Macmillan would work during his time in office.

In the event, Macmillan would have to wait over a decade to put into practice the ideas on the conduct of statecraft which he had forged during the war. Of the episodes which marked his post-war political career, without question the most significant from the point of view of shaping his conduct of foreign policy as Prime Minister was the Suez crisis of 1956. Macmillan's role as Chancellor of the Exchequer during the crisis was undoubtedly one of the most ambiguous phases of his political career. Initially among the most hawkish of the members of Eden's inner circle, Macmillan was a firm backer of military action as the only appropriate means to reverse Nasser's nationalization of the Suez Canal Company.[13] Indeed, to help ginger Eden into military action, he may well have twisted his accounts of the talks he held in Washington with Secretary of State John Foster Dulles and President Dwight D. Eisenhower towards the end of September 1956.[14] Yet, when the ill-fated Anglo-French-Israeli invasion of Egypt was launched at the end of October 1956, it was Macmillan who was the first to break ranks over the use of force. His loss of nerve followed a phone conversation with Washington on the morning of 6 November in which he was left in no doubt that US assistance would only be forthcoming to bolster the embattled Pound Sterling if an immediate ceasefire was announced. The most convincing balance that can be struck in explaining his actions is to suggest that Macmillan now believed American hostility had escalated to the point where there was no alternative but to halt operations.[15]

In terms of his future views on the conduct of foreign policy, Macmillan drew two lessons from the crisis. First, it reinforced his belief in the 'Greeks' and 'Romans' strategy for handling Anglo-American relations. Britain should not pursue her independent ambitions to the point where they brought her into an open confrontation with America. She should instead revert to the more subtle practice of the covert manipulation of the US power towards British ends. Second, Macmillan came to believe that the other key reason for the British failure over Suez had been what he later termed 'dithering'.[16] By this he meant the failure to take decisive action to resolve the crisis in its early stages. This was something of a self-serving interpretation of what had transpired during the Suez crisis, because at the time, Macmillan himself had recognized that the forces necessary to invade Egypt would take some weeks to assemble.[17] He had in any case, through his membership of the Egypt Committee, been at the heart of the decision-making process over Suez. Nevertheless, this view of the need to act decisively in the early stages of any international crisis informed Macmillan's actions at key junctures during his premiership. So, at the outset of the Cuban missile crisis, it is this concept which helps us to explain what was otherwise Macmillan's surprisingly hawkish advocacy to President Kennedy of an American invasion of Cuba. During his opening missile crisis telephone conversation with the President early on the morning of 23 October 1962, Macmillan's first comment of substance was 'what's worrying me is how do you see the way out of this? What are you going to do with the blockade? Are you going to occupy Cuba and have done with it or is it just going to drag on?' Elaborating on the point later in the conversation, Macmillan noted that 'in my long experience we've always found that our weakness has been when we've not acted with sufficient strength to start with'.[18] No doubt here, the experience of the Suez 'dithering' overlaid and reinforced the earlier lesson of the dangers of prevarication and appeasement during the 1930s. To be sure, Macmillan's belief in the utility of negotiation and summitry became the dominant refrain in his subsequent handling of the Cuban crisis, but it is fascinating to see the various political instincts drawn from earlier experience battling for supremacy in what once again could be characterized as his ambiguous reaction to the missile crisis. Here again, though, one should remark that the debate in Macmillan's mind was one over means rather than ends. In other words, drawing on his own earlier experiences, Macmillan searched for the most promising means to secure the overriding goal of averting the outbreak of war.

If these were the principal predilections which Macmillan brought with him to the highest office, the question must now be posed as to what were the main challenges which confronted him in framing British foreign policy during the years 1957 to 1963. The first point to make under this heading is that the Macmillan premiership coincided with the years of greatest Cold War tension. Michael Beschloss has dubbed the Kennedy–Khrushchev period the 'crisis years' of the Cold War,[19] but in truth the period of crisis stretched back into the final years of the Eisenhower administration. The crisis over Berlin, precipitated by Khrushchev's announcement on 27 November 1958 of a 'deadline' for the Western powers to reach agreement with the Soviet Union over the future status of the city, led to a significant escalation in Cold War tensions. On top of this core conflict came a succession of regional or peripheral Cold War crises which served to ratchet up the tension between the superpowers over the ensuing years. The Cuban revolution of 1959, the civil war in Laos from 1959 onwards, the Congo crisis from June 1960, the resumption of atmospheric nuclear testing by both superpowers during 1961 to 1962, and the Cuban missile crisis of October 1962 were but the highest profile of a series of interlocking crises which served to make this a period of the greatest international tension.

Against this global backdrop, Macmillan had to grapple with a number of specifically British problems in the making of foreign policy. Foremost among these was the economic vulnerability of the United Kingdom. The limitations this vulnerability imposed on his conduct of foreign policy can be illustrated with reference to the events of the summer of 1961. During the months of July and August 1961, the Macmillan government came under pressure to take its own measures to back up the increase in US defence spending and readiness announced by President Kennedy in a broadcast to the American people on 25 July.[20] While Macmillan faced international political pressure to demonstrate alliance unity, he fretted in private about the domestic economic consequences of any action he might take. If Britain were to announce measures similar to those adopted by Kennedy such as a call up of reservists or an increase in the defence budget, there might be a run on the Pound. This, Macmillan feared, would mean economic ruin.[21] In his diary entry for 23 July 1961, Macmillan noted that if tensions over Berlin continued to rise:

> The pound sterling, being at the moment the weakest currency, will take the strain of the panic into which the international usurers will fall. Already this has been a bad month, and I do not feel that the pressure on our reserves is all directed against our economic misdemeanours. It reflects, in part, the world's fears … .[22]

As Macmillan saw it the choice he faced during the summer crisis over Berlin was a stark one. 'I still think we are more likely to be bankrupted than to be blown up', he confided to his Principal Private Secretary Freddie Bishop, 'though of course it would not be any comfort in being blown up to know that one was bankrupt.'[23] To complicate matters still further, Macmillan was planning to unveil to the House of Commons at the end of July his intention to open negotiations for British membership of the European Economic Community. Thus, in addition to sentiment in Washington, he also had to take account of opinion in Paris and Bonn. He had to take enough action to appear to bolster alliance unity while at the same time not going so far as to alarm the financial markets still further. In the end, hedging his bets, he opted to do no more than bring British forces in Germany unobtrusively to a higher state of readiness.[24]

Kennedy's 25 July broadcast to the American people, with its announcement of increased funding for civil defence measures in the US, highlighted another of the constraints under which Macmillan worked in framing British foreign policy during these crisis years of the Cold War. A similar announcement on his part would have been unthinkable in the context of British public opinion. Put simply, the American President was the leader of a nation of continental extent, which, despite the shock of the *Sputnik* launch in October 1957, still felt itself to be comparatively invulnerable to Soviet attack. Macmillan, by contrast, was the Prime Minister of a small island nation, which, as he was to remind Kennedy during the Cuban missile crisis, had lived with the possibility of Soviet nuclear attack for over a decade.[25] While Macmillan was to prove adept at exploiting the divisions of the Labour opposition over matters nuclear, he had to keep one eye in framing his Cold War policy on the growth and influence of the Campaign for Nuclear Disarmament in domestic politics.

If the core of the Cold War conflict remained Europe and the German question, the proliferation of crises in the so called 'Third World' pointed to another uncomfortable reality facing Macmillan in the making of British foreign policy during these years. Albeit that Macmillan managed to avoid a colonial conflict of the disastrous proportions of the French involvement in

Algeria, nevertheless, the British too were battered by the waves of nationalism and anti-colonialism which swept through international politics during these years.[26] Significantly, it was these sentiments which were to be instrumental in scuppering the high hopes which Macmillan entertained at the beginning of his premiership for the maintenance of British influence on the back of leadership of the Commonwealth. Macmillan's search, during his second term as Prime Minister, for an orderly method of retreating from empire was to clash with the impatience for change in the 'Third World' evidenced by the 1960 United Nations Resolution on colonialism, and the passions aroused by the Congo crisis from the middle of that year onwards.

If these were among the principal constraints on Macmillan's freedom of manoeuvre in the framing of foreign policy, how did they affect the course of diplomacy during his premiership? Returning to the idea broached earlier of the three principal planks of Macmillan's foreign policy, it can be seen that initially the Prime Minister's pursuit of a renewed 'special relationship' with Washington yielded some dividends. Macmillan played the part of the wounded ally in his first weeks in office with sufficient skill to lure Eisenhower into approaching him with the offer of a summit on British territory at Bermuda at the end of March 1957. Then, through his past friendship and close personal relations with the President, he was able to foster the impression at the Bermuda conference of an alliance restored, albeit that beneath the surface significant differences of outlook remained on the questions of Middle Eastern policy which had brought about the rupture over Suez.[27] This was a promising opening to what might be termed the first, and most successful, of the three phases into which the foreign policy of the Macmillan premiership may be divided. This first phase ran from Macmillan's assumption of office in January 1957 through to the collapse of the Paris summit in May 1960. The second phase of Macmillan's foreign policy began and ended in Paris, running from May 1960 until January 1963, the latter month marked of course by de Gaulle's press conference in which he announced his intention to veto British entry into the European Economic Community. The third and final phase, the dog days of the Macmillan premiership, ran from January 1963 until the Prime Minister's resignation in October 1963. One may thus speak of two main watersheds in Macmillan's foreign policy: the spring of 1960 and the winter of 1962/63.

In marking out the Macmillan era into phases, the intention is not to claim that there were sudden or immediate switches in the orientation of foreign policy. Rather, what transpired was a process of evolution in the thinking of the Prime Minister and his closest advisers,[28] which in turn resulted from shifts in the domestic and international political and economic environment. What this method of approach does highlight, though, is that there were certain key events which served to crystallize thinking as to the need for a change of course in foreign policy. In particular, the significance of the 'shock and disappointment'[29] sustained by Macmillan at the Paris summit should not be underestimated when assessing his subsequent conduct of foreign policy. The collapse of the summit was the key factor in bringing about Macmillan's reassessment of the role of the Anglo-American alliance in British foreign policy. It led to his decision to apply to join the European Economic Community in 1961, a measure conceived not, as some commentators have claimed,[30] as a means to strengthen the Anglo-American alliance, but rather as a hedge against the unreliability of that alliance.

During the first year of his premiership, Macmillan could have been forgiven for thinking that the hopes he entertained for a renewed Anglo-American alliance as the foundation for his foreign policy were beginning to be realized. Although the success of the Bermuda conference was more one of presentation than of substance, Macmillan was able to seize on two opportunities during the summer and autumn of 1957 to advance the cause of Anglo-American cooperation much further. The first opportunity was provided somewhat paradoxically by events in the Middle East, the region over which the two powers had so recently and spectacularly fallen out. Here, a crisis that broke out in Syria during August 1957, created significant apprehension in Washington that a pro-Soviet coup was imminent.[31] Macmillan was able to capitalize on American fears to establish new institutional machinery for Anglo-American cooperation over Syria. The so-called Syria Working Group that held its first meetings in Washington during early September 1957 provided a flexible forum for the exchange of intelligence information, and a means of developing ideas as to how to meet a range of political and military contingencies. While no joint Anglo-American intervention in Syria transpired during the autumn of 1957, largely because the peak of the crisis passed after the landing of Egyptian troops at Latakia in northern Syria on 13 October 1957, the Working Group provided a model for the type of Anglo-American cooperation that Macmillan wanted to develop on a broader front.

The second opportunity on which Macmillan was able to capitalize to set this broader process of cooperation in train was provided by the launch of the Soviet *Sputnik* satellite on 4 October 1957. The Prime Minister seems quickly to have sensed that the *Sputnik* launch would usher in a new era of uncertainty in American public opinion and foreign policy. The apparent Soviet lead in the field of ballistic missile technology, and the American fears of surprise attack harking back to the debacle of Pearl Harbor, gave Macmillan the opportunity to press the case for much closer Anglo-American collaboration in the waging of the Cold War. In a personal letter to Eisenhower on 10 October 1957, Macmillan argued that the *Sputnik* launch had served to bring home the magnitude of the threat that the Russians posed to the Free World. In these circumstances, he posed the question as to whether the time had now come 'when we could go further towards pooling our efforts and decide how best to use them for the common good'. As Macmillan saw it, the framework established for cooperation in meeting the Soviet threat in Syria could be 'the key to a great new venture. I would like to see this sort of cooperation continued with a view to our working out together the role of the free countries in the struggle against communist Russia.'[32] Harking back to his war-time conception of the Anglo-American alliance, Macmillan seemed to be saying that the barbarians could only successfully be opposed if the Romans were now prepared unreservedly to pool their efforts with the Greeks.

The fruits of Macmillan's initiative were an invitation to Washington, and a series of talks with Eisenhower at the beginning of the final week of October 1957, during which the Prime Minister seemed to secure all that he had sought by way of Anglo-American cooperation. While Secretary of State Dulles evidently felt that any intensification of the Anglo-American relationship should only be the starting point for a broader effort to invigorate the US's alliances worldwide, Macmillan was able to capitalize on Eisenhower's own instincts to create a new foundation for Anglo-American relations.[33] He returned from Washington with what he grandly described to the Cabinet as an Anglo-American 'declaration of interdependence' in his pocket.[34] No doubt the play on words in terms of the history of relations between Great Britain and America appealed to the Prime Minister's sense of irony, but, in theory at least, Macmillan had extracted significant commitments from the President in the fields of both nuclear cooperation and broader Cold War coordination. The President had committed himself to seeking a repeal in respect of Britain of the provisions of the 1946 McMahon Act which barred the sharing of nuclear information.[35] To this end, he had agreed to the establishment of three Anglo-American Working Groups to study various aspects of bilateral nuclear relations. In addition to the nuclear groups, a second collection of three Working Groups was established to look at a set of regional Cold War questions. These concerned the Middle East (especially Syria); Hong Kong; and Algeria. Finally, a further collection of three Working Groups was established to look at Cold War countermeasures. There was to be a group to study psychological warfare questions, another to determine the criteria for strategic controls on trade, and a final one to investigate economic warfare measures.[36]

The longer-term implications of the agreements reached in October 1957 in terms of the second plank of Macmillan's foreign policy, the maintenance of Britain's independent nuclear deterrent, were wide ranging. The signature by Eisenhower of the Agreement on Atomic Energy for Mutual Defence Purposes, following the passage by Congress of the necessary amendments to the McMahon Act in July 1958, reopened the way to formal Anglo-American nuclear cooperation such as had not existed since the war years. Ian Clark has rightly termed this period a 'unique high point' in Anglo-American defence relations.[37] To augment existing British expertise, demonstrated in the hydrogen bomb test of May 1957, Britain now gained access to American technical information on the production of nuclear warheads, as well as to fissile material. This represented a significant saving in time and money for the British government. On the other hand, there was no American commitment at this stage to help with the other side of the nuclear question: that of the means of delivery of nuclear weapons. Indeed, it was to be in this field that the biggest threat to the future of the British independent deterrent was to emerge. For all his prevarication over the fate of the British-designed Blue Streak ballistic missile during the period up to February 1960, Macmillan was eventually to be forced to turn to the US to secure a reliable and affordable delivery system. This would turn interdependence into dependence. Still, in the summer of 1958, this was all very much in the future, and Macmillan could be forgiven for congratulating himself on the remarkable successes of his attempt to re-establish the Anglo-American alliance during his first 18 months in office.

This same period also seemed to mark a promising beginning in respect of the third plank of Macmillan's foreign policy, the development of Britain's role as leader of an expanding multi-racial Commonwealth. First, from 26 June to 5 July 1957, Macmillan had presided over a conference of Commonwealth Prime Ministers in London, which, he gleefully recorded in his memoirs, even *The Times* newspaper had termed 'a personal success'.[38] Despite the challenges that he believed would be posed by emerging nationalism, Macmillan felt 'inspired at least to try to guide these disparate forces into a common faith'.[39] The result, during January and February 1958, was the first and last grand tour of the Commonwealth undertaken by a British Prime Minister in office.[40] Lasting six weeks, and covering 35 000 miles with 34 different overnight stopovers, the tour was a remarkable undertaking for a Prime Minister who had barely completed his first year in power. It was made all the more remarkable by the domestic problems that Macmillan left behind him in the shape of the resignation on the day before his departure of three Treasury ministers; an incident Macmillan famously dismissed as 'little local difficulties'. Anthony Sampson, who travelled with the Prime Minister in his capacity as a journalist, described the tour as 'the most remarkable stage in Macmillan's progress', and 'a turning point in his fortune'.[41] Macmillan returned to Britain in mid-February 1958, believing that an expanding Commonwealth could still serve to enhance Britain's prestige, and perhaps maintain her standing in international politics, particularly *vis-à-vis* the Americans.[42]

So, if in respect of these three planks of foreign policy, the first 18 months of the Macmillan premiership seemed a record of remarkable success in the face of adversity, what went wrong thereafter? In respect of Anglo-American relations, the initial success of Macmillan's personal diplomacy in securing special treatment from Eisenhower perhaps led the Prime Minister to set too much store by what could be achieved through these methods. This same initial success also reinforced what proved in the end to be an exaggerated sense on Macmillan's part that he could carve out a distinctive international role for himself in Cold War diplomacy. Even before Macmillan set out on his 'voyage of discovery' to the Soviet Union in February 1959, problems with the restored Anglo-American alliance had begun to emerge. The practical results of the new administrative machinery set up to coordinate Anglo-American Cold War strategy were proving disappointing. Although a detailed Anglo-American contingency plan for intervention in the Lebanon had been developed during May 1958, when the time had come to take action in July, Eisenhower had chosen instead to shelve the plan, and send in US marines to the Lebanon unilaterally. Although the two leaders were able to maintain a common diplomatic front, with the US also agreeing to provide logistical support for a contemporaneous British intervention in Jordan, the underlying tensions that characterized the operations in the Levant in the summer of 1958 did not augur well for the development of Anglo-American interdependence.[43]

Following hard on the heels of the extraction of British and American forces from the Middle East, came the crisis precipitated by Khrushchev's 27 November 1958 declaration of a six-month 'deadline' for the Western powers to reach agreement with the Soviet Union over the future status of Berlin. The unyielding American response, together with Macmillan's belief in the scope for independent British action, led to his dramatic flight to Moscow in February 1959 to seek a negotiated settlement of the crisis. Macmillan's initiative did not find favour with Eisenhower who saw the danger that the Soviets would try to exploit divisions in the Western alliance. The President secretly hoped that the British would 'come back with their tails between their legs and then we are smart fellows'.[44] Nevertheless, Macmillan did not return from the Soviet capital empty-handed. Through his offer to accept a Foreign Ministers' meeting in Geneva in April as a prelude to a summit meeting, Khrushchev implicitly backed away from his sixth-month deadline for agreement over Berlin.[45] Whatever the impact of his visit on the Soviet leadership, Macmillan evidently believed that he had set in train a process of *détente* which might lead to a genuine and lasting relaxation in Cold War tensions. It is in this context that the collapse of the Paris summit in May 1960 had such a devastating impact on him. Indeed, those who claim that Macmillan was only motivated in his summit policy by a Machiavellian desire to accrue credit ahead of the autumn 1959 general election, must surely have difficulty in explaining the profound impact on him of the failure in Paris.[46] After all, with the election won, and a comfortable parliamentary majority behind him, there was little left to play for in the summit game in terms of domestic political stakes.

In truth, the events in Paris exposed to Macmillan the limitations of his Greeks and Romans approach to Anglo-American relations. Confronted with a direct challenge to the US's Cold War credibility in the shape Khrushchev's demand for a full apology for the U-2 incident, and the punishment of its perpetrators, Eisenhower was unbending in his refusal. Macmillan's suggestions that the President could '"say he was sorry" – or, preferably, make a formal diplomatic apology' seem to have represented a complete mis-judgement on his part of the President's resolve.[47] The collapse of the Paris summit showed that *in extremis*, Macmillan could not influence the American President. In the wake of the summit, Macmillan confided to Foreign Secretary Selwyn Lloyd that it was difficult to see the way ahead, particularly as he could no longer 'usefully talk to the Americans'.[48] To Macmillan's Private Secretary, Philip de Zulueta, Paris represented a real watershed for the Prime Minister, because 'this was the moment he suddenly realised that Britain counted for nothing; he couldn't move Ike to make a gesture towards Khrushchev ... .'[49] The Prime Minister himself put it even more simply: Paris 'was the most tragic moment of my life'.[50]

If the events of May 1960 in Paris represented a watershed in Macmillan's thinking about the role of the Anglo-American relationship in British foreign policy, contemporaneous developments were also having their effect on the other two main planks of his strategy. In February 1960, the long-delayed decision had finally been taken to abandon development of the Blue Streak ballistic missile. The abandonment of the missile meant the abandonment for the future of an independent British means of nuclear delivery. Although Eisenhower stepped in the following month at Camp David with the offer of the sale of the American Skybolt missile, which would prolong the effective operational life of the existing British V-Bomber force, the implication of the offer was British dependence in future on American largesse and good faith to keep the country in the nuclear game. As early as December 1960, Macmillan was already expressing doubts in his diary as to whether the Americans would let Britain down over Skybolt.[51] The consequences of British dependence would become all too apparent during Macmillan's winter of discontent of 1962/63.

In terms of the British role as leader of the Commonwealth, Macmillan at the beginning of the year had still seemed to be keeping ahead of events. The warning for which he is best remembered outside British shores, uttered in Cape Town on 3 February 1960, that the 'wind of change is blowing through this continent',[52] was unfortunately quickly followed by the outbreak of a crisis in the Belgian Congo in June. This was to have profound implications for the British international role. The chaotic Belgian decolonization, and the civil war which followed, dragging in the superpowers to back their respective clients, polarized African politics. Britain's evident sympathy for the secession of the rebel province of Katanga, and suspicions about the role of Sir Roy Welensky and his British-sponsored Central African Federation across the southern Congolese border, helped blacken Britain's colonial reputation. Once again, during the bleak mid-winter of 1962/63, the success of United Nations troops in forcibly reintegrating Katanga into the Congo was to prove a signal defeat for British foreign policy.[53]

It was, thus, in the midst of a multi-faceted crisis in the conduct and conception of his foreign policy during the summer of 1960 that Macmillan began to turn his mind to an alternative strategy. The development of his interest in a possible British application to join the European Economic Community was defensive in every respect. First, if Britain could not rely on promoting her interests through Anglo-American channels, then membership of the European Community would provide a welcome hedge, possibly even acting as an instrument for the exertion of pressure on the Americans. Second, if Britain could not retain her world role through leadership of the Commonwealth, she might instead do so through leadership of Europe. Third, if the Anglo-American nuclear partnership were for any reason to be called into question in the future, then cooperation with the French might provide an alternative, albeit less attractive strategy. Fourth, in economic terms, membership of the community would stave off the threat of isolation which had been worrying Macmillan more and more as he surveyed developments on the Continent during the period 1958–60.

As he hatched his European scheme during the latter months of 1960, Macmillan had to deal with a further important variable: the forthcoming change of administration in the US. Of course, the added uncertainty provided by the election of a new President was still a further argument in favour of hedging his bets on the future of the Anglo-American alliance. Whoever was elected, he could not rely on the bonds of personal friendship which had helped underpin his working relationship with Eisenhower. On the other hand, it would be foolish to sacrifice the remaining hard-won gains of his Anglo-American strategy, particularly in the field of nuclear cooperation, without at least trying to build a bridge to the new President. In the event, Macmillan felt that the election of John F. Kennedy rather than Richard Nixon to the Presidency in November 1960 was a better outcome from the point of view of Anglo-American relations.[54] Certainly, by the final weeks of December 1960, one has the sense that the Prime Minister was in fact glad to see the back of the Eisenhower administration. He confided to his diary that the American administration had 'gone mad' and 'turned nasty' over problems like the crisis in Laos.[55] Just before Christmas Macmillan annotated a note from Philip de Zulueta with the sarcastic comment: 'they have about three weeks of power. Do you think they are planning to start a war while Eisenhower is having his Christmas dinner and quail shoot?'[56]

From Macmillan's point of view, the early indications as to the intentions of the new administration in respect of Anglo-American relations were on balance positive. In respect of interdependence, the new US Secretary of Defense, Robert McNamara, expressed himself keen to coordinate efforts with the British across the whole field of weapons research, development and production. McNamara saw the parallel development of similar weapons systems by alliance partners as wasteful and inefficient. Hence, during a visit to Washington by British Minister of Defence Harold Watkinson in March 1961, two memoranda of understanding were agreed. The first expressed the general need for greater coordination in defence research and development, and confirmed the existing Skybolt deal. The second laid down terms of reference for a joint study of potential areas of coordination.[57]

Less congenial from Macmillan's point of view, were the risks he was forced to run to avoid a rupture with the new administration over policy toward Laos. As the hedging strategy implied, while he hatched his European scheme, he could not afford to fall out with the Americans. Thus, as Kennedy slid towards full-scale military intervention in the Laotian civil war during the final weeks of March 1961, Macmillan found himself dragged along on the President's coat-tails. Macmillan's attempts to wriggle his way out of a British ground force commitment to a South-East Asia Treaty Organization (SEATO) operation in Laos, resulted in what amounted to a summons from the new President to discuss the crisis at the US Key West naval base on 26 March 1961.[58] Or as Macmillan put it in his own subsequent memoir account, 'the President in his telephone message, had been very insistent ... .'[59] Macmillan's own account of what transpired at Key West was that he reinforced the cautious instincts of a President himself anxious to avoid being sucked into the Laotian quagmire.[60] This self-serving version has been largely accepted by subsequent commentators.[61] In fact, the transcripts now available of the conversations at Key West show that the President pressed Macmillan into agreeing to a British commitment to plan jointly for the possible implementation of SEATO Plan 5/61.[62] This would involve, among other measures, the introduction of a Commonwealth Brigade, including British forces, to hold bridgeheads on the Mekong River. Macmillan, who arrived at Key West ill-prepared and poorly briefed, was evidently unaware of the full scope of what he had agreed to by signing up to Plan 5/61.[63] He was rescued from the potential quagmire of a British ground force commitment in south-east Asia, not by his skilful diplomacy at Key West, but by the intervention of the Bay of Pigs fiasco. This, far more than Macmillan's arguments at Key West, convinced the new President that he should be more cautious about advice gleaned from his military and intelligence advisers as to the need for military intervention in Laos.

The unveiling of the EEC application to the House of Commons on 31 July 1961 marked the point when Macmillan committed himself publicly to his new foreign policy. During a visit to Washington at the beginning of April 1961, he had already confided his intentions to the President, although not, of course, in the terms of the argument advanced here.[64] From this point onwards, the fate of Macmillan's strategy would be tied to the development of opinion in Paris, Bonn[65] and Brussels[66] in that order. It was unfortunate in this respect that Macmillan had paid insufficient attention to opinion in all of these quarters during the first three years of his premiership. As Macmillan saw matters, the key to securing entry to the EEC would be to persuade the French President General de Gaulle that it was in France's interests to accept Britain's application. In one sense, Macmillan's rationale for the British application, when framed in terms of a disillusionment with the Anglo-American alliance, could have been appealing to the General. However, in another crucial sense the rationale for the British application was unappealing to de Gaulle. If Macmillan sought entry to the EEC so that Britain could gain the leadership of Europe to strengthen her international position, this could only come about, to the General's way of thinking, at France's expense. Macmillan's attempts to convince de Gaulle that he sought no more than joint Anglo-French leadership of Europe left the General, probably rightly, unconvinced.[67] By the autumn of 1962, Macmillan was left hoping for some sort of El Alamein, a dramatic change of fortune that might somehow circumvent the General's objections, and open the way to British entry to the Community.[68]

In Shakespearian tragedy, pathetic fallacy is a familiar device. During the winter of 1962/63, the Lear-like figure of Macmillan, stalking the heath of international politics, was to be confronted not just by the collapse of his European policy, not just by his 'betrayal' at the hands of the American President over Skybolt, not just by the discrediting of British colonial policy during the denouement of the Congo crisis, but, indignity of all, by one of the worst British winters of the century.[69] Although the snows did not begin until the New Year, the relentless fall in temperature thereafter seemed to confirm that even the elements were mocking the Prime Minister for his political impotence.

The unravelling of the fabric of Anglo-American 'interdependence' that Macmillan had stitched together during 1957–58, and repaired again at the beginning of 1961, began in earnest during the late summer and autumn of 1962. A brief prepared by the Ministry of Defence for Macmillan's April 1962 visit to Washington, had already noted that 'the United Kingdom is … having to rely on America for certain important and expensive weapons (such as Skybolt) which have proved beyond our resources to develop. This is one-sided dependence. As an earnest of their ability and willingness to help us achieve interdependence in the short term, we would urge that an effort should be made to find areas in which the United States can "depend" on the United Kingdom … .'[70] However, Macmillan's appeals for flesh to be put on the bones of interdependence had met with a 'cold and unsatisfactory' response from the President.[71]

Thereafter, two specific Anglo-American controversies arose, the first concerning the pressure exerted on NATO countries by the US authorities to buy the American 'Sergeant' surface-to-surface missile system, instead of the British-designed Blue Water alternative. Macmillan was furious when, as he saw it, 'Sergeant was imposed not preferred.'[72] Hard on the heels of the Blue Water–Sergeant dispute, came the US decision, in the middle of August 1962, to sell Hawk surface-to-air missiles to Israel. Macmillan was once again livid with rage, believing that the US administration had violated an Anglo-American agreement not to sell such weapons to Israel, as part of a deliberate ploy to prevent the British from marketing their competing Bloodhound missile system. In a fit of rage, he dashed off an extraordinary message to the President: 'I cannot believe', he wrote,

> that you were privy to this disgraceful piece of trickery. For myself I must say frankly that I can hardly find words to express my sense of disgust and despair. Nor do I see how you and I are to conduct the great affairs of the world on this basis ... I have instructed our officials to let me have a list of all the understandings in different parts of the world which we have entered into together. It certainly makes it necessary to reconsider our whole position on this and allied matters.[73]

In fact, the available US documents reveal that the decision to sell Hawk missiles to Israel had been taken with a view to regional and US domestic political considerations.[74] The Anglo-American dimension of the issue had not even been raised in the relevant meeting attended by the President. Secretary of State Rusk's comment on the affair, as reported by National Security Adviser McGeorge Bundy, was, though, to prove remarkably prescient with the Skybolt crisis a matter of four months away. 'When a married couple begin to talk about divorce, it is already too late ...'[75]

On the Skybolt crisis itself, and the 18 to 21 December 1962 Nassau conference at which Macmillan extracted from Kennedy the commitment to sell the Polaris delivery system to Britain, there is space here only to make the briefest of remarks. It was the best of times, it was the worst of times, for both Macmillan himself and the Anglo-American relationship. On the one hand, through the Nassau agreement, Macmillan managed to preserve Britain's status as a nuclear power for the foreseeable future. On the other hand, the deal struck in Nassau confirmed the British dependence on the US which the March 1960 Skybolt deal had instituted. The picture which emerges from the recently released transcripts of the conference, is also subtly different from that presented in the existing literature, including Richard Neustadt's report.[76] A principal cause of much of the bad feeling generated in the initial stages of the conference was Kennedy's surprise offer of a fifty-fifty deal over the future research and development costs of the Skybolt missile.[77] Through earlier conversations between British Minister of Defence Peter Thorneycroft, and US Defense Secretary McNamara, the British had arrived at Nassau expecting instead some sort of offer over Polaris.[78] Kennedy's persistence in pressing the fifty-fifty offer on Skybolt was such a blatant political device to cover his position in the event of a breakdown that the British side became enraged. Neustadt of course could hardly lay the blame for much of the rancour of the conference at the door of the President himself in view of the desk on which his report would land. In these circumstances, Macmillan deserves some credit for persisting with negotiations at a time when others, particularly Thorneycroft, wanted to walk out.[79]

In the end, though, while the Prime Minister managed to salvage an agreement from the wreckage, the negotiations had surely served to reinforce in his own mind the fears about the Anglo-American alliance that had led him to open the EEC negotiations. Certainly, this view is confirmed by Macmillan's hawk-like attention to the negotiations over implementation that followed the Nassau agreement. He warned Minister of Defence Thorneycroft that 'we must be prepared for some pressure to be put upon us … coming to a point where we would threaten to tear up the agreement', and asked 'whether, if we were driven into a corner, we could, either as a bluff or as a reality, make a Polaris missile, perhaps of a simpler kind, ourselves … .'[80]

Unfortunately from this point of view, President de Gaulle's choice of the aftermath of Nassau to deliver his EEC veto, left Macmillan now also bereft of his European hedge. Adding to his troubles, from the perspective of the Commonwealth dimension of his overall strategy, the Nassau conference immediately preceded the UN decision to launch the decisive Operation 'Gland Slam'. This brought about the reintegration by force of the rebel Congolese province of Katanga, a move the British government had done its best to block for more than two years. The British response to the UN action, as Alan James memorably terms it, amounted to no more than 'diplomatic mumbling'.[81]

The final phase of the Macmillan premiership, from January 1963 through to the Prime Minister's resignation for reasons of ill-health in October, must have been one of the loneliest periods of the post-war decades in which to face up to the task of making British foreign policy. Macmillan himself was honest enough to quote the relevant passage of his diary, summing up his feelings in his memoirs:

> All our policies at home and abroad are in ruins. Our defence plans have been radically changed, from air to sea. European unity is no more; French domination of Europe is the new and alarming feature; our popularity as a Government is rapidly declining. We have lost everything, except our courage and determination.[82]

In these circumstances, it is something of a credit to Macmillan that he managed to carry on at all. Nor was the final phase of his premiership totally bereft of all achievement. His continued pursuit of a nuclear test ban treaty, for instance, particularly in the shape of his promptings of the US President during the spring of 1963,[83] finally bore fruit in the form of the Partial Nuclear Test Ban Treaty of 5 August 1963. Nevertheless, it is clear that during this final phase, there was no grand strategy left to speak of, merely the diplomatic equivalent of marking time.

On balance, when considering Macmillan's role as a 'maker of British foreign policy', one is confronted with a legacy that, like the man himself, is a study in ambiguity. In respect of Anglo-American relations, Macmillan, on the one hand, maintained a closer working relationship with his American counterparts than virtually any other post-war British Prime Minister despite the challenge posed by the 'crisis years' of the Cold War. On the other hand, though, from the Paris summit onwards, he was plagued by fears of British impotence in the face of American arrogance and even duplicity. In respect of the British 'independent' nuclear deterrent, Macmillan was able, through Anglo-American channels, to secure for Britain the most modern and invulnerable means of delivery through arrangements that hold fast nearly 40 years on. But, as the Ministry of Defence brief for his April 1962 talks in Washington acknowledged, these arrangements could equally well be termed 'one-sided dependence' of Britain on the US. In respect of colonial affairs and the Commonwealth, Macmillan on the one hand presided over an accelerated and relatively smooth dismantling of the African empire. On the other, his hopes for the Commonwealth as a future instrument for the maintenance of Britain's international status were to prove wishful thinking. Finally, over Europe, Macmillan's application to the EEC was, on the one hand, an historic departure in British foreign policy, just as its collapse was, on the other, an historic failure.

Notes

1. Note for the Record, meeting between the Prime Minister, Foreign Secretary, Minister of Defence, and Chiefs of Staff, 6pm, 22 October 1962, PRO PREM11/3877.
2. Horne, A., *Macmillan, 1894–1956: Volume I of the Official Biography* (London: Macmillan, 1988), pp. 80–1; Sampson, A., *Macmillan: A Study in Ambiguity*, (London: The Penguin Press, 1967), p. 6. Although Alistair Horne's two-volume official biography of Macmillan is the standard work, Anthony Sampson's much earlier portrait provides a thought-provoking analysis of his character.
3. Macmillan's diary entry, 15 September 1961, quoted in Horne, A., *Macmillan, 1957–1986: Volume II of the Official Biography* (London: Macmillan, 1989), pp. 313–14.
4. Richard Aldous in his essay 'A Family Affair: Macmillan and the Art of Personal Diplomacy' argues that Macmillan's attempts to forge *détente*, and, in particular his visit to Moscow, were 'driven almost entirely by domestic imperatives, notably to avert imminent defeat at the next general election'. (Aldous, R. and Lee, S., *Harold Macmillan and Britain's World Role* (London: Macmillan, 1996), p. 17.)
5. Sampson, *Macmillan: A Study in Ambiguity*.
6. Macmillan to Kennedy, T5/62, 5 January 1962, Public Record Office (PRO), PREM11/4041. Macmillan also quoted the full text of his letter in his memoirs, Macmillan, H., *At the End of the Day* (London: Macmillan, 1973), pp. 154–63. For a recent account which strikes a judicious balance in assessing Macmillan's motives in the pursuit of a nuclear test ban see Oliver K., *Kennedy, Macmillan and the Nuclear Test Ban Debate, 1961–63* (London: Macmillan, 1998).
7. Horne, *Macmillan, 1957–86*, p. 113.
8. Ibid.

9. Macmillan's annotation on Beeley to Home, 25 February 1963, PRO PREM11/4173.

10. Crossman quoted in Sampson, *Macmillan: A Study in Ambiguity*, p. 61.

11. Macmillan, H., *The Blast of War, 1939–1945* (London: Macmillan, 1967), p. 242.

12. Ibid., p. 243.

13. Kyle, K., *Suez* (London: Weidenfeld & Nicholson, 1991), p. 155.

14. Ashton, N.J., *Eisenhower, Macmillan and the Problem of Nasser* (London: Macmillan, 1996), pp. 90–1.

15. For various perspectives on Macmillan's 6 November 'loss of nerve' see Horne, *Macmillan, 1896–1956*, pp. 440–5; Rhodes James, R., *Anthony Eden* (London: Weidenfeld & Nicholson, 1986), p. 573; and Kyle, *Suez*, p. 465.

16. For the impact of this concept on Macmillan's subsequent crisis management see, for example, Ashton, N., 'Britain and the Kuwaiti Crisis, 1961', *Diplomacy and Statecraft*, Vol. 9, No. 1, March 1998, p. 169.

17. Horne, *Macmillan, 1894–1956*, p. 398.

18. Record of a Conversation between the Prime Minister and President Kennedy, 12.30am, 23 October 1962, PRO PREM11/3689.

19. Beschloss, M.R., *Kennedy v. Khrushchev: The Crisis Years, 1960–63* (London: Faber & Faber, 1991).

20. After much deliberation, Kennedy had finally decided on a request to Congress for an increase of $3.2bn in the defense budget, including an extra $207m for civil defense, together with a series of measures to improve military readiness, including the movement of six extra divisions to Europe. (Tusa, A., *The Last Division: Berlin and the Wall* (London: Hodder and Stoughton, 1996), p. 252.)

21. Macmillan to Bishop enclosing draft minute to the Foreign Secretary, M.200/61, 24 June 1961, PRO PREM11/3348.

22. Macmillan, H., *Pointing the Way, 1959–1961* (London: Macmillan, 1972), pp. 390–1.

23. Macmillan to Bishop, M.207/61, 24 June 1961, PRO PREM11/3348.

24. Gearson, J.P.S., *Harold Macmillan and the Berlin Wall Crisis, 1958–62: The Limits of Interest and Force* (Basingstoke: Macmillan, 1998), p. 182. It should be noted that Gearson is a staunch critic of Macmillan's Berlin policy.

25. Macmillan to Kennedy, T.492/62, 22 October 1962, PRO PREM11/3689.

26. It is arguable that Macmillan himself showed a degree of foresight into this process. In a speech delivered at Bedford in July 1957 he spoke of nationalism becoming 'a tidal wave surging from Asia across the ocean to the shores of Africa … Of all political forces, the new rise of nationalism is the most powerful, swift and elemental … It can be led: but it cannot be driven back.' (Quoted in Hemming, P.E., 'Macmillan and the End of the British Empire in Africa' in Aldous, R. and Lee, S., *Harold Macmillan and Britain's World Role* (London: Macmillan, 1996), pp. 99–100.)

27. Ashton, *Eisenhower, Macmillan and the Problem of Nasser*, pp. 117–20.

28. It should be noted that throughout the Macmillan premiership, a 'kitchen cabinet' of advisers, among whom the most important figures were Philip de Zulueta and Freddie Bishop, exerted significant influence over the formation of foreign policy. Of Macmillan's two Foreign Secretaries, Alec Douglas-Home (July 1960 to October 1963) proved far more influential than Selwyn Lloyd (January 1957 to July 1960).

29. Macmillan used these words in describing his feelings about the collapse of the summit in a letter to the Queen (Macmillan, *Pointing the Way*, p. 213).

30. For instance, Wolfram Kaiser has argued that the EEC application 'would help to appease the United States government into continuing special treatment of Britain'. (Kaiser, W., *Using Europe, Abusing the Europeans: Britain and European Integration, 1945–63* (Basingstoke: Macmillan, 1996), p. 108.)

31. For more on these developments see Ashton, *Eisenhower, Macmillan and the Problem of Nasser*, pp. 125–30.

32. Macmillan to Eisenhower, 10 October 1957, PRO PREM11/2461.

33. Briefing paper for the Washington Conference, undated [October 1957], Eisenhower papers, Dwight D. Eisenhower Library [DDEL], Box 74, White House Central File, Confidential Series, Subject Sub-Series; Meeting with the President, 22 October 1957, DDEL, Box 2, White House Office, Office of the Staff Secretary, Subject Series, State Department Sub-Series.

34. Cabinet Conclusions, 28 October 1957, PRO CAB128/31 Part 2.

35. Horne, *Macmillan, 1957–1986*, pp. 56–7.

36. Elbrick to Dulles, 'Establishment of Working Groups to Implement the Eisenhower-Macmillan Talks', US State Department, Central Decimal File, 611.41/10–2957; Chiefs of Staff Committee, Confidential Annex, 29 October 1957, PRO DEFE4/101.

37. Clark, I., *Nuclear Diplomacy and the Special Relationship: Britain's Deterrent and America, 1957–62* (Oxford: OUP, 1994), p. 3.

38. Macmillan, H., *Riding the Storm* (London: Macmillan, 1971), p. 378.

39. Ibid, p. 380.

40. Horne, *Macmillan, 1957–1986*, p. 83.

41. Sampson, *Macmillan: A Study In Ambiguity*, p. 136.

42. Ibid, p. 139.

43. Ashton, *Eisenhower, Macmillan and the Problem of Nasser*, pp. 150–89.

44. Aldous, R., 'A Family Affair: Macmillan and the Art of Personal Diplomacy', in Aldous, R. and Lee, S., *Harold Macmillan and Britain's World Role* (Basingstoke: Macmillan, 1996), pp. 18–19; Horne, *Macmillan, 1957–1986*, pp. 120–1.

45. Whether it was Macmillan's visit to Moscow, or the contemporaneous signals given by Washington of a determination to stand fast over Berlin which changed Khrushchev's mind remains a matter for debate. See the comments by Sir Bernard Ledwidge in Gearson, J.P.S., 'British Policy and the Berlin Wall Crisis, 1958–61', *Contemporary Record*, Vol. 6, No. 1, Summer 1992, p. 134.

46. For example, Richard Aldous argues that Macmillan's summit strategy during 1959 was inexorably linked to his election chances. But this argument cannot explain why, with the election won, Macmillan remained so wedded to the pursuit of *détente*. (Aldous, 'A Family Affair: Macmillan and the Art of Personal Diplomacy', in Aldous and Lee, *Harold Macmillan and Britain's World Role*, p. 17.)

47. Macmillan, *Pointing the Way*, p. 208.

48. Macmillan to Lloyd, 24 May 1960, PRO FO371/152128.

49. Horne, *Macmillan, 1957–1986*, p. 231.

50. Ibid.

51. Diary Entry, 1 December 1960, dep. C.21/1, p. 135, Harold Macmillan Diary [HMD], Bodleian Library, Oxford.

52. Macmillan, *Pointing the Way*, p. 156.

53. James, A., *Britain and the Congo Crisis, 1960–3* (Basingstoke: Macmillan, 1996), pp. 184–95.

54. Diary Entry, 28 October 1960, dep. C.21/1, p. 122, HMD, Bodleian Library, Oxford.

55. Diary Entry, 19 December 1960, dep. C.21/1, HMD, Bodleian Library, Oxford.
56. Macmillan's annotation, (dated '23/12') on a memorandum from De Zulueta, 22 December 1960, PRO PREM11/2961.
57. Watkinson to Macmillan, 21 March 1961, Washington telegrams nos 726, 727, 728, PRO PREM11/3715.
58. Ambassador Harold Caccia's account of his telephone conversation with the President conveys something of the pressure which Kennedy exerted. (Caccia to Foreign Office, 24 March 1961, Washington telegram no. 765, PRO PREM11/3280.)
59. Macmillan, *Pointing the Way*, p. 335.
60. Macmillan, *Pointing the Way*, pp. 335–8.
61. Horne, *Macmillan, 1957–86*, pp. 292–4; Lamb, R., *The Macmillan Years, 1957–1963 : The Emerging Truth* (London: John Murray, 1995), p. 394.
62. Or, as the President himself put it, 'if action were worth taking by the United States it was worth taking by other countries too'. (Record of a discussion at the US Naval Base at Key West, Florida, 12.10pm, Sunday, 26 March 1961, p. 5, PRO PREM11/3280.)
63. Minister of Defence Harold Watkinson subsequently warned the Prime Minister that Plan 5/61 was wider ranging than he had realized, involving the possible participation of SEATO forces in extended operations beyond the mere holding of bridgeheads (Watkinson to Macmillan, 30 March 1961, T.196/61, PRO PREM11/3280).
64. Record of a Meeting held at the White House, Wednesday 5 April 1961, 11am, 'International Economic Problems', pp. 3–4, PRO CAB133/244.
65. John Gearson has argued that 'the chance for West German support on … British entry into the EEC (if any existed) was thrown away by Macmillan's limited support for Adenauer on Berlin.' (Gearson, *Harold Macmillan and the Berlin Wall Crisis*, p. 32.) However, it seems highly unlikely that whatever Macmillan had done, Adenauer would have chosen to stand up to de Gaulle on his behalf.
66. Piers Ludlow has argued that through the use of more astute tactics in the Brussels negotiations, the British government might have made it impossible for de Gaulle to veto its EEC application. However, this view perhaps underestimates the lengths to which the General was prepared to go in blocking British entry, and overestimates the potential political significance of any momentum that might have been established in Brussels (Ludlow, P., *Dealing With Britain: the Six and the First UK Application to the EEC* (Cambridge: CUP, 1997), pp. 244–9.
67. Ludlow, P., 'Le Paradoxe Anglais: Britain and Political Union', *Revue d'Allemagne et des Pays de langue allemande*, Vol. 29, No. 2, April–June 1997, pp. 266–7.
68. W. Kaiser, *Using Europe*, pp. 167–8.
69. Macmillan, *At the End of the Day*, pp. 388–90.
70. 'Anglo-American Interdependence in Military Research and Development', 12 April 1962, P.M.(W)(62)3, PRO CAB133/246.
71. Shuckburgh to Stephenson, 6 June 1962, PRO FO371/166311.
72. Macmillan, *At the End of the Day*, pp. 335–6.
73. Macmillan to Kennedy, 18 August 1962, T.406/62, PRO PREM11/4933.
74. Notes of Conference, 14 August 1962, *Foreign Relations of the United States*, [*FRUS*] 1961–1963, Vol. XVIII, pp. 54–8.
75. Bundy to Kennedy, 19 August 1962, *FRUS*, 1961–1963, Vol. XVIII, pp. 63–4.
76. British Records of the Nassau Conference are in PRO PREM11/4147. US records can be found in *FRUS*, 1961–1963, Vol. XIII, pp. 1091–1101. The full text of

Neustadt's declassified 'Report to the President: Skybolt and Nassau: American Policy-Making and Anglo-American Relations', 15 November 1963, is available in the National Security File, Staff Memoranda, Box 322, John F. Kennedy Library, Boston, Mass.

77. Macmillan (*At the End of the Day*, pp. 357–8) termed this offer 'startling' and 'a somewhat astonishing suggestion'.

78. Notes of a Conversation with Mr McNamara by Thorneycroft, 15 December 1962, PRO PREM11/4147.

79. Thorneycroft to Macmillan, 19 December 1962, PRO PREM11/4147.

80. Macmillan to Thorneycroft, M.343/62, 26 December 1962, PRO PREM11/4147.

81. James, *Britain and the Congo Crisis*, p. 190.

82. Diary entry, 28 January 1963, quoted in Macmillan, *At the End of the Day*, p. 367.

83. In particular Macmillan's 16 March 1963 letter to the President helped to move the process of negotiation forward at a difficult stage (Macmillan to Kennedy, 16 March 1963, T.130/63, PRO PREM11/4555).

12
British Foreign Policy under Margaret Thatcher

Paul Sharp

Introduction

Does an assessment of British foreign policy under Margaret Thatcher belong in this collection? The question is worth asking for three reasons. First, Thatcher remains recent, not only in archival terms, but also in the sense that she is still very much argued about at the political level. Second, even Thatcher regarded the Britain over which she presided as greatly changed from that of her predecessors. As a famous, if atypical, line in her autobiography expresses it, Britain '... was a middle-ranking power, given unusual influence by virtue of its historical distinction, skilled diplomacy, and versatile military forces – but greatly weakened by economic decline ...' [1] None of her predecessors covered in this volume would have thought of Britain in these terms, let alone spoken of it thus. Third, the world in which she presided over British foreign policy appeared also to be in the throes of unprecedented change.

By this, I do not mean the end of the Cold War and the resulting shifts in the balance of power between states. Others among Thatcher's predecessors had dealt with the problems posed by the rise and fall of great powers. What they had not had to confront was the sense that Britain's international environment itself might be changing, both in terms of globalization and its effects on states in general, and in terms of Europe, Britain's near abroad, in which changes increasingly seemed to call into question the very nature of the British state and its prospects for survival as a sovereign, political community. British Prime Ministers before Thatcher had confronted the prospect of Britain's defeat and even annihilation at the hands external enemies, but none of them had confronted the prospect of its translation and absorption at the hands of its friends. In terms of the other subjects of this volume, therefore, Thatcher is special, a Constantine among emperors certainly, but whether the first or the last remains as unclear.

Foreign policy discovers Thatcher

To understand Thatcher's foreign policy, it is necessary to realize that she was both an economic liberal and a political nationalist. This combination, while as common as anything on the High Street, is widely regarded by intellectuals and experts as a prescription for incoherence, or worse, in statecraft unless economic 'sense' is allowed to prevail over political 'sentiment'. What makes Thatcher's foreign policy so interesting, however, is that during her time in office the tension between the two orientations became manifest and she attempted to resolve it, indeed felt bound to resolve it, in favour of the requirements of the sentiment over the sense.[2]

When she was elected to office in 1979, however, all this was far ahead. Whatever received images we now have of the catastrophes which beset Britain during the years of her Labour predecessors, their handling of British foreign policy was not one of them. Callaghan was widely judged to have handled foreign policy well. Perhaps there had been a little too much tilt towards the US, but Thatcher was widely expected to redress the balance in favour of Europe. Robert Conquest's opinion that, under Thatcher, we should expect the British Lion to roar again was a lonely one to which not even the lady herself appears to have given much credence.[3] Indeed, the prevailing sense during the 1979 election campaign was that whatever was wrong with Britain, foreign policy had nothing much to do with it, either as a cause or as a solution, because British foreign policy did not matter much any more.

To judge by her appointments and priorities once in office, Thatcher seemed to share this consensus. 'Her' people went to the economic ministries; the 'power' ministries could be safely left in the hands of prominent 'wets', leaders of sections and sentiments within the Conservative Party who did not yet accept what she was attempting to do. How so? Thatcher's own answer, to borrow from a later American President, might have been 'it's the economy, stupid' or, to begin with, 'it's the money supply'. Take care of the money supply and you squeeze out inflation. Squeeze out inflation and investment returns. Investment returns and the economy begins to grow. Then, perhaps, we might think about what, if anything, we might like to do with the extra tax revenues.

Foreign policy played no part in this strategy for recovery. Surprisingly, given the bewildering combination of inflation and stagnation which was afflicting the economies of the advanced industrial nations at the time and the disintegration of the post-war economic order, one gets no sense that Thatcher had given any attention to how the resulting chaos might be shaped to accommodate British preferences and interests. To the longstanding preference of the Foreign Office for freer trade wherever it suited Britain, she added only the ending of currency controls to allow British capital to flow more freely. Less surprisingly, one gets no sense that Thatcher realized that the attempts of others to shape the terms on which international economic relations were conducted might impinge on her own agenda, British interests or, indeed, the existence of Britain as a sovereign state. Like nearly everybody else, she took the political communities which existed at the time as givens. One talked about what happened within them and between them, but otherwise one did not need to talk about them.

For the liberal intellectuals on whom Thatcher drew for her own analysis, this might have been because particular political communities do not matter. Particular political communities come and go; all we should care about is whether they safeguard liberty within and advance it abroad. For everybody else and Thatcher (and one suspects for many liberal intellectuals, too, outside their conferences and studies), however, the existing political communities simply seemed more solid and real at the start of her period in office than they do now. Existential threats emanated only from the world of high politics, at this time from an outwardly resurgent and apparently powerful USSR bullying a dithering and incompetent US. This sort of stuff, together with the day-to-day problems posed by selling arms to China, constructing joint European declarations on the big diplomatic questions of the day, and nursing Rhodesia and a host of other residual problems posed by obscure territories and islands dotted around the word, could be safely left to the patricians of the Tory Party and the mandarins of the Foreign Office with whom they seemed to get on so well.

The Argentine invasion of the Falkland Islands changed all this. By Thatcher's opponents, it was presented as a challenge to her claim to be returning Britain to greatness by rediscovering its traditional virtues. To hair shirts and heartlessness at home could now be added incompetence and failure abroad. By her friends, the loss of the islands was presented as consequence of all Thatcher was against from foreign bullies to those at home who were all too ready to appease them rather than do the right thing. For Thatcher, herself, the invasion presented a great test in which the fate of her own political career, the legitimacy of her government, the status and credibility of her country, and the future of international law were all intertwined. It was one thing to be abrasive and forthright with one's European colleagues in arguments over Britain's contribution to the finances of the European Community (EC). It was quite another to respond effectively to the invasion of British territory at the other end of the world.

About the merits of the war, there is little to say. Given the islands' lack of intrinsic value, the expressed wishes of their inhabitants, and the frailty of Argentina's claim to them in any but the most formal of senses, it had no case for claiming that circumstances dictated that the normal restrictions on using force to settle disputes should be relaxed. This being so, the only question placed over Britain's response was a practical one. Could it recover the islands expeditiously by its own efforts or would it require the help of the international community?

Anecdotal evidence suggests that the initial professional advice which Thatcher received to the affirmative on this question may have involved some heroic assumptions about the scale of the operation which would be needed.[4] We know that it was provided by an officer whose duty it would not normally have been to provide such advice, and that the enthusiasm with which he advocated his position was probably fuelled by his desire to demonstrate the indispensability of the Royal Navy when deep cuts in its budget had been proposed. None of this was widely known at the time. As a consequence, arguments about whether the Falkland Islands could be recovered were not given a good public airing at the time, and the eventual success of the operation ensured that the initial assumptions upon which it had been based became a matter of interest for those with professional and historical interests alone.

This is not to say that the war did not spark a heated debate in Britain, but the narrow range of the options covered by that debate is remarkable in retrospect. Ostensibly, it was about whether and when Britain should go to war but, in fact, virtually everybody in the mainstream of British politics was agreed that Britain should go to war if all else failed. This being so, the heat was generated principally by arguments over whether all else had failed yet, whether the government, and Thatcher in particular, were prepared to give peaceful measures a fair chance, and by the anger of her political opponents as they began to realize that a national disaster was being transformed into a personal political triumph through military success backed by diplomatic skill. Even before success became manifest, however, those who retained their doubts about the necessity of the operation found it increasingly difficult to maintain that peaceful measures should be given more time when the government could fairly respond that further delay would impinge upon operational considerations in the south Atlantic.

Whether or not the risks were reasonable, the costs justifiable, and all other options had been exhausted, the operation was launched and, after a burst of intense but contained violence and some very worrying moments, the Falkland Islands were recaptured, the Argentinians were defeated, and Thatcher's political fortunes were completely reversed. It is very difficult to overestimate the consequences of this success for what she subsequently attempted. Thatcher caught, in David Watt's phrase, the 'foreign bug', but not in the sense that domestic failure and disappointment had driven her to the attractions and distractions of foreign policy.[5] The worst, in terms of domestic disappointment, had passed just before the Argentinian invasion with both Britain's economic indicators and Thatcher's own standing in the opinion polls beginning to recover. Rather, she caught the bug by having her convictions about how the world worked confirmed by the Falklands War but, more importantly, making a discovery about the extent and potential for British power and influence which not even she had anticipated.

The war had confirmed her sense, shared by all good liberals, of how utterly alone one can be, both as an individual in society and as a country in the international society when things go wrong. Thatcher's own political survival was clearly at stake and, as she makes clear in her memoirs, had she failed to recover the islands she would have resigned.[6] As the actions of others in her own party and government at the time make clear, had she not resigned, she would almost certainly have been forced to do so. Similarly, Britain found itself alone (so, too, did Argentina). The international community might condemn the initial aggression. Close friends might offer words of sympathy and adopt measures of symbolic significance to show where their sympathies lay. Beyond that, however, existed only the desire that the antagonists should settle their differences peacefully, since conflict introduces an element of unpredictablity for everyone else in terms of its demands upon their own interests, and an almost voyeuristic concern with the terms upon which a peaceful settlement would be reached. Thus, both Argentina and Britain were subjected to a barrage of peace plans and diplomatic pressure to make concessions, the former to let a British presence back on to the islands, the latter to let an Argentine presence remain there, while they talked.

Making the first concession was a matter of great importance. Whoever did would doubtless have been showered with praise for its statesmanship from the UN Secretary General's Office and from almost every diplomatic chancellory in the world. At the same time, however, the chancellories, the world's mass media, and that element of international public opinion which pays attention to this sort of thing would have made a judgement about the new balance of power and the new place of both countries in the international pecking order.

An Argentine concession, while still leaving it with a net gain, a presence on the islands, would have undermined its bid to obtain recognition as a new and effective regional power by the dramatic act of national self-assertion in seizing the islands. If it was to obtain them now, it would be by courtesy of the international community and British diplomatic flexibility. A British concession, in contrast, would have undermined its claim to be a great power and one of the principal underwriters of international order on the UN Security Council for, no matter how the concession would have been obscured by international praise and expressions of relief, it would have been precipitated by an act of violence from a lesser power.

Neither Thatcher nor any other British Prime Minister would have found it easy to respond other than they did to such a challenge. However, Thatcher also discovered that being alone, if you happen to be the leader of a wealthy country of nearly 60 million people with a strong military tradition, was not necessarily a bad thing in an international system which remains in its essential respects anarchical. One might not be able to rely on much help from self-interested foreigners, but this same self-interest resulted in a generally permissive system. If a country was prepared to act decisively, there were few who would stand in its way, and many who would praise it should it be successful. While the Cold War still had several years to run, what the Falklands War allowed Thatcher to discover was that the old sanction against the use of force by great powers without superpower approval, the 'lesson' learned from the Suez crisis, was no longer in force. It was not failure which drove Thatcher on to the international stage, but success, both her country's and her own, which transformed it into a new front in the pursuit of her political, economic and social agendas.

The American connection

Of course, US policy was a major factor in Britain's success. Collaboration between the military and intelligence communities of the two countries, in particular, was very important to the eventual outcome. It is important to recall, however, that the Thatcher–Reagan relationship which many regard as the keystone of her statecraft did not yet exist. As her speeches on her visits to Washington after Reagan's victory in 1980 suggest, Thatcher was pursuing such a relationship,[7] but as the initial US response to the Argentine invasion – arguments within the administration between hemisphere-first people such as Kirkpatrick and traditionalists like Haig, followed by the latter's failed mediation between two friends – underlines, she had not secured it. The important thing at the start was that US diplomacy did not oppose Britain. Beyond that, it was Thatcher's success in the Falklands which landed the relationship with Reagan and not the other way around.

Thatcher's relationship with Reagan was, in some respects, both unlikely and complex.[8] It was, first and foremost, a political relationship, a matter of interests for both parties. The chemistry, such as it was, came only with time and the experience of success. They were not like each other. More importantly, Reagan lacked qualities which Thatcher usually sought in those with whom she worked and he possessed some which she did not value. He was neither quick nor particularly ruthless, or 'resolute' as she might have expressed it. Thatcher's economic policy, for example, was rooted in notions of hard choices and being unable both to have one's cake and eat it. Reagan's, particularly on the relationship between federal deficits and increased defence spending, and especially after he had seen the consequences of Thatcher's hard choices for Britain, was not.

However, three reasons helped Thatcher override these differences with Reagan. First, he was sound on what was becoming the big question for her of standing up to the Russians. Second, he was the US President, *ex officio*, leader of the Free World. European leaders can choose between standing up to the American President or demonstrating their excellent relationship with them. The choice is greatly influenced by the composition of one's own domestic political constituency and, as Edward Heath had convincingly demonstrated, there were few domestic rewards to be obtained for a Tory leader by blowing cold on the Americans. Third, and crucially, however, an opportunity seemed to exist for a close relationship with this particular American President. For reasons which range from the geostrategic and political to the personal and psychological, Reagan was interested in Thatcher. The fact that he was is of vital importance for, as British Prime Ministers seem to have to learn over and over again, the opportunity of a special relationship with the US is in the gift of the American President. All British Prime Ministers can do is seek to exploit the opportunity if it is on offer, and this Thatcher did very well.

She did so by departing from the normal pattern by which British Prime Ministers have sought a role in Washington, suggested so well by Macmillan's image of Greeks in a latter-day Roman empire.[9] This image rested on the conceits that the British, because of their 'smarts' and because of their greater experience of, and greater cultural affinity for, the real world of power politics, were in a position to advise the Americans about how to pursue and, perhaps, even how to define US interests abroad. Within the image, two forms of advice or influence predominate: that of restraining the good-hearted but simple Americans from clumsy, impulsive and even cruel actions which, while domestically satisfying, hurt its interests and those of its allies abroad; for example US policy during the Vietnam War; and that of persuading them to maintain difficult, but important, commitments abroad when the American public were hostile to them, for example, committing forces to Europe.

Whatever one may think about the merits of the claim, there is little evidence to suggest that the Americans ever bought it. The relationship was close because of a real coincidence of interests and ways of seeing things, and on the occasions when the British may have thought they were being listened to out of deference to their experience, this was invariably because they had been mobilized by one faction in the American government which already agreed with them to credential its position in fights over policy in Washington. Instead of the diplomacy of influence, therefore, Thatcher built her US policy on the diplomacy of support, that is, encouraging the American administration to do what it wanted to do anyway.

Most obviously, she provided strong rhetorical and political support for Reagan's desire to pursue a more confrontational policy with the USSR enabling him, at critical moments, to demonstrate to both domestic and foreign audiences that he was not alone in the stand he wished to take. How successful this was in actually generating more support for Reagan's policy, especially abroad, is questionable. On the critical question of modernizing NATO's theatre nuclear forces, apparently in response to the Soviet deployment of SS-20 missiles in Europe, for example, the sense remains that

Thatcher helped polarize positions within the attentive public rather than secure additional support for what Washington, London and (although less obviously) what the other NATO governments wanted to do.

Given that there seemed very little scope for changing minds on this difficult issue, however, it may be reasonably countered that the quest for consensus in these circumstances was far less important than ensuring the resolve and commitment of one's own side on the issue. At this Thatcher excelled by putting Britain at the front of the line to receive the new systems, and by underlining the willingness of her government to pay the domestic price. The confrontations between women activists of the Peace Movement who were camped around the bases for the missiles at Greenham Common and Molesworth and the smart, but unarmed, paratroopers who stood at ease around the airfield as the systems were flown in may have been an exercise in the politics of imagery and confronting the spectacle but, if so, it was conducted thus from both sides and with multiple purposes. Much of the British public might have focused on the women and the worst fears about the missile deployment which they sought to amplify. Most Americans focused on the licks that Thatcher was prepared to take on behalf of an American conception of the general good.

Whatever else it accomplished, the diplomacy of support gave Britain, and especially Thatcher, a standing in US government circles (and with Reagan in particular) which no one else had, and which Britain had not enjoyed since the Second World War. The actual payoff from this privileged standing in terms of British influence over American policy was, as always, very hard to identify. As we shall see, attempts to influence the Americans which ended in disappointment are much more easily identified. The reward in terms of influence came with third parties who would turn to Britain as part of their efforts to find out what the Americans were 'really' thinking and, for Thatcher herself, in terms of her domestic standing. Being 'in' with the Americans had been successively incorporated into British strategic planning, British foreign policy interests and, finally, Britons' sense of their country's identity as it had declined as an international force and American power had grown during the twentieth century. Only a minority, drawn from the most dedicated Europhiles, the unreconstructed left, and a few British 'national-ists', were uncomfortable with this dimension to what post-imperial Britain was all about, and they constituted an unpromising coalition for challenging Thatcher's success.

Ephemeral international influence, however, was not what Thatcher was particularly interested in. Aside from helping the Americans do what both they and she thought was right, how did Thatcher's close relationship with Reagan serve specifically British interests? It did so in only one, but supremely important, respect: securing American acceptance of a measure of nuclear proliferation and, thus, her own government's policy of maintaining Britain as a nuclear weapons power of the first rank, if not in quantity then in quality. Britain had been closely involved in the research to develop nuclear weapons during the Second World War and, once the US had denied it access to the practical side of producing warheads, it had embarked on developing its own. By the late 1950s, however, it had become clear that Britain could no longer afford the costs of keeping up with developments in the warheads delivery systems as aircraft gave way to missiles, and missile range, accuracy and security were improved by a constant stream of technical innovations in the US and the USSR. The solution, worked out between Macmillan, Eisenhower and Kennedy, was that the US would provide Britain with rockets to deliver the warheads while Britain would continue to develop the bombs and the platforms from which they could be launched.

The Nassau agreement by which the arrangements were finalized was symptomatic of both the closeness of the Anglo-American relationship and the difficulties which it, nevertheless, posed for British governments. Britain obtained Polaris missiles with the ability to deliver multiple warheads from submerged nuclear-powered submarines plus some of the technical knowledge essential to develop the latter; in short, the very latest in the US nuclear armoury. The principal reason it did so, however, was because the Americans had cancelled development of the original system, Skybolt missiles to be launched from British aircraft, without consulting the British government.

By the time Thatcher came to office the Polaris system was nearing the end of its operational life. Her Labour predecessors had set in motion the procedure for acquiring the more modern Trident 1 or C4 system from the Americans and, while there had been some doubts about whether such a powerful system was necessary for Britain, the Thatcher government had continued what appeared to be relatively uncontroversial negotiations. Then, in an embarrassing re-run of the Skybolt crisis, the Americans cancelled C4 and offered Britain the considerably more powerful (in terms of range and warheads carried) and more expensive (in terms of the rockets themselves and the new generation of submarines which would be required to handle them) D5 or Trident 2 system.

This change, taking place as it did in the midst of a deteriorating international situation, re-opened two debates: in Britain about whether something less threatening to the USSR could be obtained and, indeed, about whether Britain needed nuclear weapons at all; and in the US administration about whether it was wise to keep sharing nuclear secrets in a way which fuelled proliferation and diluted American influence in NATO. The argument in Britain was a very difficult one with the question of unilateral nuclear disarmament becoming an election issue between the two principal political parties. Two benefits flowed from it, however. First, politicians learned that while very few people liked nuclear weapons the majority opinion, to judge by the result of the 1987 election where Labour adopted a unilateralist position, was clearly that Britain should keep them.

Second, Thatcher was forced to work out her own distinctive and robust position on nuclear deterrence. It was pointless and wrong to try to get rid of them. Pointless, because in the event of a serious war threatening, countries would race to re-acquire nuclear weapons and the country which would win the race would be that which had cheated and kept a few in the first place.[10] Wrong, because nuclear weapons frightened potential aggressors and provided life insurance against the possibility of Britain finding itself alone again[11] and because rich, liberal democracies were unable or unwilling to make the sort of conventional effort which would have anything approaching the same effect.

The debate in the US was necessarily more muted for it took place mainly within the administration. That it did not ever seriously get going, however, was a tribute both to Thatcher's close relationship with Reagan and her stature in the eyes of American public opinion. How could one possibly let down the one ally who was willing to stand with the US in all sorts of difficult circumstances by denying her substitutes for promised weapons no longer available purely because of changes in American policy? As a result, Britain continued to remain privy to some of the most important US military secrets and sole external beneficiary of some of its most sophisticated and destructive weapons. Nuclear weapons remain a matter of great controversy and opinions may differ over whether it is wise for Britain to retain them, especially in their most powerful form. However, the capacity to wield force remains one of the pillars of state power and, thus, it is hard to disagree with the proposition that America's willingness to share these weapons with Britain is evidence of an extraordinary closeness between them to which the Thatcher–Reagan relationship contributed greatly.

Nevertheless, Anglo-American closeness came with costs both for Britain in general and for Thatcher in particular, for the two leaders did not by any means always agree. Their first major difference emerged over the plan to construct a pipeline from the natural gas fields in the heart of the USSR to Germany and Western Europe. The Europeans wanted to see this proposal, rather than the arguments over missiles and troop levels as the real indicator of where the Second Cold War was going in a world of increasing interdependence. The Americans, by contrast, regarded the idea as folly, for it would increase Western Europe's energy dependence on and vulnerability to the USSR, provide the latter with scarce hard currency, and send entirely the wrong message about 'business as usual' just as the West had decided to stand up to the Russians and condemn their support for attempts to intimidate Polish nationalists and democrats seeking reform. In 1981 the Americans had decided to forbid their own companies from having any role in the construction of the pipeline, but the real difficulties emerged the following year when they decided to extend this prohibition to the involvement of US subsidies based abroad, a measure which affected a number of British engineering firms.

This placed Thatcher in a very difficult position, for she had strongly supported the US position in the pipeline debate before it was extended to foreign companies as part of her diplomacy of support for a strong US stand against the USSR. Now she shifted to opposition in defence of the British interests which were at stake, justifying her shift not by European arguments about engagement and interdependence, but by claims about the sanctity of contracts and expressions of regret that the Americans had not been clearer about the approach they intended to take before the contracts had been signed.[12]

The dispute dragged on for several months, threatening at one point to become enmeshed with another argument between the Europeans and the US over steel imports and being cited as a possible reason for US support of a General Assembly resolution calling for the resumption of talks between Britain and Argentina over the future of the Falkland Islands, but in the end it fizzled out. The Europeans promised to tighten their restrictions on credit and technology transfers to the Eastern bloc and to reduce their dependency on raw materials from it. The Poles released Lech Walesa and the Americans dropped their objections to the activities of the subsidiaries.

This was a European victory of sorts although mitigated by the fact that the Russians refused to buy any pipeline equipment until the US lifted its ban on its own companies some months later. For Thatcher, however, the episode was an exercise in damage control conducted with some skill. Her emphasis on poor transatlantic communications pre-empted any claim that their was a serious disagreement between the US and Britain on how to tackle the big questions, while her decision to justify her resistance to American pressure by arguing that contracts entered into in good faith should be honoured allowed her to stand up for British interests even when these came into conflict with American grand geo-economic strategy.

Another high political issue on which the two countries differed with costs, if not to Britain, then certainly to Thatcher, was on the question of ballistic missile defences. In 1983, Reagan announced his Strategic Defense Initiative (SDI), a programme for researching and developing a variety of rockets and directed energy weapons which would be capable of destroying ballistic missiles before they reached their targets. He hoped that these would be so effective that they would eventually render ballistic missiles and the nuclear warheads they delivered obsolete and maintained that if the US was successful in developing such defences, it would share them with the USSR.

The resulting debate revolved around two issues, the technical feasibility of such a conception and the costs, in terms of money and strategic stability, of trying to realize the conception. Within the US, a consensus soon developed against the technical feasibility of Reagan's own hopes and the debate narrowed to arguments over whether a more modest system was worth developing. The same issues were debated in Britain with similar constella-tions grouping around the two principal positions, although the coalition of arms controllers and peace campaigners was much larger than the coalition of strategists and neo-conservatives in Britain than it was in the US. However, the British debate was complicated by the fact that Britain was, in quantitative terms, a lesser nuclear power. Added to the fear that the US might waste a great deal of money in pursuing a chimera, therefore, was the even greater worry that ballistic missile defences might work well enough to cause the Americans to become either more isolationist or adventurist or both, and to cause the USSR to develop its own defences. The effectiveness of these against a British strike, even one using the new systems to which billions of pounds had been committed, would be far higher than against a US one.

Again, Thatcher was placed in a difficult position. In her own view, the idea that there was any alternative to nuclear deterrence in the near future was a 'perilous pretence',[13] but Reagan was deeply committed both personally and politically to SDI in its grandest conception. Accordingly, she was content to follow the European lead in regarding research into ballistic missile defences as prudent whilst opposing any move to go beyond research to development. The Americans sweetened this choice by promises of money for sharing in the research. However, as the offensive potential of these systems combined with the new 'theater nuclear forces' in Europe and the fear which this potential generated in the USSR became clearer, British and European hostility to the idea increased.

Whatever Thatcher may have thought of the offensive aspects of ballistic missile defence against the USSR, she was able to remain a member of the coalition of European sceptics primarily because she saw Reagan's attachment to SDI as an aspect of a far more worrying aspiration, to rid the world of nuclear weapons. In 1984, she travelled to Washington to secure Reagan's reaffirmation that the US sought no advantage over the USSR, would consider ballistic missile defence only within the context of existing arms control treaties, would do nothing to undermine deterrence, and would seek reductions in offensive systems.[14]

This was the first episode in what was to become the legend of Thatcher's keeping Reagan on the straight and narrow when it came to NATO security policy. By the times of her more famous visit in 1986, after Reagan had come close to agreeing at Reykjavik to deep cuts in nuclear arsenals with an eventual target of zero, her worries about SDI had been replaced by the need to remind the President of the vital role on nuclear weapons in NATO's strategy for countering the advantage in conventional forces of the Warsaw Pact. His commitment to retaining SDI had prevented Reagan from accepting Gorbachev's proposal, but SDI itself was in difficulties caused by technical problems and was becoming overshadowed, for the rest of Thatcher's term of office at least, by the ending of the Cold War. This posed new problems for advocates of nuclear deterrence like Thatcher, but the technical (though not the political) threat to the effectiveness of Britain's own nuclear deterrent posed by SDI subsided.

Both the pipeline and the SDI issues were long running affairs with complex subplots and themes which intertwined with other concerns. Accordingly, whatever strains they imposed on the Anglo-American relationship, in general and the Thatcher–Reagan partnership, in particular, could generally be muffled or obscured either by design or accident. It is for this reason, perhaps, that the sharpest and hardest to conceal of disagreements between the two occurred over the direct and forceful use of US military power, an aspect of American policy on which one might expect Thatcher's diplomacy of support to have been running at full throttle. The first instance of such a breach resulted from the US administration's decision to adopt a new and more forceful response to international terrorism. Acts of terrorism against American nationals or facilities would be punished by retaliatory air strikes against those whom the US believed to be supporting the terrorists. As a result, in 1986 US forces in the Mediterranean became involved in a series of armed confrontations with Libya culminating in air raids on Tripoli in which US aircraft flown from Britain participated.

The other European great powers had refused to allow their bases or even their airspace to be used for this attack, believing that it would encourage further terrorist attacks upon themselves. As a result, Britain enjoyed the kudos in the US of being America's only supporter and, arguably a more concrete benefit, the Senate opposition to legislation making it harder for IRA fugitives to claim asylum in the US disappeared shortly after. However, Britain also paid the price in terms of three British hostages in the Lebanon being murdered in retaliation for the 1986 attack. At the time, Thatcher herself appeared to relish the confirmation of her tough image by US expressions of gratitude and domestic protests from the usual sources. However, two years later, after the destruction of a Pan Am aircraft over Scotland by a terrorist bomb, she made it very clear that bringing the perpetrators to justice was far more important than looking for ways of obtaining revenge, a point which was reiterated two days later after the Americans shot down two Libyan aircraft.[15]

Thatcher's distancing from US unilateral counter-terrorist strikes may have been prompted by her greater sensitivity and, indeed, vulnerability, to the political and security costs, but she made her case primarily in legal terms. She did this also in perhaps the sharpest, if by no means most important, disagreement between Thatcher and Reagan which took place as a result of the US invasion of Grenada in 1983. At the time, the island was under the control of a Marxist group which had putsched and murdered their predecessor and one-time ally and who, according to the Americans, posed a threat to American students at a medical school on the island. The Reagan administration regarded Grenada, like Cuba and Nicaragua, as an outpost for Soviet influence in the region. The putsch provided the opportunity for intervention. The possibility of a hostage crisis provided the rationale. The obliteration of over two hundred US marines by a suicide bomber in Beirut in the midst of the crisis may have stiffened the Reagan administration's determination to act.

However, the US did so without telling Britain, and this was a problem because Grenada was a member of the Commonwealth. To make matters worse, the US invaded while giving Thatcher's Foreign Secretary, Sir Geoffrey Howe, the impression that it was not going to before further consultations with Britain and others. Thatcher set little store by the Commonwealth. Whatever attractions it might hold as a reminder of the glories of empire were completely overshadowed by her sense of it as an incubator of lame left-wing ideas for economic and social policy in the Third World and as an increasingly troublesome source of humbug regarding South Africa, *apartheid*, and her policy towards them. However, she could not ignore the protests of those in Britain who took the Commonwealth more seriously. Nor could she ignore the dent to her claim to be at the heart of American counsels delivered by their decision not to tell Thatcher what was going on, despite their *post hoc* explanations that they had not realized the Commonwealth dimension was so important, and had decided to keep her out of the loop to spare her embarrassment.

Thatcher had called Reagan once she knew the invasion was underway, but to no avail. In the aftermath, she faced criticism from those to her political right who maintained that Thatcher should have supported it since, in their view, it had broadly been the correct thing to do. Her response was that invading countries where Communism came to power through internal struggles was both dangerous in itself and provided real aggressors with a very helpful precedent.[16] For Thatcher, it was one thing to play a robust and sometimes dubious hand against terrorists who were out to get you and yours on your own soil, whether this be south Armagh, Brighton, or Gibraltar. It was another to play the same fast and loose game in relations between states, where the ground for support had to be prepared more carefully and the stakes were potentially much higher. Thatcher was prepared to speak out to this effect even when the source of such conduct was her own closest ally, but her willingness was fuelled by the embarrassment of being ignored by an ally on an issue in which she had a stake.

While it occurred relatively early on in Thatcher's period as Prime Minister, and certainly at an early stage in the otherwise quickly warming relationship between herself and Reagan, the Grenada episode was emblematic of the limits of the American card in Thatcher's diplomacy. When she supported the Americans doing what they wanted to do, this could be rewarding even if, sometimes especially if, Thatcher had to pay an obvious political price at home for providing this support. On occasions, when the Americans were uncertain, as during the Falklands War, or distracted, as in the immediate aftermath of the arms-for-hostages scandal, Thatcher was able to acquire a defining role among the NATO allies bordering on leadership.

In both respects, Thatcher was very effective, the success of her role as a Washington insider equalling and at times exceeding that of Macmillan's Edwardian statesman. However, when the Americans were determined on a particular course on which Britain did not approve – for example, invading Grenada, accepting the logic of their own 'zero option' and negotiating away all theatre nuclear forces in Europe, and eventually accepting a unified Germany – Thatcher enjoyed no more success than her predecessors in changing American minds.

Nothing she achieved with Reagan could alter the fact that she was aspiring to influence the government of a country with four times the population of her own and with an economy up to eight times as big. The benefits of closeness with such a giant, and they were considerable, could only be obtained at the price of a degree of insecurity engendered by a sense of dependence on people whom if they changed their mind or simply forgot about you in their calculations, there was nothing you could do about it unless they let you. Thatcher was able to exploit the climate of emergency which the US confronted and contributed to in the early 1980s, but she could not create such a climate if the US refused to recognize it as such and, more importantly, she could not ensure the election of a President with whom she got on. Hence, while she had exploited the opportunity presented by Reagan to the full, her initial disappointment with Bush and the resulting need to start again almost from scratch with him demonstrated just why the legacy of Thatcher's American policy to her successors would be virtually empty. Rather than in the realm of an American opportunity dependent as it was on the ebbing and flowing of the domestic politics of that country, her legacy was to be amassed in Europe, the realm of necessity for Britain where, as Thatcher had always maintained, its future lay.

Thatcher's European policy

From the European Union's origins in the Rome treaties in 1957 and the European Community (EC) a decade later, the real question had never been whether Britain would be 'in' Europe, but what kind of Europe would it be and what kind of place would Britain occupy within it. Even if the call made by some American and British conservatives for an English Speaking Union or British membership of the North American Free Trade Area (NAFTA) should bear fruit, this would not alter the fact that Britain is primarily a European great power with its fundamental commercial and strategic interests located there.[17] What complicates matters is that the question, 'what kind of Europe?' has not received a definitive answer, because such an answer has been, and remains, impossible to make.

The European Union (EU) is an excellent example of what some theorists invite us to regard as the constructed character of all social life. We tend to see ourselves as living within social structures, for example, the anarchic international society of states, which impose a certain logic of behaviour upon us. What the constructivists seek to draw to our attention is the extent to which these structures are neither just there nor produced and reproduced by anything but our own behaviour.[18] The EU conforms to this view in a number of ways. First, it is a work in progress, rather than a set of arrangements which are apparently settled. Second, it can be seen to be the product of pushing and pulling, arguing and compromising, between members with different, uncertain and sometimes ambiguous agendas, rather than as a project under the strategic direction of any one dominant group. And finally, the strength of what is achieved in terms of principles, laws, and institutions is unclear, contested and, therefore, sometimes fragile.

Post-war British policy towards Europe had been distinguished by a remarkable continuity in both preferences and the inability to realize them. British governments have, until recently, sought to advance the common market aspect of the European idea while restraining or opposing attempts to create a pan-European community with its own political authority and social policy. Whereas many Europeans have seen the creation of such an entity as a way of escaping both their own history of destructive rivalry and external domination by continent-sized superpowers, the British have worried that a united Europe would, at worst, amount to the very threat against which their balance of power policy has been historically directed and, at best, be a barrier to the effective pursuit of their commercial and financial interests in the wider world.

Accordingly, in the three attempts that Britain made to join the EC between 1960 and 1973, its governments stressed the importance of access to European markets to secure British growth and competitiveness and presented it as a sort of congress on behalf of which Britain would speak in the wider world, with membership amplifying Britain's voice. The only shift in Britain's approach over the period, arising from its relative international decline and increasingly disappointing economic performance, was from presenting membership as a desirable way of supercharging Britain's performance to stressing that joining might be a matter of necessity.[19]

It is often argued that by not being a founder member of the EC, Britain 'missed the bus', that is, it missed out on both the economic growth of the early years and on being in a position to set some of the ground rules upon which the EC was subsequently to develop. In retrospect, however, it might be argued that joining when it did, in 1973, was just as unfortunate, for this was in the midst of a long period of dormancy in institutional development following the great arguments between de Gaulle and others over sovereignty and the resulting recognition of an informal right of veto agreed to by the Luxembourg compromise.

What had happened seemed to confirm British scepticism about the practicality, let alone the desirability, of Continental grand designs for Europe. It appeared that the EC was primarily a vehicle for inter-governmental collaboration with some annoying, but essentially stymied, common policies whose costs were outweighed by the benefits of membership. It also seemed as if the EC posed no threat to Britain's preference for European security being maintained by NATO and underwritten by the US, and that this was the way it would stay.

Thus, notwithstanding the predictions during the 1979 election campaign about a tilt towards Europe if the Conservatives won, the European policy of the new Thatcher government was characterized by business as usual. Carrington, the new Foreign Secretary, devoted himself to constructing a common diplomatic voice for Europe with its own distinctive position on the Middle East and the Soviet intervention in Afghanistan.[20] Especially after the Reagan administration embarked on its own version of what Carrington called 'megaphone diplomacy', confronting and condemning the Russians, he emphasized that the European approach was to keep talking to the USSR in order to help it to find a way out of the mess into which it had blundered. In this, he enjoyed some success, although not with the Russians. As so often happens with European diplomacy, the criteria of success were focused on the ability to construct a common position and not on whether that position resulted in the desired effect.

Meanwhile, Thatcher herself addressed the 'bread-and-butter' or common market aspects of Britain's membership of the EC, specifically the question of its contributions to the EC's finances. She did so for a number of reasons. First, the formulae by which members' contributions and receipts were determined favoured countries with larger agricultural sectors and more intra-Community trade over countries with larger industrial sectors and more extra-Community trade. As a result, Britain was a net contributor to the budget while France, a country of comparable economic size and arguably better economic health, was a net beneficiary. Whether the actual sums of money which were at stake were significant rather depends upon one's point of view on other questions. If one saw them as the price of participating in the most exciting political project of the era, as Carrington tended to, then they were negligible, and the resulting arguments were about what former German Chancellor Helmut Schmidt called '... ridiculous, parochial, third rate matters'.[21] If one saw them, as Thatcher did, as politically embarrassing at a time of economic difficulties at home, as economically questionable since the bulk of the money went into agricultural price supports from which uncompetitive foreign producers benefited, and as a matter which her European colleagues had promised to monitor at the time of her Labour predecessors' renegotiation of the terms of Britain's membership of the EC in 1975, then important principles were at stake. Further, according to the worst predictions, even with the budget correction mechanism established in 1975, which generated rebates for net contributors when their economic performance fell below the EC average on certain indicators, Britain's bill for membership was still scheduled to rise disproportionately.

Thatcher demanded that something should be done in a way which, according to many of her colleagues, both European and British, transgressed the norms of accepted conduct at Council meetings. It was not what she threatened, blocking rises in the Value Added Tax (VAT) which provided the EC revenues, blocking other Community business and withholding the VAT revenues which Britain collected, but the manner in which Thatcher argued with and lectured other heads of government which they apparently found difficult.

Whatever its influence, however, Thatcher's approach to the budget had three important consequences. First, and perhaps least importantly, after many false dawns, it resulted in a settlement by which Britain got more money back, although precisely how much depended on the nationality of the accountants consulted and the diplomatic and political requirements of those for whom they worked. Second, it moved Britain away from its accustomed role as a country prepared to pay a price in terms of its immediate interests for maintaining the international order and patterns of collaboration in which it had a broader interest, towards the more unfamiliar role of a *demandeur*, a country which extracted a price, not only for its own participation in collaborative schemes, but for allowing those schemes to go ahead even without its own direct involvement. Finally, and perhaps most importantly for Thatcher's fortunes, the emphasis on the budget contributed to Britain's misreading of measures intended to relaunch the EC.

It seems remarkable in retrospect that the British saw the Stuttgart EC summit in 1983 as significant for having provided the principles for a final settlement of the budget problem and not for the Solemn Declaration by which the members committed themselves to the relaunch and '... construction of Europe'. Thatcher's own lack of response to this development resulted from a combination of factors in addition to her budget victory. Winning her second term of office, the British predisposition to emphasize the rhetorical over the substantive in their European colleagues' pronouncements on the future of the EC and, increasingly, the sense that progress could be steered in the direction of a single and open European market, rather than a single European polity and society, may have all been contributory factors. Nevertheless, a series of initiatives followed which removed any ambiguity about what was happening and which quickly forced the British out of their position as a *demandeur* and eventually into that of a *résistant*.

The same Fontainebleau meeting in 1984 at which Britain's budget settlement was agreed also saw the establishment of two committees to examine ways of creating a common European identity for the citizens of the Community and to explore the question of institutional reform. Political union, it was argued by the resulting Dooge Report, could be achieved only by shifting the balance of power within the Community away from the Council of Ministers at which the member governments were represented and towards the Commission and the Parliament. The report was followed by a Franco-German draft treaty on European Union and, after the Luxembourg summit, the Single European Act in 1986. This committed the EC to achieving a single market by 1992, but the commitment was buttressed by talk of the harmonization of tax laws and social policy, the subordination of members' laws to EC law in many areas and, by Jacques Delors, the president of the Commission since 1985, the call for monetary union.

The initial British response to these measures was to offer their own more pragmatic proposals and to call for more, real, practical cooperation on internal issues like unemployment and reforming the Common Agricultural Policy from which, they argued, talk of grand designs for the future of Europe was but a distraction. Once it became clear that this approach was not working and, indeed, that some of her leading colleagues were not sure it could work, Thatcher decided on a more explicit response signalled by the speech she gave in Bruges in 1988.

In this, she argued that successful European cooperation had to be built upon the existing sovereign, national states and not around or in spite of them, for it would be impossible to fit them '... into some sort of Identikit European personality'. In addition, Thatcher argued that her government would oppose Continental corporatism and collectivism because '... it had not successfully rolled back the frontiers of the state in Britain only to see them reimposed at a European level ...'[22] This was a nationalist or, more properly, statist call to resistance, yet it was in itself testimony to how much Britain's external environment had changed; for in making it Thatcher effectively acknowledged that domestic debates in Britain about how much the government should intervene in the economy was already an issue to be fought over on the European stage as well.

The Bruges speech positioned Thatcher, and arguably everybody else as well, to enter unfamiliar territory. More than this, however, it did not do because she still presented the argument about nations, states and sovereignty in essentially pragmatic and instrumental terms. One built on, and not against, national states because they were the basic facts of international political reality, and to '... suppress nationhood' would be '... highly damaging and would jeopardize the objectives we seek to achieve'.[23] There is no moral imperative in the Bruges call to work with independent, sovereign states, simply a presentation of them as facts which cannot be ignored. Similarly, the justification for Britain's refusal to participate in Delores' conception of European Union rests not on the claim that Britain is a sovereign state which is free to do what it likes, so much as the claim that it is doing the right thing whereas the European Union in prospect will do the wrong thing. As it stands, this is not a particularly strong defence of sovereignty for the question then arises, supposing Britain had remained an unreformed, collectivist state and the European Union in prospect had been a Thatcherite, marketizing deregulator, of what would Thatcher have had to say in defence of British sovereignty then.

In fact, she was forced into answering a variant of this question surprisingly quickly by the progress the EC made on moving towards economic and monetary union, with a single currency and a single central bank administering it. From the 1970s and the collapse of the Bretton Woods international monetary system, the members of the EC had experimented with various measures designed to create a zone of monetary stability within the Community. The European Monetary System (EMS) agreed upon by most of the members in 1978 incorporated an Exchange Rate Mechanism (ERM) by which participants pegged their currencies' values relative to one another and committed themselves to intervene if their own currency's value fluctuated by more than a percentage point or so in either direction.

Britain did not participate; its official position being that it had no objection in principle to ERM but would join only when conditions were right for Britain. In fact, Thatcher did not like the ERM. In principle, she was attracted to the idea of a clean float. One of her first steps when coming to power had been to abolish exchange rate controls, thereby exposing Sterling to the judgements of the international money markets. Pegged rates would involve countries using their interest rates and reserves to maintain a particular and arbitrary value, when the right thing to do was to use interest rates to maintain a monetary supply which was not inflationary.[24]

As concerns about the high value of the Pound and as inflationary pressures increased from 1985 onwards, however, Britain's official position, that it would enter when conditions were right, was increasingly used to cover differences between those, like Thatcher, who did not wish to join the ERM at all, and others who believed that there were no longer good reasons for staying out. The arguments, difficult and technical in themselves were fuelled by political and personal disagreements which were exacerbated as it became clear that the ERM was rapidly becoming a stopping station on the road to full economic and monetary union anchored by a single independent monetary authority operating on economic, indeed bankers', priorities rather than political priorities.

As this final destination became clearer, so too did Thatcher's opposition to it, although the grounds for her opposition were, initially, less clear. To begin with, she argued that central banks had '... a total and absolute duty to protect the value of currency ...', which meant they had, what was for her, an unhealthy obsession with exchange rates rather than the monetary supply, and would require complete control over economic policy.[25] This argument was implausible both in its claim about the necessary priority of central banks and in its implied and counter-intuitive corollary that they needed political minders to keep them focused on what was important.

Thatcher's position quickly evolved, however, into the more plausible, yet still essentially pragmatic, claim that a really independent European central bank was an impossibility because it would be subject to multiple political influences from national finance ministers, in which case it would be able to impose neither monetary nor fiscal discipline. Worse, as some of her supporters maintained, the bank might be subject to a single political influence, that of Germany, in which case it would impose a discipline which even with the best will in the world, which was unlikely, would suit German interests rather than British ones.[26] Italians, given their history of fiscal profligacy and monetary slackness, might welcome the prospect of German discipline as opposed to no discipline at all, but Britain was capable of taking care of itself. This was a very different order of argument for it implied the subordination of economic reasoning to political and, indeed, national priorities.

Under intense political pressure both at home and abroad, which resulted in the resignation of two of her senior ministers, Thatcher finally agreed to Britain's joining the ERM but, at the same time, she crossed the line from purely economic reasoning to opposing monetary union on political grounds. Britain, she claimed, was

a great and ancient citadel behind whose walls the peoples of these islands have sheltered for almost four centuries. Within these walls, liberty, justice and human progress have flourished in a manner unsurpassed anywhere else in the world.[27]

All this was threatened by the prospect of British participation in European economic and monetary union, for within such a union, Britain would lose its sovereignty. However, Thatcher's defence of sovereignty in these terms was not allowed to run its full course. Indeed, it played an important part in the arguments of those who forced her out of office in 1990 by leading a revolt within her own political party.

That it did so was due, in great part, to the fact that her argument was incomplete. As a proponent of liberal economics, Thatcher had taken the political framework within which economic policies are pursued as a given. Arguments about the right or the wrong course of action took place within particular countries. Now, she was the first British Prime Minister to be confronted by what was, in theory, an entirely reasonable economic proposal consistent with her own economic beliefs, which would end her country's sovereignty. Instinct and common sense drove her to defend sovereignty, but Thatcher's intellectual foundations provided no way of getting from why it was correct to defend Britain's sovereignty when it was doing the right thing in her view, to defending its sovereignty *per se*, indeed its right to do even the wrong thing by her own narrow economic criteria.

The elements of an answer to this problem were present in Nicholas Ridley's claims about Britain never being able to match German productivity and, less embarrassingly, arguments about the different requirements of British and German business cycles, which implied that there were such things as national economies and that, by further implication, while national economies might not have intrinsic economic value in liberal terms, they might have value as sustainers of liberal political values in an illiberal world. However, Thatcher was gone before this argument gained momentum, a victim of her European policy in part, but also of larger developments which contributed to her difficulties while, at the same time, giving weight to the grounds on which she resisted European union.

Gorbachev, Germany and the end of the Cold War

One of the reasons why Thatcher did not develop a convincing intellectual case for her defence of British sovereignty was that she, and everybody else, was operating on utterly unfamiliar territory. However, another reason for this failure was quite simply that there were a lot of other things going on. Arguments about European union and British sovereignty took place against a backdrop, the Cold War political settlement, which, after 45 years of providing the boundaries to what was politically possible, first flapped alarmingly and then collapsed completely. While the end of the Cold War and the end of the USSR did result in a radical transformation of the balance of power in Europe, however, it did not present the same sort of challenge as European union to what people thought international relations were supposed to be about. The resultant manoeuvring into which Thatcher was drawn, while exciting, was familiar and reinforced her sense that international political reality was still to be found in the interplay of sovereign states, and not in schemes for transcending them.

Post-war British Prime Ministers had all tried, without much success, to make a contribution to East–West relations as a 'catalyst of common sense' with a more flexible approach to the USSR than the one the US was prepared to take.[28] This flexibility derived from a greater willingness to accept the USSR as a fact of international life, and this was a reasonable assumption so long as one saw the USSR as no more than a manifestation of Russia, a view which was not always maintained. Under Thatcher, East–West bridge building had been left to her Foreign Secretaries. Carrington enjoyed a measure of success in building up a distinctly European approach to handling the USSR. His successor, Howe, undertook a series of missions to Eastern Europe seeking to identify and widen gaps between the local leaderships and Moscow, but the little fruit that this bore was to be lost in the deluge of windfalls which was to come. Thatcher, herself, made a trip to Hungary, but as a leading protagonist in the arguments over SS-20s, Cruise and Pershing missiles, she had avoided the Brezhnev funeral in 1982, content to retain the sobriquet of 'Iron Lady' which the Russians had conferred on her earlier. Two years later, however, she went to Andropov's funeral and a year later, Chernenko's.

That she was seeking some part to play there can be little doubt, for she had met Gorbachev the year before and had committed herself by declaring that he was a man with whom the West could do business. Nevertheless, little happened primarily because Gorbachev, like his predecessors was focused on the centre of power in the Western alliance, the US and Reagan, but also because the Americans were very strongly signalling that they did not appreciate British attempts to become involved, especially at a time when British scepticism about SDI was playing into Soviet hands.

This all changed with the Reykjavik summit and the emergence of the Iran-Contra scandal in the US in 1986. With Reagan apparently politically paralyzed and Thatcher apparently the senior person in the West capable of giving an authoritative rendition of the place of nuclear weapons in NATO's strategy, she went to Moscow in 1987, ostensibly to discuss upcoming negotiations on intermediate nuclear forces (INF) but, in the event, to have her role as spokesperson for the West credentialled by lavish treatment. Gorbachev reciprocated by visiting Britain on his way to Washington to finalize the INF agreement, and Thatcher was able to present herself as speaking for Europe on the agreement. Briefly, it appeared as though bipolarity had given way to a troika in world affairs and that Thatcher had succeeded, where Macmillan had failed, in speaking for Europe and speaking with a very British accent.

This was, of course, a temporary state of affairs and for the simple reason that, as always, Britain had a role to play between the superpowers only in so far as at least one of them was prepared to let it. Thatcher's relationship with Gorbachev was quickly hampered by their differences on the fate of intermediate nuclear forces in Europe. Thatcher had been prepared to back Reagan's zero option and then raising the stakes by linking the agreement to a similar reduction in other systems whenever the USSR looked likely to comply, as a bluff. When the bluff was called, she argued for a slowdown in reductions for she believed that the Cruise and Pershing force modernization had given NATO an advantage in such systems. The Americans, now under George Bush, were not interested and, more importantly, the Russians were angered by her willingness to maintain this tough position.

Nevertheless, another opportunity for Anglo-Soviet cooperation briefly appeared in 1990 as the movement for German unification gathered pace. German unification served neither British nor Soviet interests and Thatcher took the lead in trying to slow the process down. Gorbachev, however, embarked on his last great gamble offering Chancellor Kohl Soviet support for German unity in return for German distance from NATO, a development in which Thatcher had no interest at all. Gorbachev's own weakness, however, enabled Kohl to pocket the concession and, with US support, he was able to ignore the tentative coalition of doubters which Thatcher was struggling to create. She was left having overplayed Britain's hand, overestimated the strength of Gorbachev's, and miscalculated what he intended to do with it. A new US–German axis appeared in the making and Thatcher's

Britain appeared to have been sidelined with the limits to her statecraft clearly exposed by the episode.

Conclusions

However, a final assessment of Thatcher's statecraft remains premature. She faced challenges which her predecessors did not. She remains recent, and many of the arguments which surrounded her remain unresolved. One of the advantages of this is that it reminds us that the coherence with which we imbue our accounts of the great is made possible by the passage of time, but not always because we are thus able to obtain a more accurate and complete account. No doubt, with the passage of time it will be tempting to conclude an assessment of Thatcher with her German failure. Tempting possibly, but inaccurate for, as Anglo-American collaboration in response to the Iraqi invasion of Kuwait showed later in the year, neither Britain nor Thatcher were sidelined for very long. And the continuing difficulties of Thatcher's successors, Conservative and Labour alike, on the question of whether or not Britain should participate in monetary union show how that argument was not merely the product of a single, forceful and increasingly cranky political personality resisting the inevitable.

Thatcher's place in this volume should serve as a reminder that political careers do not progress thematically towards the natural closure provided by their biographers but, rather, like ordinary life, keep going along multiple fronts until they come to a stop. They are driven by the big forces, but they are also spurred by smaller ambitions, fights and slights and, as Thatcher's career clearly demonstrates, in foreign policy, above all, they are shaped by things happening and the opportunities they create. For Thatcher, the poorly timed decisions of some desperate Argentine generals and the election of an unusual American President were of critical importance to her catching the foreign bug and for how she will be remembered. She will not be remembered for the Anglo-Irish agreement which arguably began the process of extracting the sting from Northern Irish politics, nor for negotiating a reasonably secure future for Hong Kong, both of which occurred on her watch. Nor, perhaps, in any eventual assessment of her European policy will the crippling effects of her own failure to create a good working relationship with most of her foreign ministers and her professional diplomats be given sufficient weight. However, we live in a world in which peoples' appetites for living separately do not seem to be diminishing, while their need to have dealings with each other and to accept certain basic principles about how these dealings are best undertaken is increasing. In confronting the tension between the requirements of British sovereignty, the requirements of liberty and the requirements of good economic practice head on, Thatcher was speaking to one of the central problems of globalization. That is why she belongs in this collection and, indeed, in any study addressing the problems of diplomacy and statecraft in a postmodern and globalizing world.

Notes

1. Margaret Thatcher, *The Downing Street Years* (London: Harper Collins, 1993), p. 9.
2. For an earlier but more extensive treatment of this theme see Paul Sharp, *Thatcher's Diplomacy*, (Basingstoke: Macmillan, reprinted 1999).
3. *Daily Telegraph*, 7 April 1979.
4. Max Hastings and Simon Jenkins, *The Battle for the Falklands* (London: Pan, 1983), p. 90 and pp. 393–403, still provides the best account of the decision to send the task force and has been confirmed by senior ministers subsequently.
5. *The Times*, 1 July 1982.
6. Sharp, *Thatcher*, p. 208.
7. *The Times*, 30 January and 24 July 1981, and 24 November 1982.
8. For a study of the relationship which emphasizes 'chemistry' rather than political interests, see Geoffrey Smith, *Reagan and Thatcher* (New York and London: WW Norton, 1991).
9. See Anthony Sampson, *Macmillan: A Study in Ambiguity* (Harmondsworth: Penguin, 1968), p. 205 for a consideration of this theme.
10. *The Times*, 29 May 1986.
11. *The Times*, 2 April 1982.
12. *The Times*, 23 September 1982.
13. Thatcher to the UN cited in Sir Geoffrey Howe, 'Defence and Security in the Nuclear Age', an address to the Royal United Services Institute, London, 15 March 1985.
14. Smith, *Reagan and Thatcher*, pp. 222–3.
15. *The Times*, 2 January 1999.
16. *The Times*, 31 October 1983. For a critical view of Britain's reaction see, George Shultz, *Turmoil and Triumph* (New York: Charles Scribner's Sons, 1993), pp. 340–4.
17. See, for example, Robert Conquest, 'An English-Speaking Union', *The National Interest*, No. 57, Fall 1999, pp. 64–70 and 'Britain and NAFTA: Dream On?', *The Economist*, April 15 2000. See also P. Sharp, 'Time for America to join the Commonwealth', *International Journal*, Summer, 2000, pp. 497–509.
18. See, for example, Alexander Wendt, 'Anarchy Is What States Make of It: The Social Construction of Power Politics', *International Organization*, 46, 2, (1992) pp. 391–425.
19. See P. Sharp, 'The Place of the European Community in British Foreign Policy', *Millennium: Journal of International Studies'*, 11, 2, (1998), pp. 155–71.
20. For his own account see Peter Carrington, *Reflect On Things Past* (Glasgow: Fontana, 1989).
21. Former Chancellor Schmidt on arguments within the EC, *The Times*, 13 June 1984.
22. *The Times*, 21 September 1988.
23. *The Times*, 21 September 1988.
24. Sharp, *Thatcher*, pp. 688–726.
25. *The Times*, 26 October 1988.
26. This view was expressed by Nicholas Ridley who eventually called the ERM a 'German racket' and had to resign. *The Times*, 13 and 16 July, 1990.
27. *The Times*, 13 May 1989.
28. George Walden, *The Times*, 5 October 1983.

Index